The Sacred Blacksmith
聖剣の刀鍛冶
VOLUME 1
story by Isao Miura
art by Kotaro Yamada
Character Design Luna

STAFF CREDITS

translation Adrienne Beck
adaptation Janet Houck
lettering Roland Amago
layout Bambi Eloriaga-Amago
cover design Nicky Lim
copy editor Shanti Whitesides
editor Adam Arnold

publisher Jason DeAngelis
Seven Seas Entertainment

THE SACRED BLACKSMITH VOLUME 1

First published in Japan in 2009 by MEDIA FACTORY, Inc.

ISBN: 978-1-937867-32-4

Printed in Canada

First Printing: May 2013

10 9 8 7 6 5 4 3 2 1

Seven Seas

READING DIRECTIONS

This book reads from ***right to left***, Japanese style. If this is your first time reading manga, you start reading from the top right panel on each page and take it from there. If you get lost, just follow the numbered diagram here. It may seem backwards at first, but you'll get the hang of it! Have fun!!

7
6
13
10
12
11
14

Experience all that *SEVEN SEAS* has to offer!

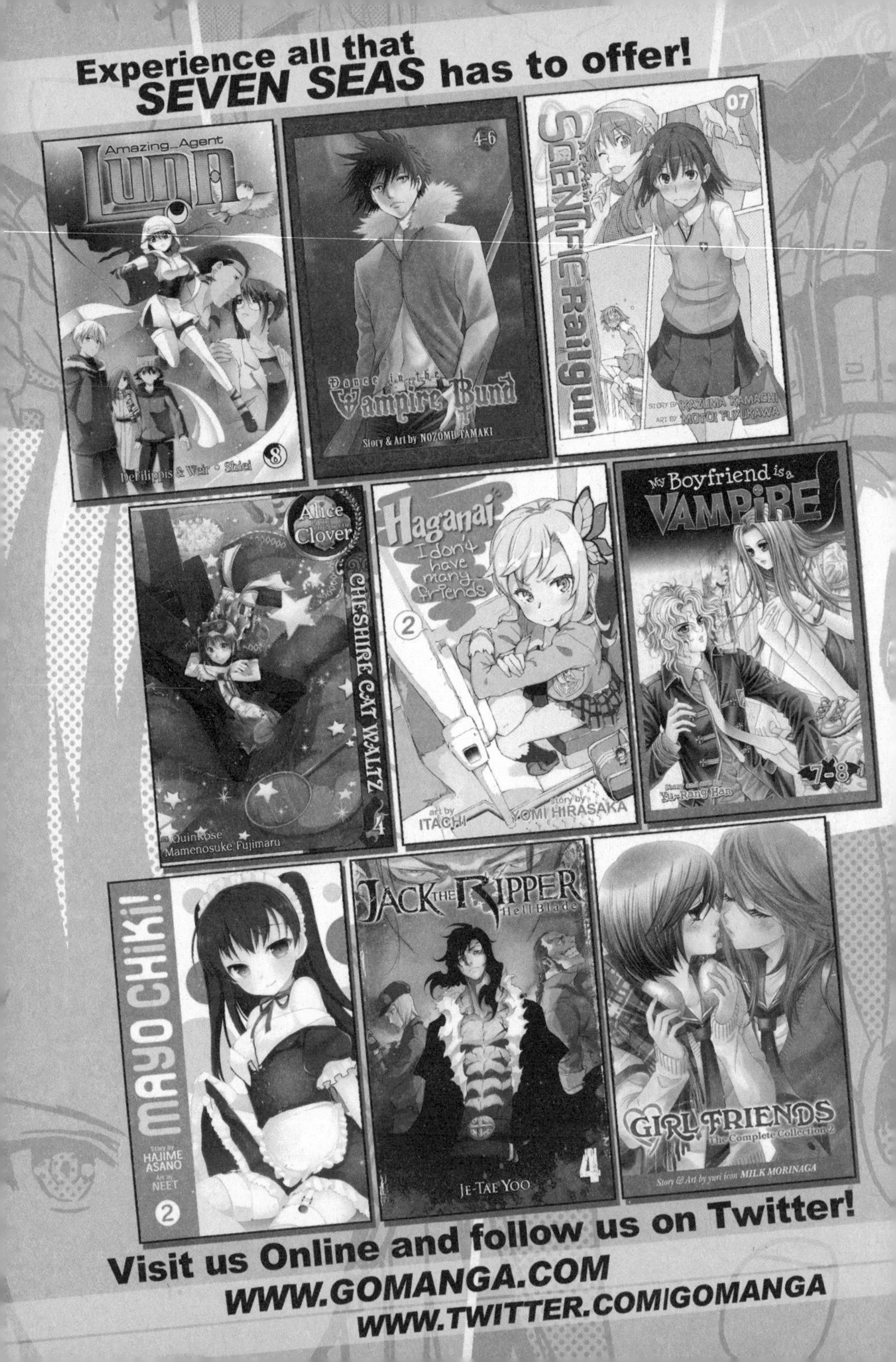

Amazing_Agent Luna
DeFilippis & Weir • Shiei
8
4-6
Dance in the Vampire Bund
Story & Art by NOZOMU TAMAKI
07
Scientific Railgun
Story by KAZUMA KAMACHI
Art by MOTOI FUYUKAWA
Alice
Clover
CHESHIRE CAT WALTZ
4
QuinRose
Mamenosuke Fujimaru
Haganai
I don't have many friends
2
art by ITACHI
story by YOMI HIRASAKA
My Boyfriend is a VAMPIRE
7-8
Yu-Rang Han
MAYO CHIKI!
Story by HAJIME ASANO
Art by NEET
2
JACK THE RIPPER
Hell Blade
JE-TAE YOO
4
GIRL FRIENDS
The Complete Collection 2
Story & Art by yuri icon MILK MORINAGA

Visit us Online and follow us on Twitter!

WWW.GOMANGA.COM

WWW.TWITTER.COM/GOMANGA

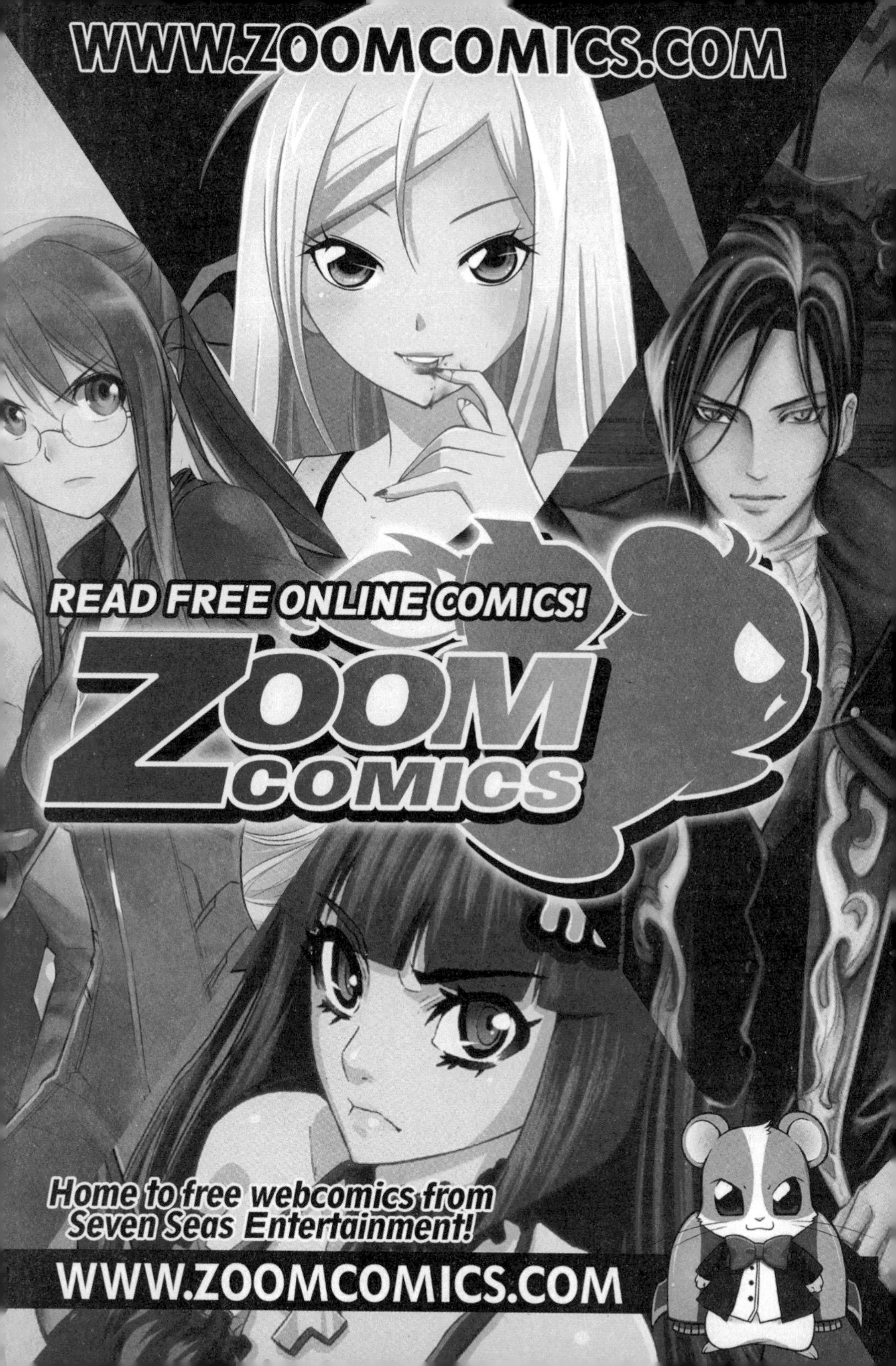

WWW.ZOOMCOMICS.COM
READ FREE ONLINE COMICS!
ZOOM COMICS
Home to free webcomics from
Seven Seas Entertainment!
WWW.ZOOMCOMICS.COM

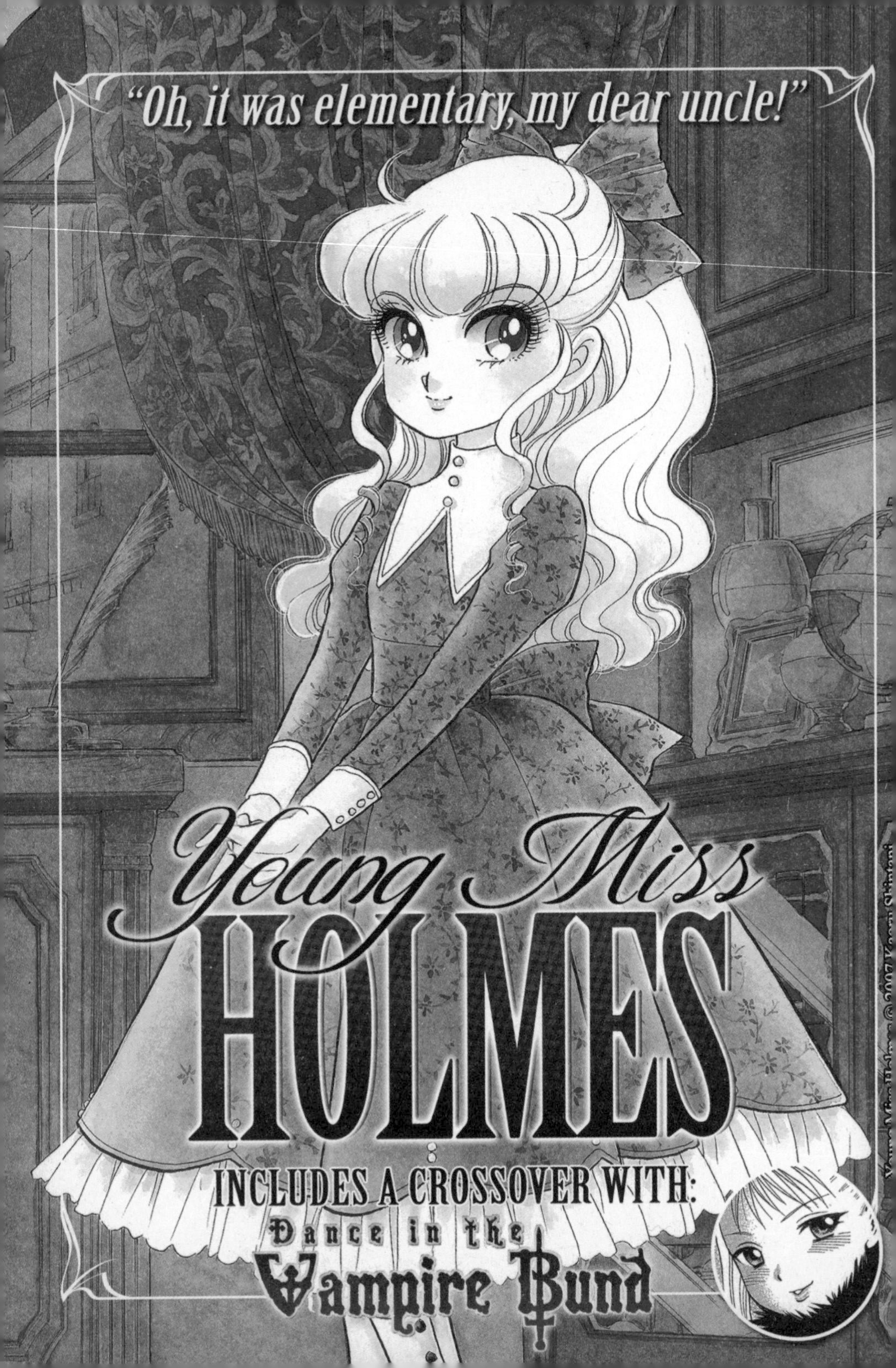
"Oh, it was elementary, my dear uncle!"
Young Miss
HOLMES
INCLUDES A CROSSOVER WITH:
Dance in the
Vampire Bund

TO ALL CREATURES OF THE NIGHT: YOUR SALVATION HAS ARRIVED!

Dance in the Vampire Bund

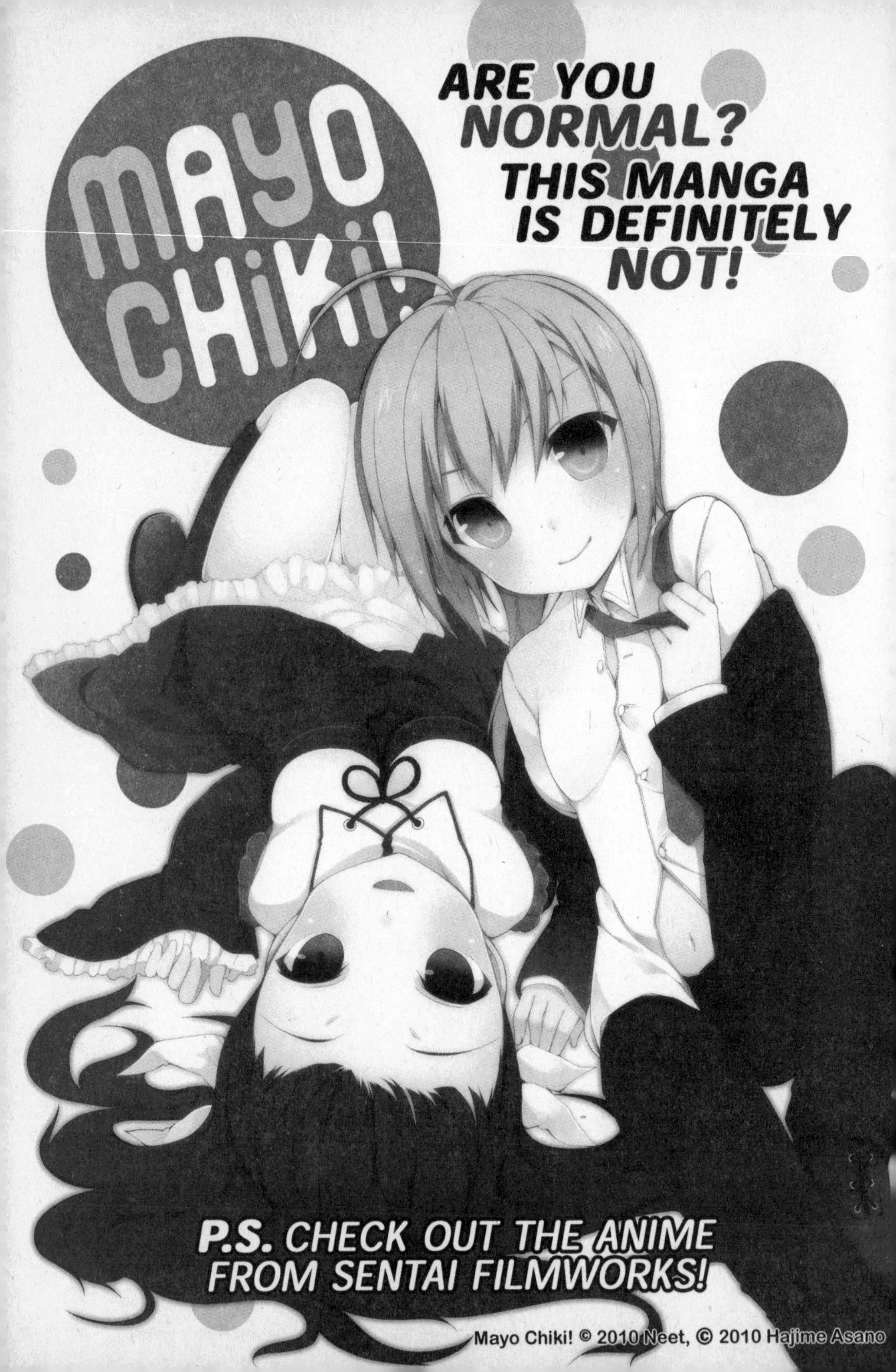
MAYO CHIKI!
ARE YOU NORMAL? THIS MANGA IS DEFINITELY NOT!
P.S. CHECK OUT THE ANIME FROM SENTAI FILMWORKS!
Mayo Chiki! © 2010 Neet, © 2010 Hajime Asano

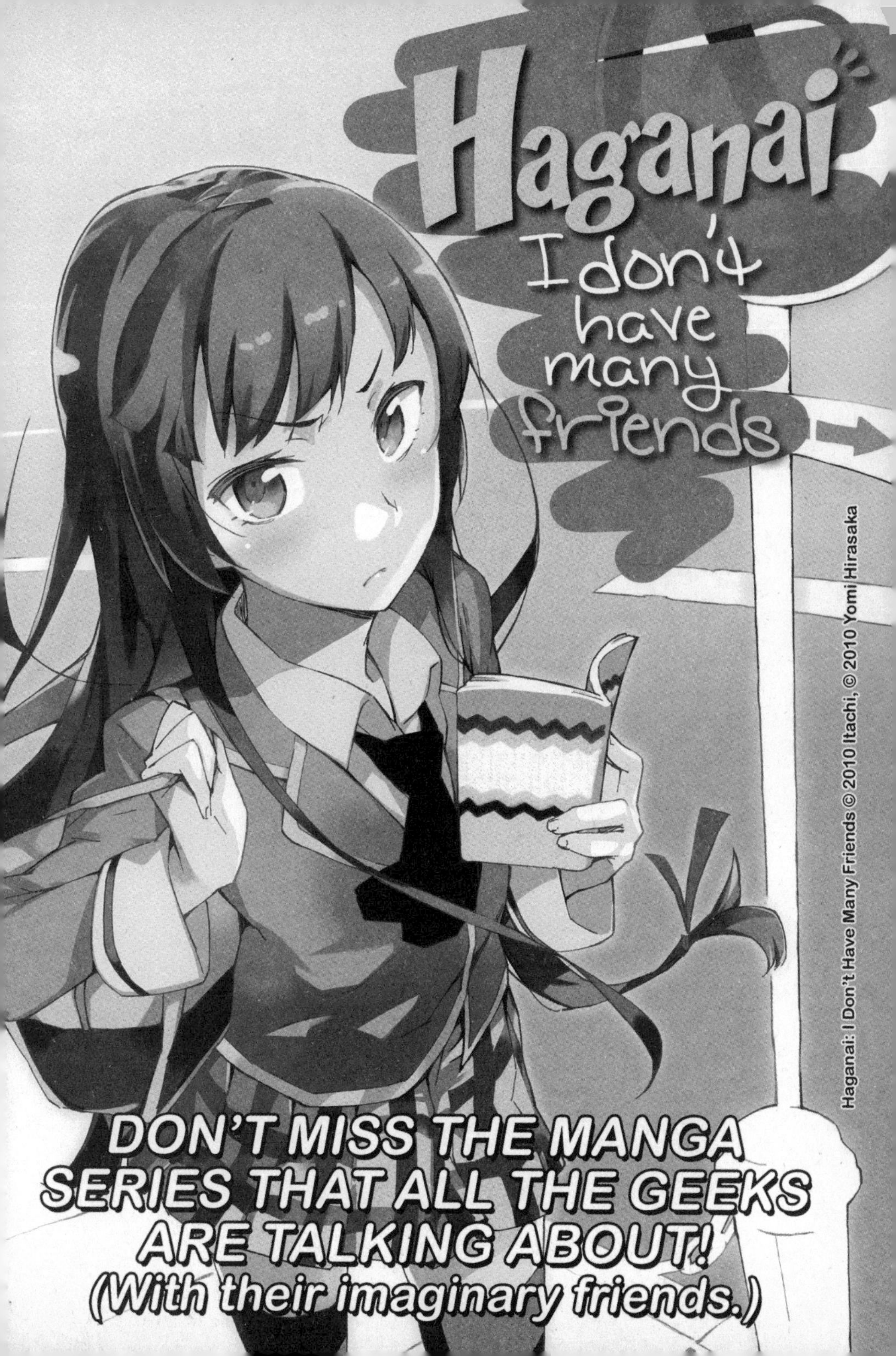
Haganai
I don't have many friends
Haganai: I Don't Have Many Friends © 2010 Itachi, © 2010 Yomi Hirasaka
DON'T MISS THE MANGA SERIES THAT ALL THE GEEKS ARE TALKING ABOUT!
(With their imaginary friends.)

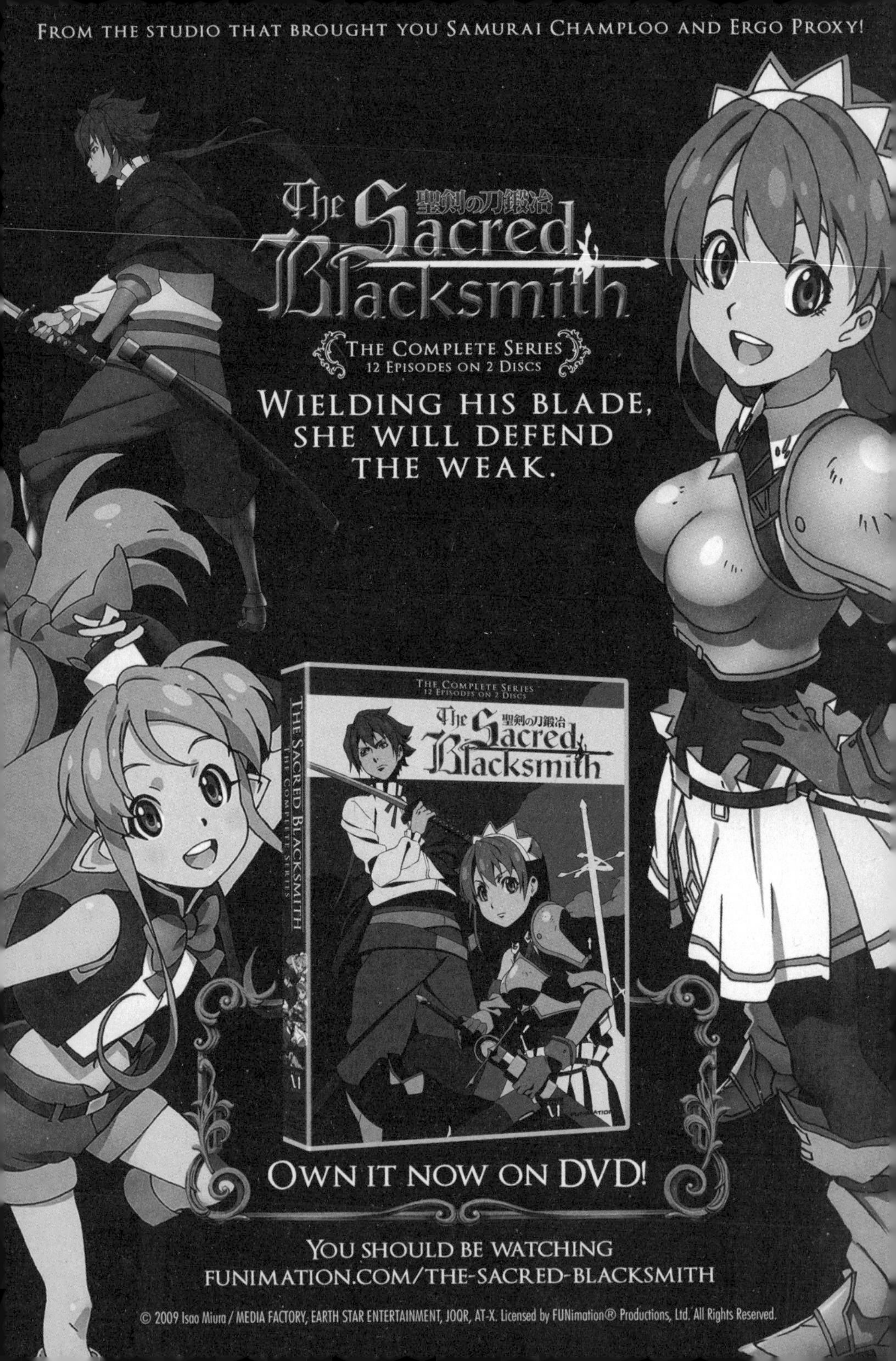

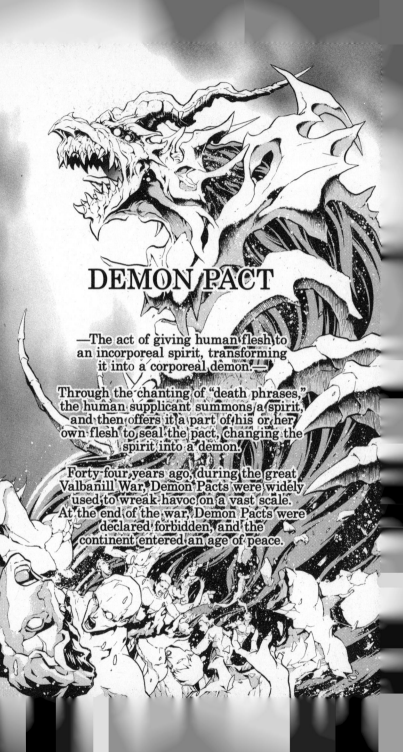

DEMON PACT

—The act of giving human flesh to an incorporeal spirit, transforming it into a corporeal demon.—

Through the chanting of "death phrases," the human supplicant summons a spirit, and then offers it a part of his or her own flesh to seal the pact, changing the spirit into a demon.

Forty-four years ago, during the great Valbanill War, Demon Pacts were widely used to wreak havoc on a vast scale. At the end of the war, Demon Pacts were declared forbidden, and the continent entered an age of peace.

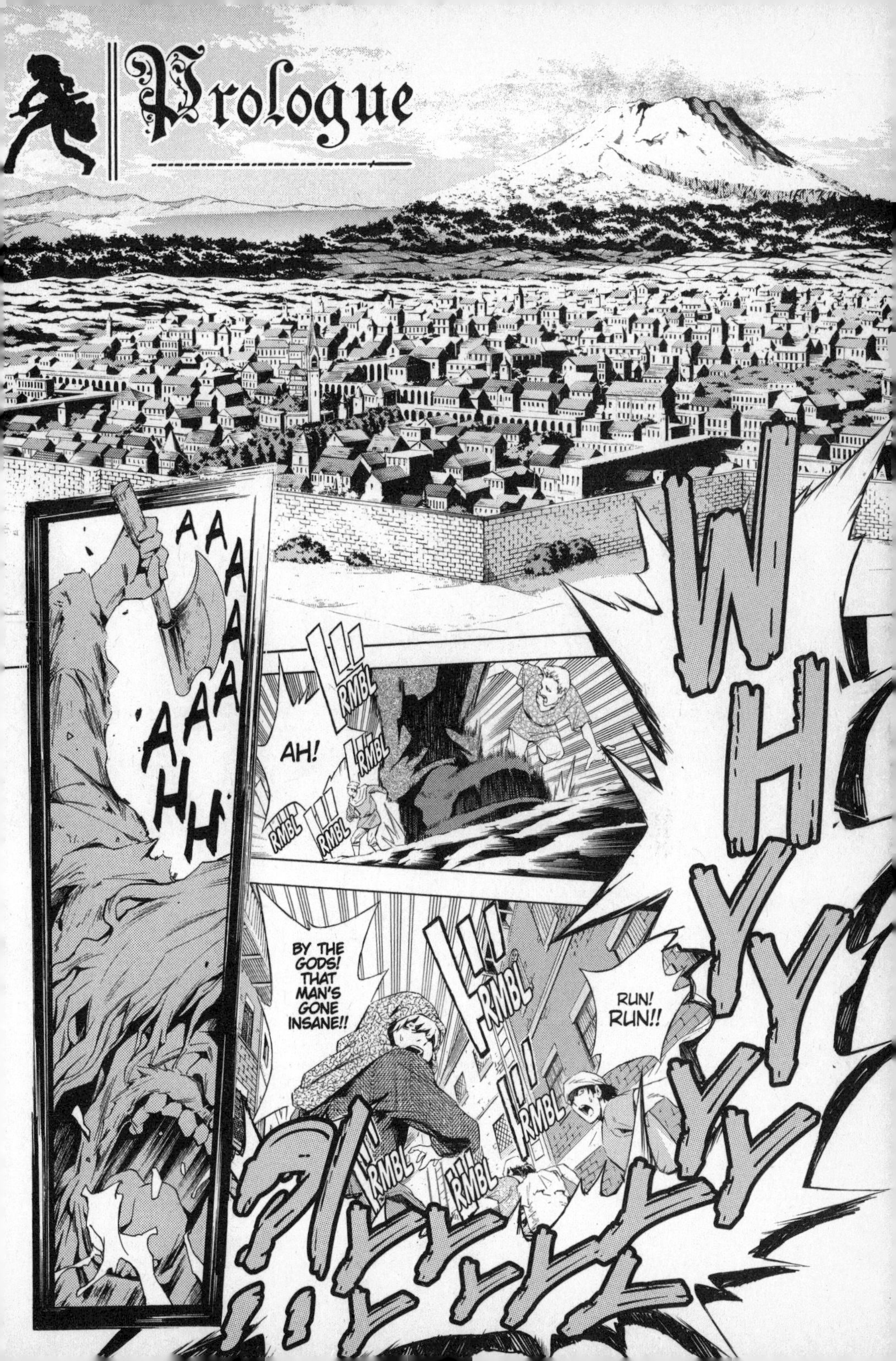
Prologue
RMBL
RMBL
AH!
RMBL
RMBL
RUN! RUN!!
BY THE GODS! THAT MAN'S GONE INSANE!!
RMBL
RMBL
RMBL
RMBL
AAAAAAAAAHH

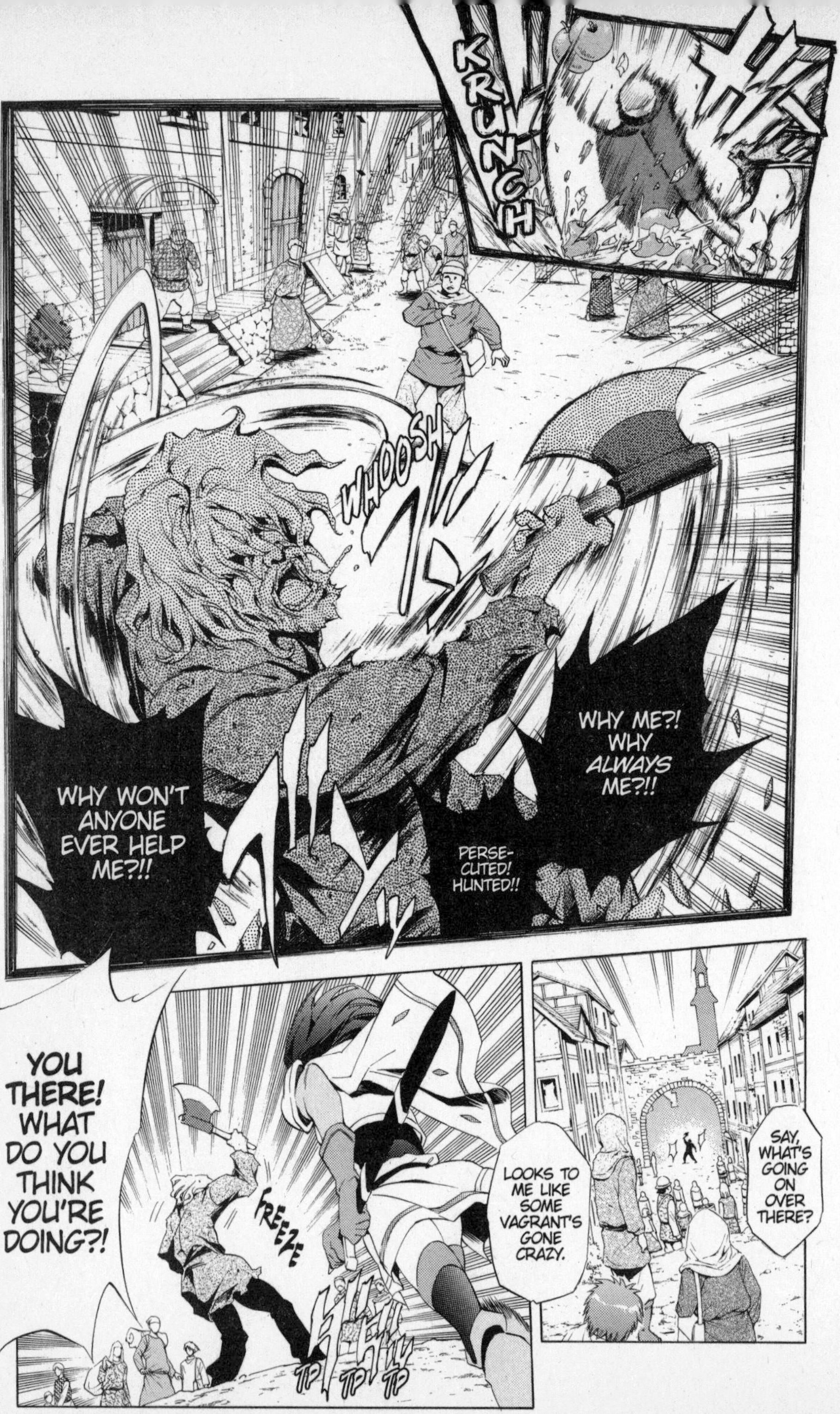
KRUNCH
WHOOSH
WHY ME?! WHY ALWAYS ME?!!
PERSE-CUTED! HUNTED!!
WHY WON'T ANYONE EVER HELP ME?!!
SAY, WHAT'S GOING ON OVER THERE?
LOOKS TO ME LIKE SOME VAGRANT'S GONE CRAZY.
YOU THERE! WHAT DO YOU THINK YOU'RE DOING?!
FREEZE
TP TP TP

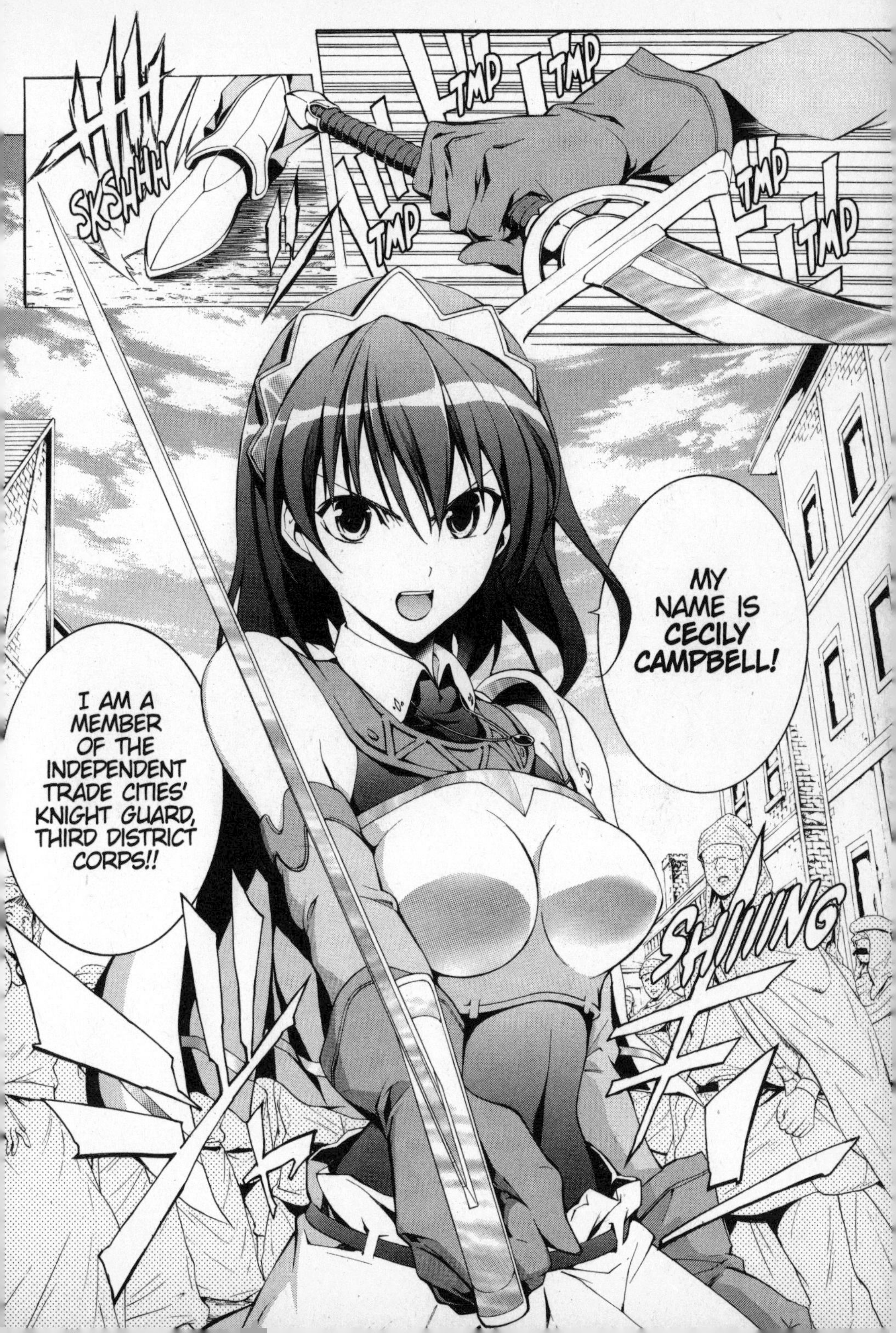

TMP
TMP
TMP
TMP
TMP
TMP
SKSHHH
MY NAME IS CECILY CAMPBELL!
I AM A MEMBER OF THE INDEPENDENT TRADE CITIES' KNIGHT GUARD, THIRD DISTRICT CORPS!!
SHIIING

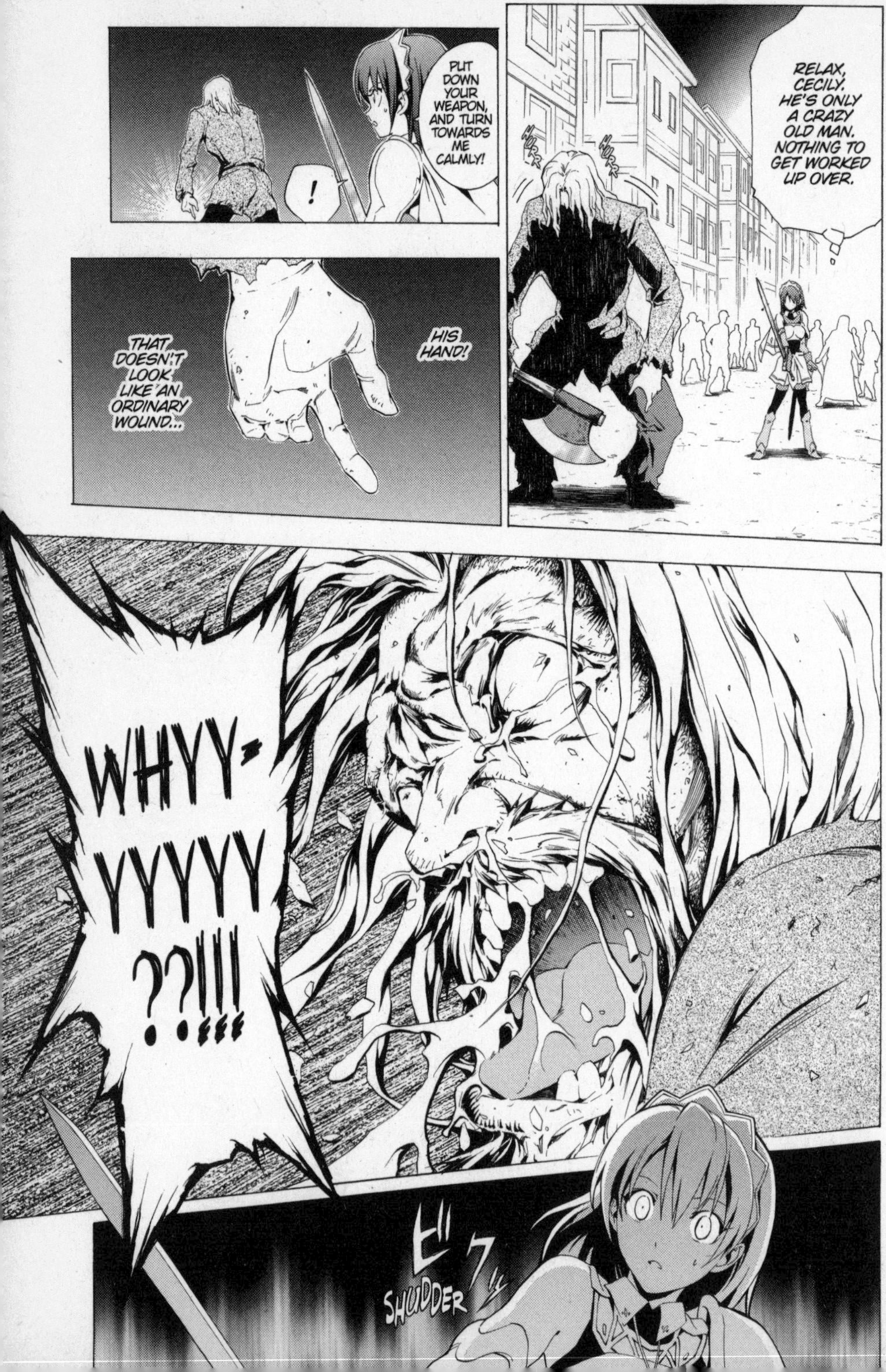
RELAX, CECILY. HE'S ONLY A CRAZY OLD MAN. NOTHING TO GET WORKED UP OVER.
HURR
HURR
PUT DOWN YOUR WEAPON, AND TURN TOWARDS ME CALMLY!
!
HIS HAND!
THAT DOESN'T LOOK LIKE AN ORDINARY WOUND...
WHYY-YYYYY??!!!!
ビクッ
SHUDDER

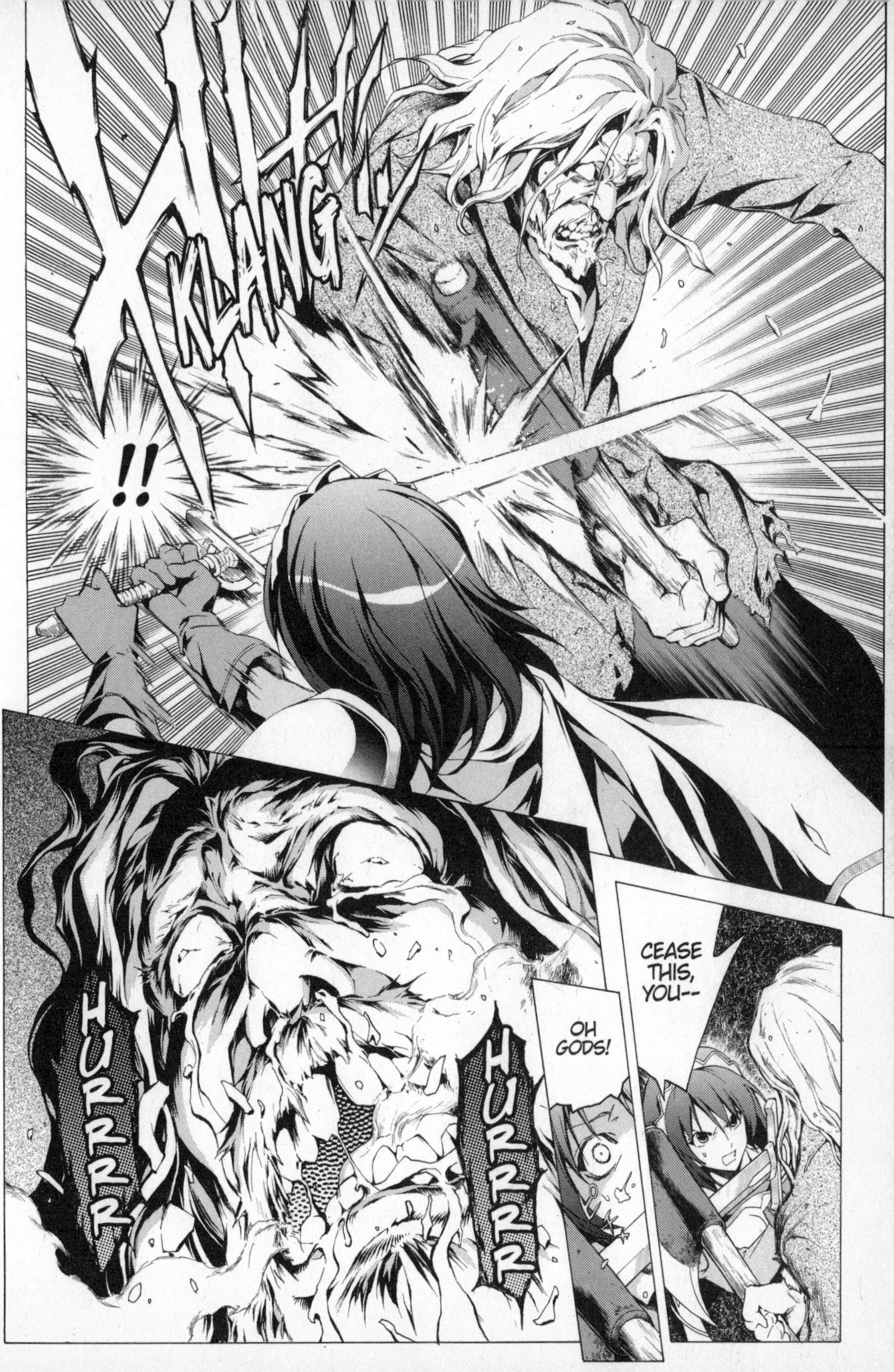
KLANG
!!
CEASE THIS, YOU--
OH GODS!
HURRRR
HURRRR

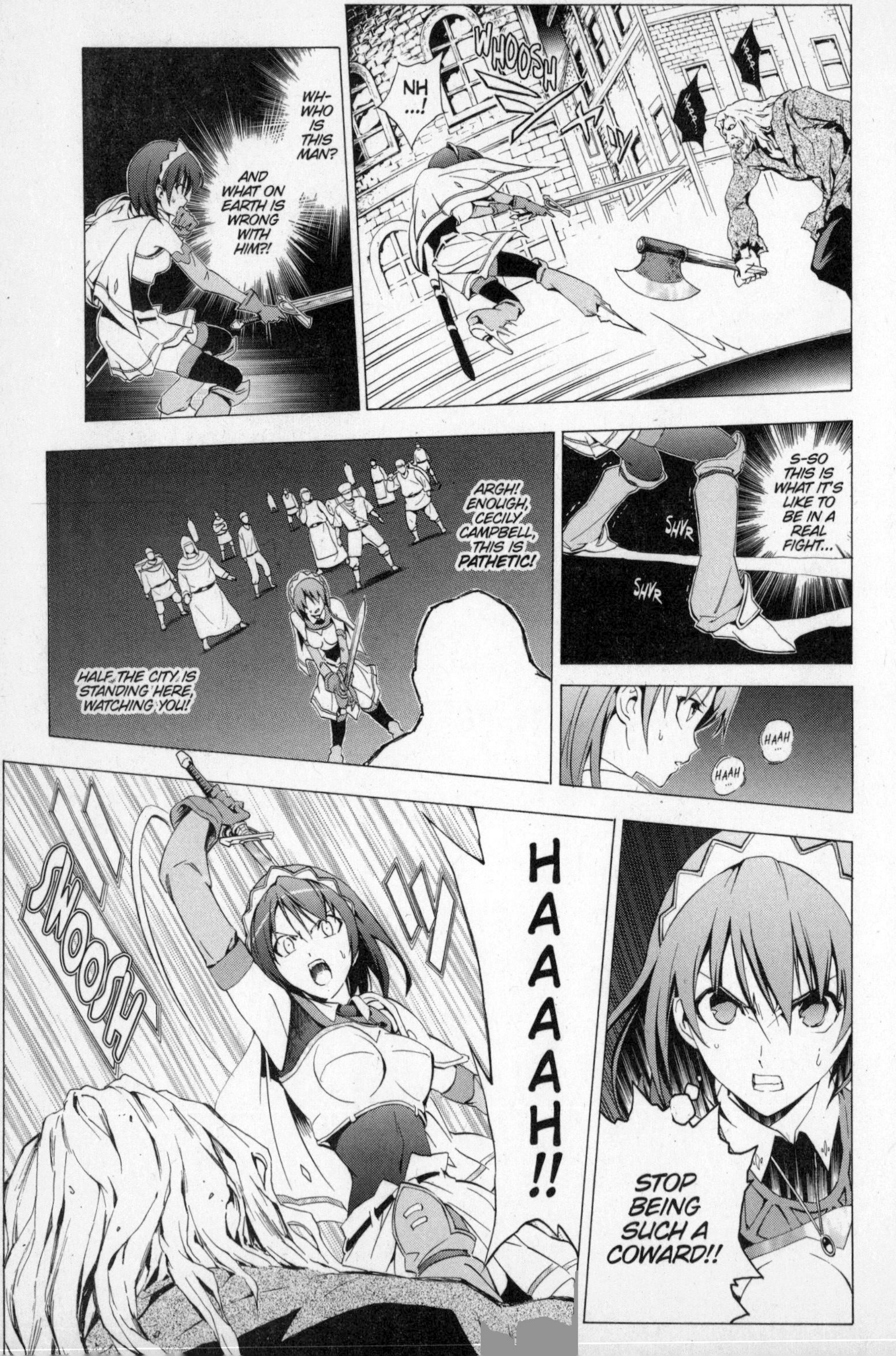

WHOOSH
NH ...!
WH- WHO IS THIS MAN?
AND WHAT ON EARTH IS WRONG WITH HIM?!
S-SO THIS IS WHAT IT'S LIKE TO BE IN A REAL FIGHT...
SHVR
SHVR
HAAH ...
HAAH ...
ARGH! ENOUGH, CECILY CAMPBELL, THIS IS PATHETIC!
HALF THE CITY IS STANDING HERE, WATCHING YOU!
STOP BEING SUCH A COWARD!!
HAAAAAH!!
SWOOSH

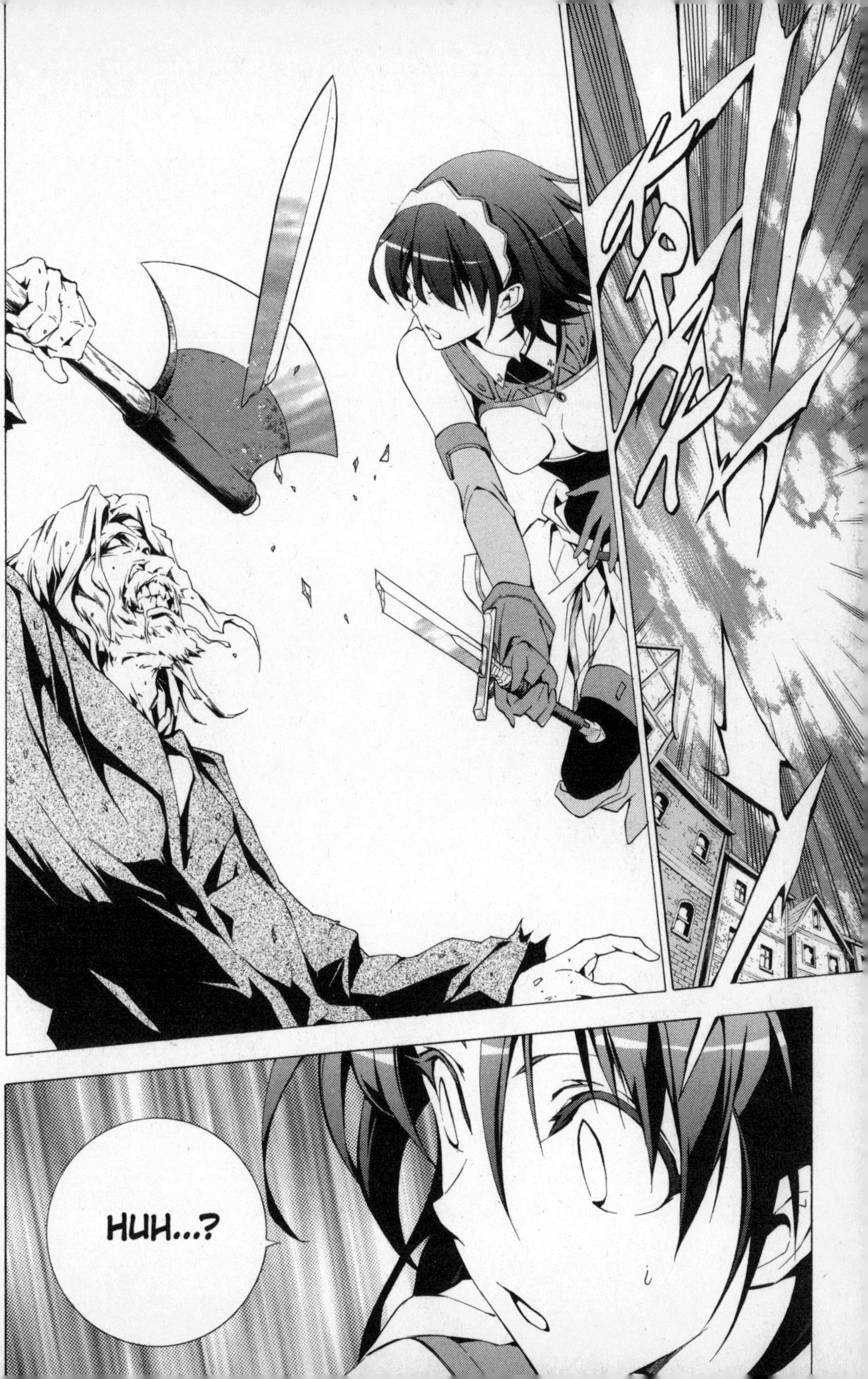
HUH...?

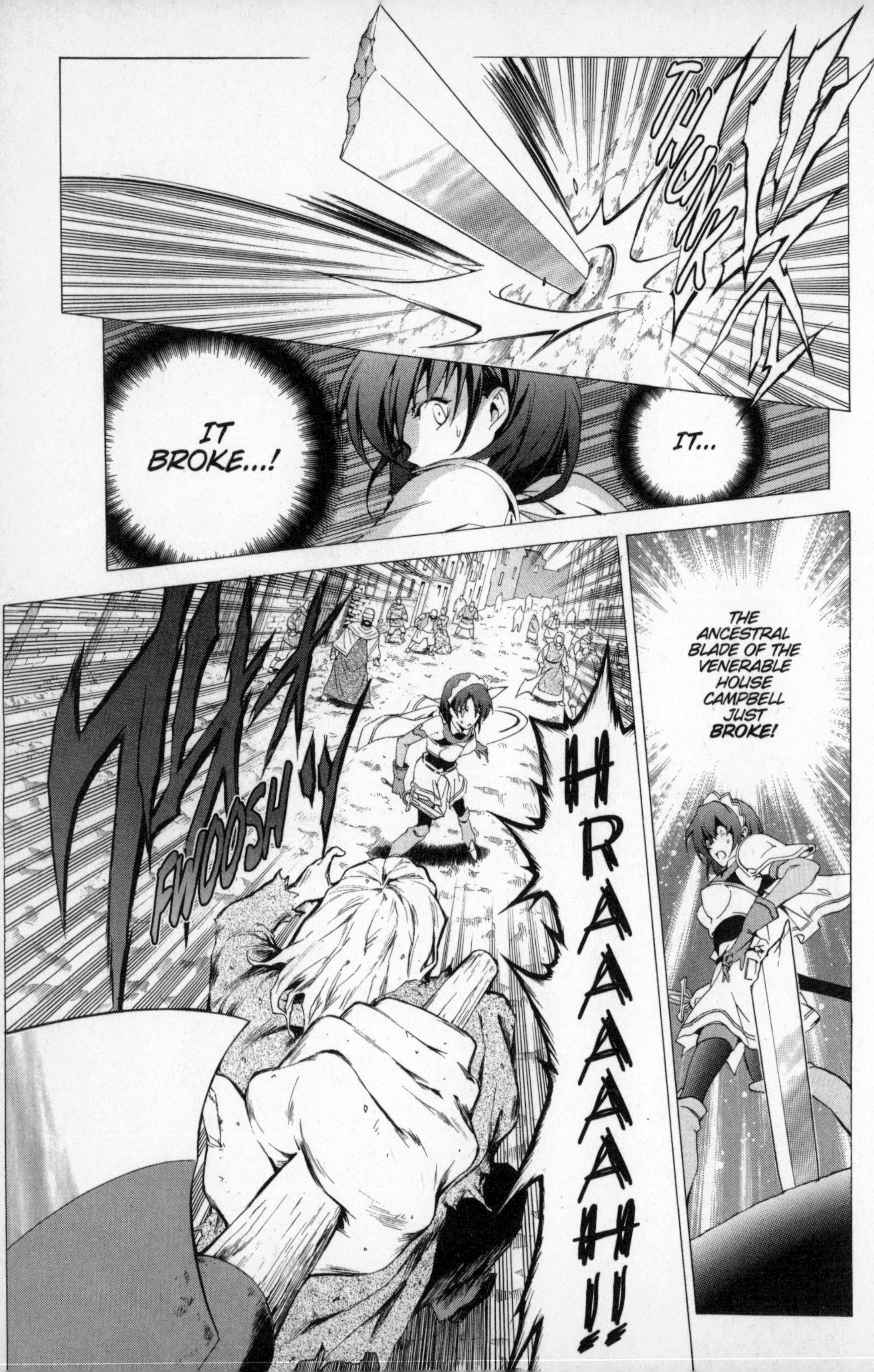
THUNK
IT...
IT BROKE...!
THE ANCESTRAL BLADE OF THE VENERABLE HOUSE CAMPBELL JUST BROKE!
HRAAAAAAH!!
FWOOSH

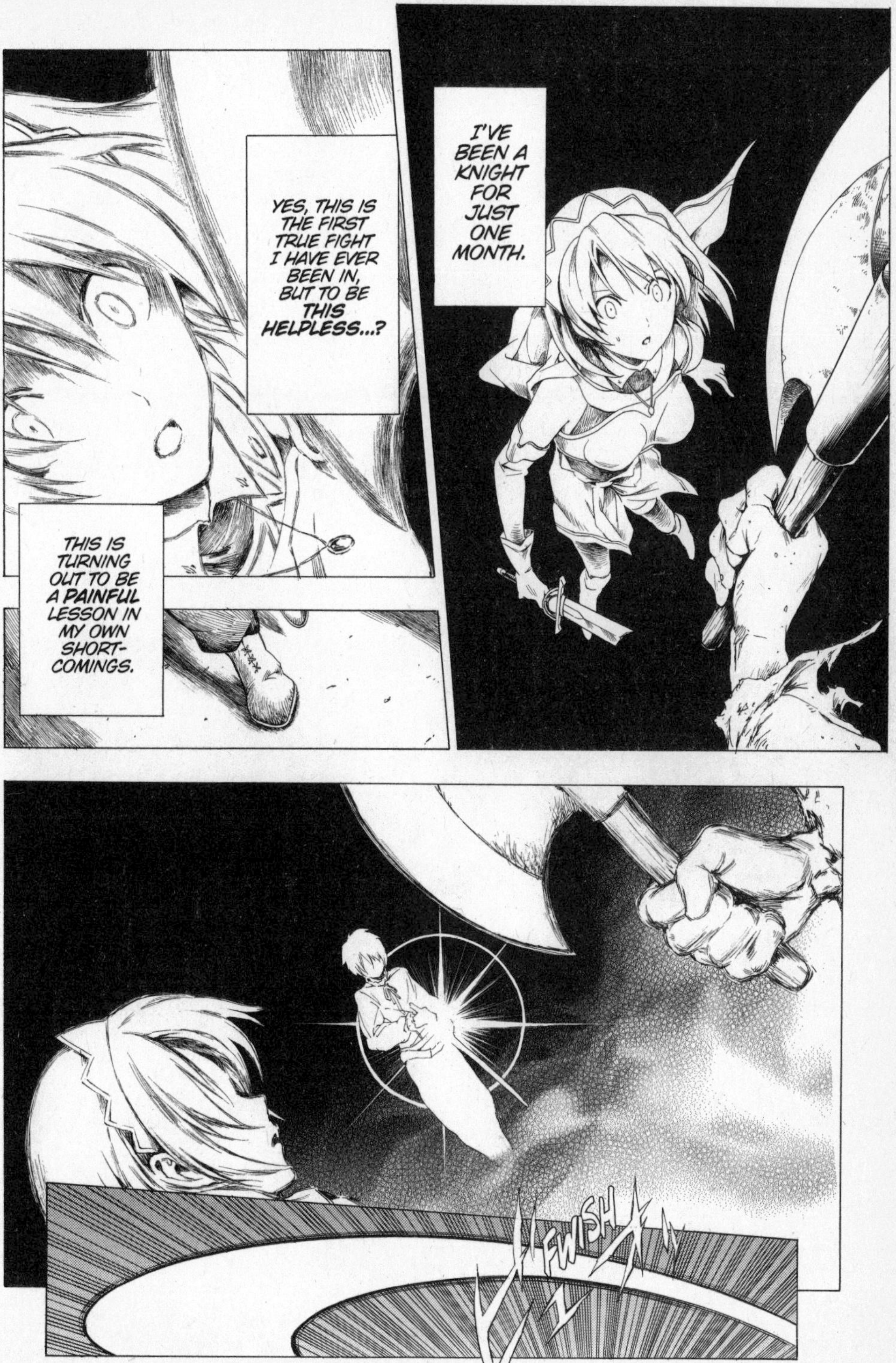
I'VE BEEN A KNIGHT FOR JUST ONE MONTH.
YES, THIS IS THE FIRST TRUE FIGHT I HAVE EVER BEEN IN, BUT TO BE **THIS HELPLESS...?**
THIS IS TURNING OUT TO BE A **PAINFUL** LESSON IN MY OWN SHORT-COMINGS.
FWISH

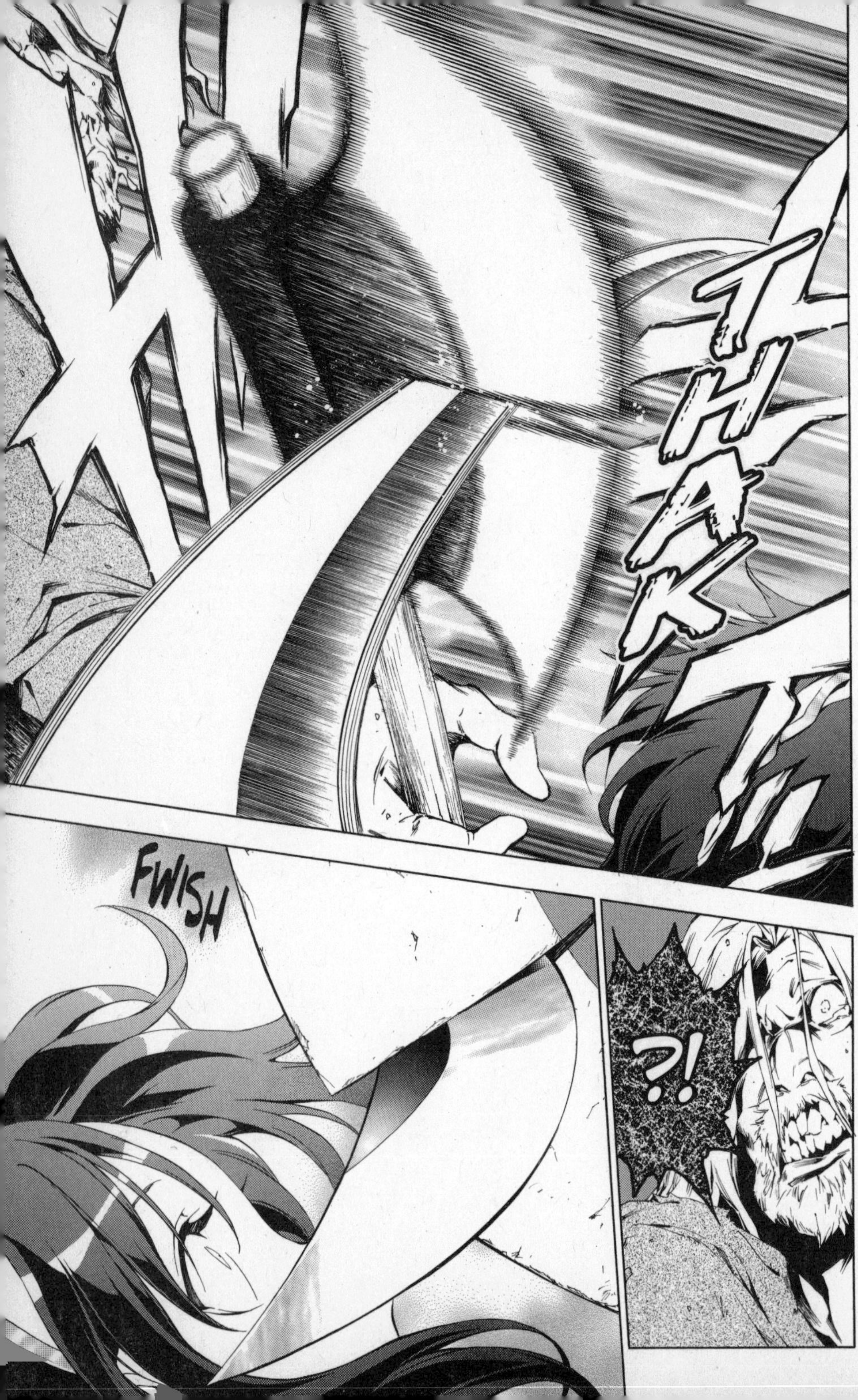
THACK
?!
FWISH

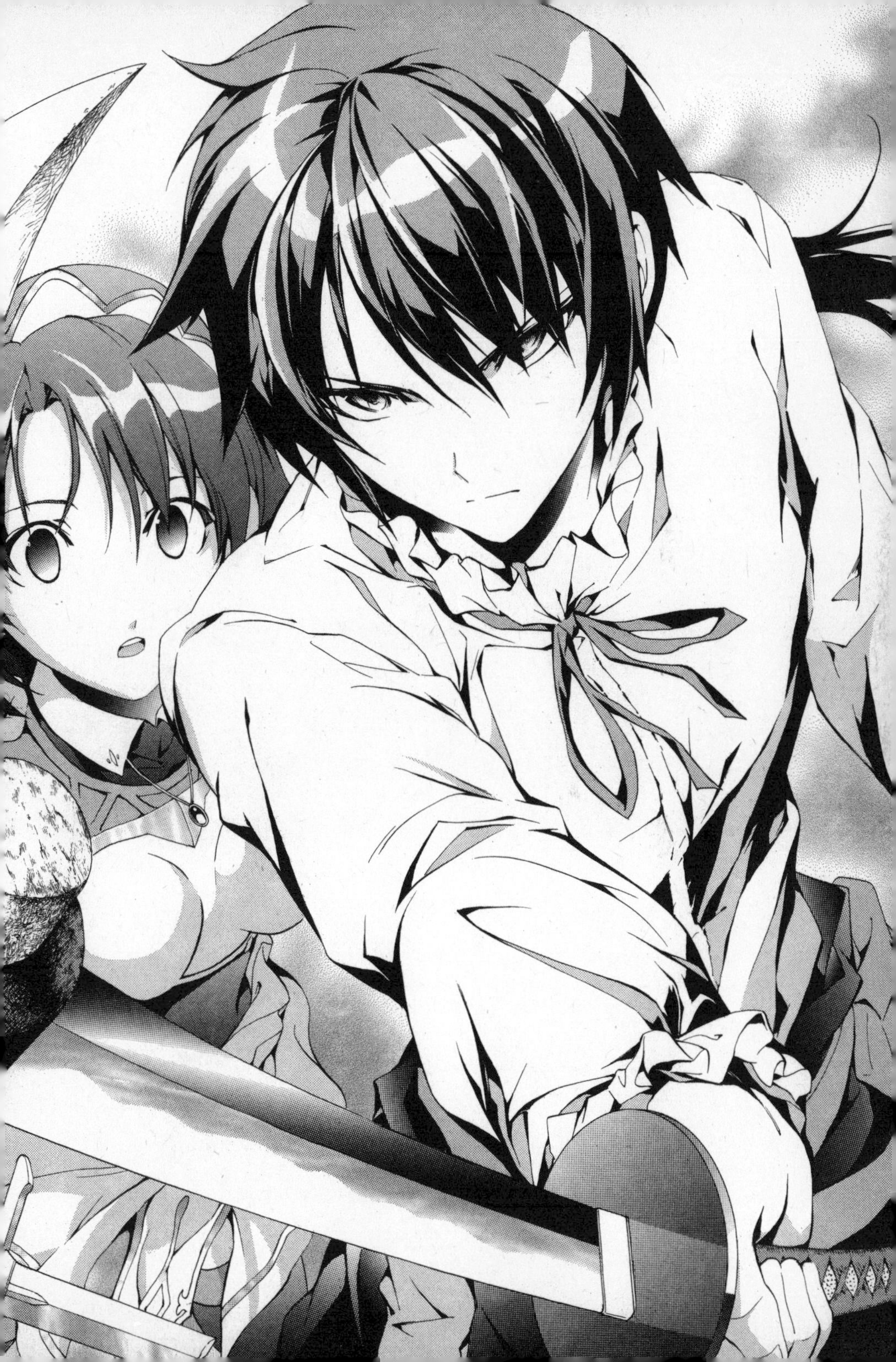

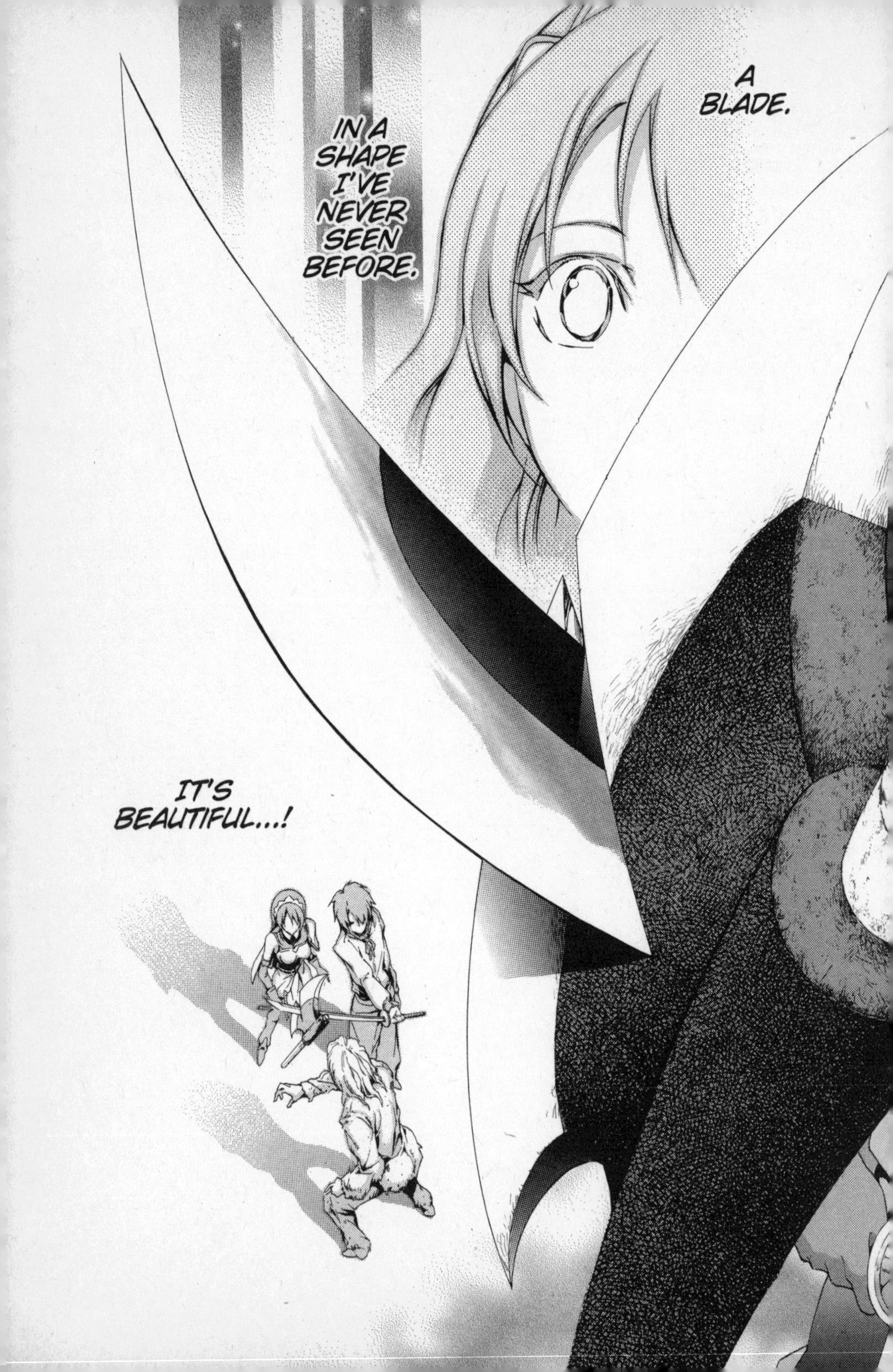
A BLADE.
IN A SHAPE I'VE NEVER SEEN BEFORE.
IT'S BEAUTIFUL...!

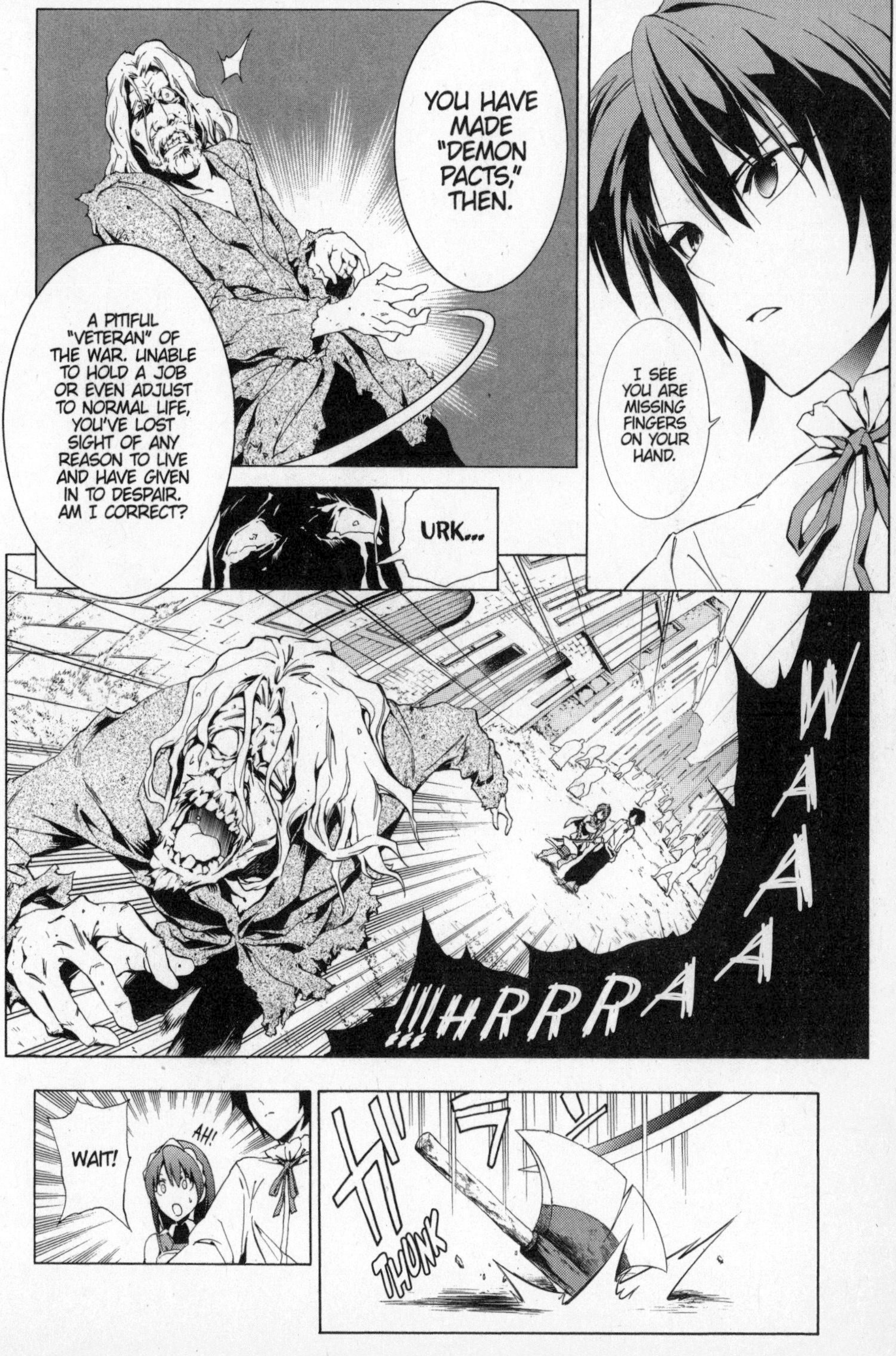
I SEE YOU ARE MISSING FINGERS ON YOUR HAND.
YOU HAVE MADE "DEMON PACTS," THEN.
A PITIFUL "VETERAN" OF THE WAR. UNABLE TO HOLD A JOB OR EVEN ADJUST TO NORMAL LIFE, YOU'VE LOST SIGHT OF ANY REASON TO LIVE AND HAVE GIVEN IN TO DESPAIR. AM I CORRECT?
URK...
WAAAAARRRRH!!!
THUNK
AH!
WAIT!

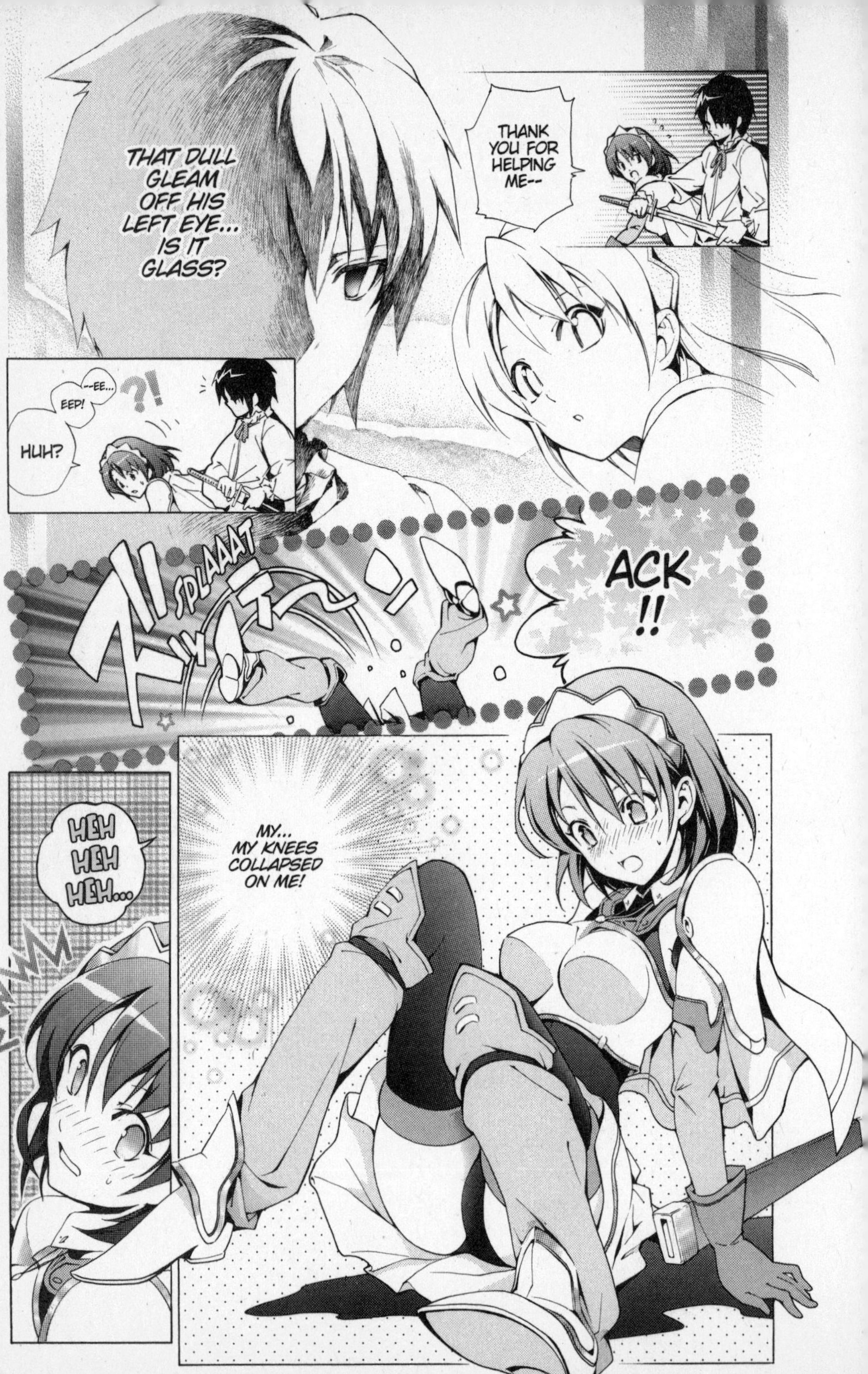
THANK YOU FOR HELPING ME--
THAT DULL GLEAM OFF HIS LEFT EYE... IS IT GLASS?
?!
--EE...
EEP!
HUH?
ACK !!
SPLAAAT
MY... MY KNEES COLLAPSED ON ME!
HEH HEH HEH...

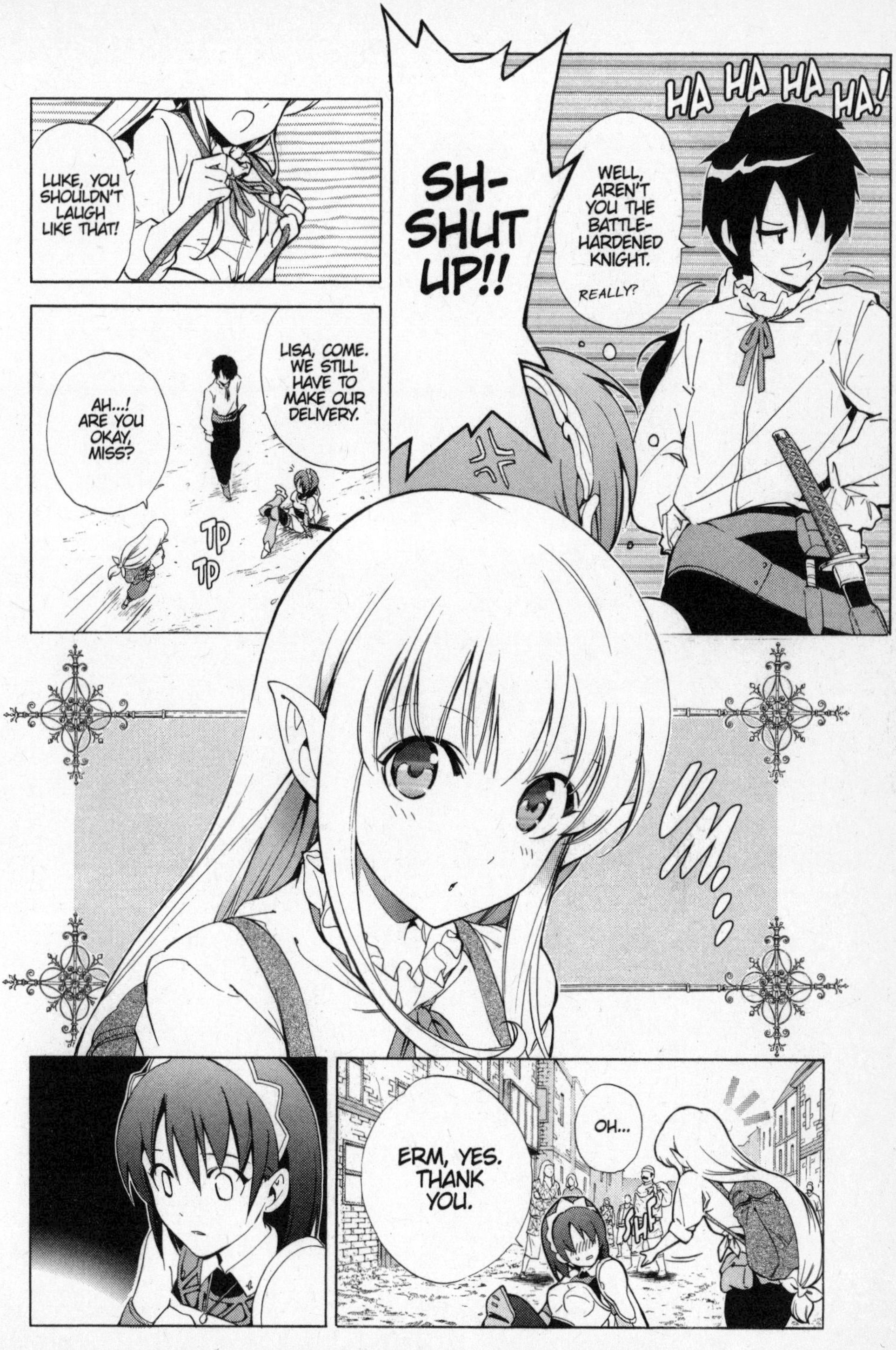
HA HA HA HA HA!
WELL, AREN'T YOU THE BATTLE-HARDENED KNIGHT.
REALLY?
SH-SHUT UP!!
LUKE, YOU SHOULDN'T LAUGH LIKE THAT!
LISA, COME. WE STILL HAVE TO MAKE OUR DELIVERY.
AH...! ARE YOU OKAY, MISS?
TP TP
UM...
OH...
ERM, YES. THANK YOU.

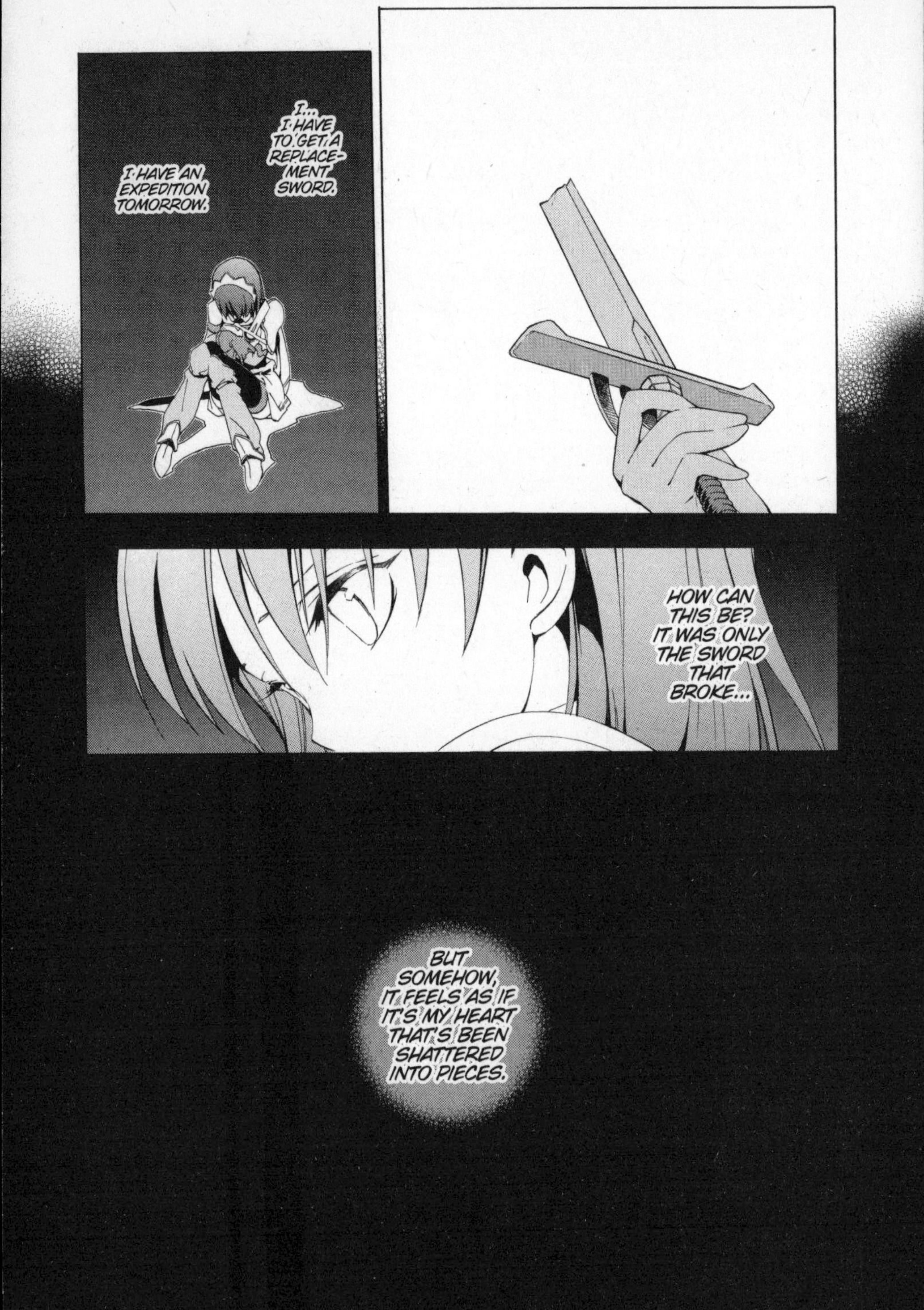
I... I HAVE TO GET A REPLACEMENT SWORD.
I HAVE AN EXPEDITION TOMORROW.
HOW CAN THIS BE? IT WAS ONLY THE SWORD THAT BROKE...
BUT SOMEHOW, IT FEELS AS IF IT'S MY HEART THAT'S BEEN SHATTERED INTO PIECES.

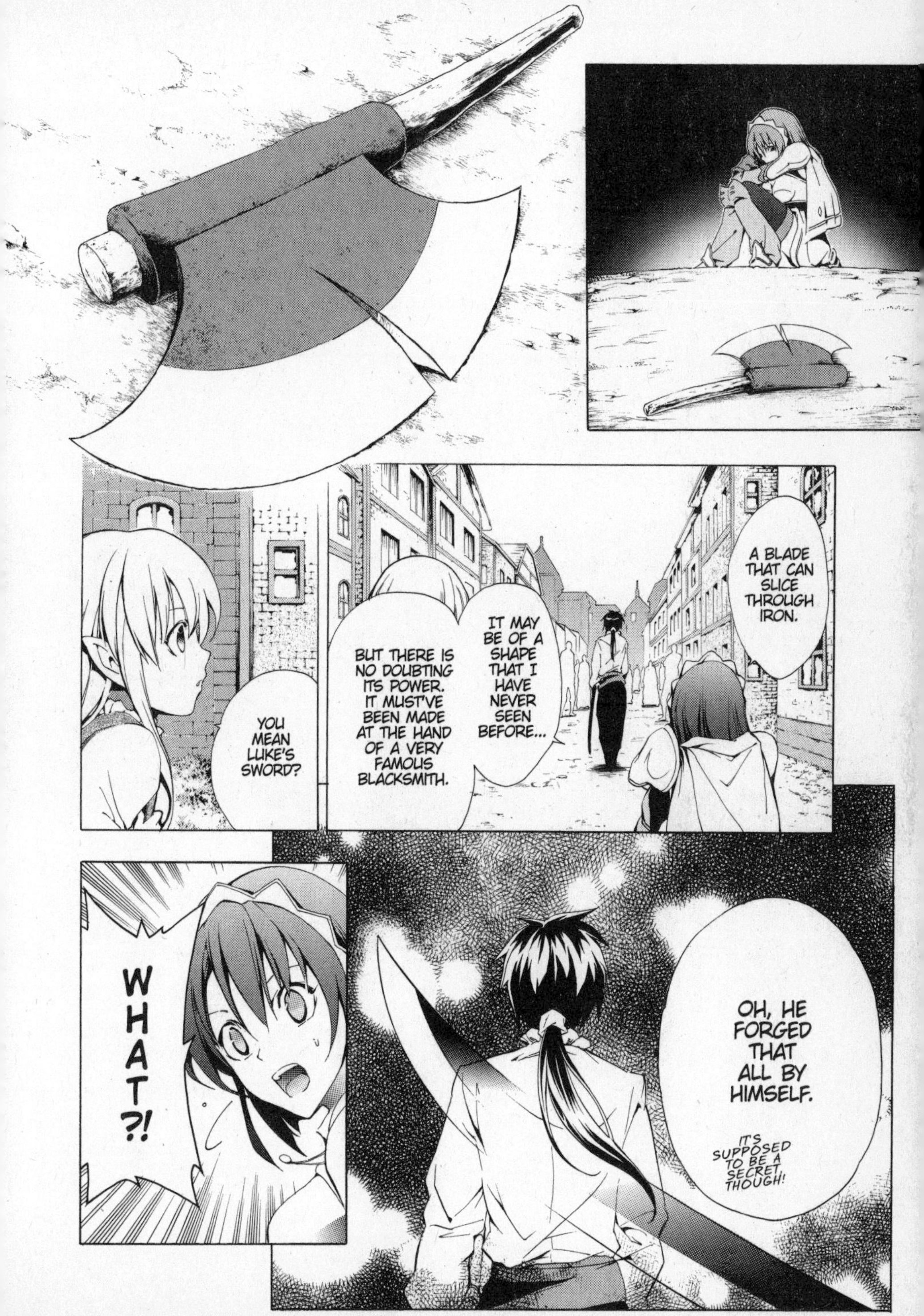
A BLADE THAT CAN SLICE THROUGH IRON.
IT MAY BE OF A SHAPE THAT I HAVE NEVER SEEN BEFORE...
BUT THERE IS NO DOUBTING ITS POWER. IT MUST'VE BEEN MADE AT THE HAND OF A VERY FAMOUS BLACKSMITH.
YOU MEAN LUKE'S SWORD?
OH, HE FORGED THAT ALL BY HIMSELF.
IT'S SUPPOSED TO BE A SECRET, THOUGH!
WHAT?!

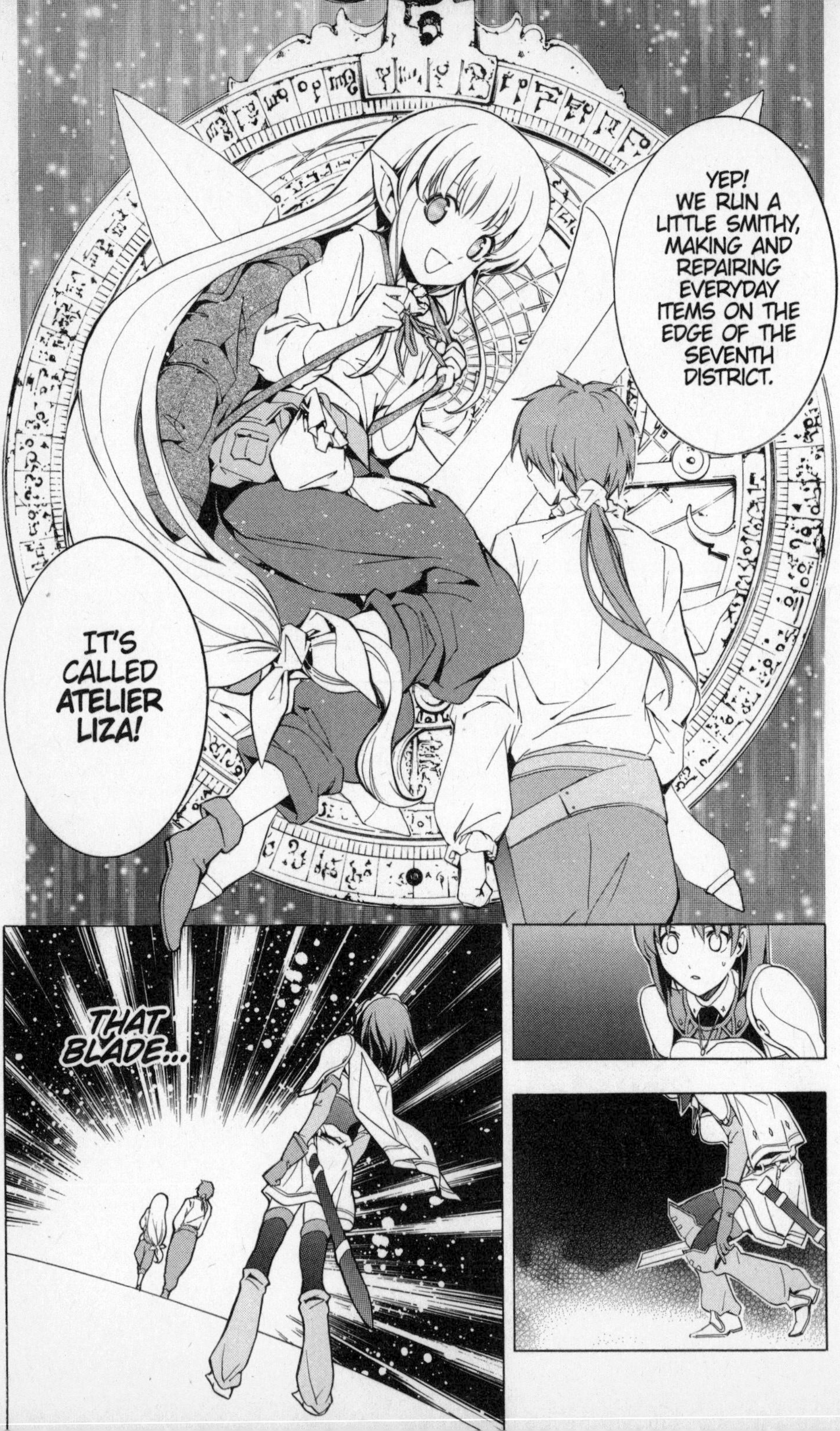
YEP! WE RUN A LITTLE SMITHY, MAKING AND REPAIRING EVERYDAY ITEMS ON THE EDGE OF THE SEVENTH DISTRICT.
IT'S CALLED ATELIER LIZA!
THAT BLADE...

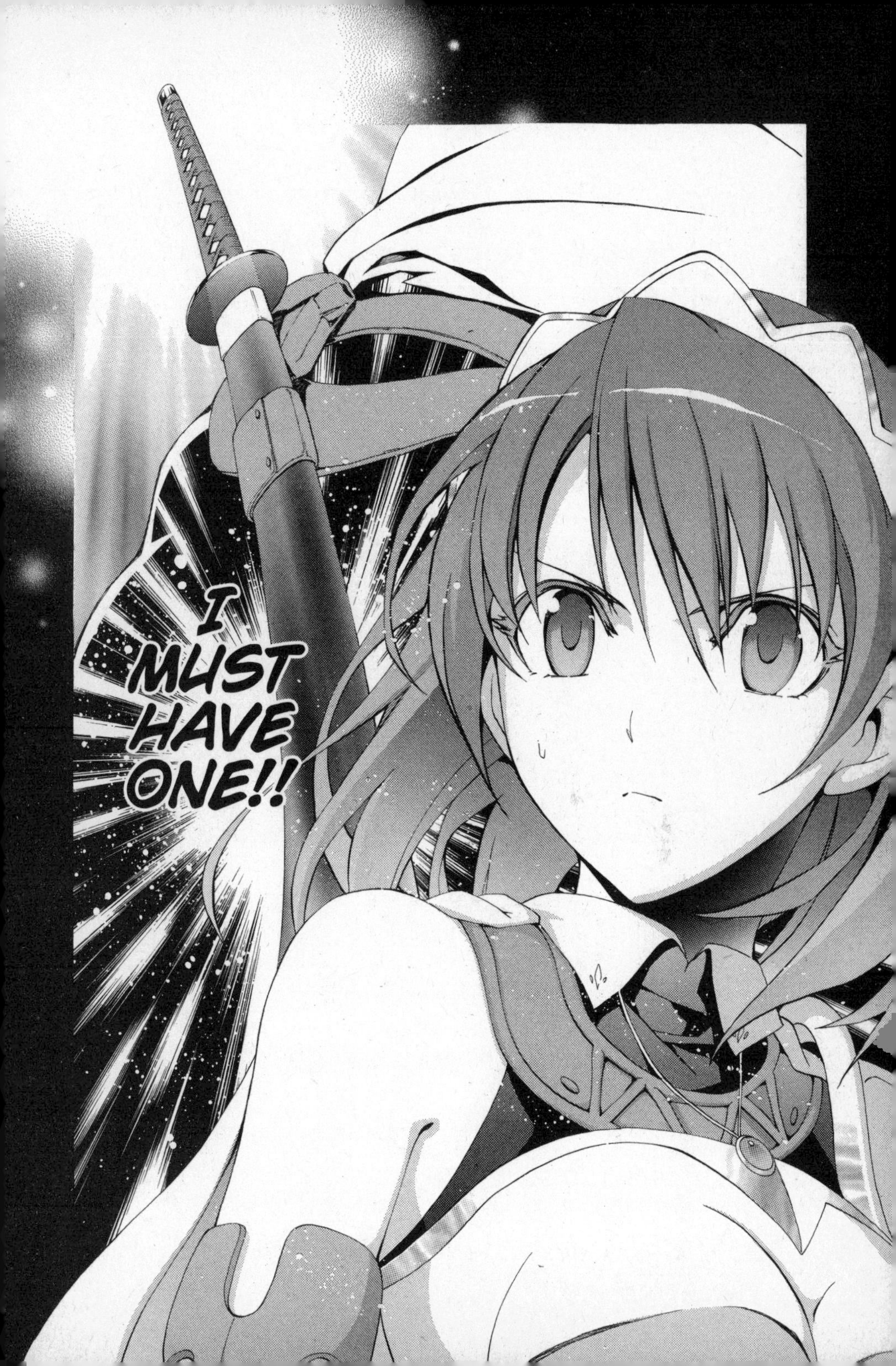
I MUST HAVE ONE!!

Continent

A volcanic zone
"Blair Volcano"

"Housman's Forest"

Independent Trade Cities
"Housman"

Empire
(Imperial Territory)

The Crowd Powers

a militant nation
(& A territory of a militant nation)

Forty-four years after the
close of the Valbanill War—
The Empire, the Crowd Powers, and the
Militant Nation have all withdrawn,
segregating themselves from each other.
And so, the continent entered an age of peace.

Tucked away in a corner of the
continent, one of the independent
Trade Cities, "Housman."

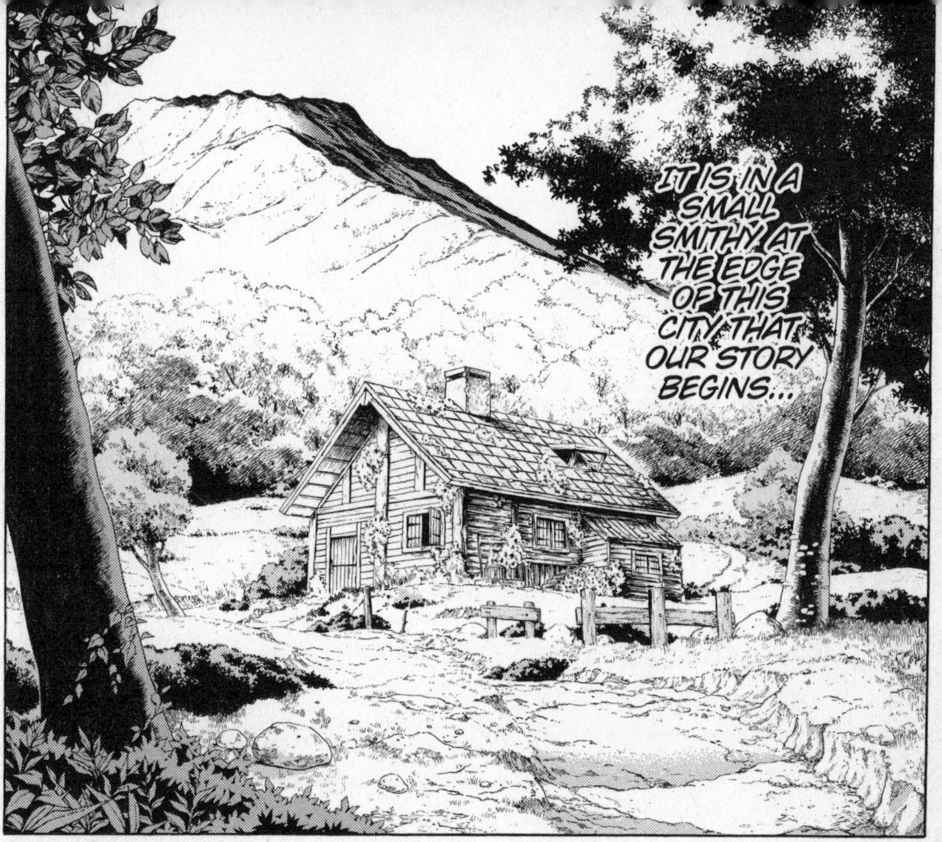
IT IS IN A SMALL SMITHY AT THE EDGE OF THIS CITY THAT OUR STORY BEGINS...

Chapter 1 Knight (Part 1)

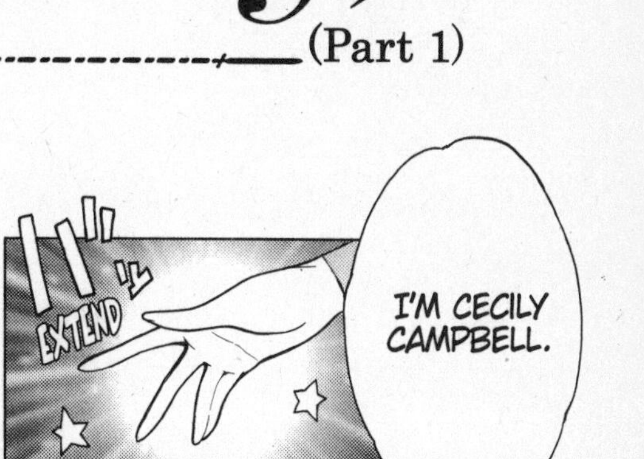
I'M CECILY CAMPBELL.
EXTEND

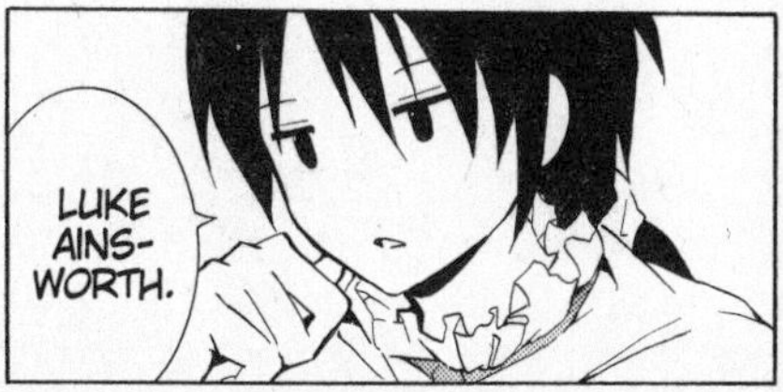
LUKE AINS-WORTH.

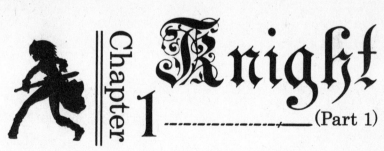

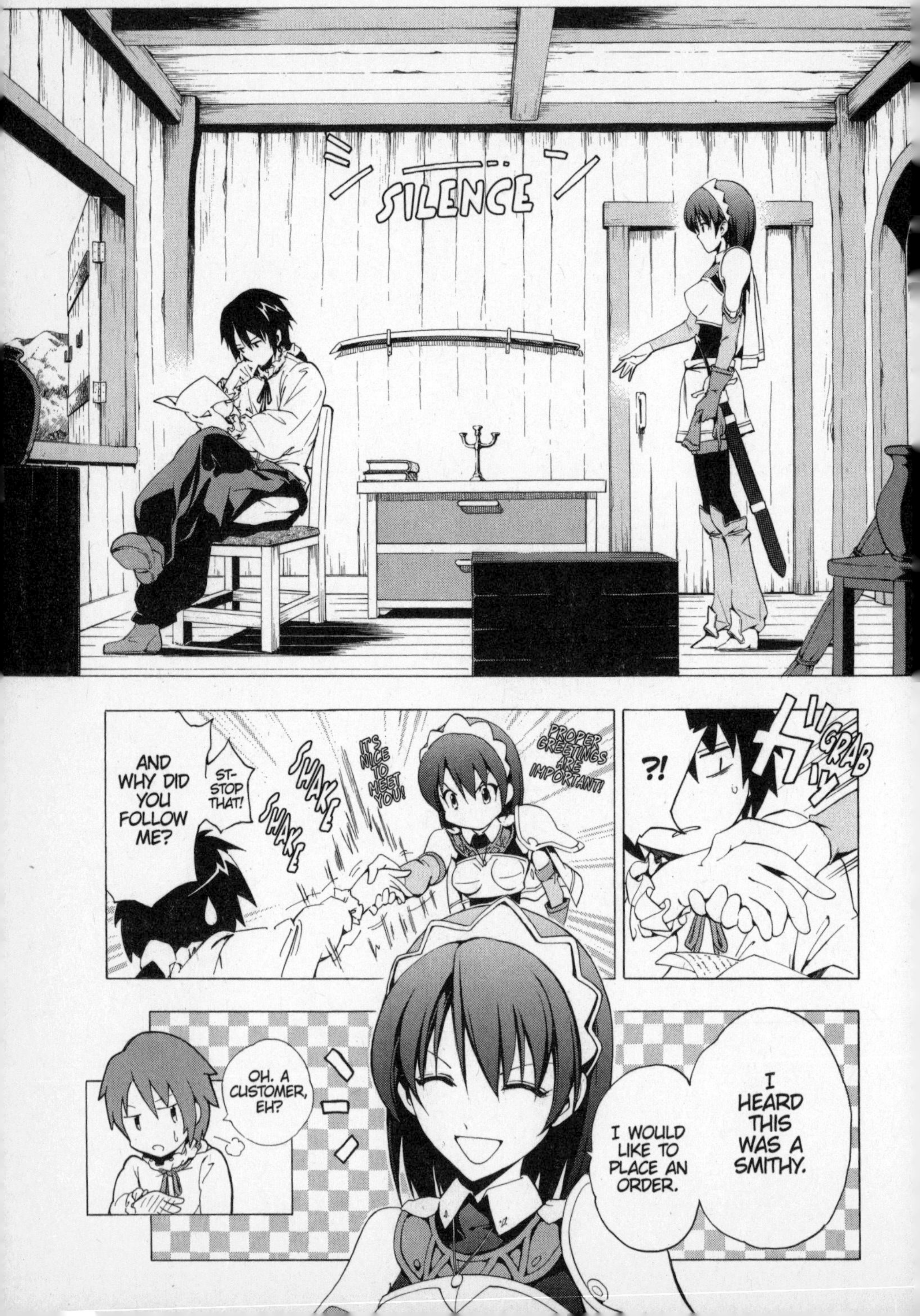
SILENCE
?!
GRAB
PROPER GREETINGS ARE IMPORTANT!
IT'S NICE TO MEET YOU!
SHAKE
SHAKE
ST-STOP THAT!
AND WHY DID YOU FOLLOW ME?
I HEARD THIS WAS A SMITHY.
I WOULD LIKE TO PLACE AN ORDER.
OH. A CUSTOMER, EH?

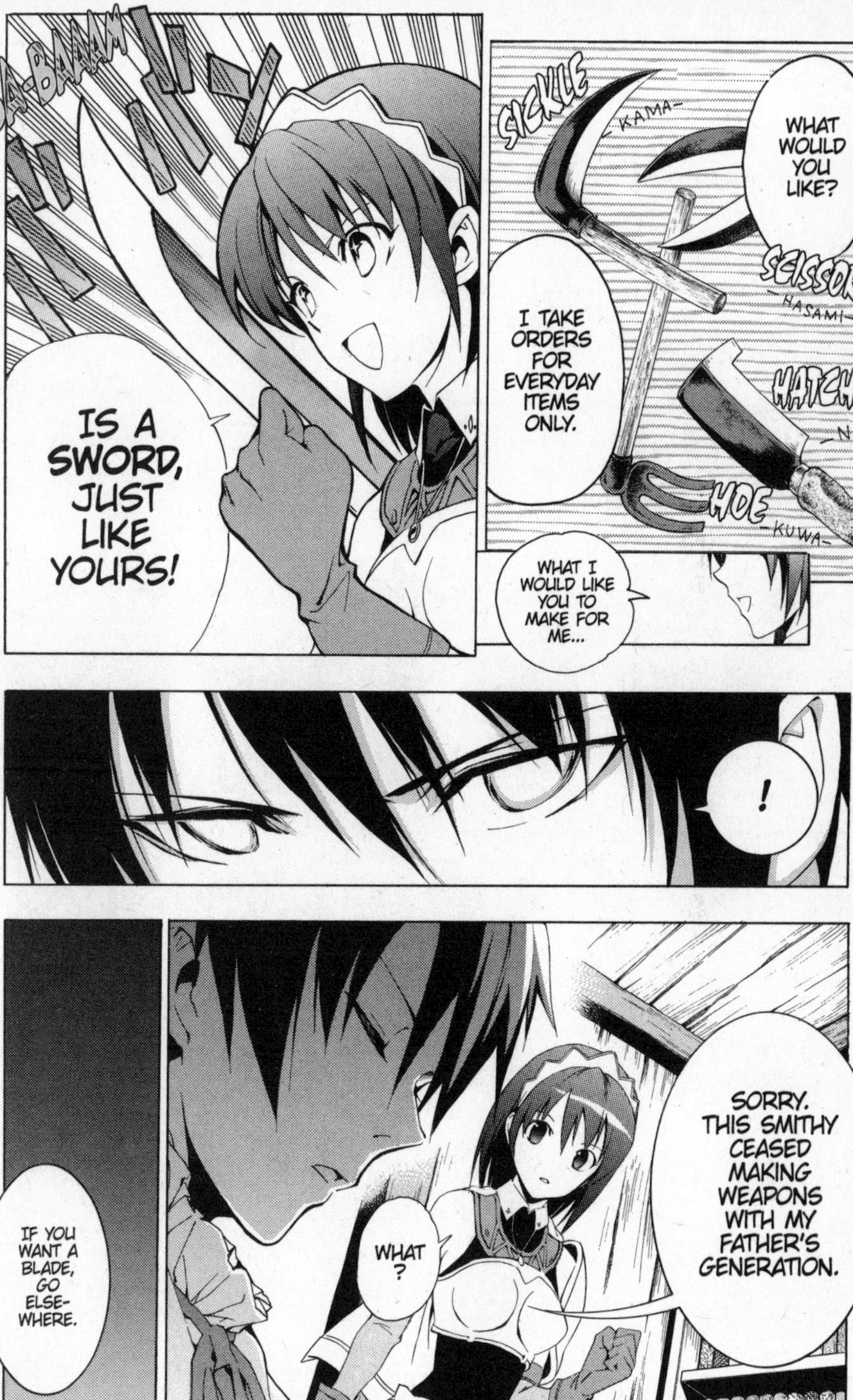
WHAT WOULD YOU LIKE?
SICKLE
—KAMA—
SCISSORS
—HASAMI—
I TAKE ORDERS FOR EVERYDAY ITEMS ONLY.
HATCHET
—NATA—
HOE
—KUWA—
WHAT I WOULD LIKE YOU TO MAKE FOR ME...
BA-BAAAM
IS A SWORD, JUST LIKE YOURS!
!
SORRY. THIS SMITHY CEASED MAKING WEAPONS WITH MY FATHER'S GENERATION.
WHAT?
IF YOU WANT A BLADE, GO ELSE-WHERE.

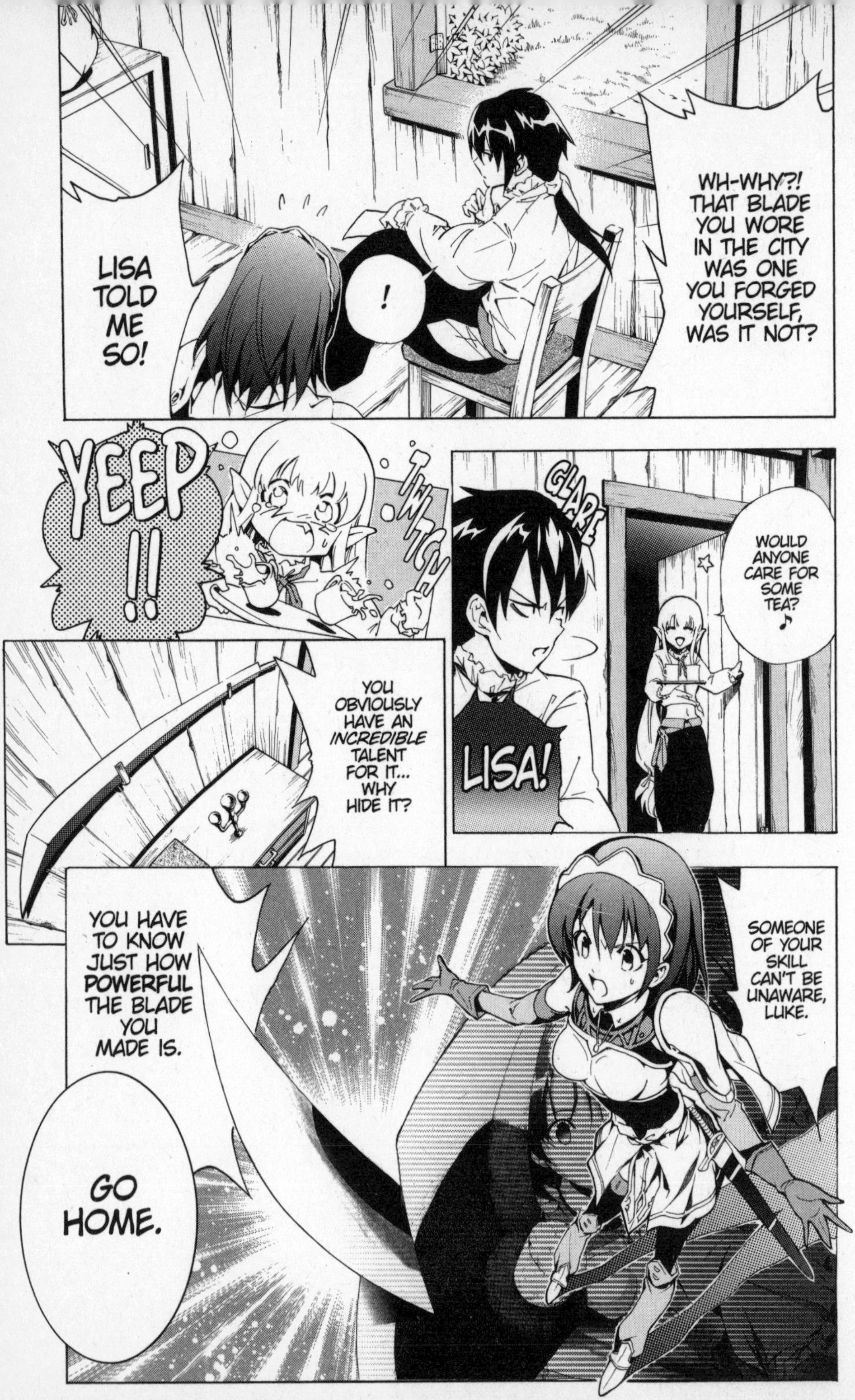
WH-WHY?! THAT BLADE YOU WORE IN THE CITY WAS ONE YOU FORGED YOURSELF, WAS IT NOT?
!
LISA TOLD ME SO!
WOULD ANYONE CARE FOR SOME TEA? ♪
GLARE
LISA!
YEEP!!
TWITCH
YOU OBVIOUSLY HAVE AN *INCREDIBLE* TALENT FOR IT... WHY HIDE IT?
SOMEONE OF YOUR SKILL CAN'T BE UNAWARE, LUKE.
YOU HAVE TO KNOW JUST HOW **POWERFUL** THE BLADE YOU MADE IS.
GO HOME.

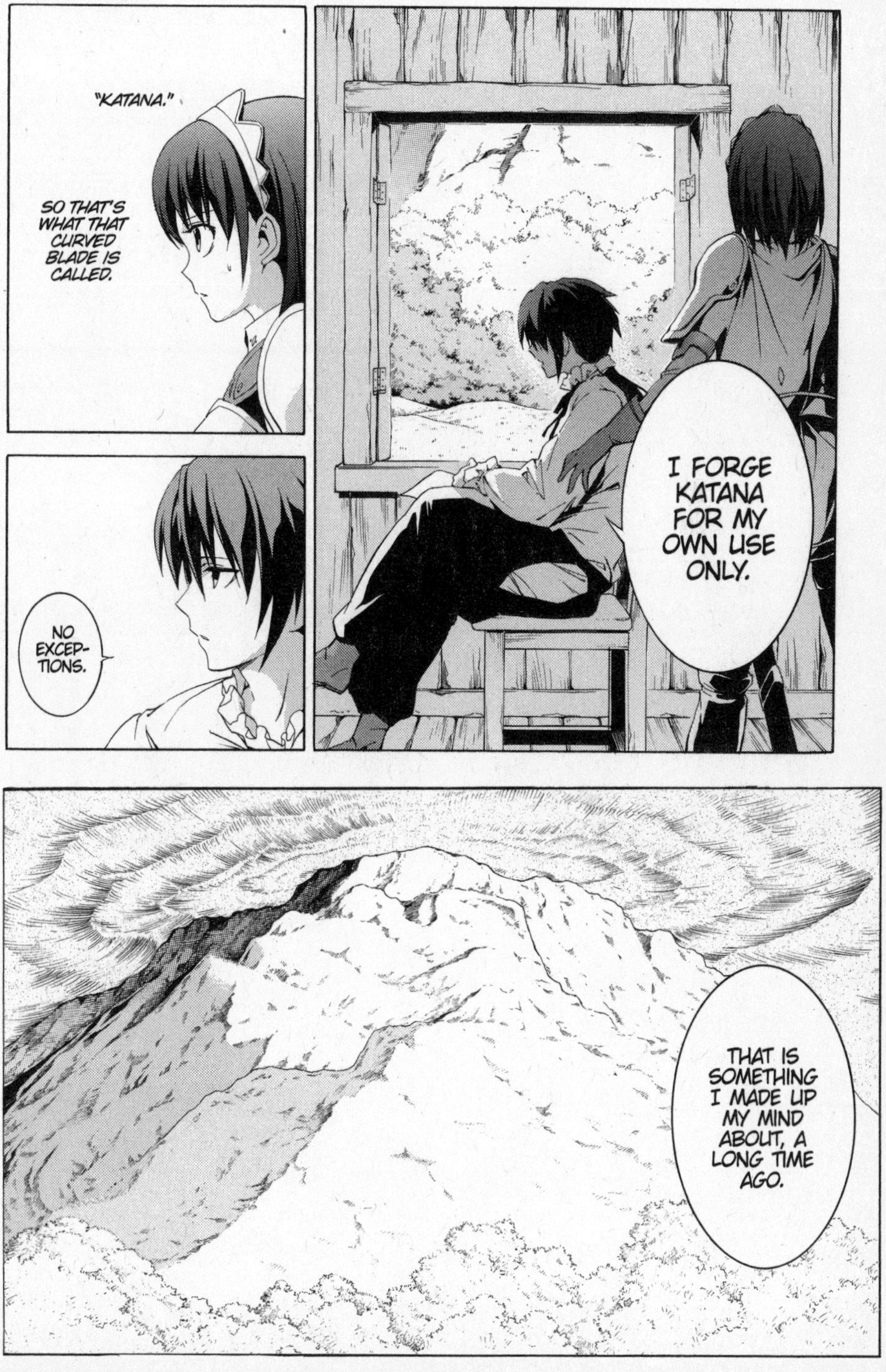
I FORGE KATANA FOR MY OWN USE ONLY.
"KATANA."
SO THAT'S WHAT THAT CURVED BLADE IS CALLED.
NO EXCEPTIONS.
THAT IS SOMETHING I MADE UP MY MIND ABOUT, A LONG TIME AGO.

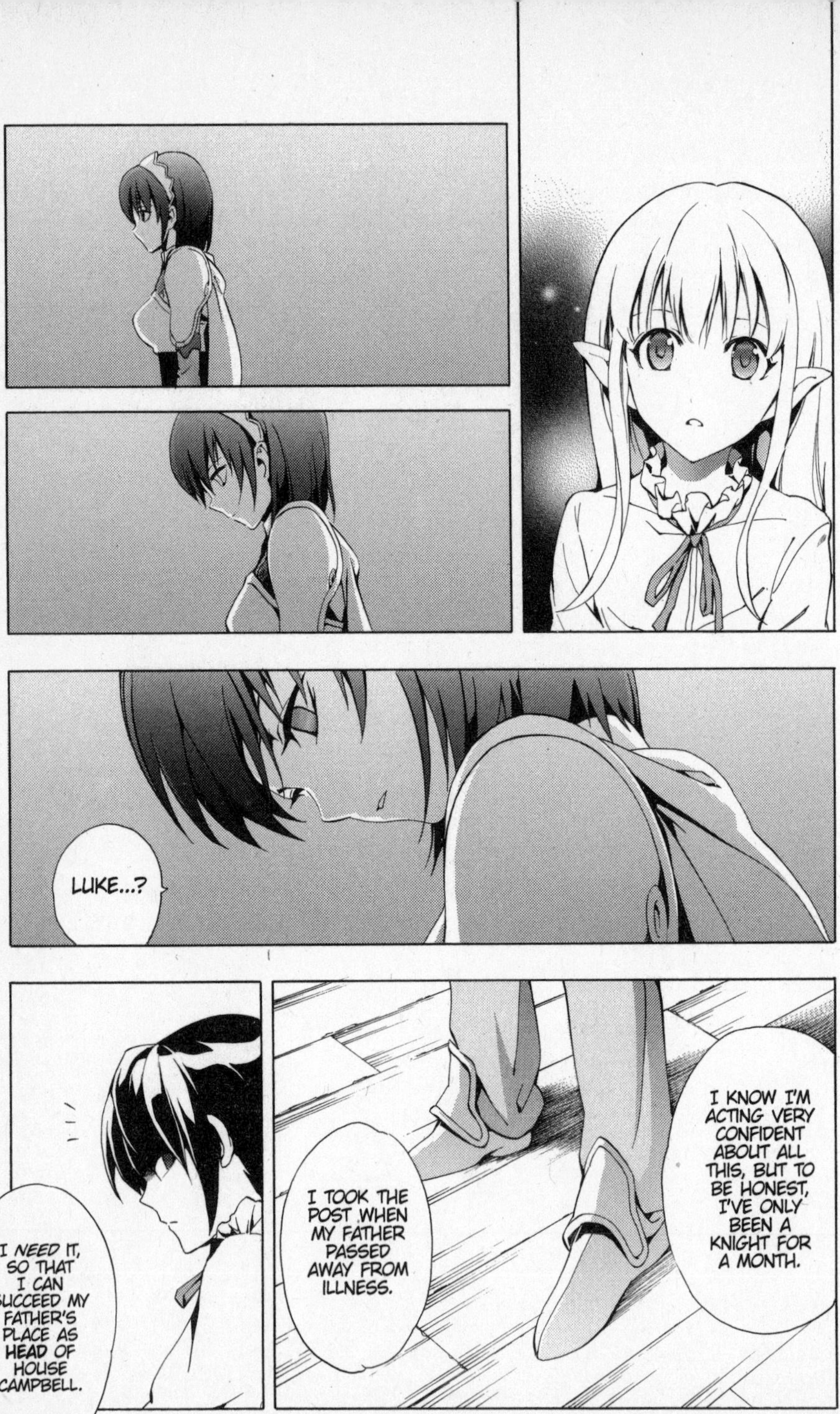
LUKE...?
I KNOW I'M ACTING VERY CONFIDENT ABOUT ALL THIS, BUT TO BE HONEST, I'VE ONLY BEEN A KNIGHT FOR A MONTH.
I TOOK THE POST WHEN MY FATHER PASSED AWAY FROM ILLNESS.
I *NEED* IT, SO THAT I CAN SUCCEED MY FATHER'S PLACE AS **HEAD OF HOUSE CAMPBELL.**

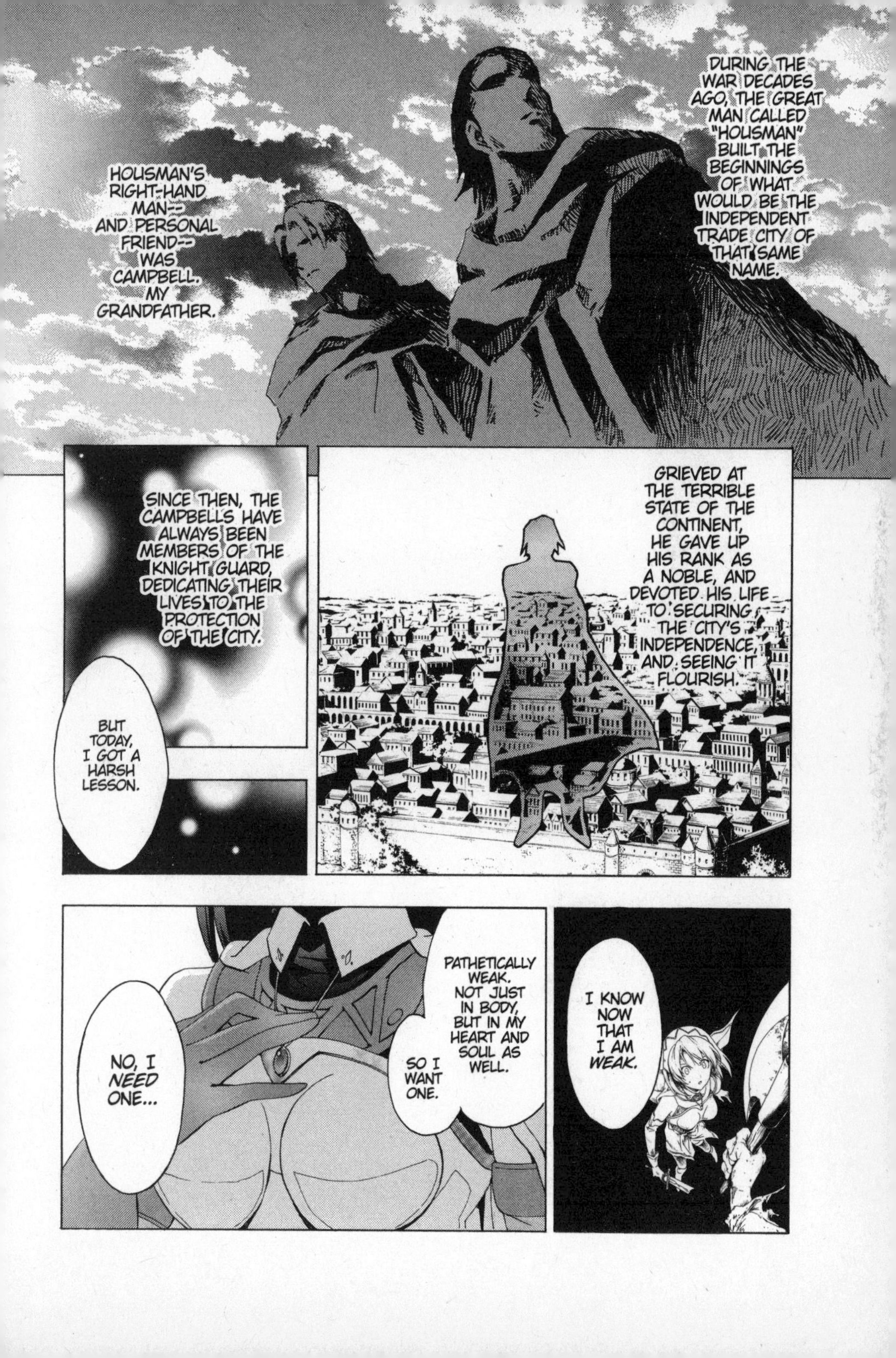
DURING THE WAR DECADES AGO, THE GREAT MAN CALLED "HOUSMAN" BUILT THE BEGINNINGS OF WHAT WOULD BE THE INDEPENDENT TRADE CITY OF THAT SAME NAME.
HOUSMAN'S RIGHT-HAND MAN-- AND PERSONAL FRIEND-- WAS CAMPBELL. MY GRANDFATHER.
GRIEVED AT THE TERRIBLE STATE OF THE CONTINENT, HE GAVE UP HIS RANK AS A NOBLE, AND DEVOTED HIS LIFE TO SECURING THE CITY'S INDEPENDENCE, AND SEEING IT FLOURISH.
SINCE THEN, THE CAMPBELLS HAVE ALWAYS BEEN MEMBERS OF THE KNIGHT GUARD, DEDICATING THEIR LIVES TO THE PROTECTION OF THE CITY.
BUT TODAY, I GOT A HARSH LESSON.
I KNOW NOW THAT I AM *WEAK*.
PATHETICALLY WEAK. NOT JUST IN BODY, BUT IN MY HEART AND SOUL AS WELL.
SO I WANT ONE.
NO, I *NEED* ONE...

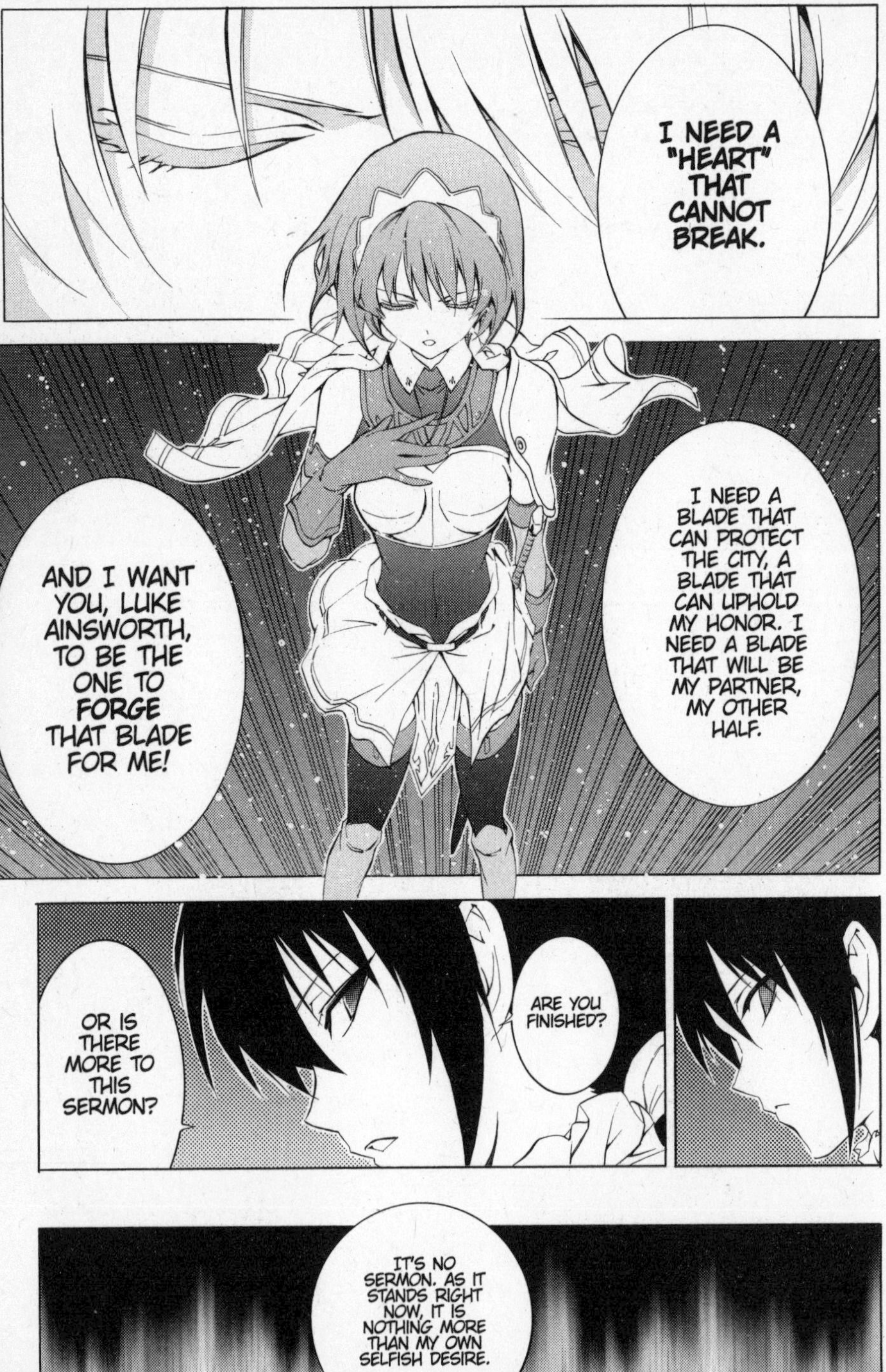
I NEED A "HEART" THAT CANNOT BREAK.
I NEED A BLADE THAT CAN PROTECT THE CITY, A BLADE THAT CAN UPHOLD MY HONOR. I NEED A BLADE THAT WILL BE MY PARTNER, MY OTHER HALF.
AND I WANT YOU, LUKE AINSWORTH, TO BE THE ONE TO **FORGE** THAT BLADE FOR ME!
ARE YOU FINISHED?
OR IS THERE MORE TO THIS SERMON?
IT'S NO SERMON. AS IT STANDS RIGHT NOW, IT IS NOTHING MORE THAN MY OWN SELFISH DESIRE.

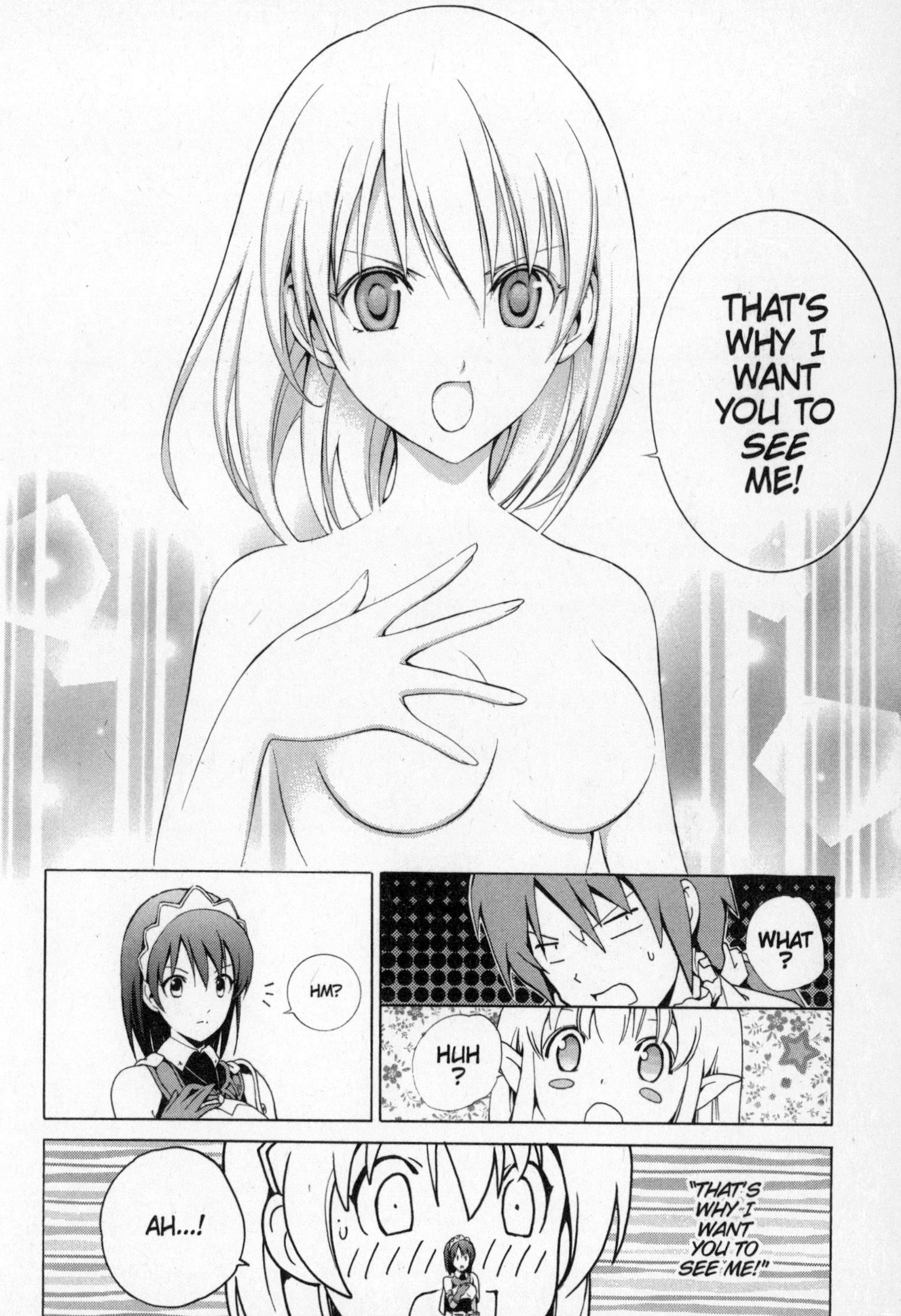
THAT'S WHY I WANT YOU TO SEE ME!
WHAT?
HUH?
HM?
"THAT'S WHY I WANT YOU TO SEE ME!"
AH...!

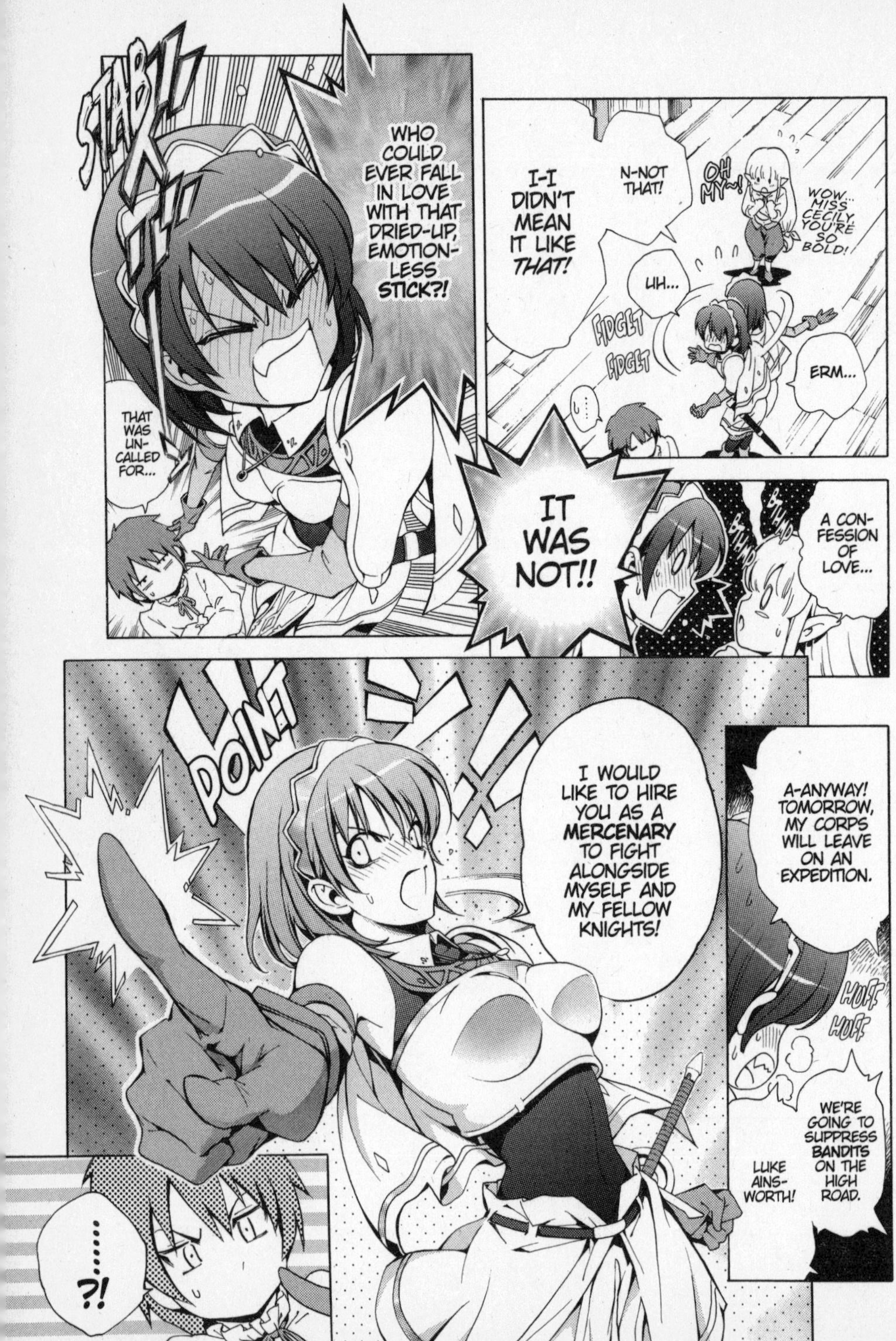

WOW... MISS CECILY, YOU'RE SO BOLD!
OH MY~!
N-NOT THAT!
I-I DIDN'T MEAN IT LIKE *THAT!*
UH...
ERM...
FIDGET FIDGET
...
A CON-FESSION OF LOVE...
IT WAS NOT!!
STAB!!
WHO COULD EVER FALL IN LOVE WITH THAT DRIED-UP, EMOTION-LESS STICK?!
THAT WAS UN-CALLED FOR...
A-ANYWAY! TOMORROW, MY CORPS WILL LEAVE ON AN EXPEDITION.
HUFF HUFF
WE'RE GOING TO SUPPRESS BANDITS ON THE HIGH ROAD.
LUKE AINS-WORTH!
I WOULD LIKE TO HIRE YOU AS A **MERCENARY** TO FIGHT ALONGSIDE MYSELF AND MY FELLOW KNIGHTS!
POINT
......?!

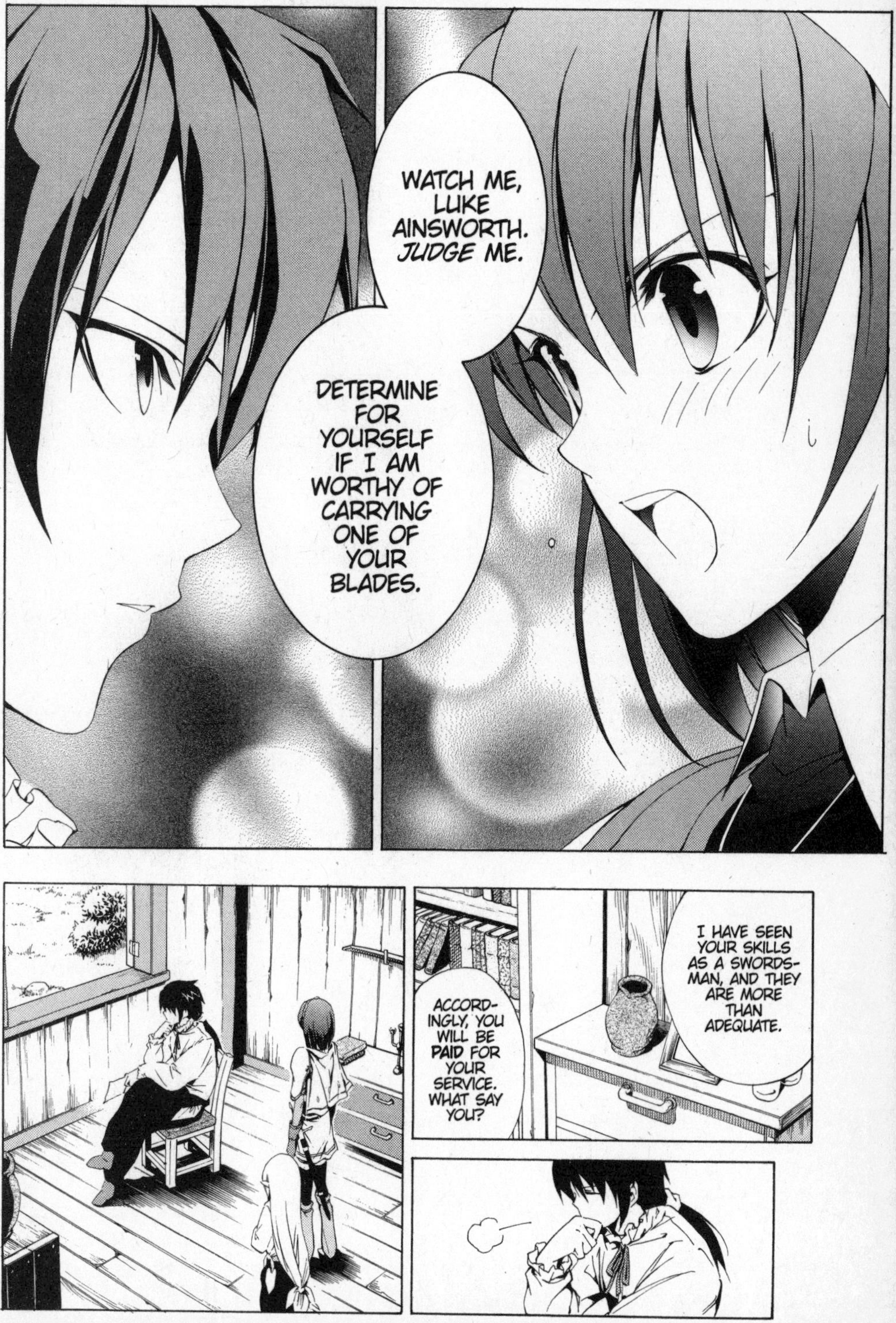
WATCH ME, LUKE AINSWORTH. JUDGE ME.
DETERMINE FOR YOURSELF IF I AM WORTHY OF CARRYING ONE OF YOUR BLADES.
I HAVE SEEN YOUR SKILLS AS A SWORDS-MAN, AND THEY ARE MORE THAN ADEQUATE.
ACCORD-INGLY, YOU WILL BE PAID FOR YOUR SERVICE. WHAT SAY YOU?

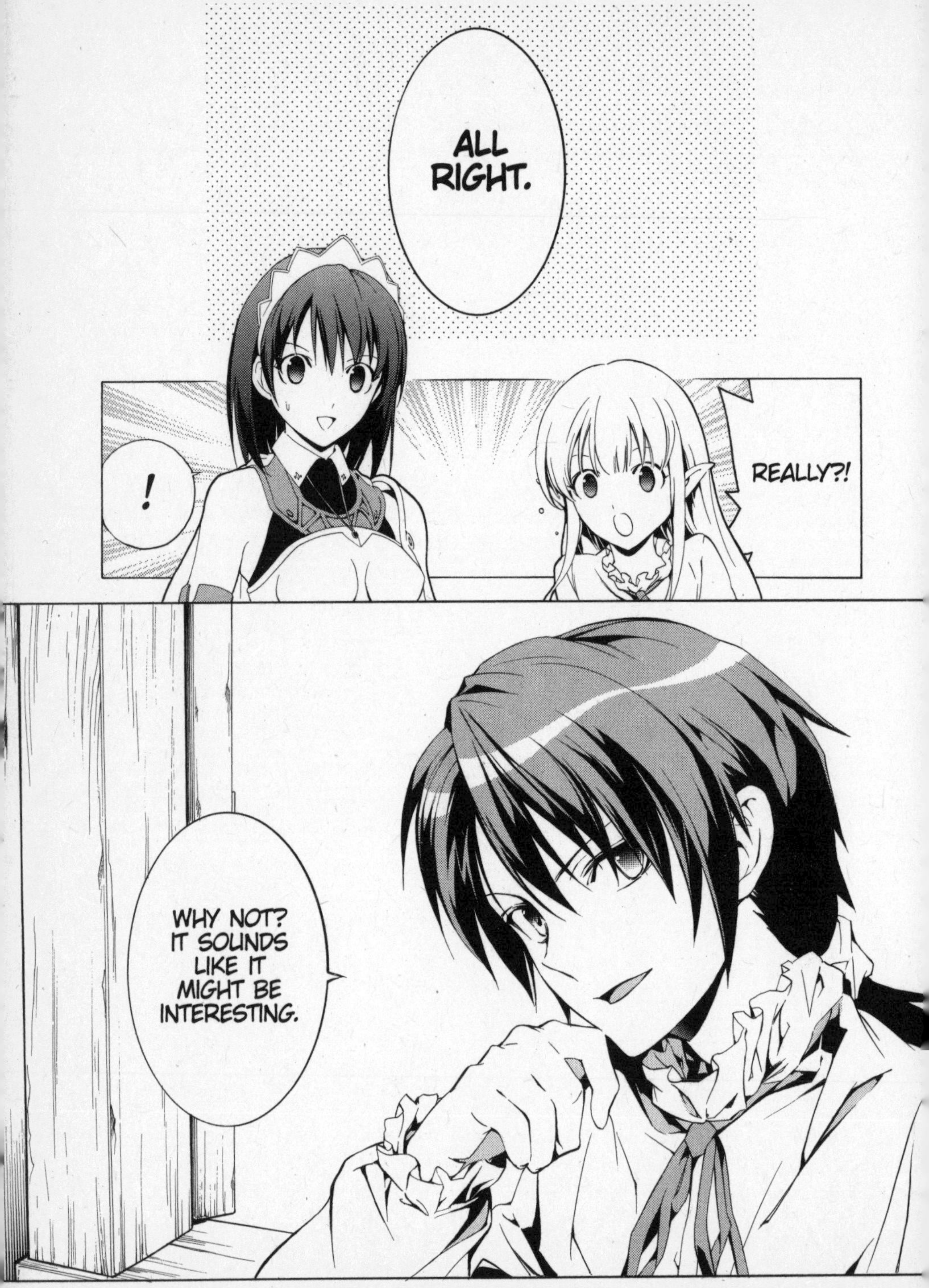
ALL RIGHT.
REALLY?!
!
WHY NOT? IT SOUNDS LIKE IT MIGHT BE INTERESTING.

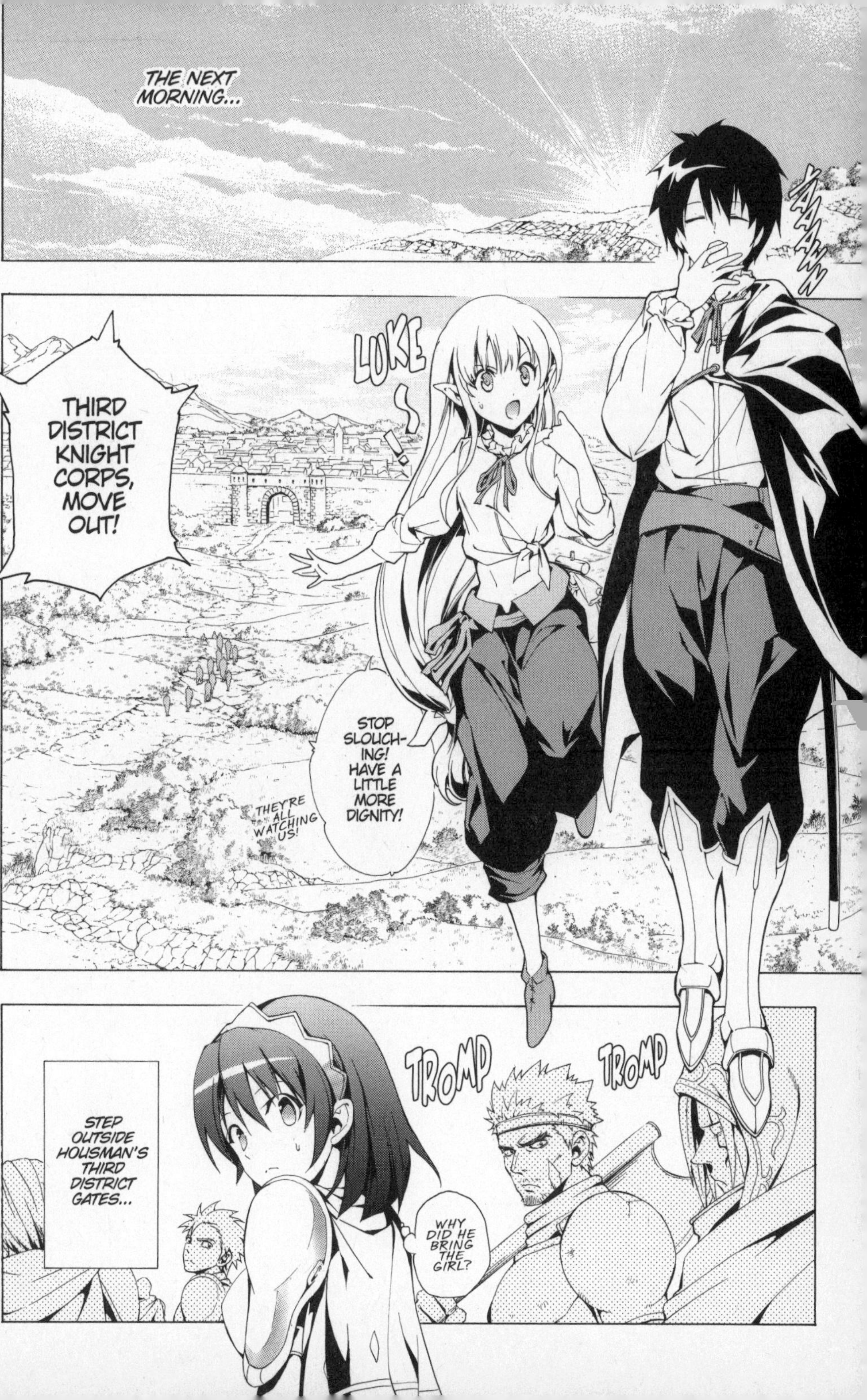
THE NEXT MORNING...
YAAAWN
LUKE~!
THIRD DISTRICT KNIGHT CORPS, MOVE OUT!
STOP SLOUCHING! HAVE A LITTLE MORE DIGNITY!
THEY'RE ALL WATCHING US!
TROMP
TROMP
STEP OUTSIDE HOUSMAN'S THIRD DISTRICT GATES...
WHY DID HE BRING THE GIRL?

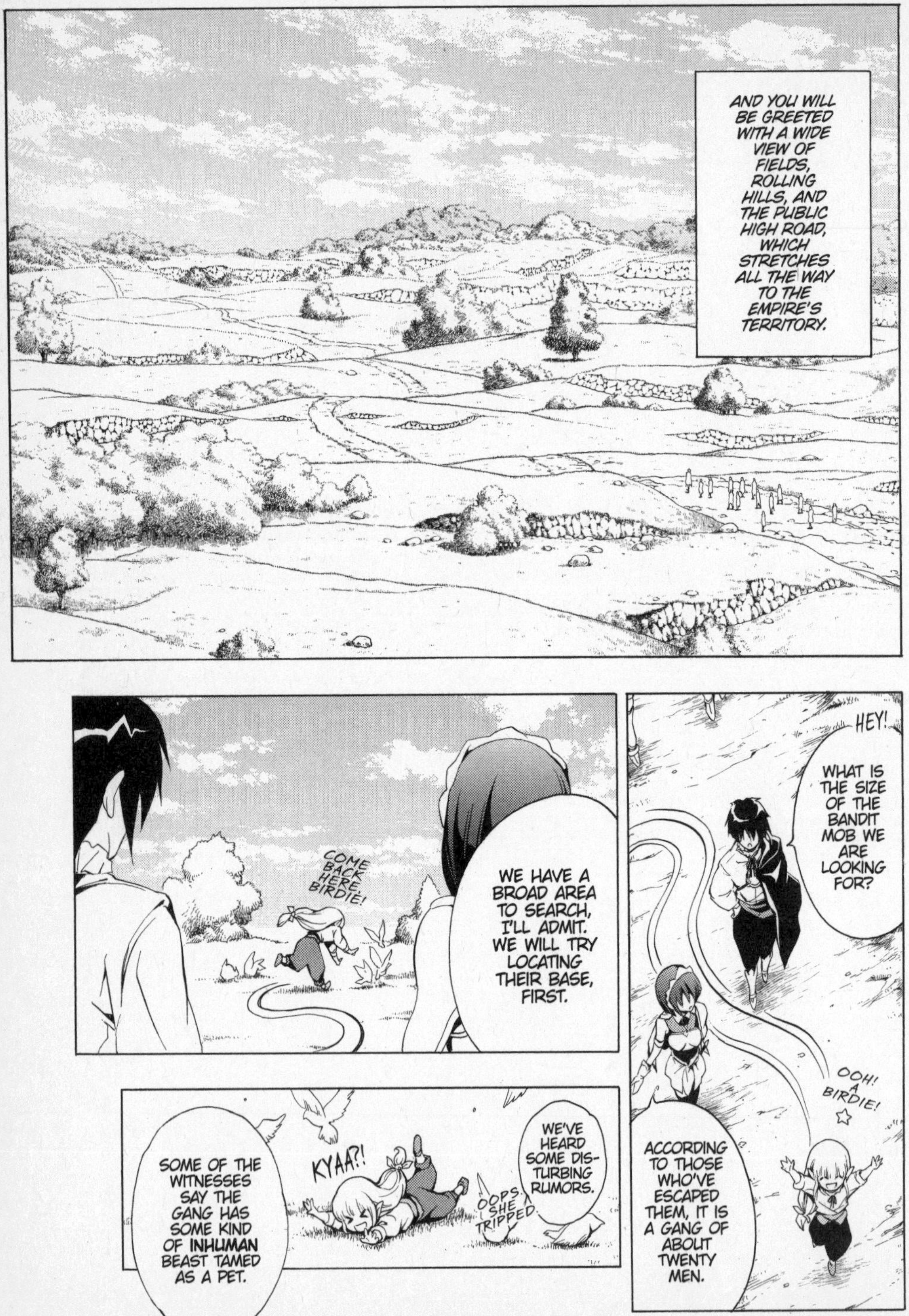
AND YOU WILL BE GREETED WITH A WIDE VIEW OF FIELDS, ROLLING HILLS, AND THE PUBLIC HIGH ROAD, WHICH STRETCHES ALL THE WAY TO THE EMPIRE'S TERRITORY.
HEY!
WHAT IS THE SIZE OF THE BANDIT MOB WE ARE LOOKING FOR?
OOH! A BIRDIE!
ACCORDING TO THOSE WHO'VE ESCAPED THEM, IT IS A GANG OF ABOUT TWENTY MEN.
WE HAVE A BROAD AREA TO SEARCH, I'LL ADMIT. WE WILL TRY LOCATING THEIR BASE, FIRST.
COME BACK HERE, BIRDIE!
WE'VE HEARD SOME DIS-TURBING RUMORS.
OOPS, SHE TRIPPED.
KYAA?!
SOME OF THE WITNESSES SAY THE GANG HAS SOME KIND OF INHUMAN BEAST TAMED AS A PET.

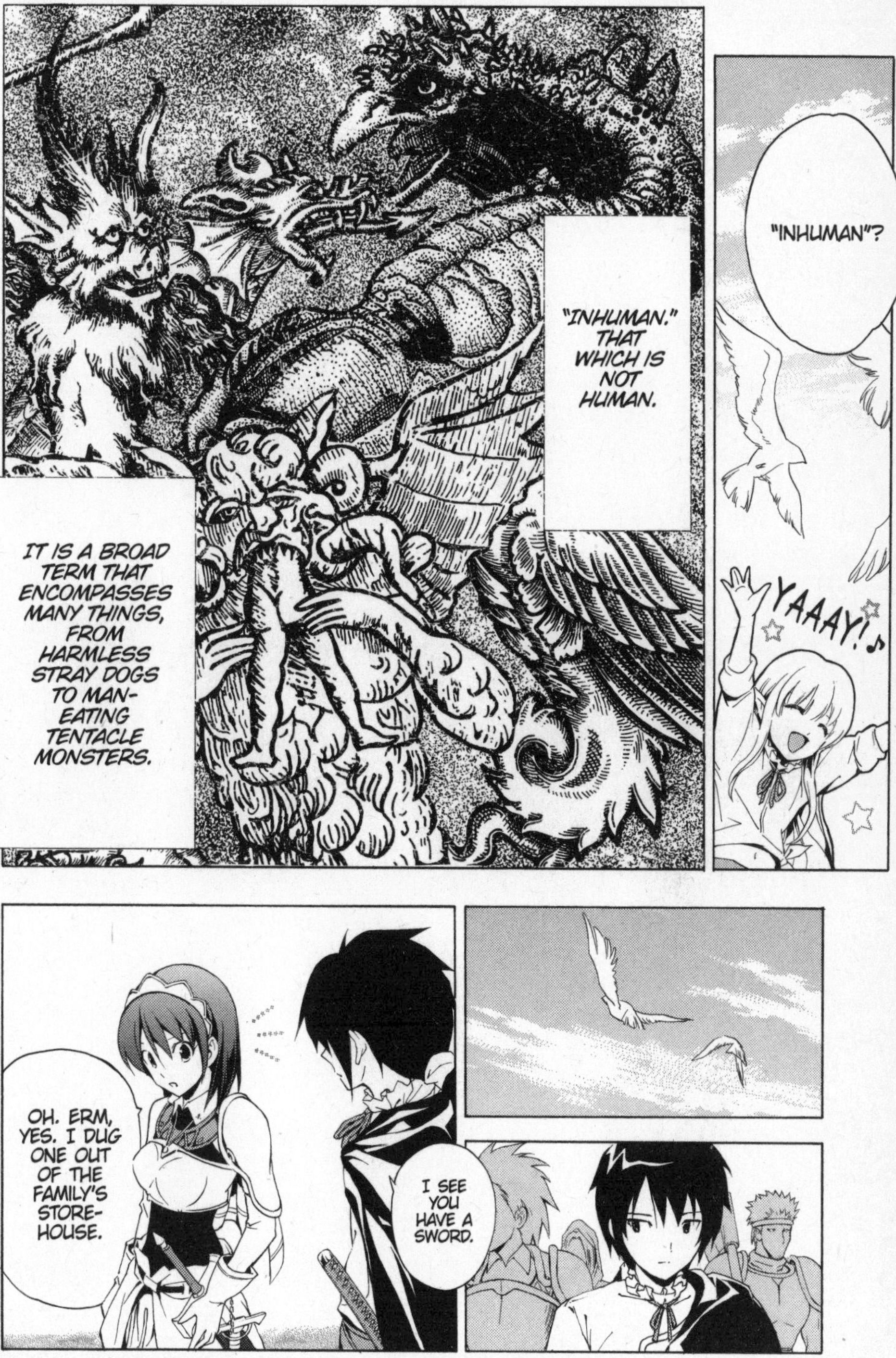
"INHUMAN"?
YAAAY!
"INHUMAN." THAT WHICH IS NOT HUMAN.
IT IS A BROAD TERM THAT ENCOMPASSES MANY THINGS, FROM HARMLESS STRAY DOGS TO MAN-EATING TENTACLE MONSTERS.
I SEE YOU HAVE A SWORD.
OH. ERM, YES. I DUG ONE OUT OF THE FAMILY'S STORE-HOUSE.

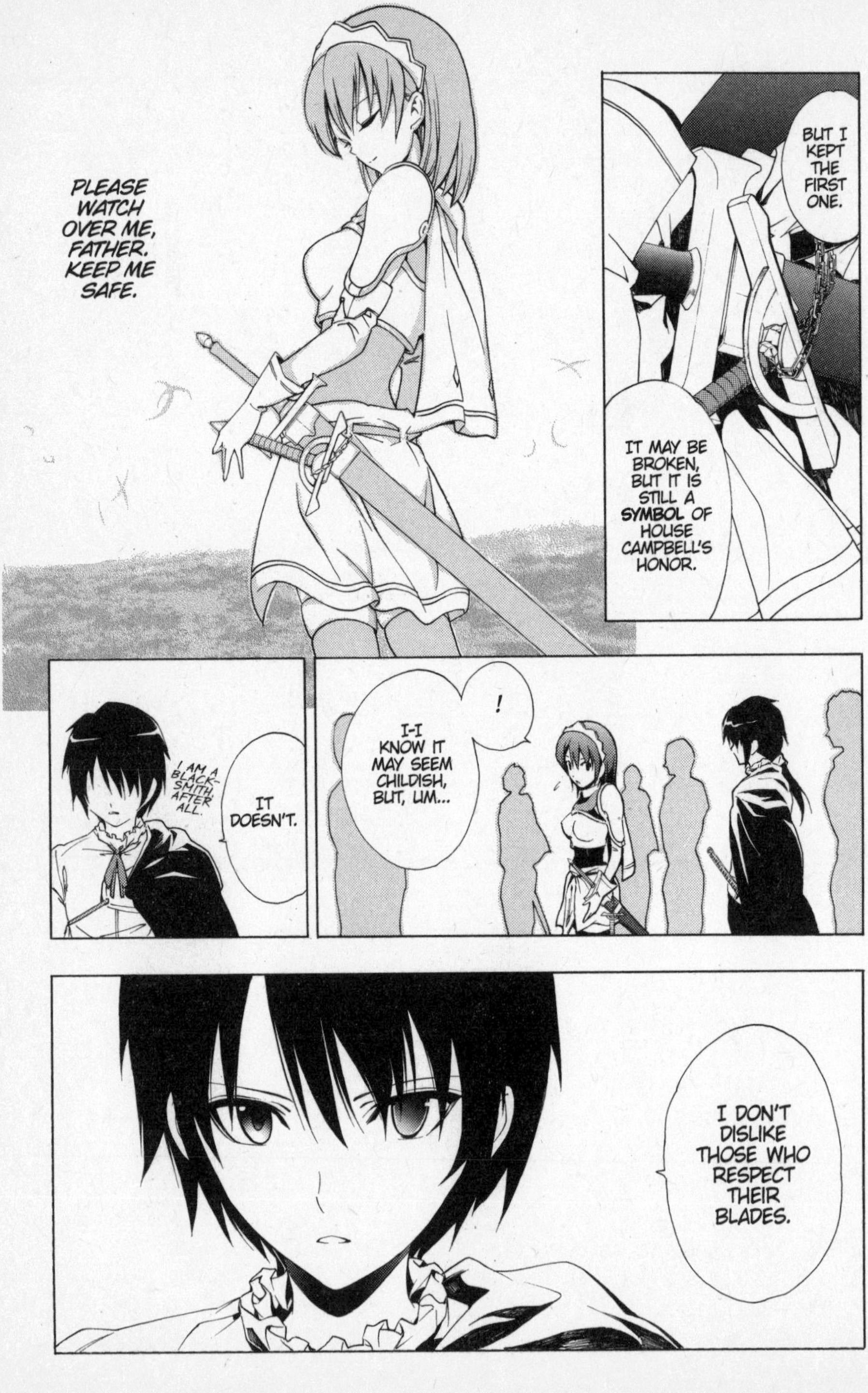
BUT I KEPT THE FIRST ONE.
IT MAY BE BROKEN, BUT IT IS STILL A **SYMBOL** OF HOUSE CAMPBELL'S HONOR.
PLEASE WATCH OVER ME, FATHER. KEEP ME SAFE.
!
I-I KNOW IT MAY SEEM CHILDISH, BUT, UM...
IT DOESN'T.
I AM A BLACKSMITH AFTER ALL.
I DON'T DISLIKE THOSE WHO RESPECT THEIR BLADES.

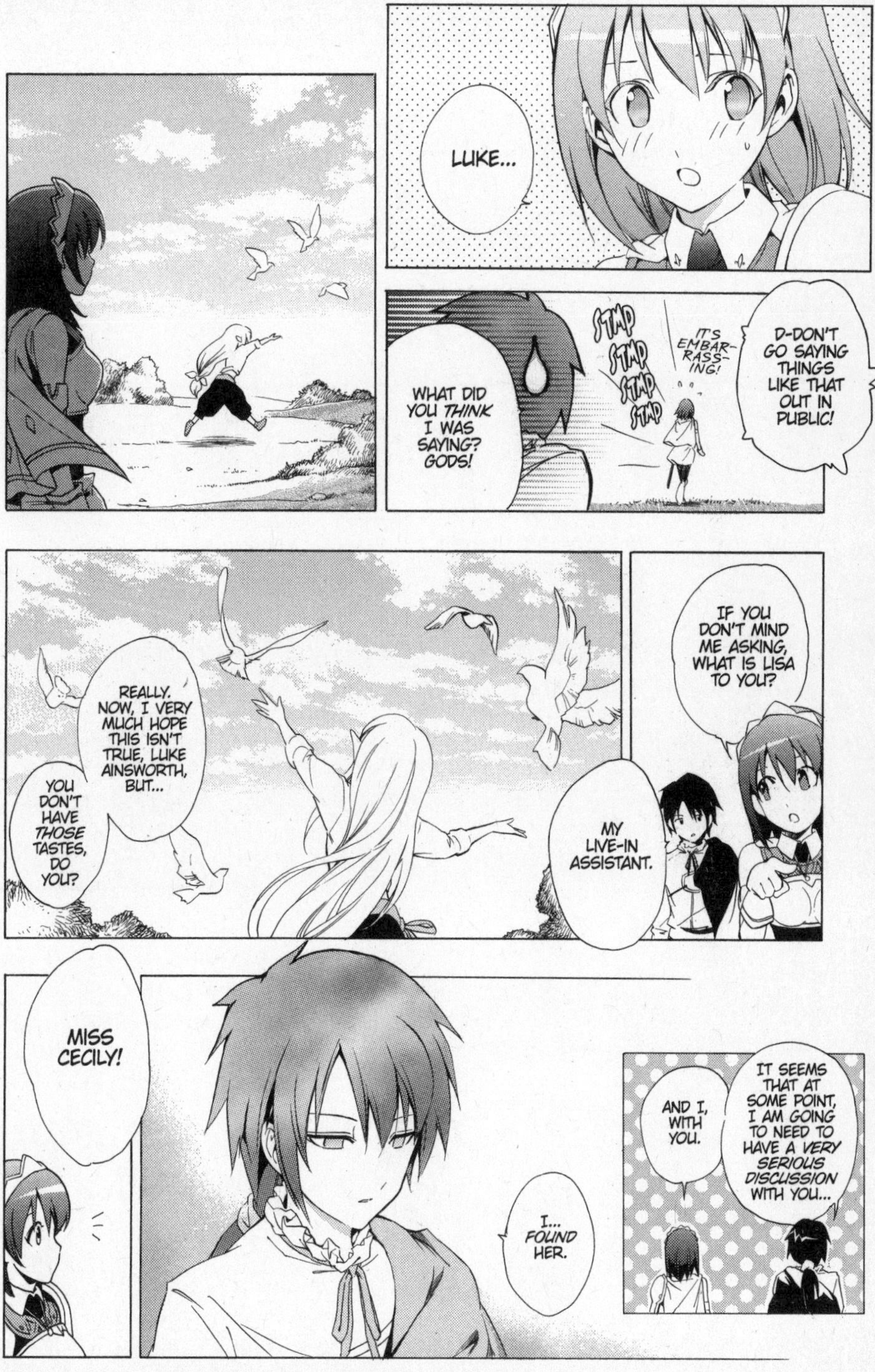

LUKE...
D-DON'T GO SAYING THINGS LIKE THAT OUT IN PUBLIC!
IT'S EMBARRASSING!
STMP STMP STMP STMP
WHAT DID YOU *THINK* I WAS SAYING? GODS!
IF YOU DON'T MIND ME ASKING, WHAT IS LISA TO YOU?
MY LIVE-IN ASSISTANT.
REALLY. NOW, I VERY MUCH HOPE THIS ISN'T TRUE, LUKE AINSWORTH, BUT...
YOU DON'T HAVE *THOSE* TASTES, DO YOU?
IT SEEMS THAT AT SOME POINT, I AM GOING TO NEED TO HAVE A *VERY SERIOUS DISCUSSION* WITH YOU...
AND I, WITH YOU.
I... *FOUND* HER.
MISS CECILY!

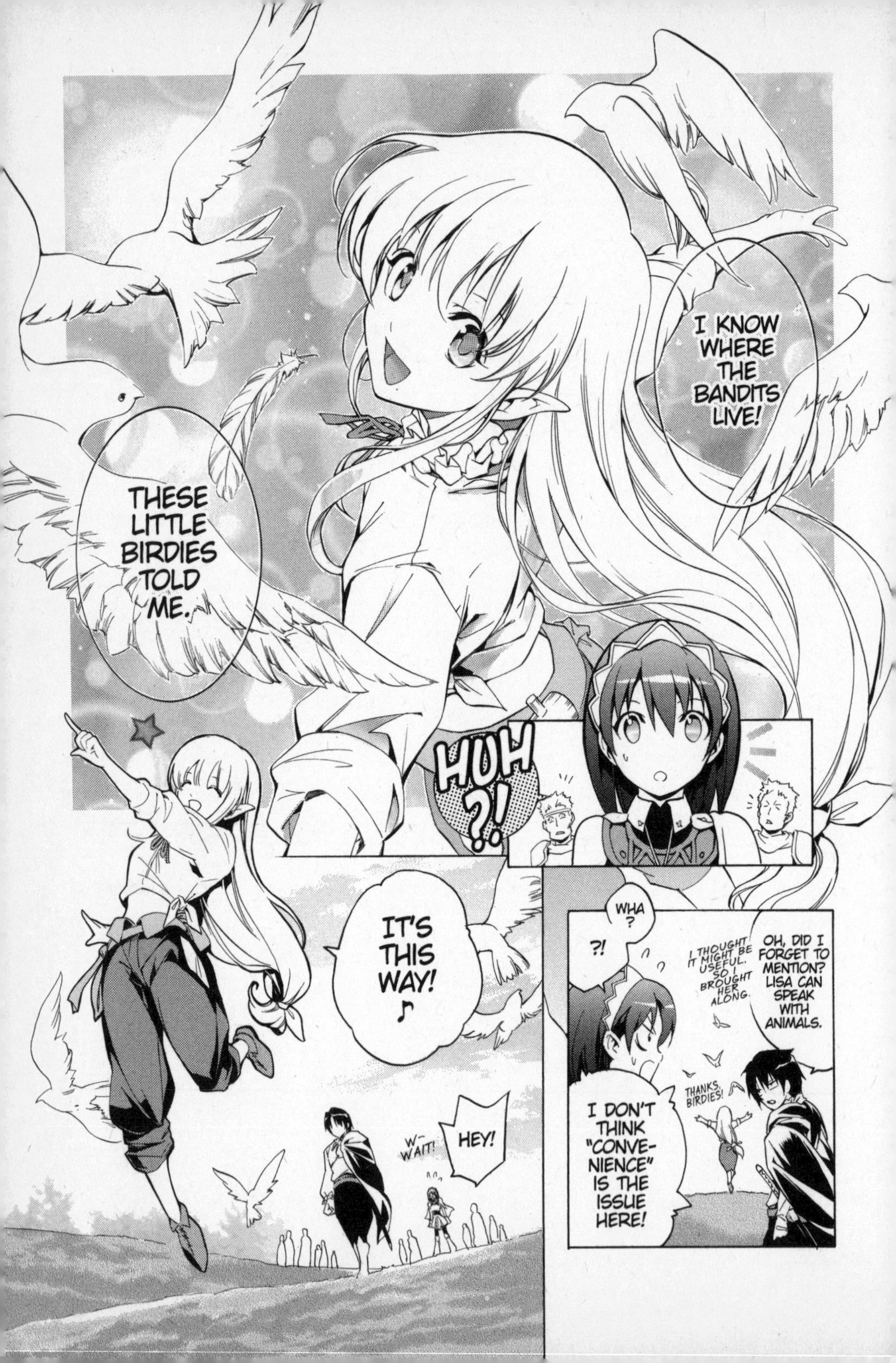
I KNOW WHERE THE BANDITS LIVE!
THESE LITTLE BIRDIES TOLD ME.
HUH?!
OH, DID I FORGET TO MENTION? LISA CAN SPEAK WITH ANIMALS.
I THOUGHT IT MIGHT BE USEFUL, SO I BROUGHT HER ALONG.
WHA?
?!
THANKS, BIRDIES!
I DON'T THINK "CONVENIENCE" IS THE ISSUE HERE!
IT'S THIS WAY! ♪
HEY!
W-WAIT!

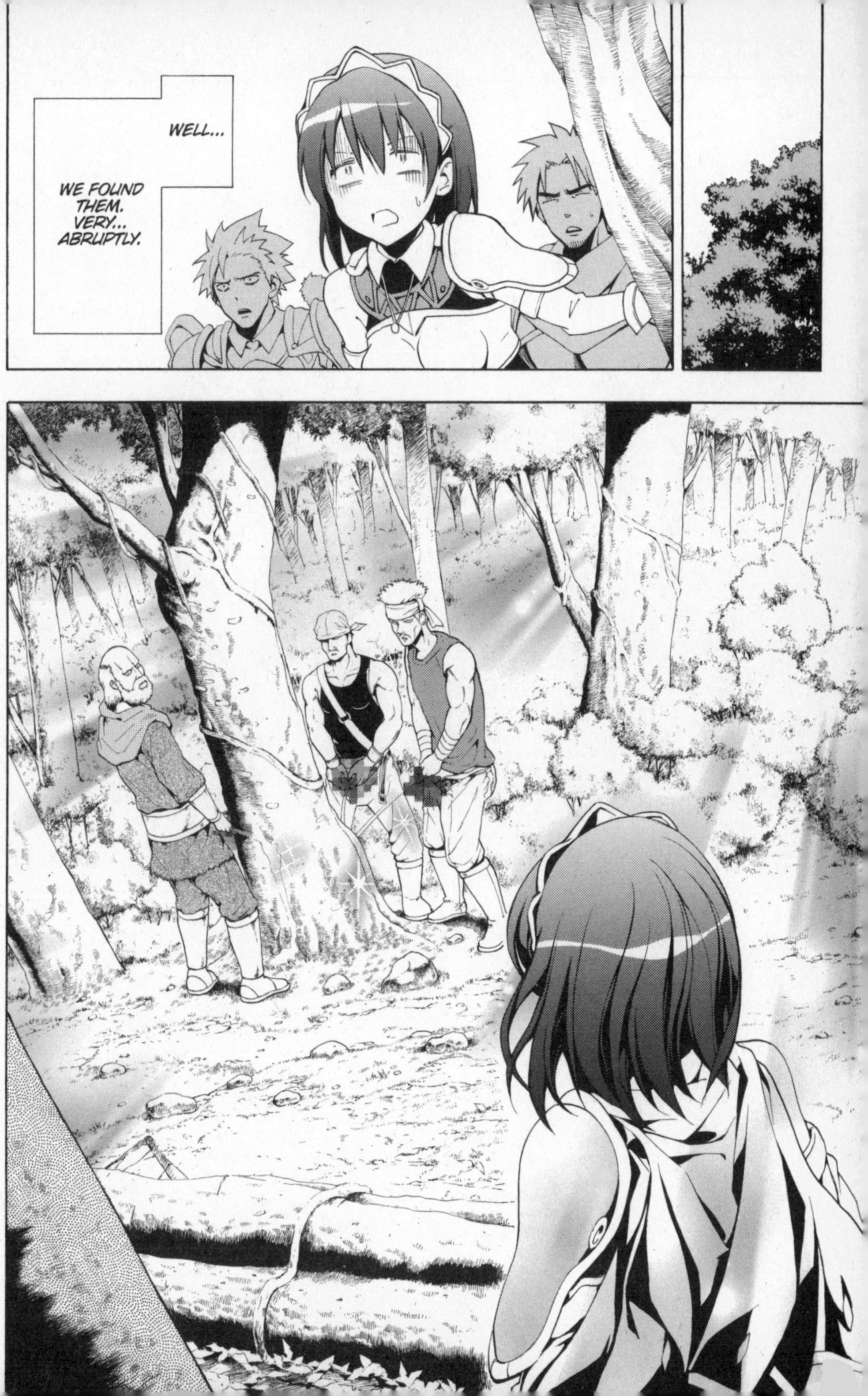
WELL...
WE FOUND THEM. VERY... ABRUPTLY.

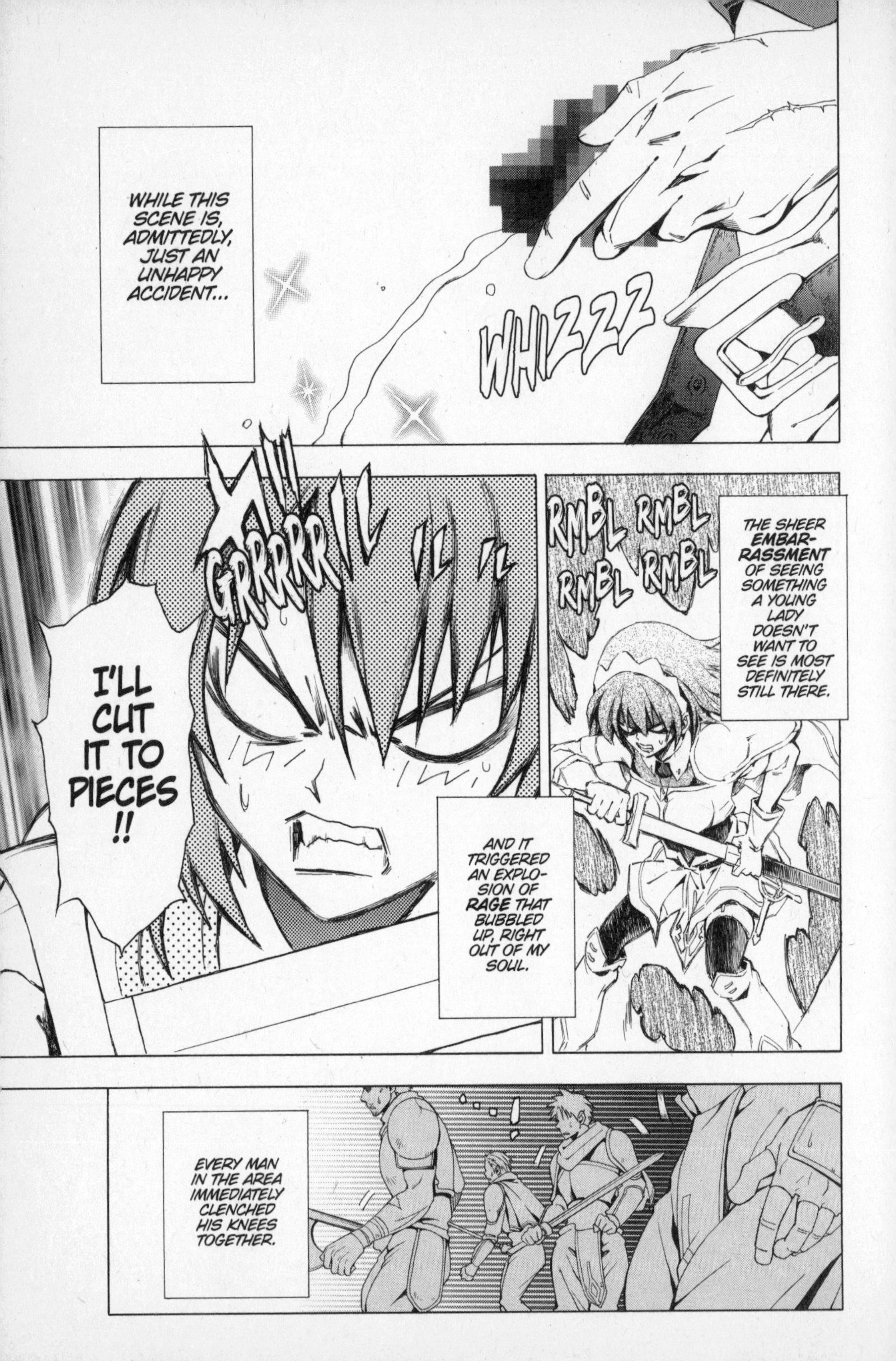
WHILE THIS SCENE IS, ADMITTEDLY, JUST AN UNHAPPY ACCIDENT...
WHIZZZ
RMBL RMBL RMBL RMBL
THE SHEER EMBARRASSMENT OF SEEING SOMETHING A YOUNG LADY DOESN'T WANT TO SEE IS MOST DEFINITELY STILL THERE.
AND IT TRIGGERED AN EXPLOSION OF RAGE THAT BUBBLED UP, RIGHT OUT OF MY SOUL.
GRRRRR
I'LL CUT IT TO PIECES!!
EVERY MAN IN THE AREA IMMEDIATELY CLENCHED HIS KNEES TOGETHER.

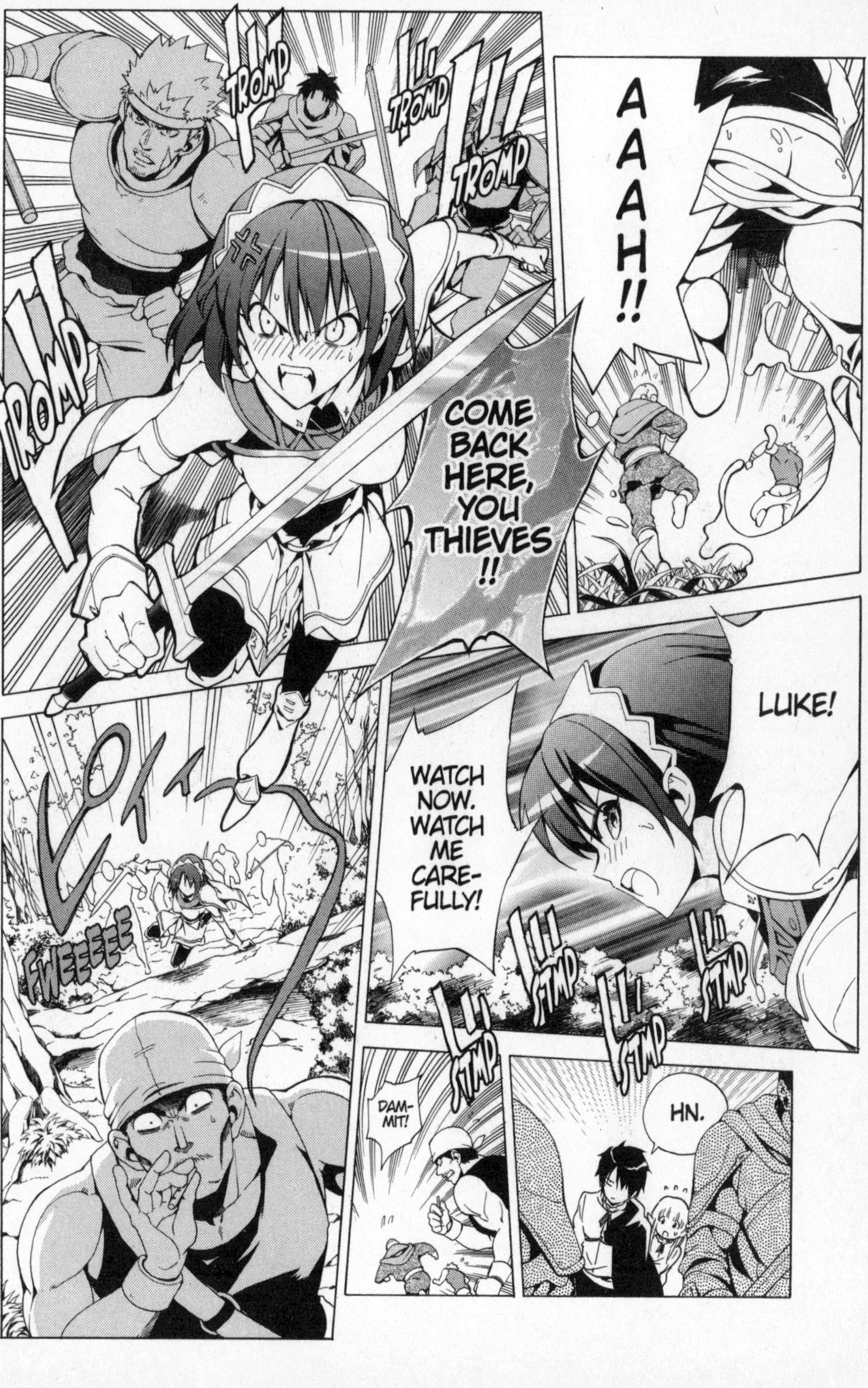
AAAH!!
TROMP
TROMP
TROMP
COME BACK HERE, YOU THIEVES!!
TROMP
LUKE!
WATCH NOW. WATCH ME CARE-FULLY!
STMP
STMP
STMP
STMP
FWEEEEEE
HN.
DAM-MIT!

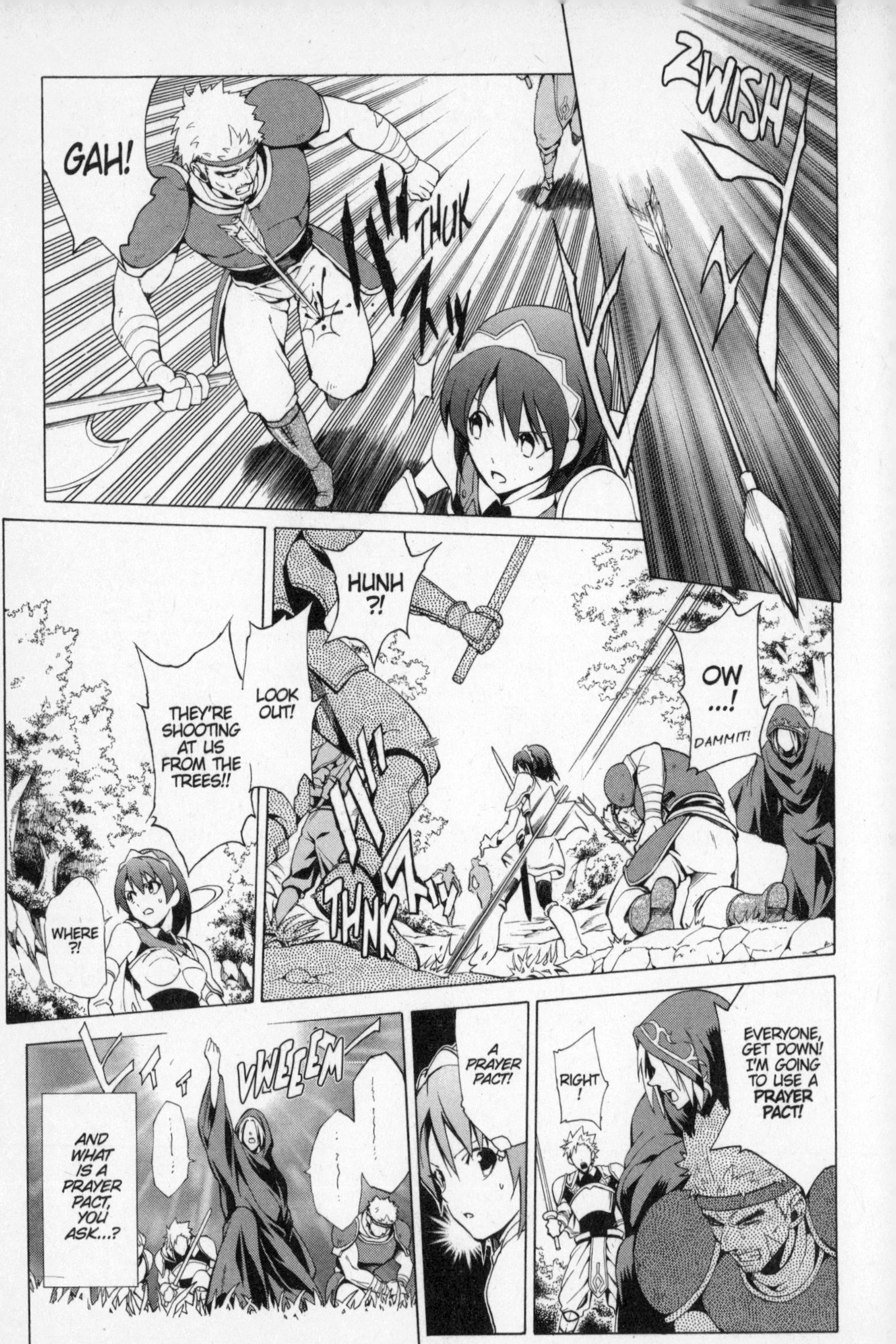
ZWISH
GAH!
THUK
OW ...!
DAMMIT!
HUNH ?!
LOOK OUT!
THEY'RE SHOOTING AT US FROM THE TREES!!
THNK
WHERE ?!
EVERYONE, GET DOWN! I'M GOING TO USE A PRAYER PACT!
RIGHT !
A PRAYER PACT!
VWEEEM
AND WHAT IS A PRAYER PACT, YOU ASK...?

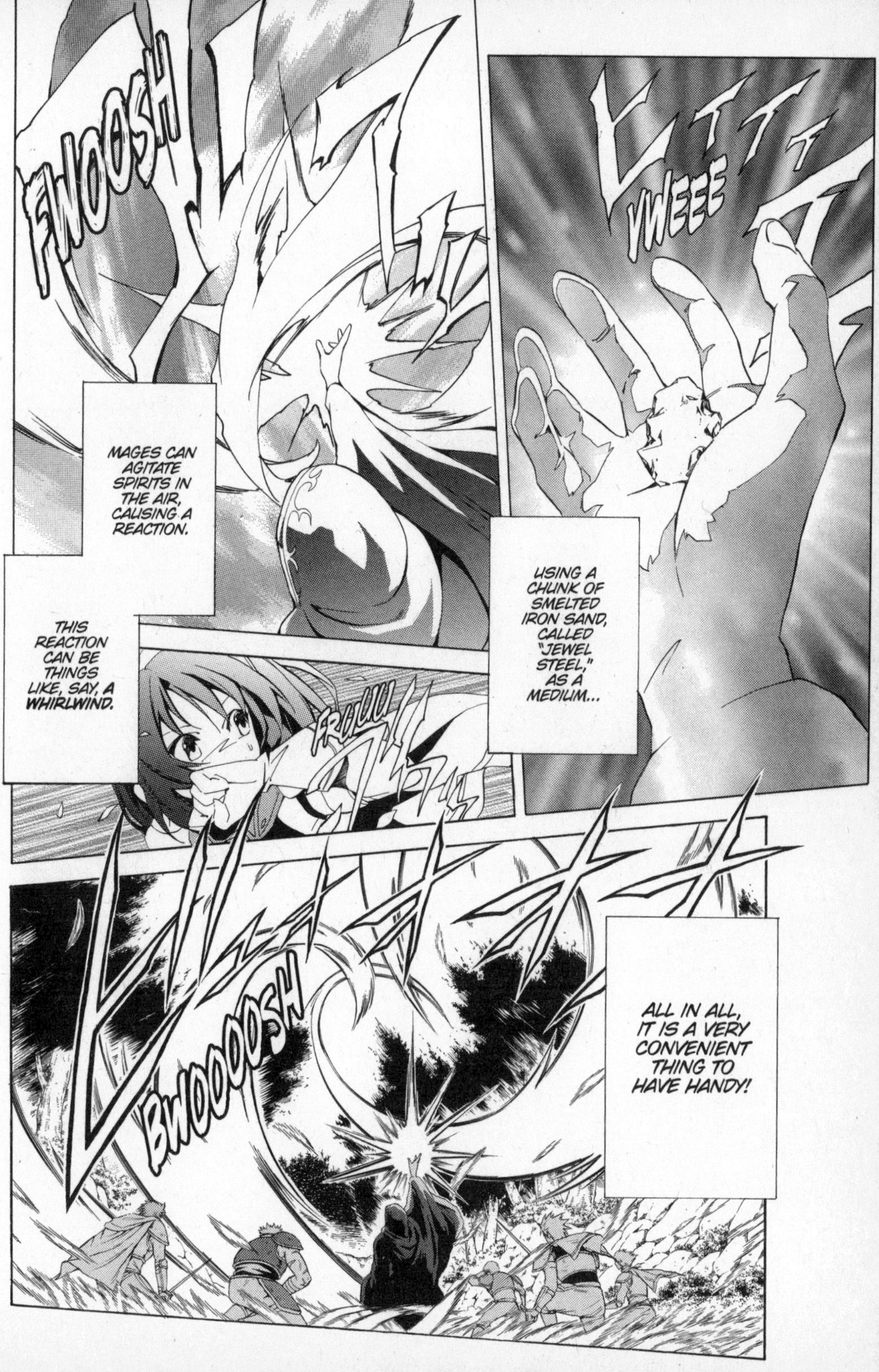
VWEEE
USING A CHUNK OF SMELTED IRON SAND, CALLED "JEWEL STEEL," AS A MEDIUM...
FWOOSH
MAGES CAN AGITATE SPIRITS IN THE AIR, CAUSING A REACTION.
THIS REACTION CAN BE THINGS LIKE, SAY, A WHIRLWIND.
FRUUU
BWOOOOSH
ALL IN ALL, IT IS A VERY CONVENIENT THING TO HAVE HANDY!

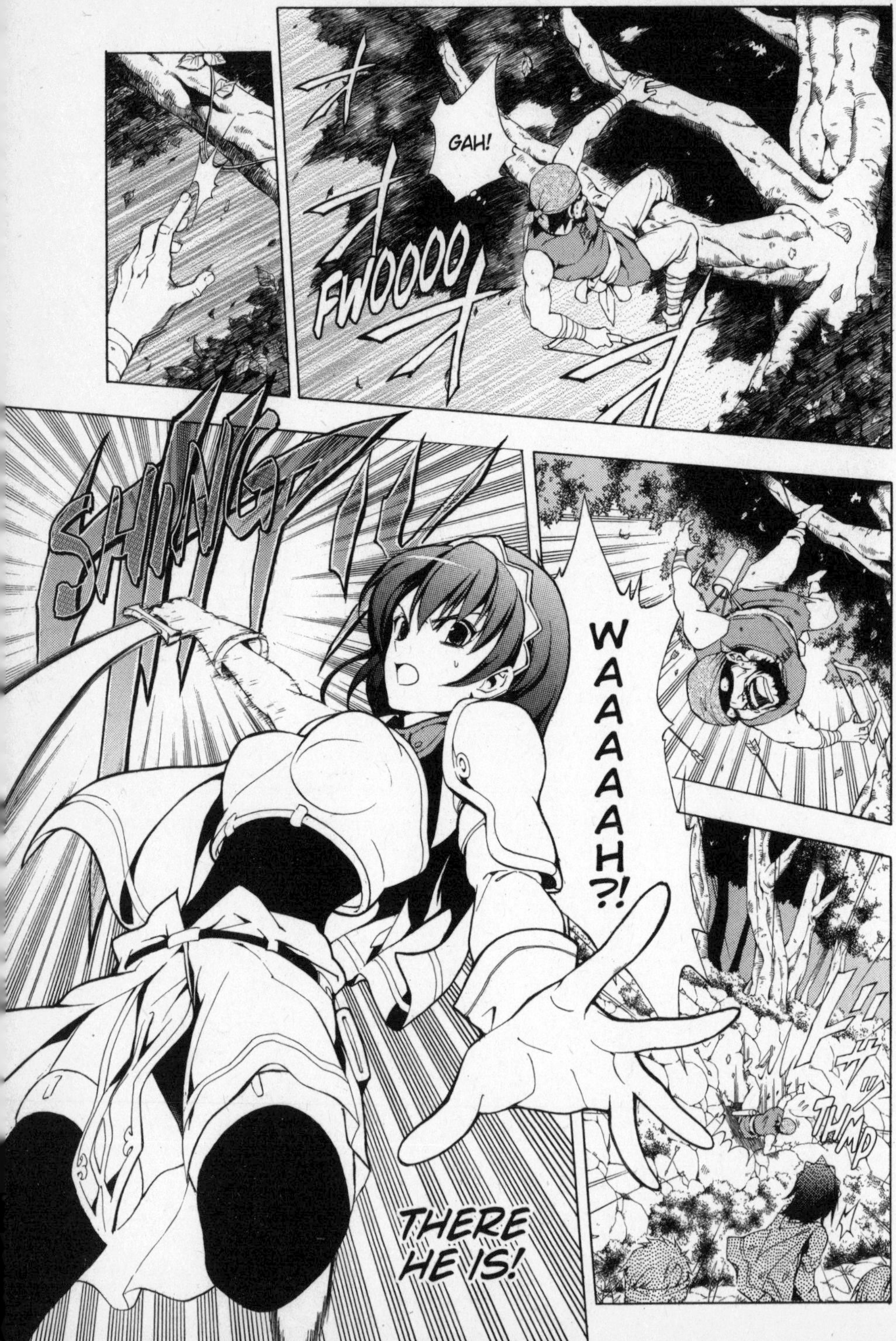

GAH!
FWOOOO
WAAAAAAH?!
THUMP
THERE HE IS!

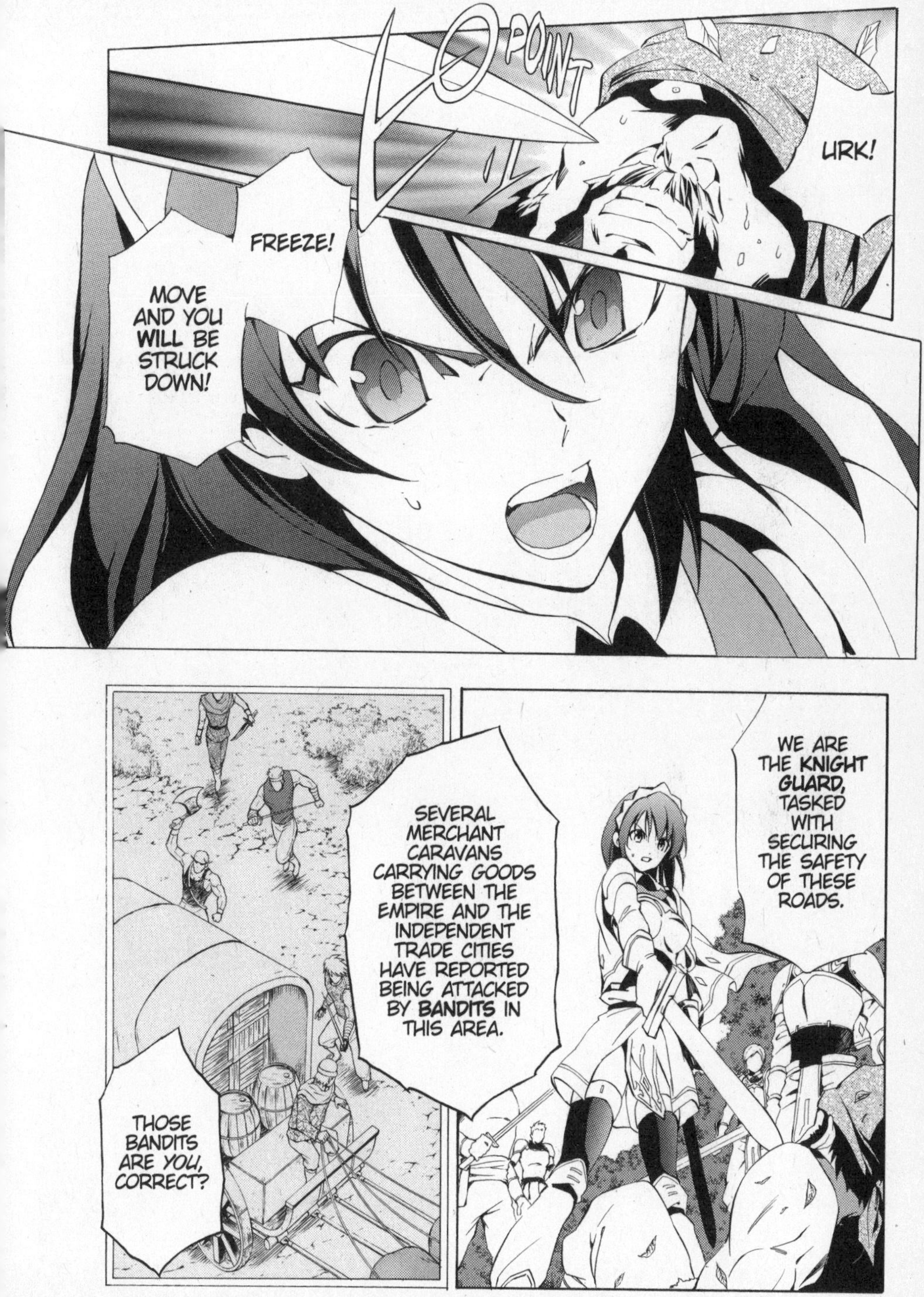
POINT
URK!
FREEZE!
MOVE AND YOU WILL BE STRUCK DOWN!
WE ARE THE KNIGHT GUARD, TASKED WITH SECURING THE SAFETY OF THESE ROADS.
SEVERAL MERCHANT CARAVANS CARRYING GOODS BETWEEN THE EMPIRE AND THE INDEPENDENT TRADE CITIES HAVE REPORTED BEING ATTACKED BY BANDITS IN THIS AREA.
THOSE BANDITS ARE YOU, CORRECT?

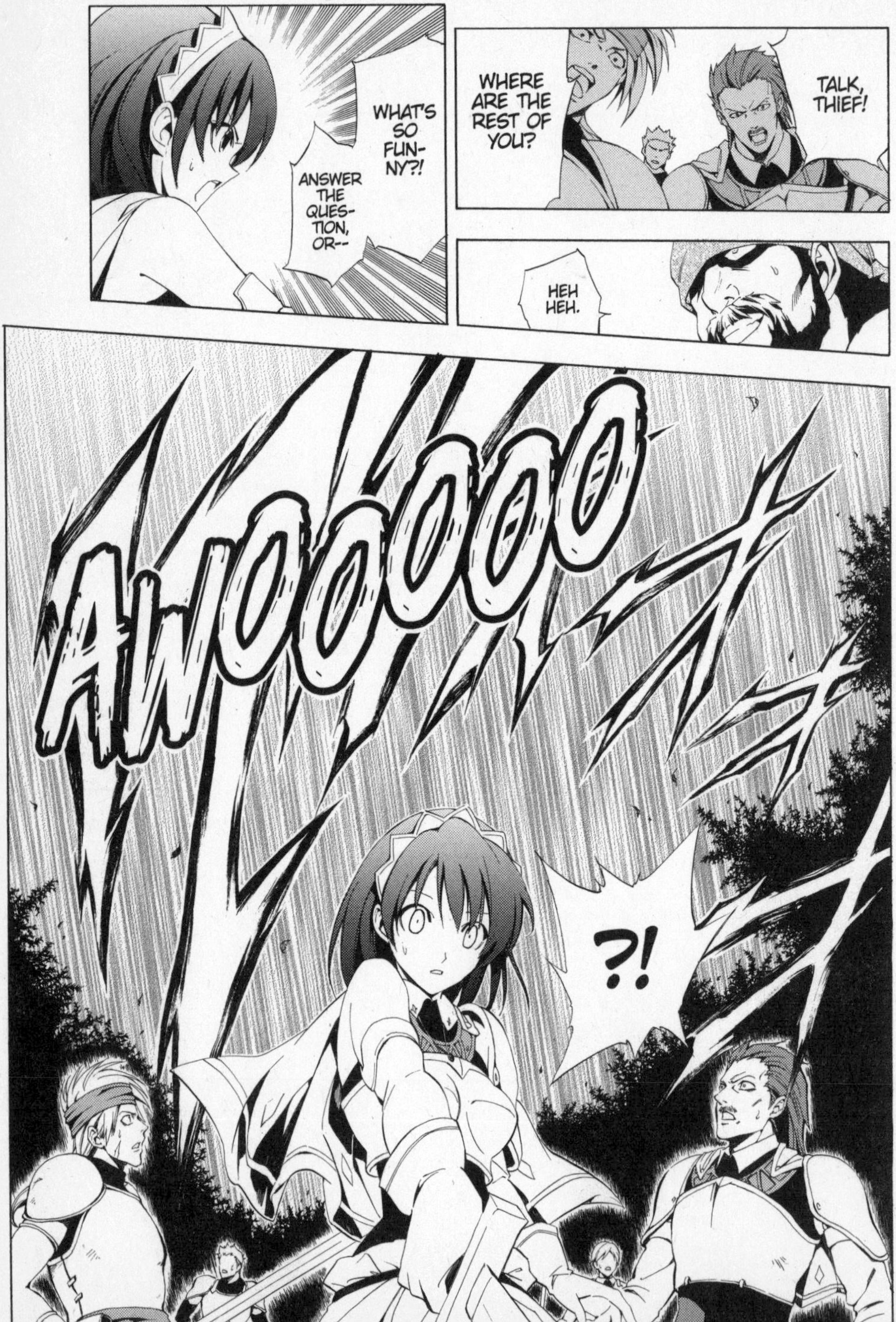
TALK, THIEF!
WHERE ARE THE REST OF YOU?
HEH HEH.
WHAT'S SO FUN-NY?!
ANSWER THE QUES-TION, OR--
AWOOOOOO
?!

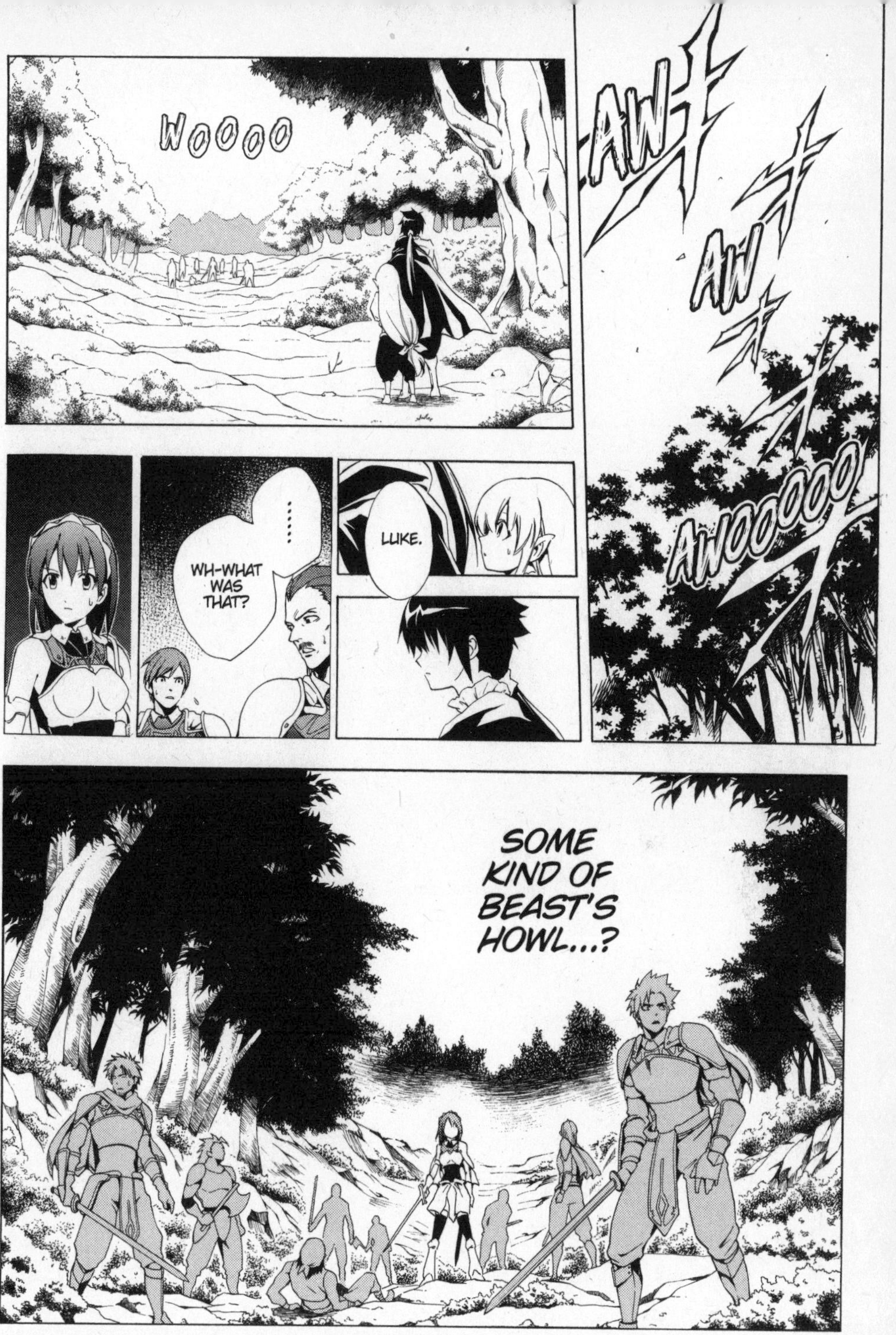
AW
AW
AWOOOOO
WOOOO
LUKE.
......
WH-WHAT WAS THAT?
SOME KIND OF BEAST'S HOWL...?

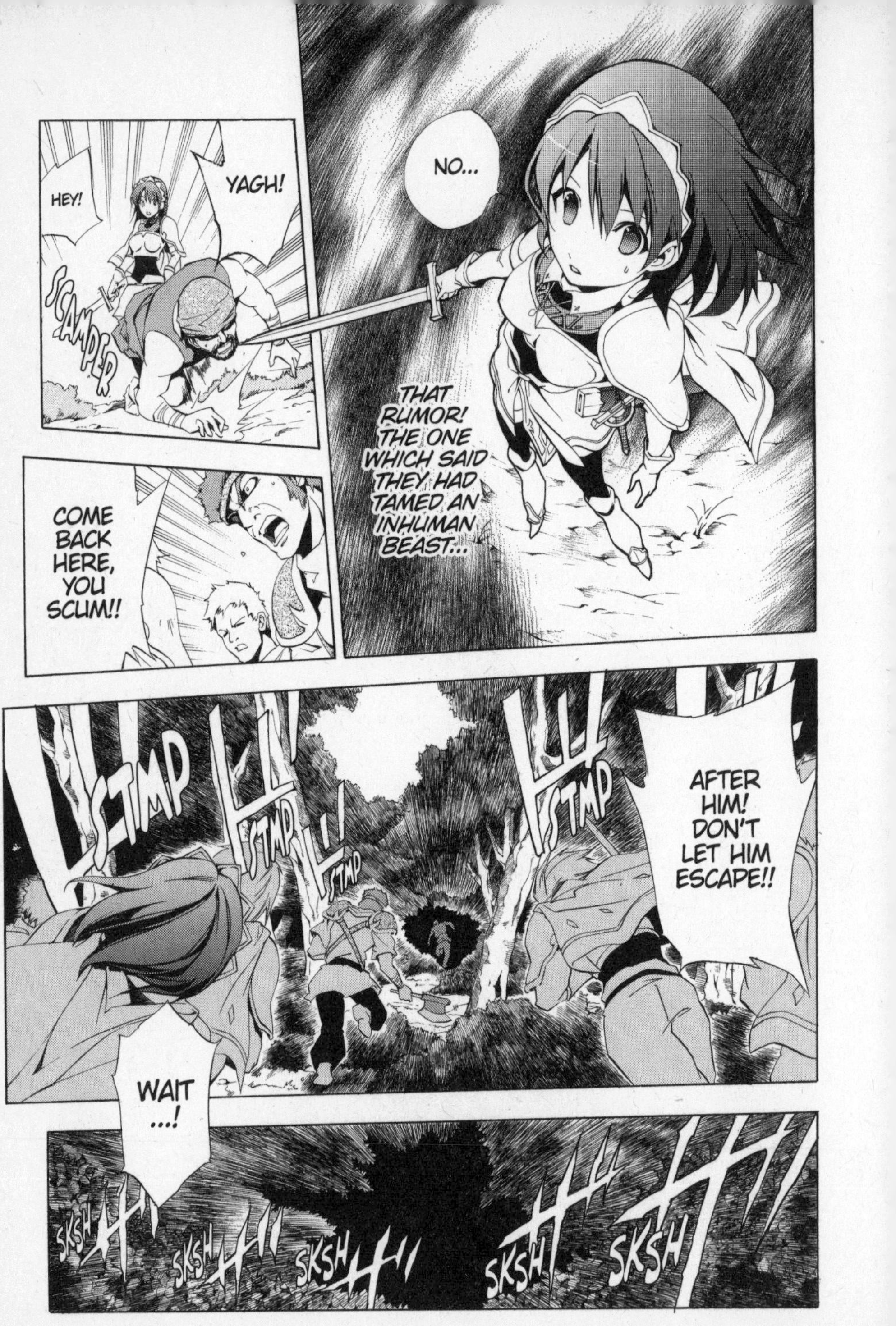
NO...
THAT RUMOR! THE ONE WHICH SAID THEY HAD TAMED AN INHUMAN BEAST...
YAGH!
HEY!
SCAMPER
COME BACK HERE, YOU SCUM!!
AFTER HIM! DON'T LET HIM ESCAPE!!
STMP
STMP
STMP
STMP
WAIT ...!
SKSH
SKSH
SKSH
SKSH
SKSH

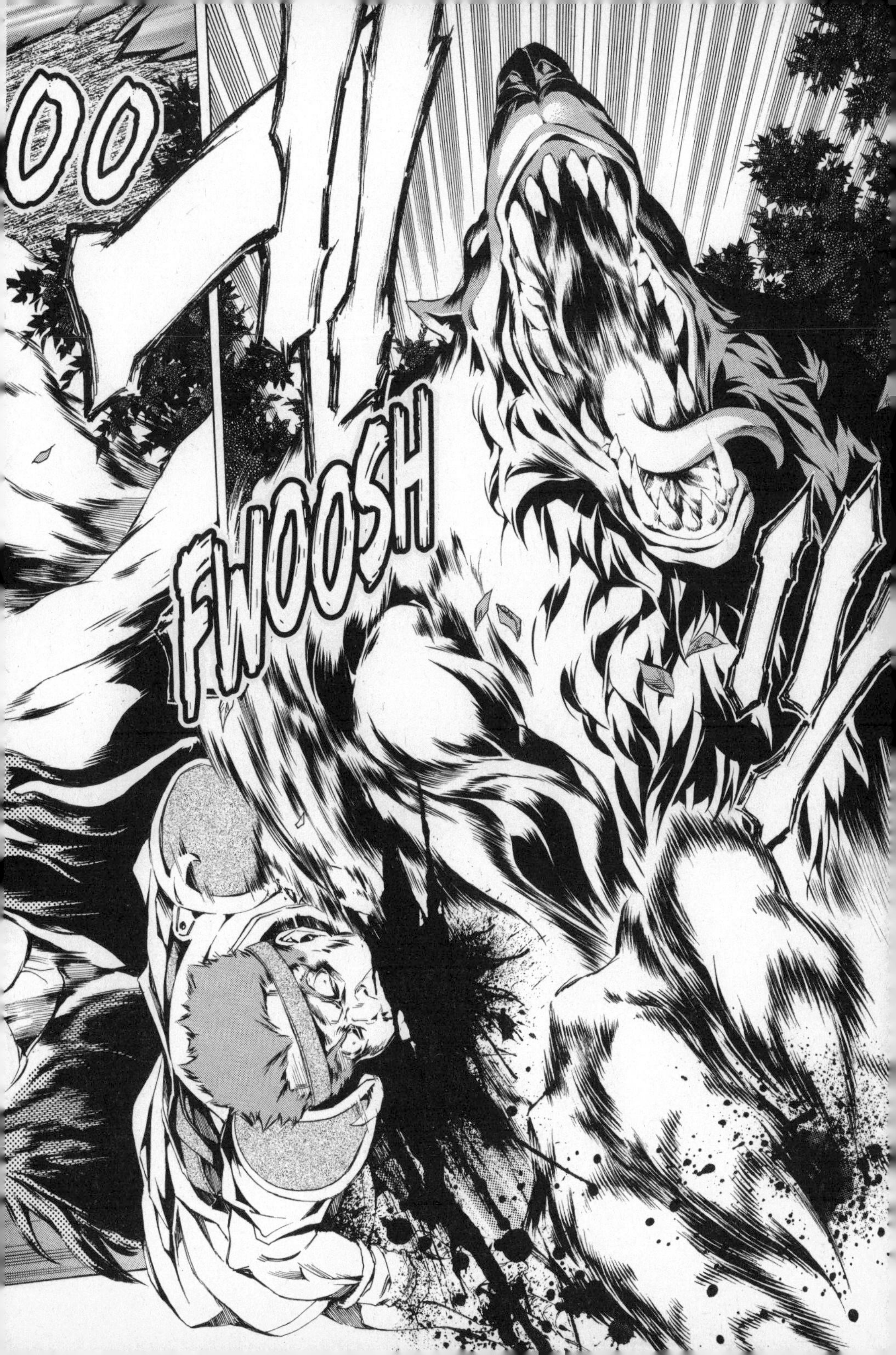
OO
FWOOSH

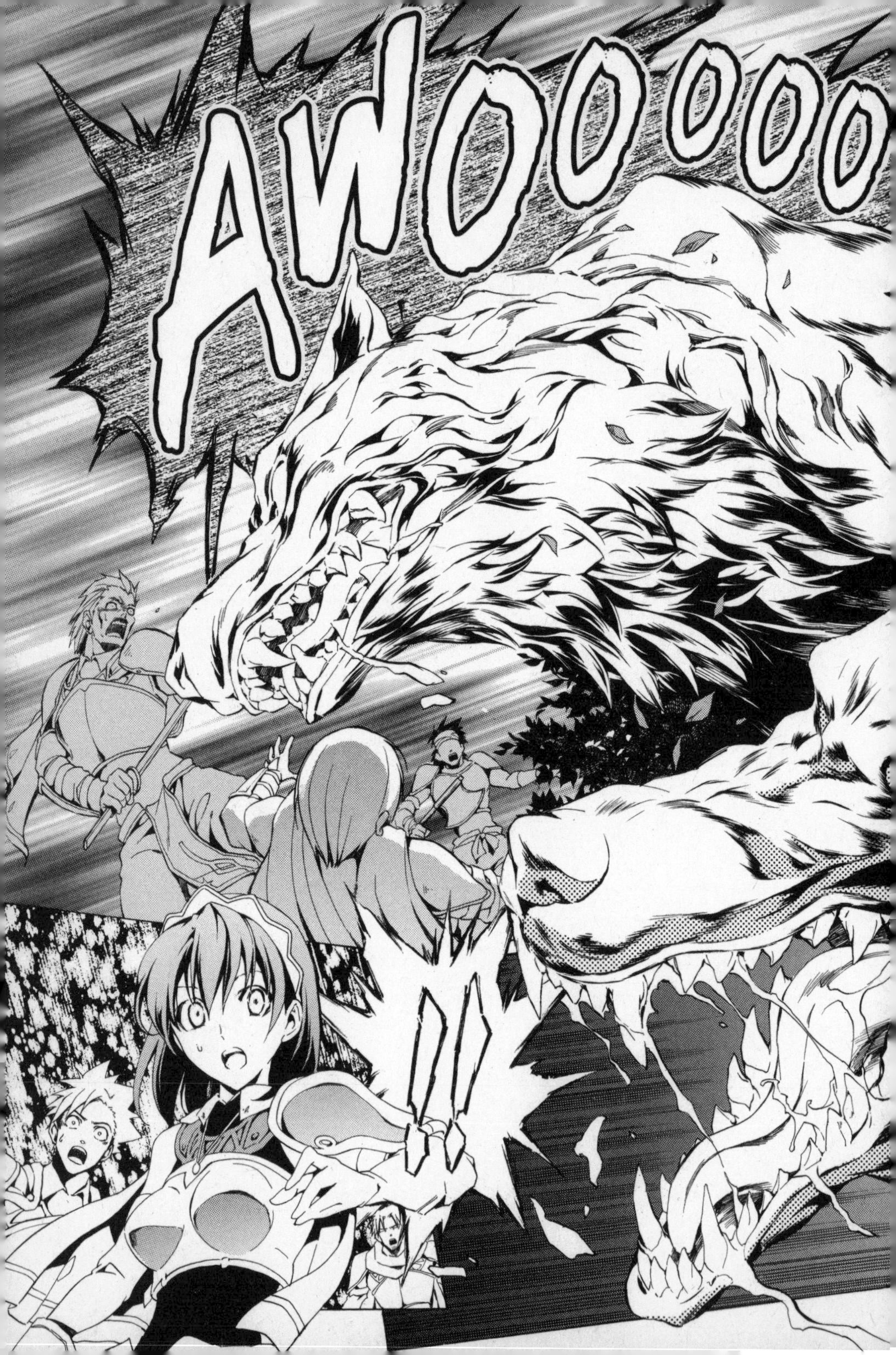
AWOOOOOO
!!

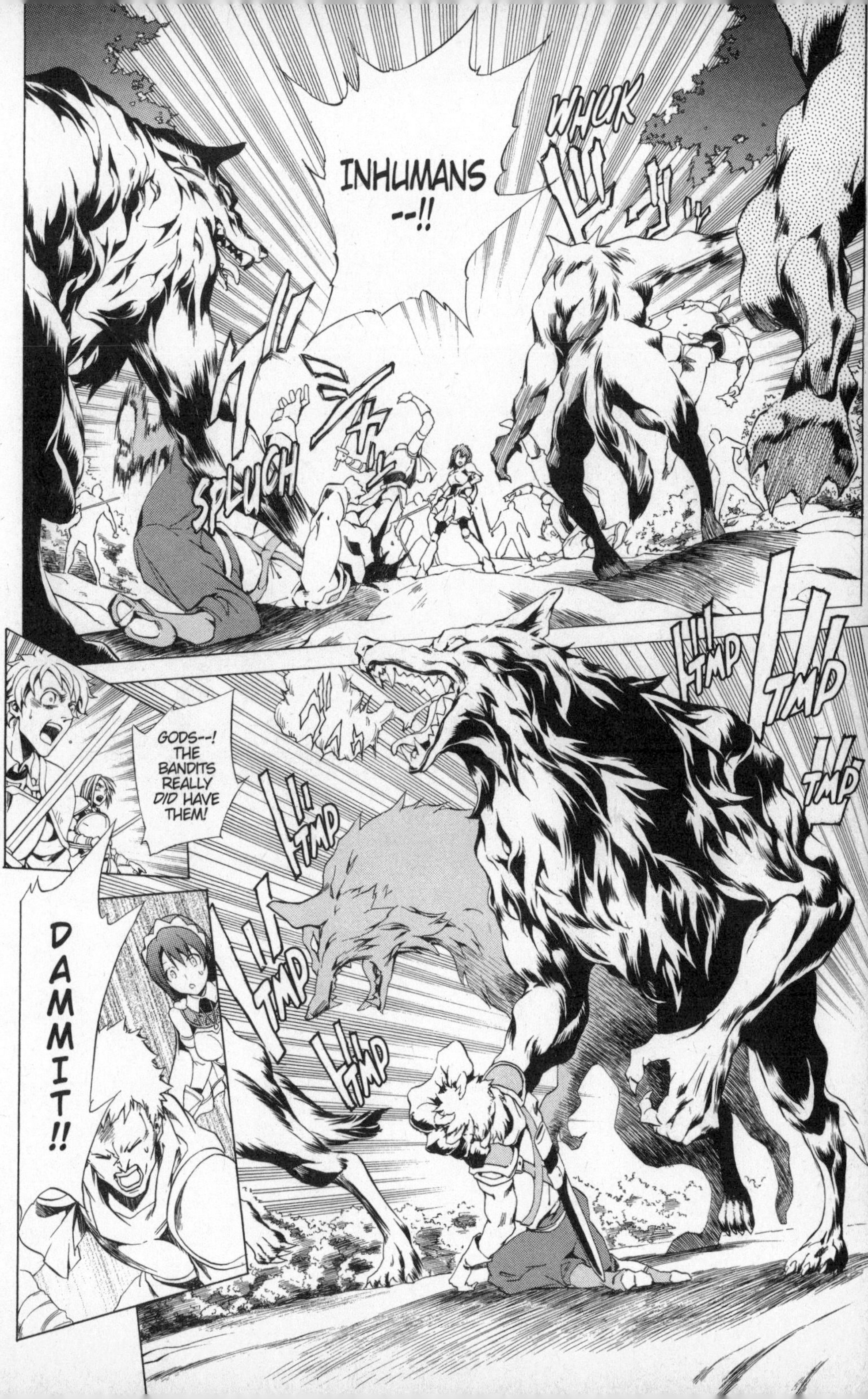
WHUK
INHUMANS --!!
SPLUCH
TMP
TMP
TMP
TMP
TMP
TMP
GODS--! THE BANDITS REALLY DID HAVE THEM!
DAMMIT!!

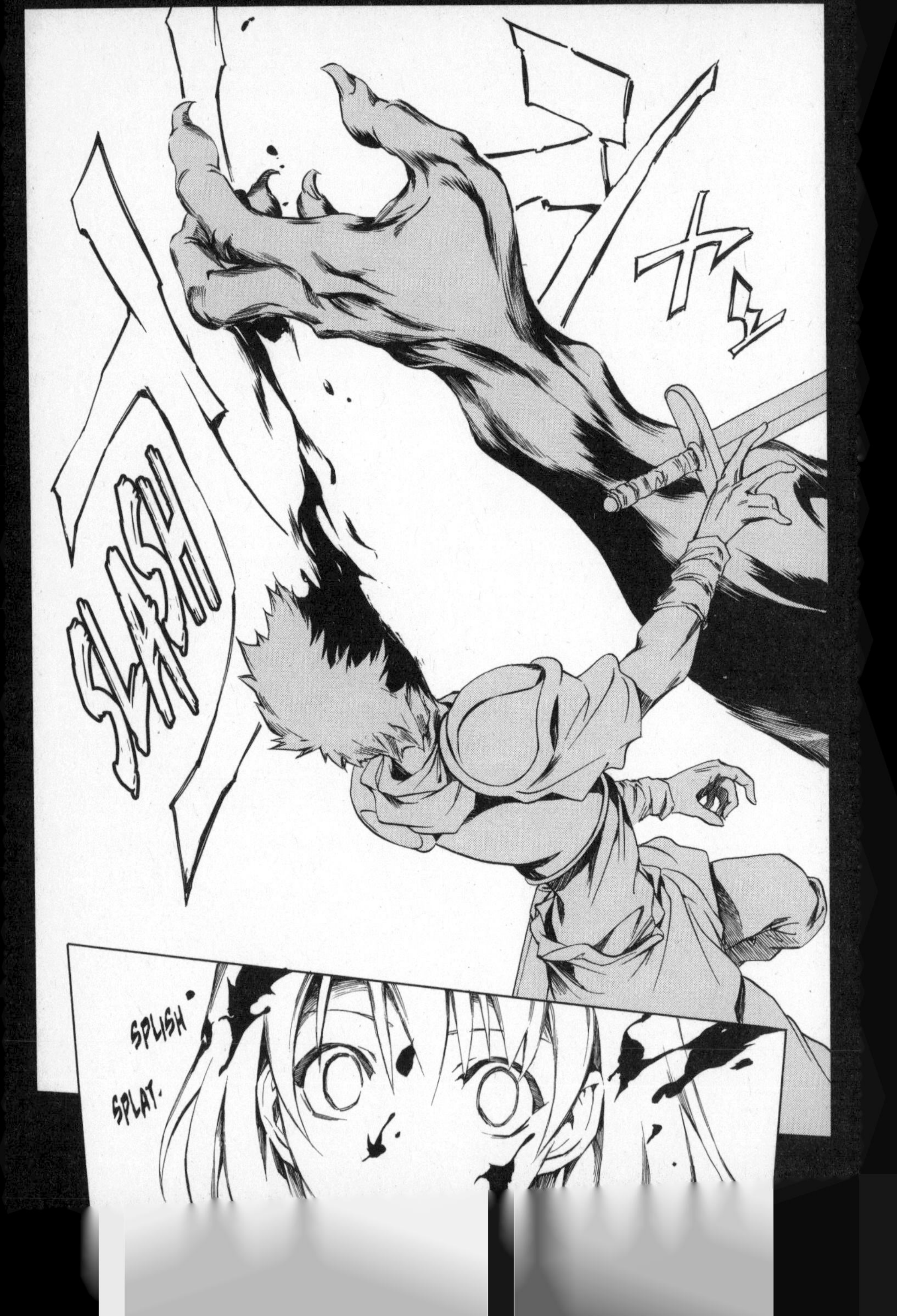
SLASH
SPLISH
SPLAT.

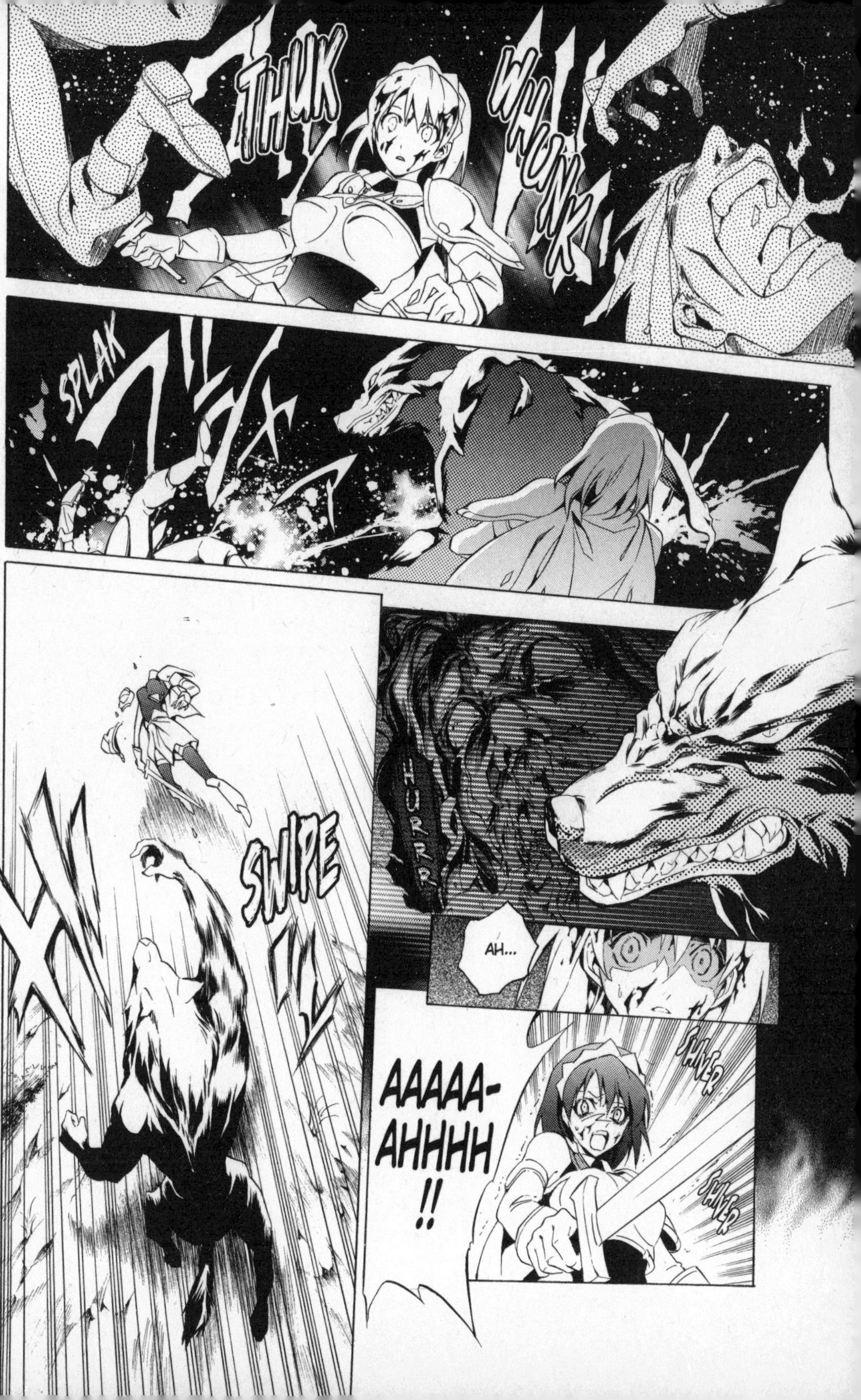
WHUNK!
THUK
SPLAK
HURRR
AH...
SHIVER
AAAAA-AHHHH!!
SHIVER
SWIPE

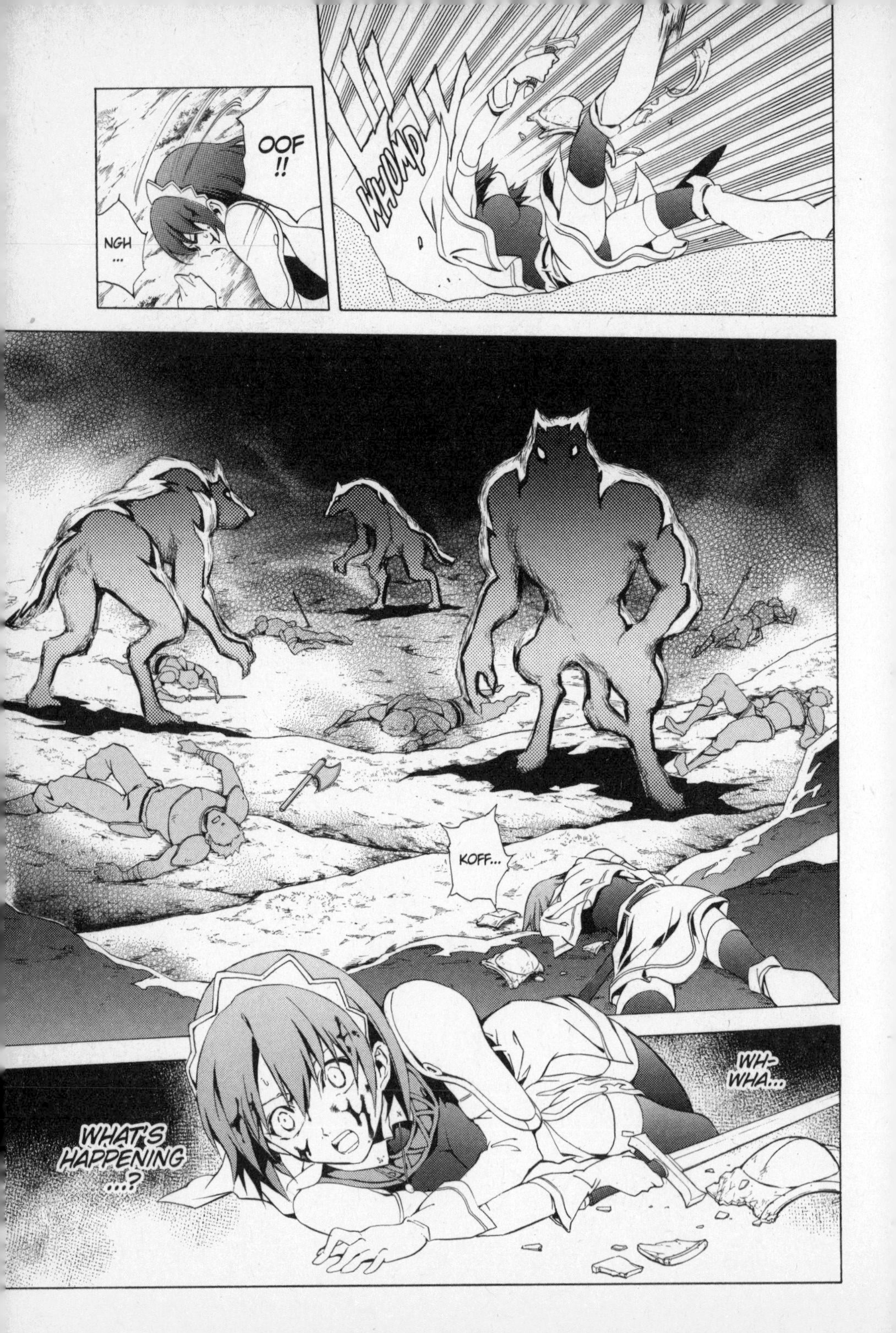
WHOMP
OOF !!
NGH ...
KOFF...
WH-WHA...
WHAT'S HAPPENING ...?

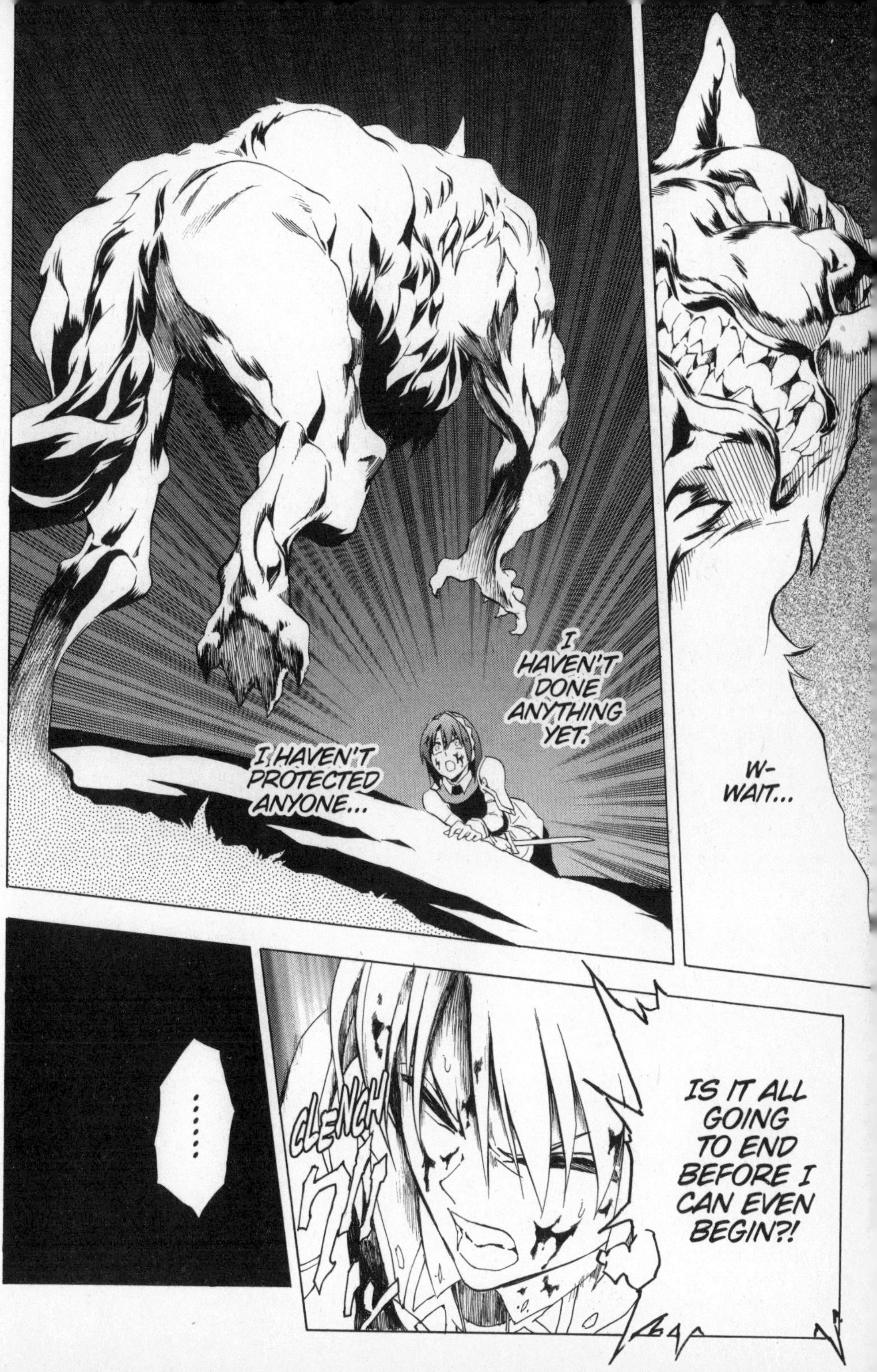
W- WAIT...
I HAVEN'T DONE ANYTHING YET.
I HAVEN'T PROTECTED ANYONE...
IS IT ALL GOING TO END BEFORE I CAN EVEN BEGIN?!
CLENCH
......

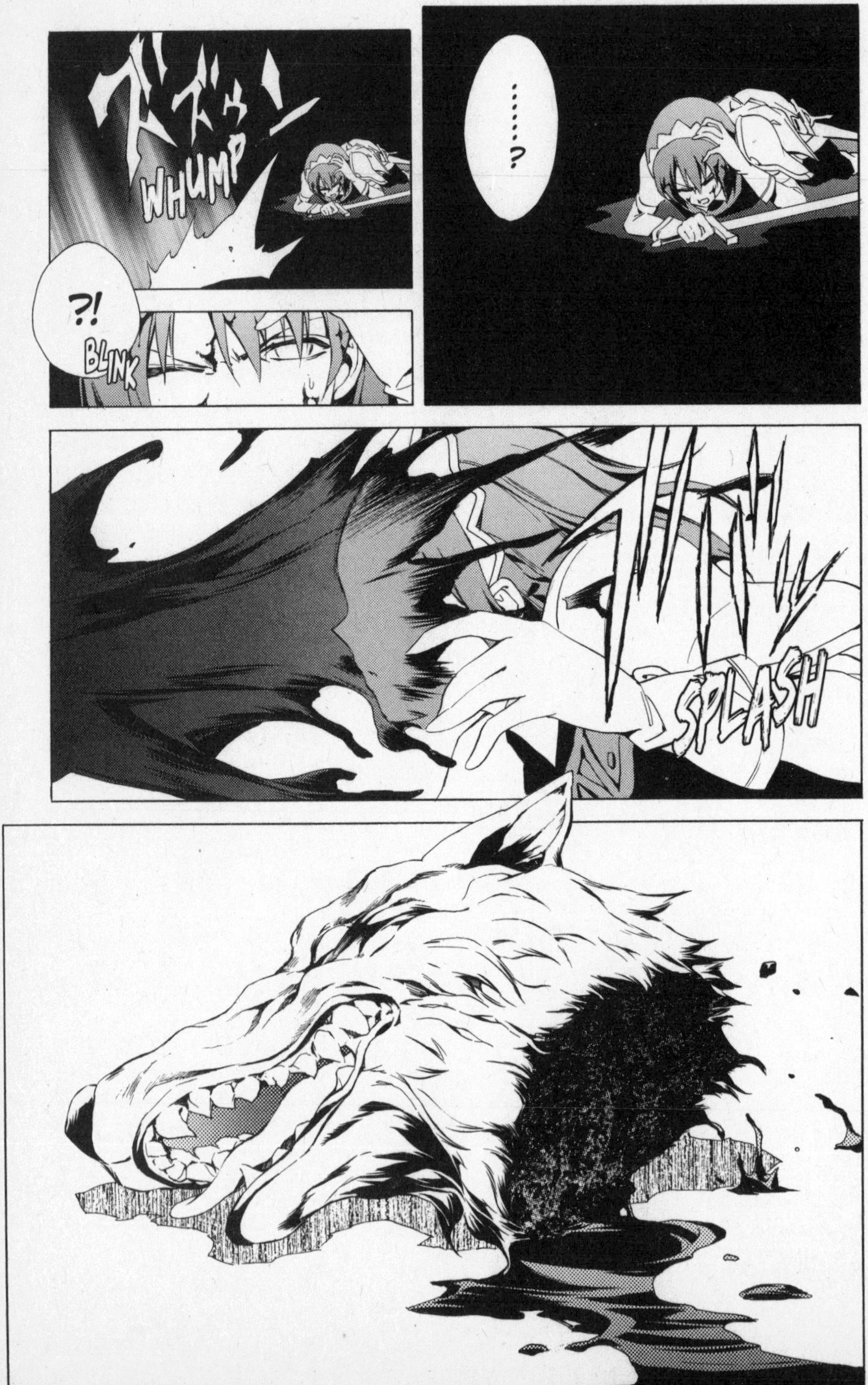
......?
WHUMP
?!
BLINK
SPLASH

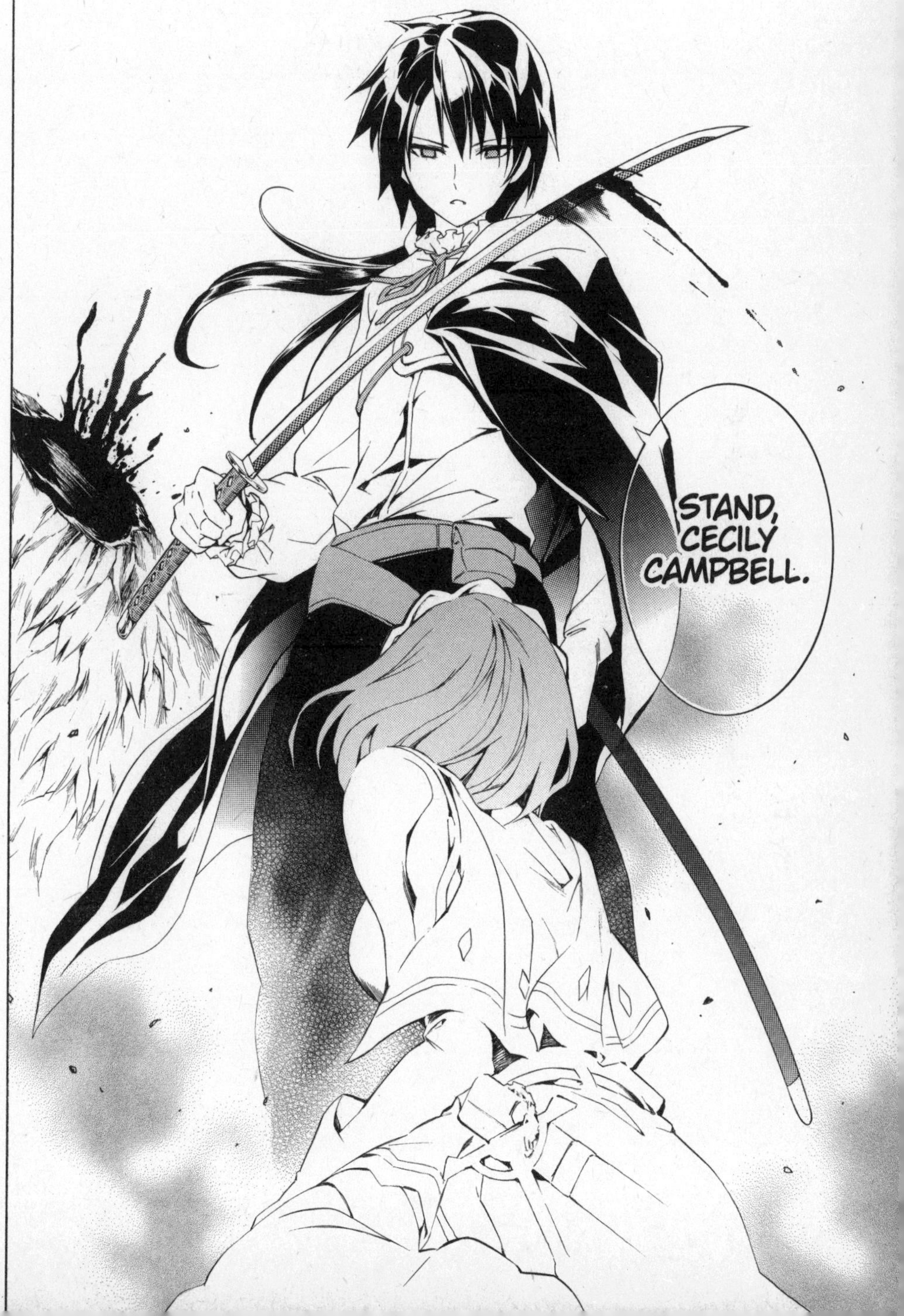
STAND, CECILY CAMPBELL.

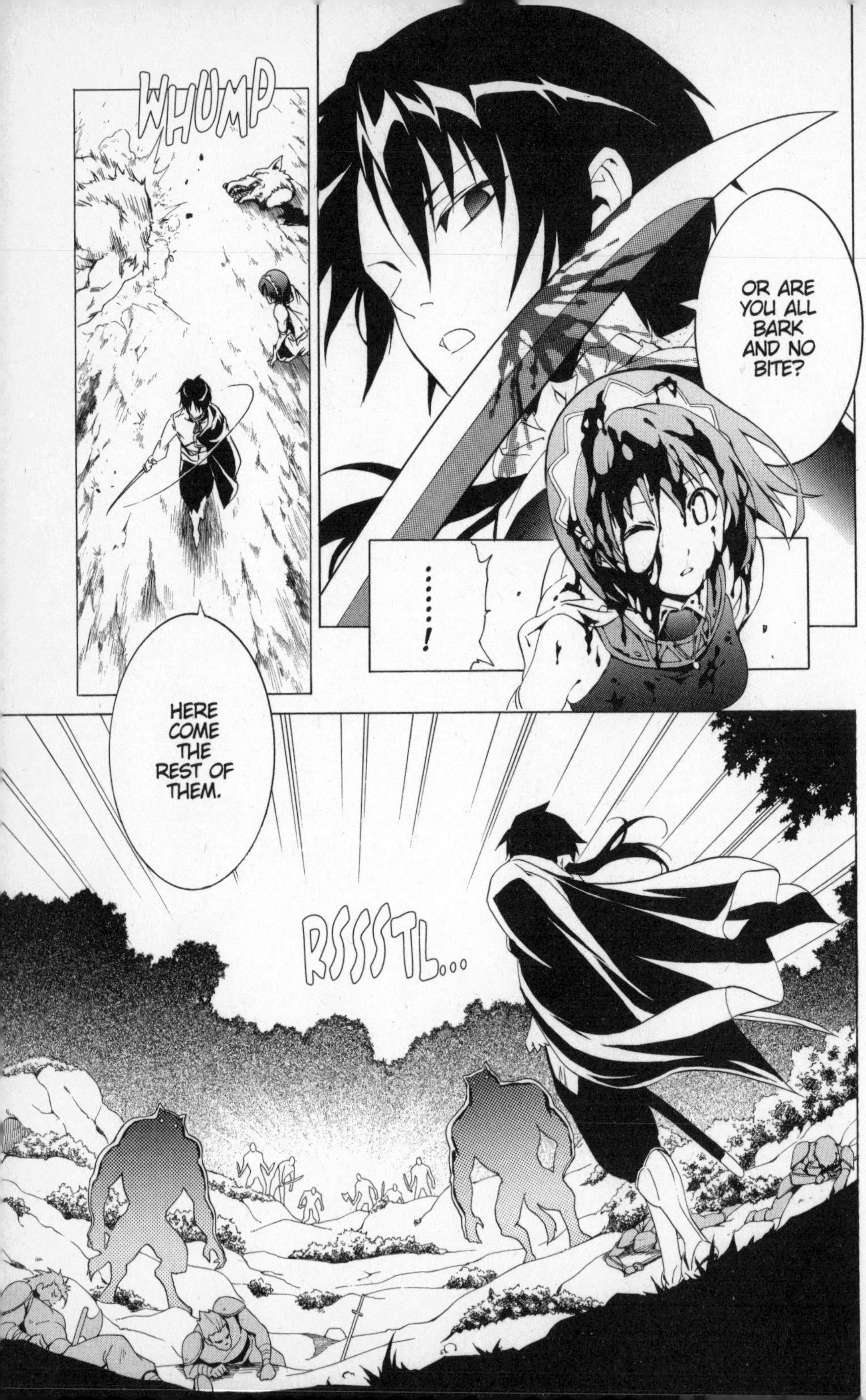
OR ARE YOU ALL BARK AND NO BITE?
......!
WHUMP
HERE COME THE REST OF THEM.
RSSSTL...

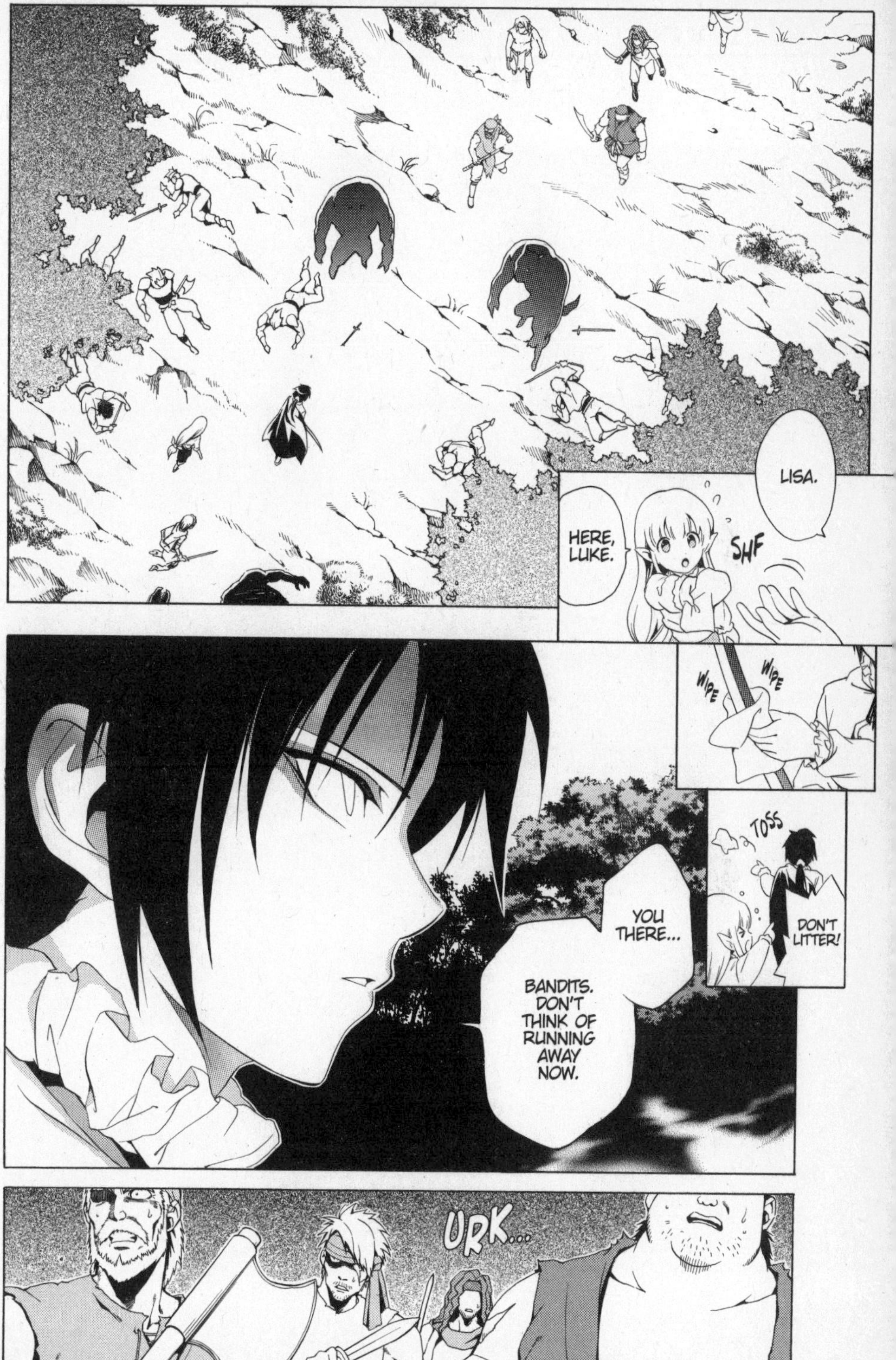
LISA.
SHF
HERE, LUKE.
WIPE
WIPE
TOSS
DON'T LITTER!
YOU THERE...
BANDITS. DON'T THINK OF RUNNING AWAY NOW.
URK...

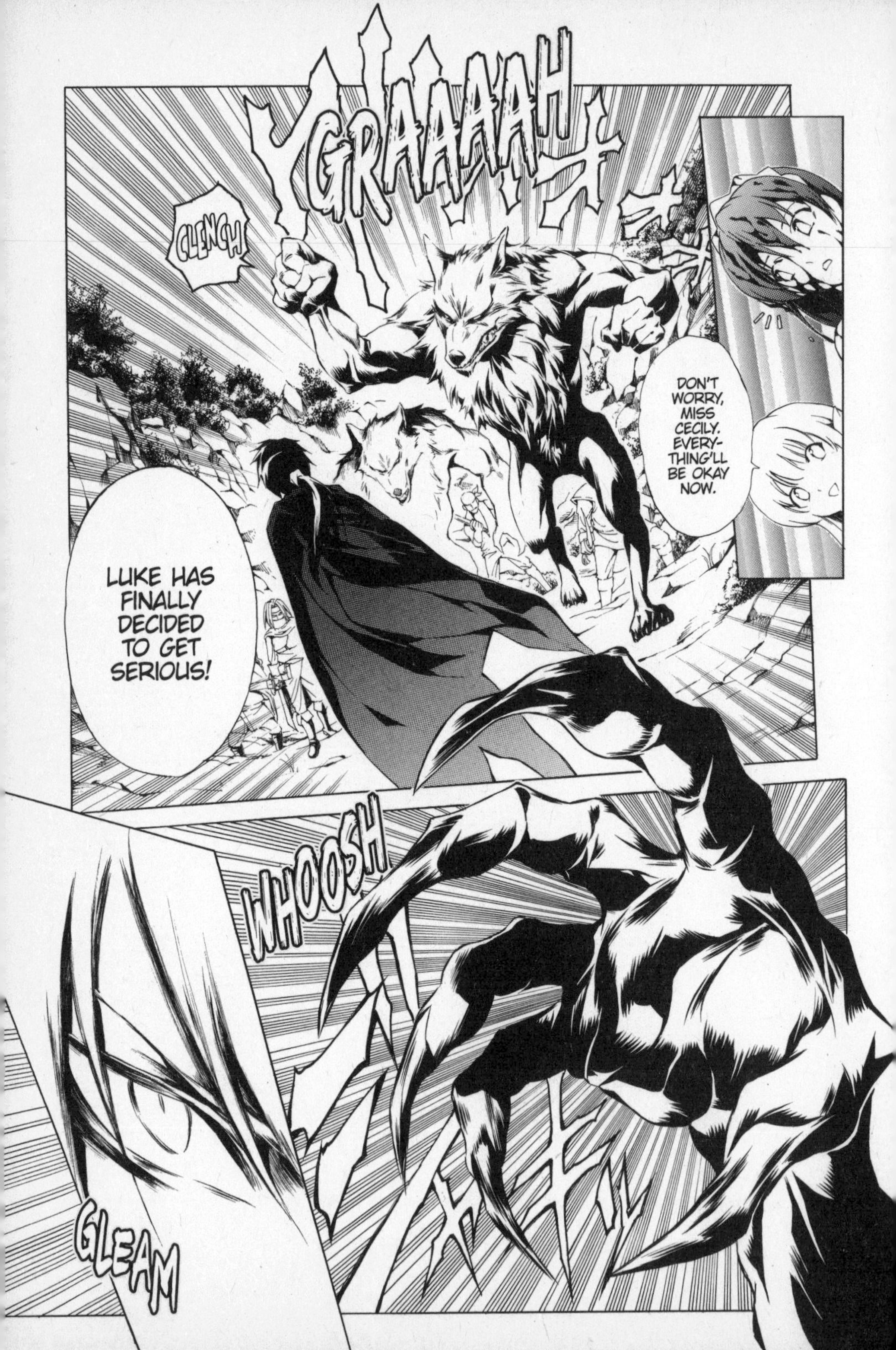
GRAAAAH
DON'T WORRY, MISS CECILY. EVERYTHING'LL BE OKAY NOW.
CLENCH
LUKE HAS FINALLY DECIDED TO GET SERIOUS!
WHOOSH
GLEAM

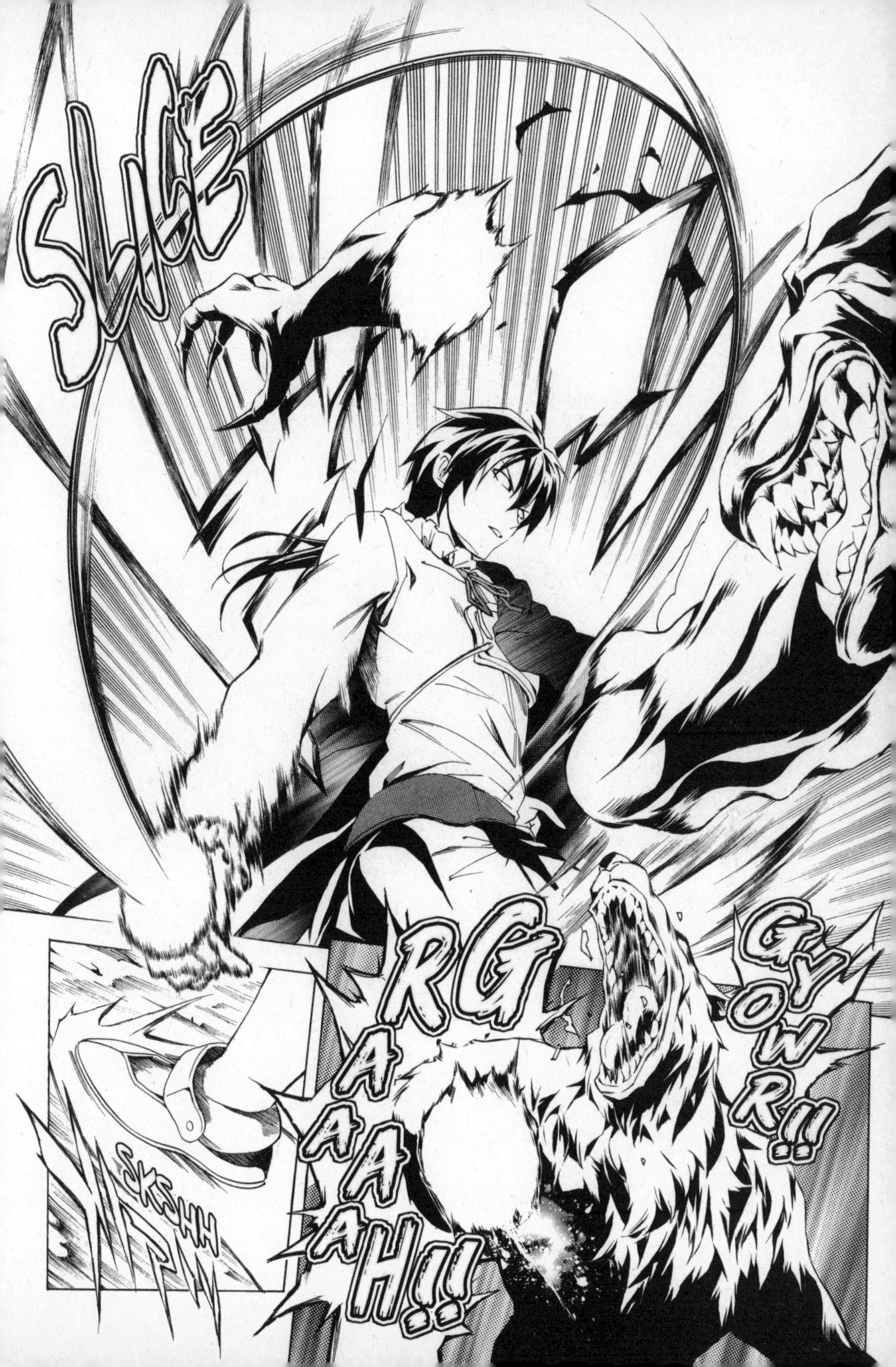
SLICE
GYOWR!!
RGAAAAH!!
SKSHH

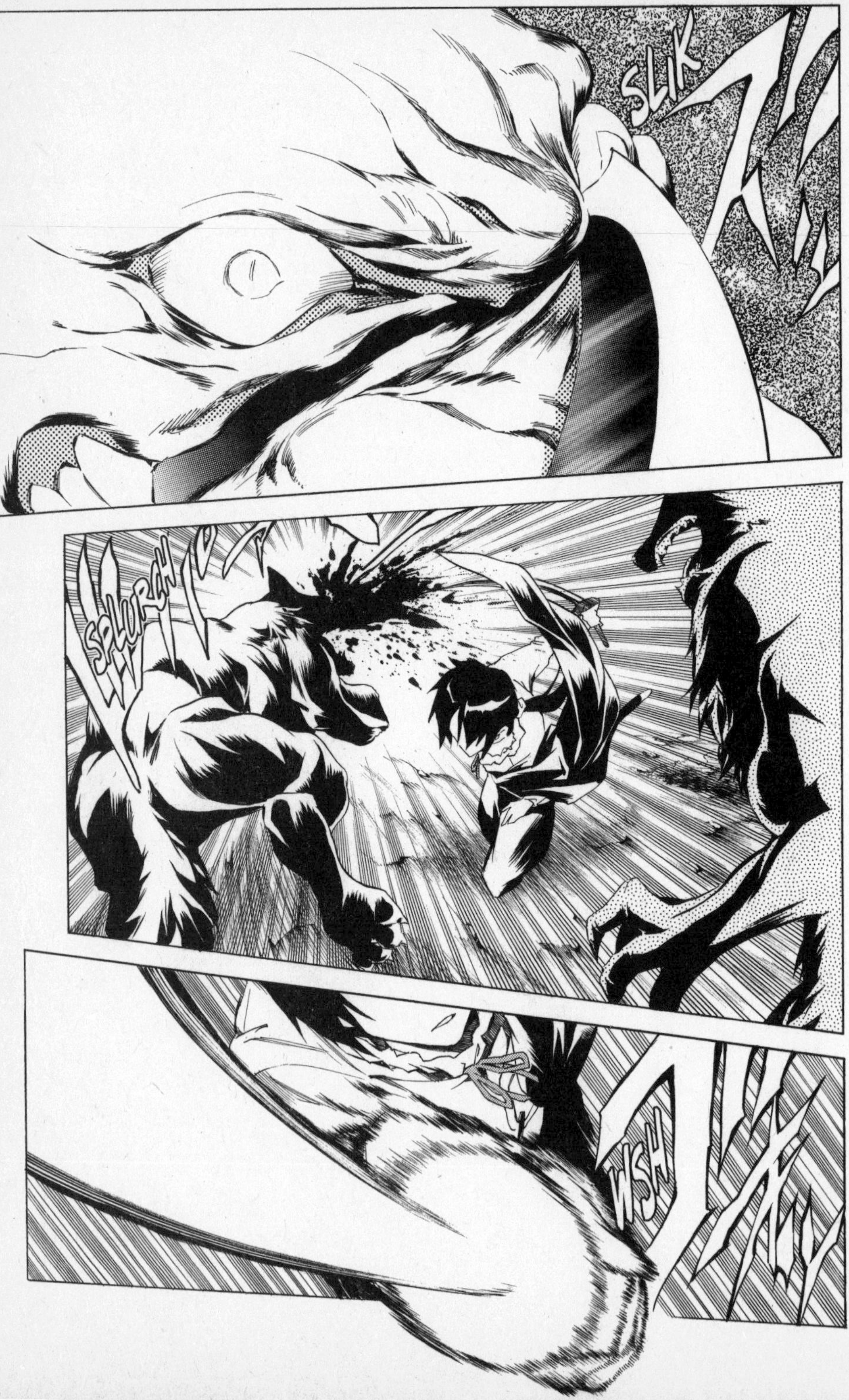
SLIK
SPLURCH
WSH

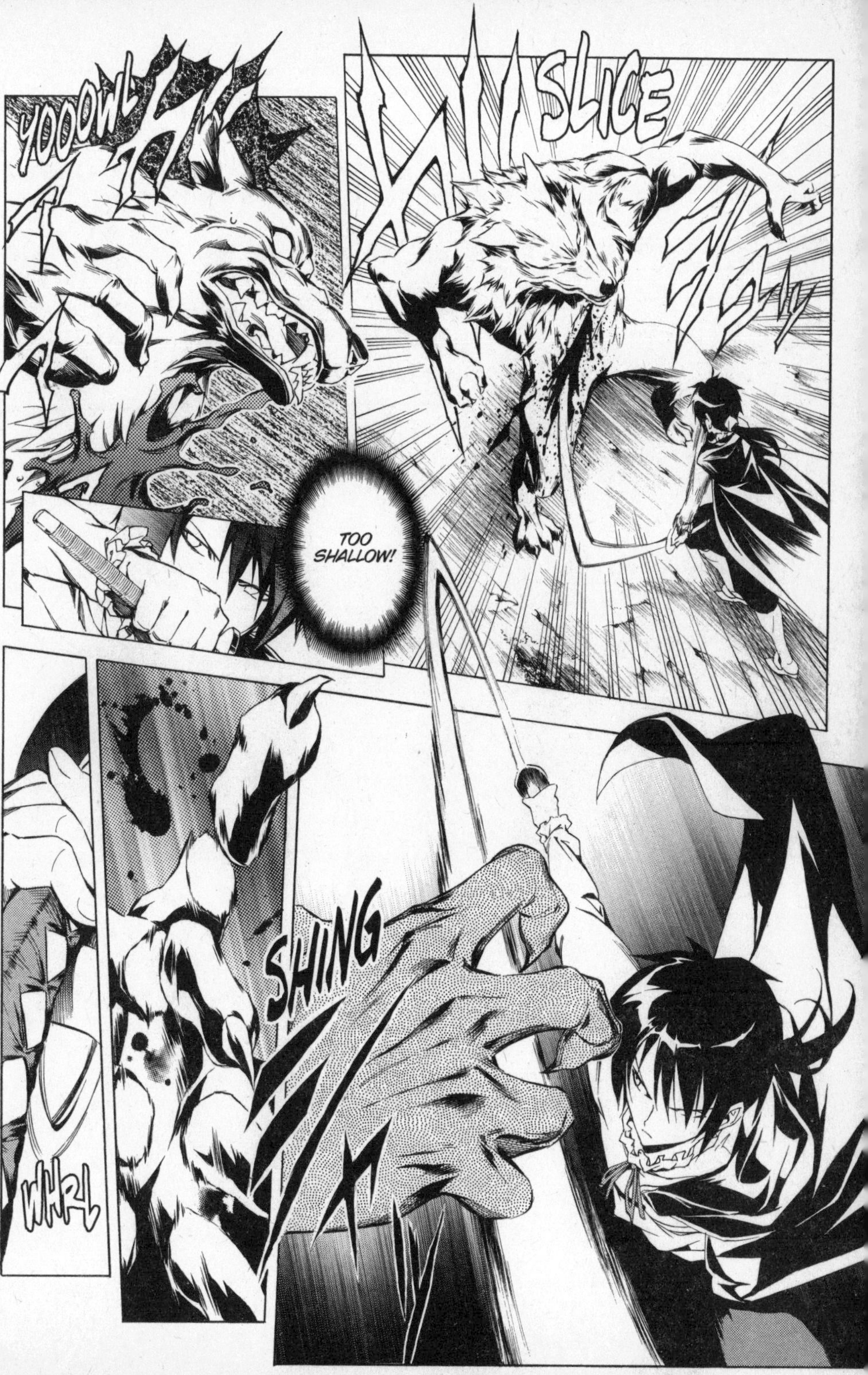

SLICE
YOOOWL
TOO SHALLOW!
SHING
WHRL

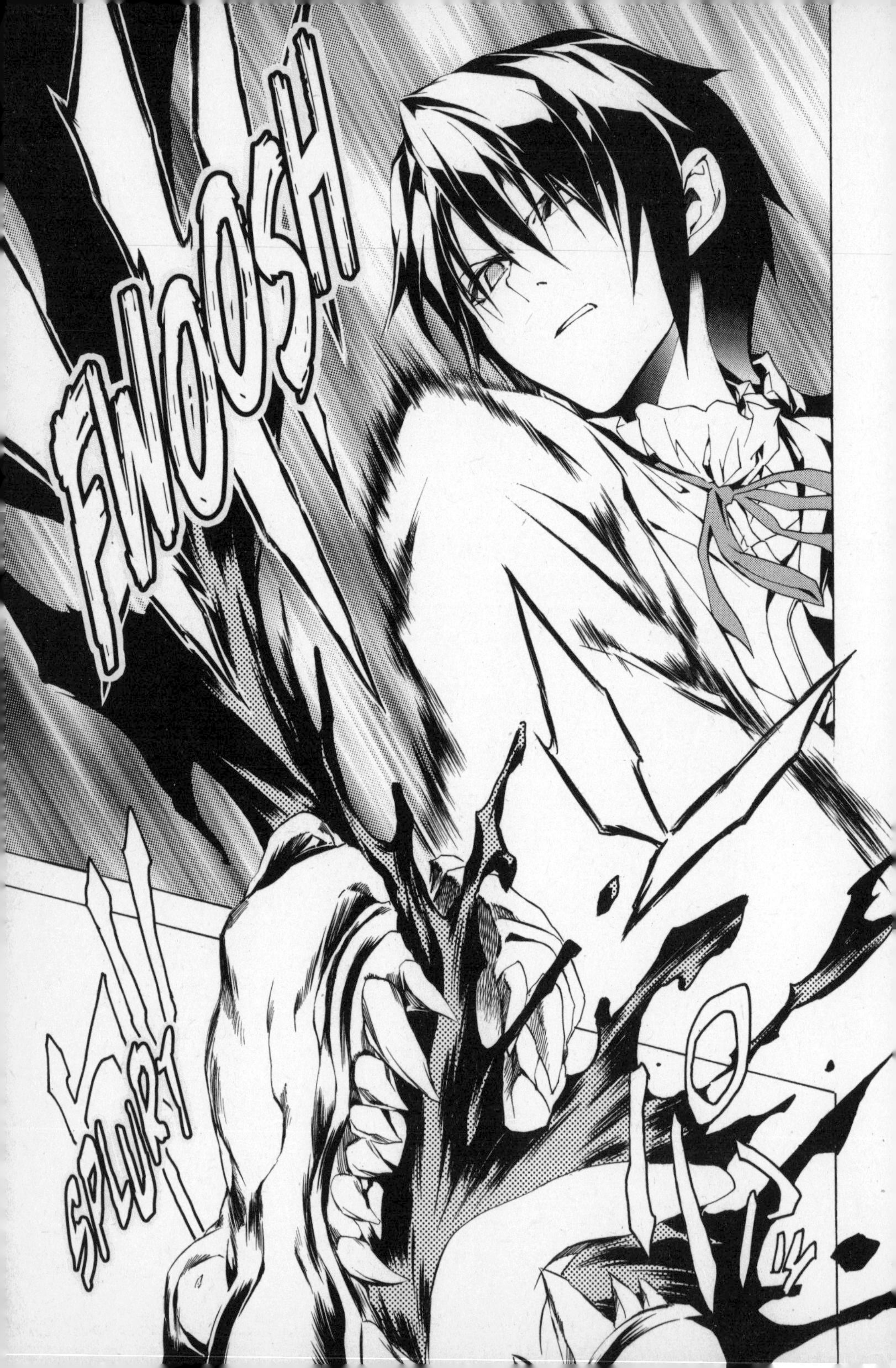
FWOOSH
SPLURT

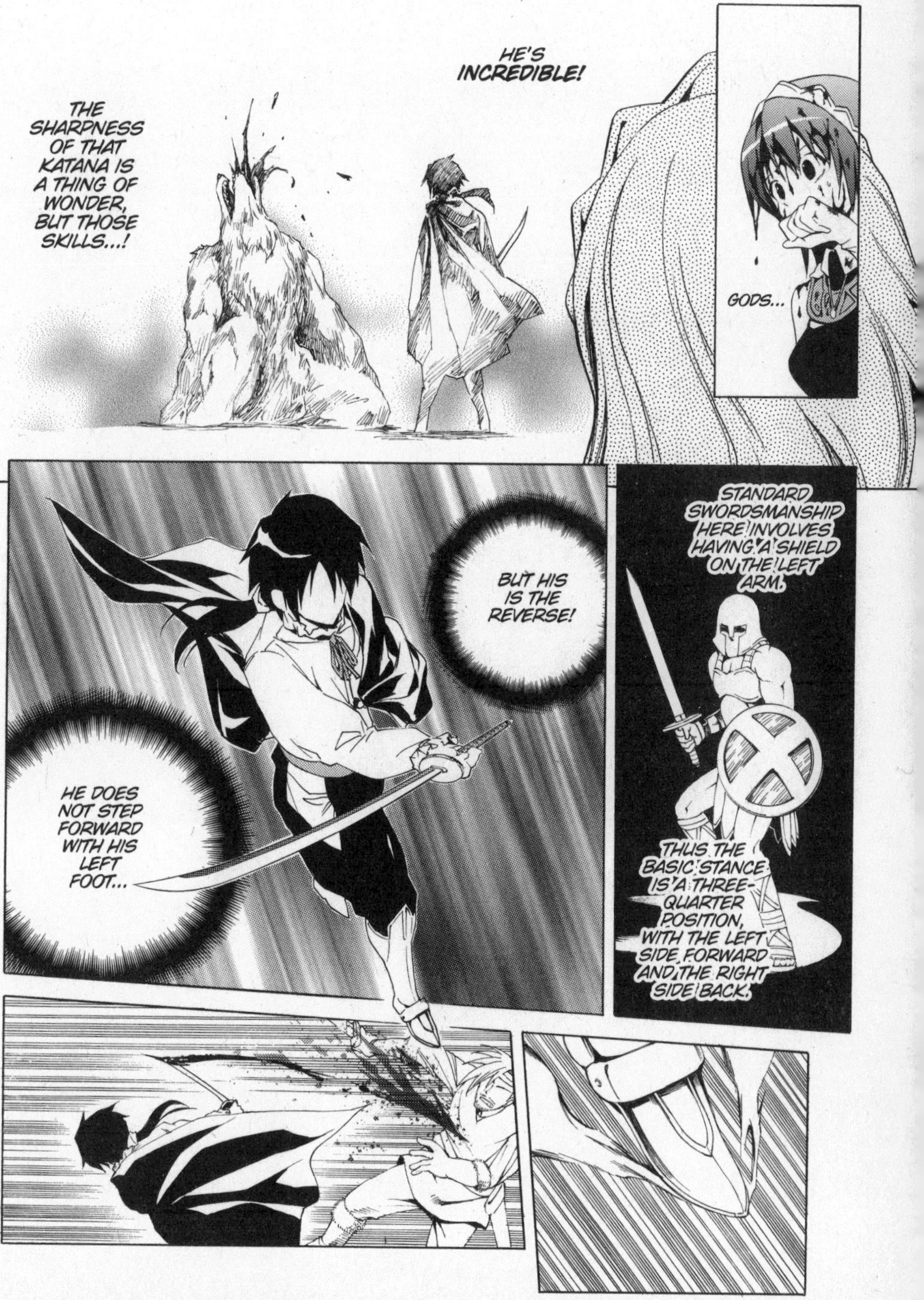
GODS...
HE'S INCREDIBLE!
THE SHARPNESS OF THAT KATANA IS A THING OF WONDER, BUT THOSE SKILLS...!
STANDARD SWORDSMANSHIP HERE INVOLVES HAVING A SHIELD ON THE LEFT ARM.
THUS THE BASIC STANCE IS A THREE-QUARTER POSITION, WITH THE LEFT SIDE FORWARD AND THE RIGHT SIDE BACK.
BUT HIS IS THE REVERSE!
HE DOES NOT STEP FORWARD WITH HIS LEFT FOOT...

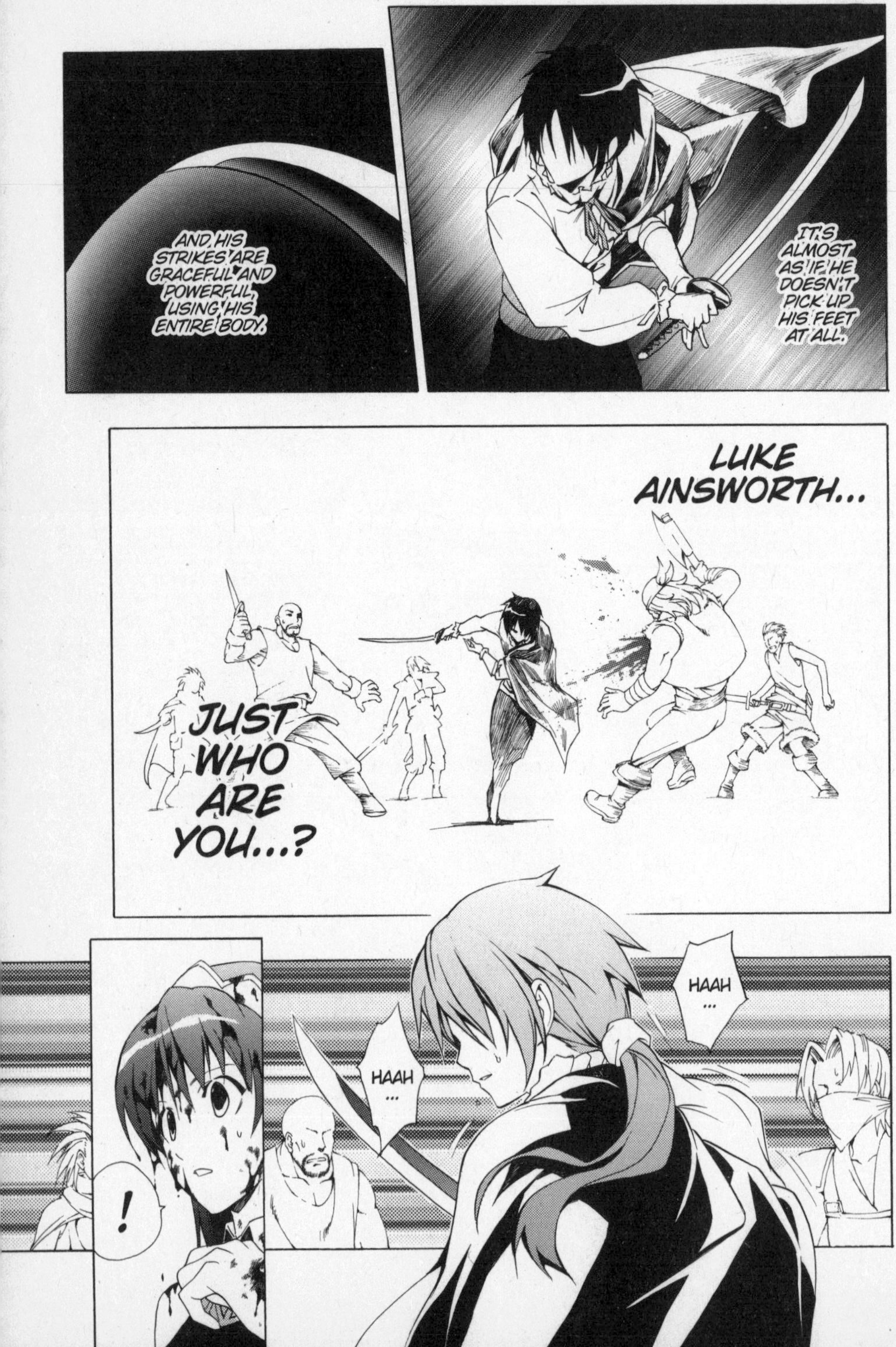
IT'S ALMOST AS IF HE DOESN'T PICK UP HIS FEET AT ALL.
AND HIS STRIKES ARE GRACEFUL AND POWERFUL, USING HIS ENTIRE BODY.
LUKE AINSWORTH...
JUST WHO ARE YOU...?
HAAH ...
HAAH ...
!

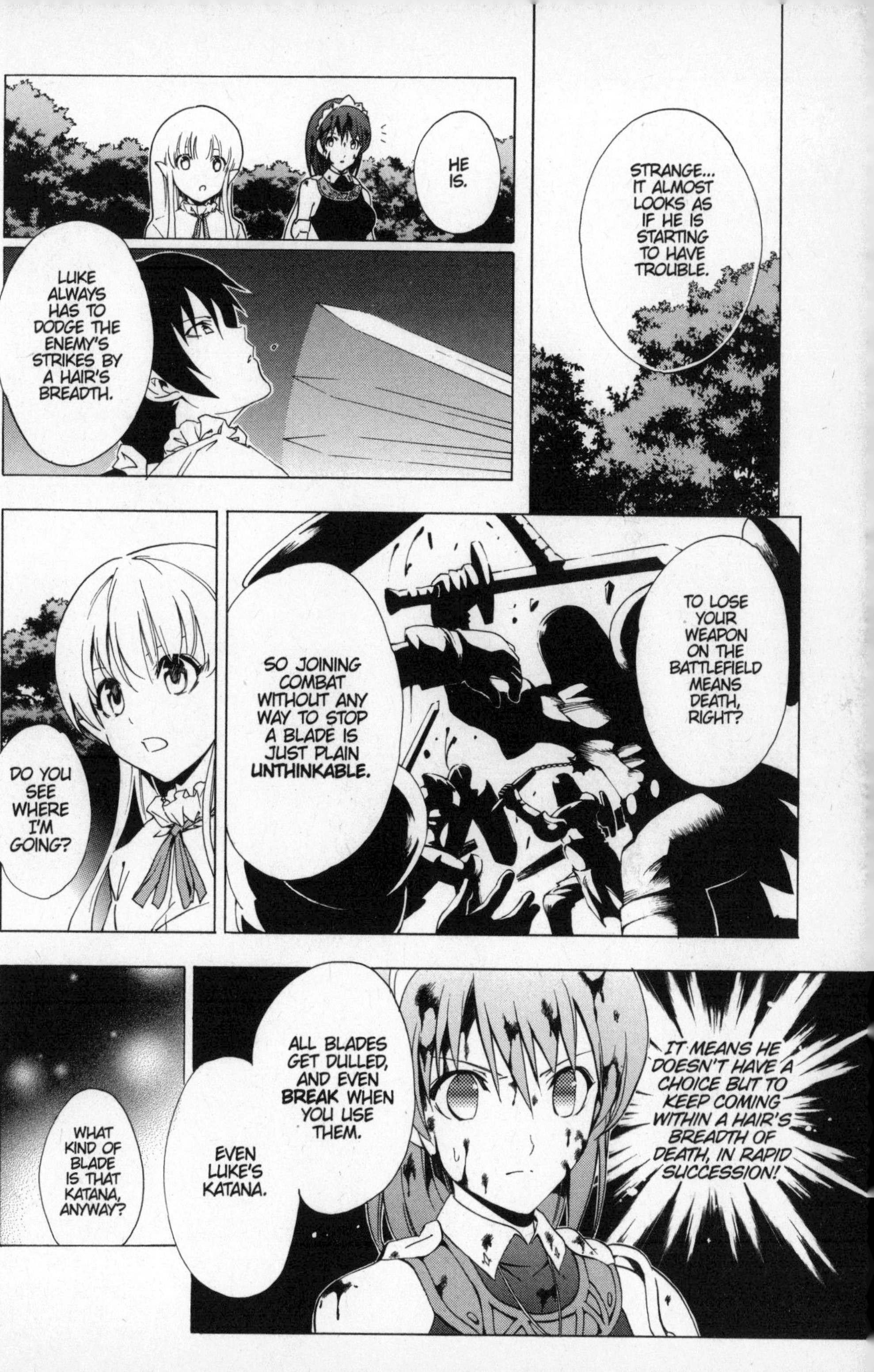
STRANGE... IT ALMOST LOOKS AS IF HE IS STARTING TO HAVE TROUBLE.
HE IS.
LUKE ALWAYS HAS TO DODGE THE ENEMY'S STRIKES BY A HAIR'S BREADTH.
TO LOSE YOUR WEAPON ON THE BATTLEFIELD MEANS DEATH, RIGHT?
SO JOINING COMBAT WITHOUT ANY WAY TO STOP A BLADE IS JUST PLAIN UNTHINKABLE.
DO YOU SEE WHERE I'M GOING?
IT MEANS HE DOESN'T HAVE A CHOICE BUT TO KEEP COMING WITHIN A HAIR'S BREADTH OF DEATH, IN RAPID SUCCESSION!
ALL BLADES GET DULLED, AND EVEN BREAK WHEN YOU USE THEM.
EVEN LUKE'S KATANA.
WHAT KIND OF BLADE IS THAT KATANA, ANYWAY?

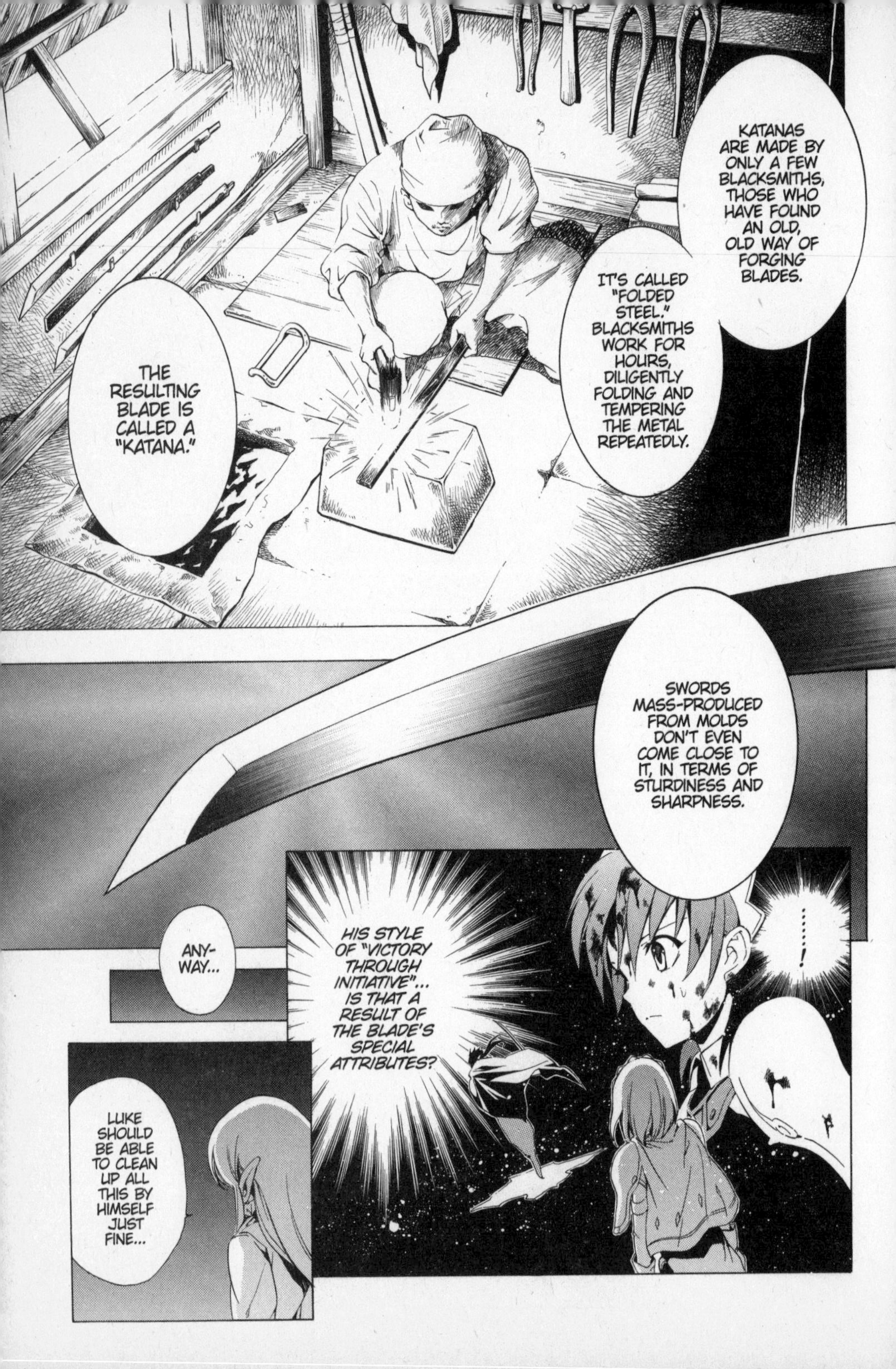
KATANAS ARE MADE BY ONLY A FEW BLACKSMITHS, THOSE WHO HAVE FOUND AN OLD, OLD WAY OF FORGING BLADES.
IT'S CALLED "FOLDED STEEL." BLACKSMITHS WORK FOR HOURS, DILIGENTLY FOLDING AND TEMPERING THE METAL REPEATEDLY.
THE RESULTING BLADE IS CALLED A "KATANA."
SWORDS MASS-PRODUCED FROM MOLDS DON'T EVEN COME CLOSE TO IT, IN TERMS OF STURDINESS AND SHARPNESS.
......!
HIS STYLE OF "VICTORY THROUGH INITIATIVE"... IS THAT A RESULT OF THE BLADE'S SPECIAL ATTRIBUTES?
ANY-WAY...
LUKE SHOULD BE ABLE TO CLEAN UP ALL THIS BY HIMSELF JUST FINE...

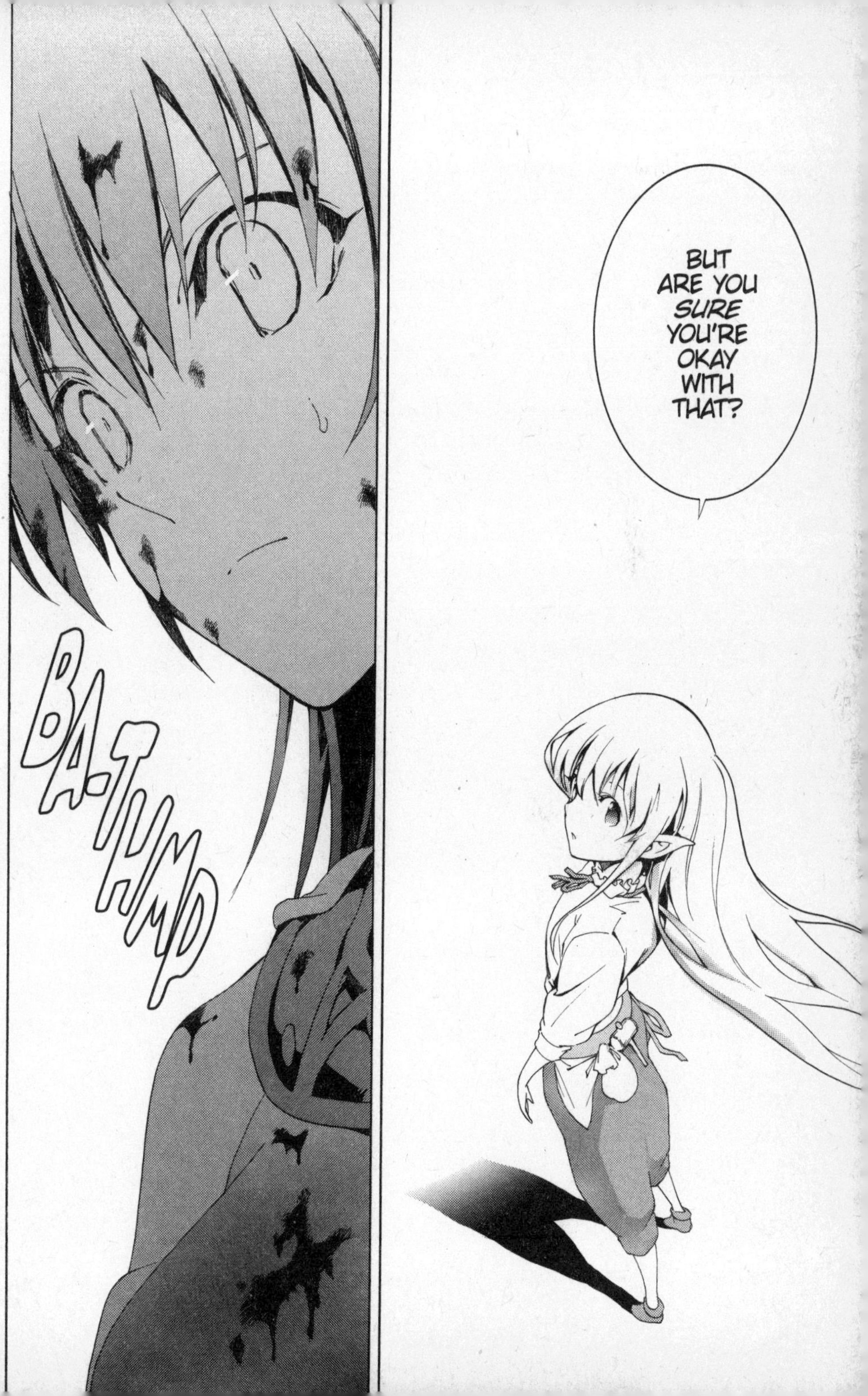
BUT ARE YOU *SURE* YOU'RE OKAY WITH THAT?
BA-THUMP

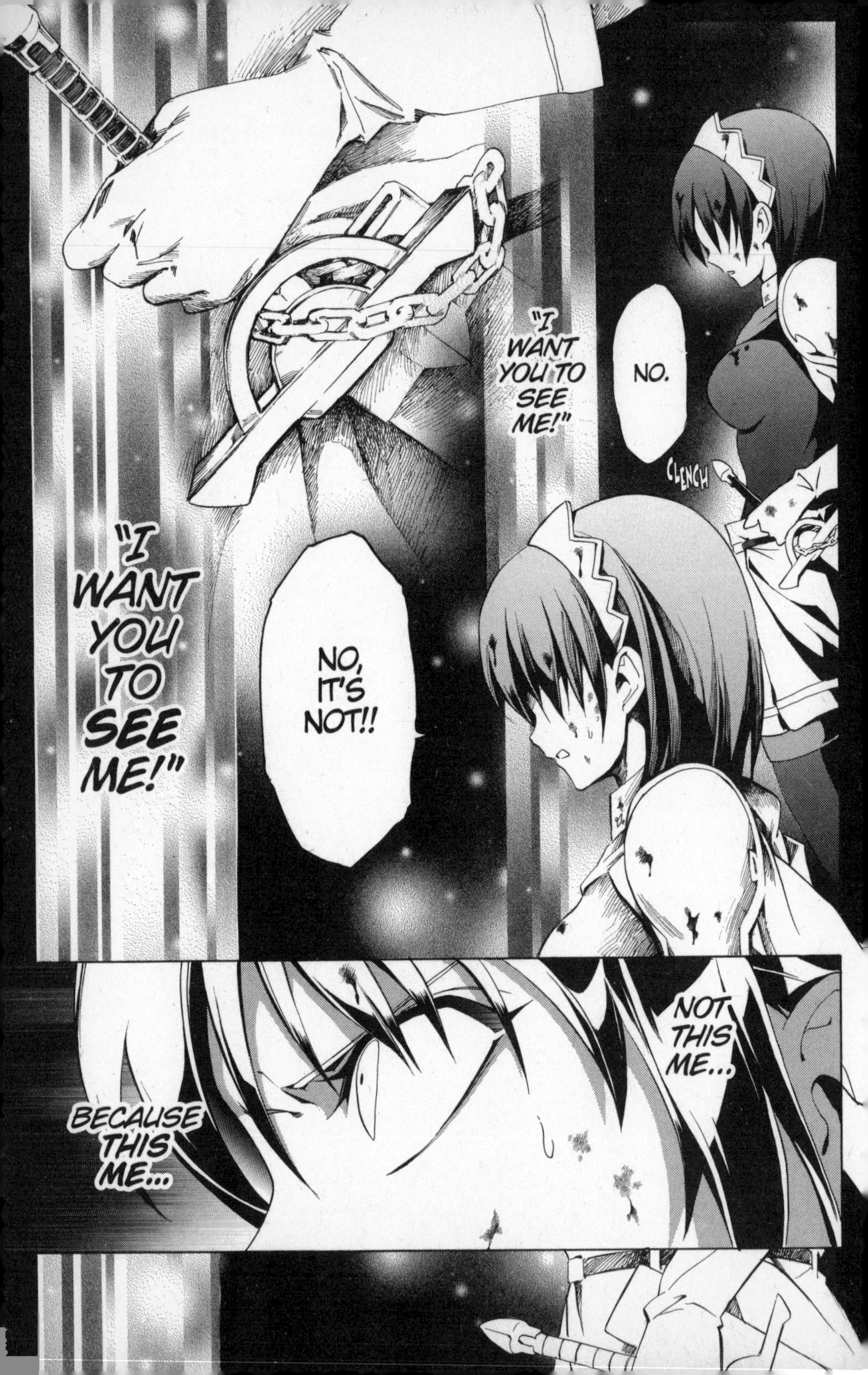
"I WANT YOU TO SEE ME!"
NO.
CLENCH
"I WANT YOU TO SEE ME!"
NO, IT'S NOT!!
NOT THIS ME...
BECAUSE THIS ME...

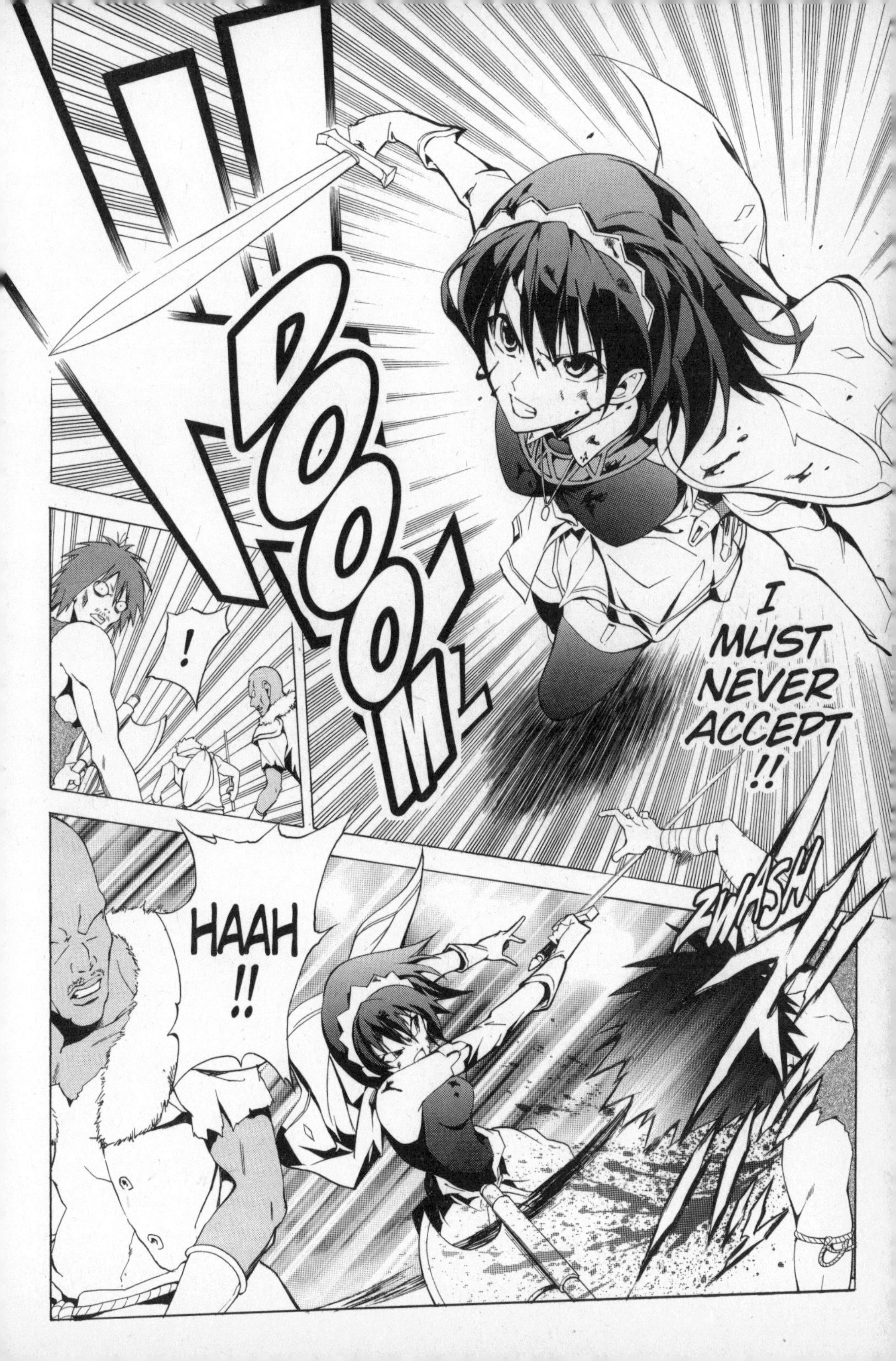
DOOOM
I MUST NEVER ACCEPT!!
!
ZWASH
HAAH!!

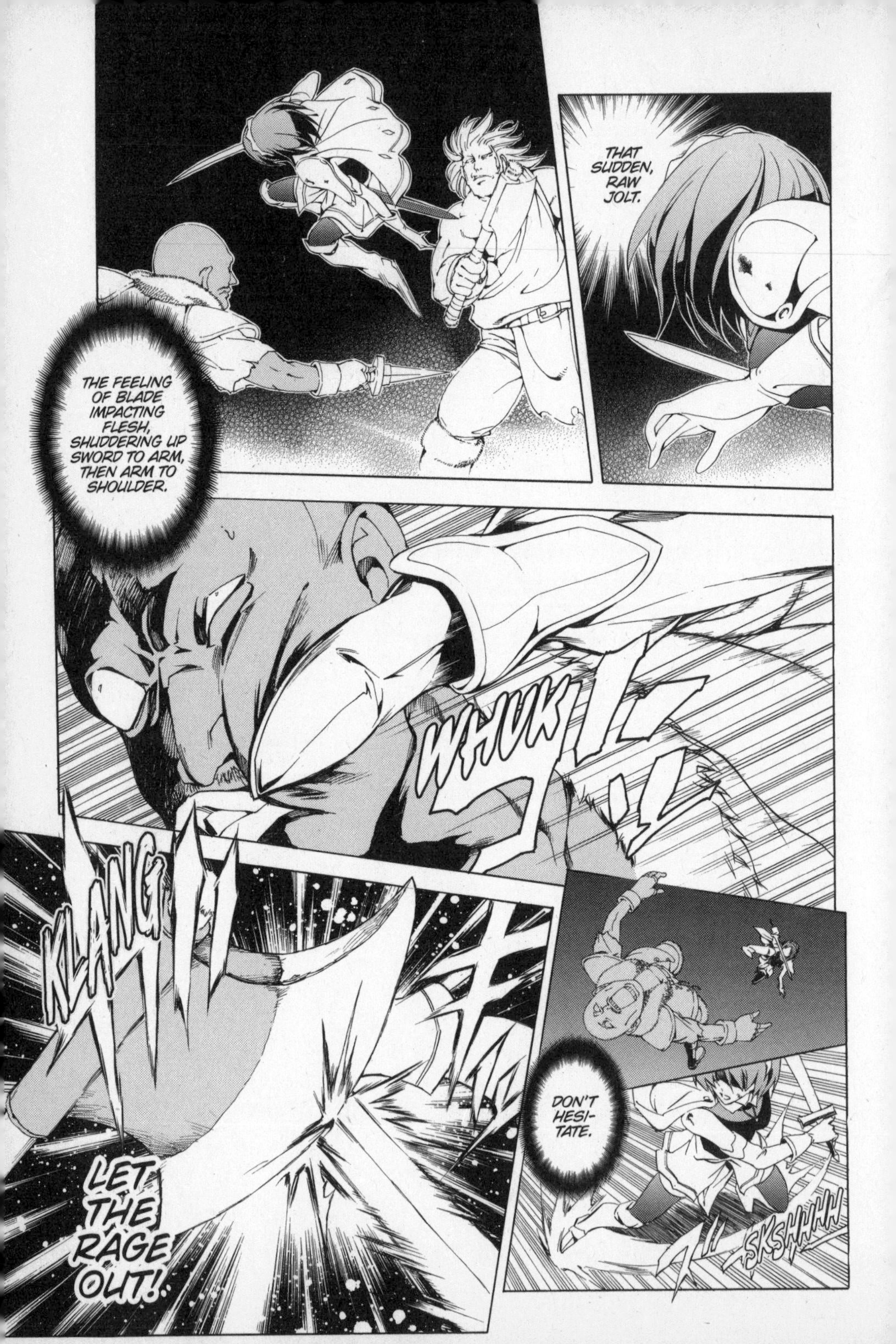
THAT SUDDEN, RAW JOLT.
THE FEELING OF BLADE IMPACTING FLESH, SHUDDERING UP SWORD TO ARM, THEN ARM TO SHOULDER.
WHUK!!
DON'T HESI-TATE.
SKSHHHH
KLANG!!
LET THE RAGE OUT!

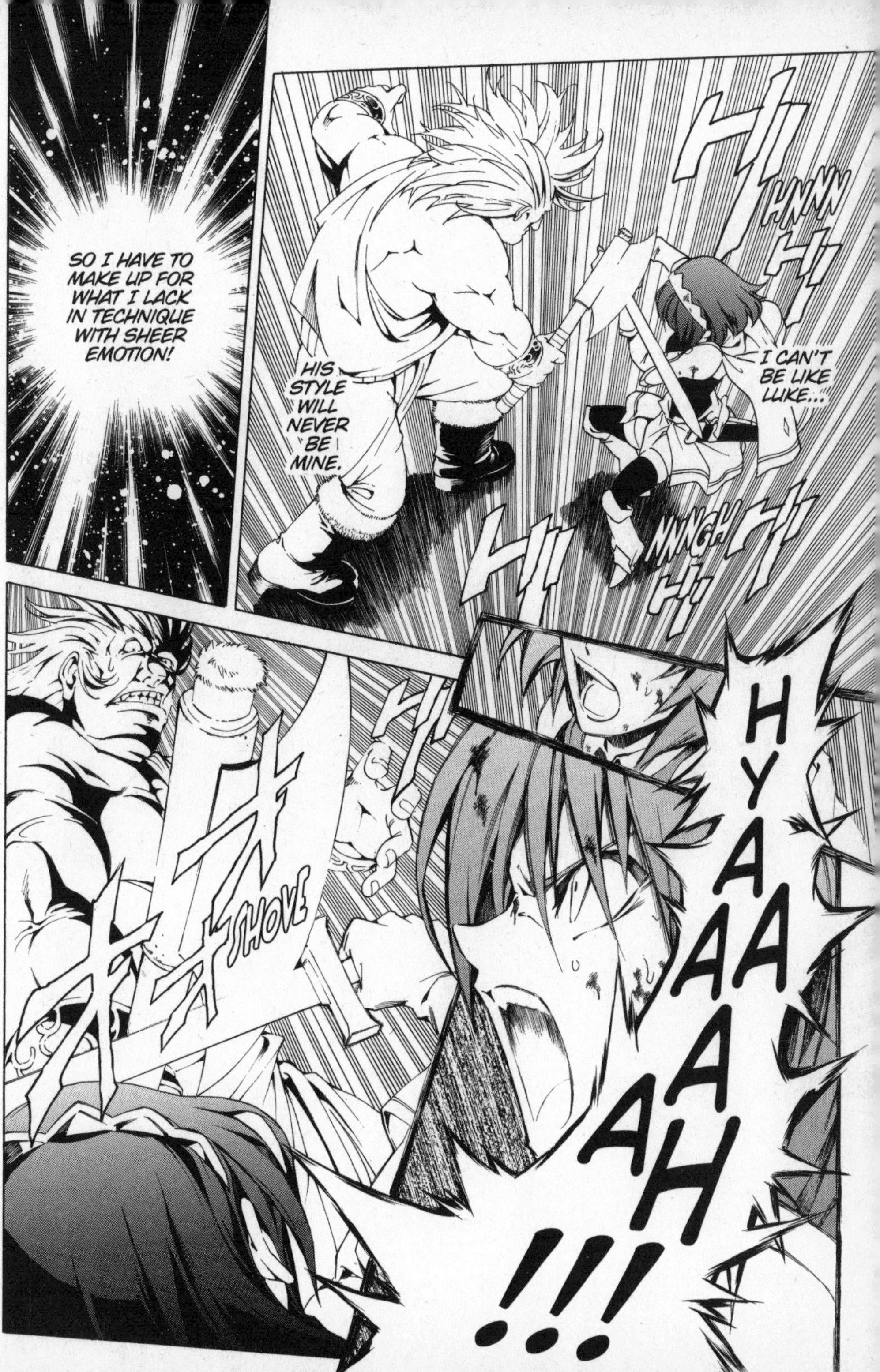
HNNNN
I CAN'T BE LIKE LUKE...
HIS STYLE WILL NEVER BE MINE.
NNNGH
SO I HAVE TO MAKE UP FOR WHAT I LACK IN TECHNIQUE WITH SHEER EMOTION!
HYAAAAAAH!!!
SHOVE

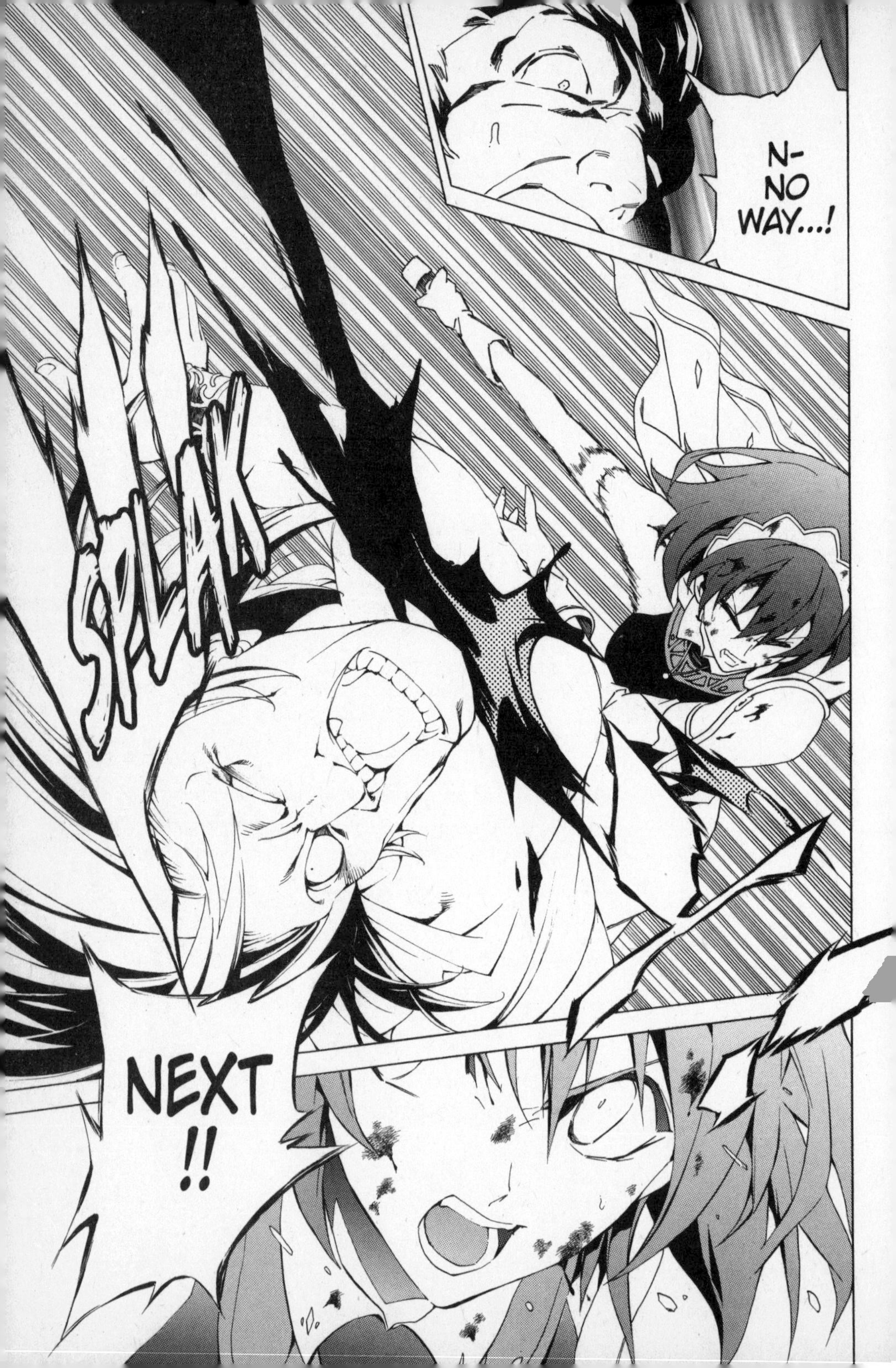
N-
NO
WAY...!
SPLAK
NEXT
!!

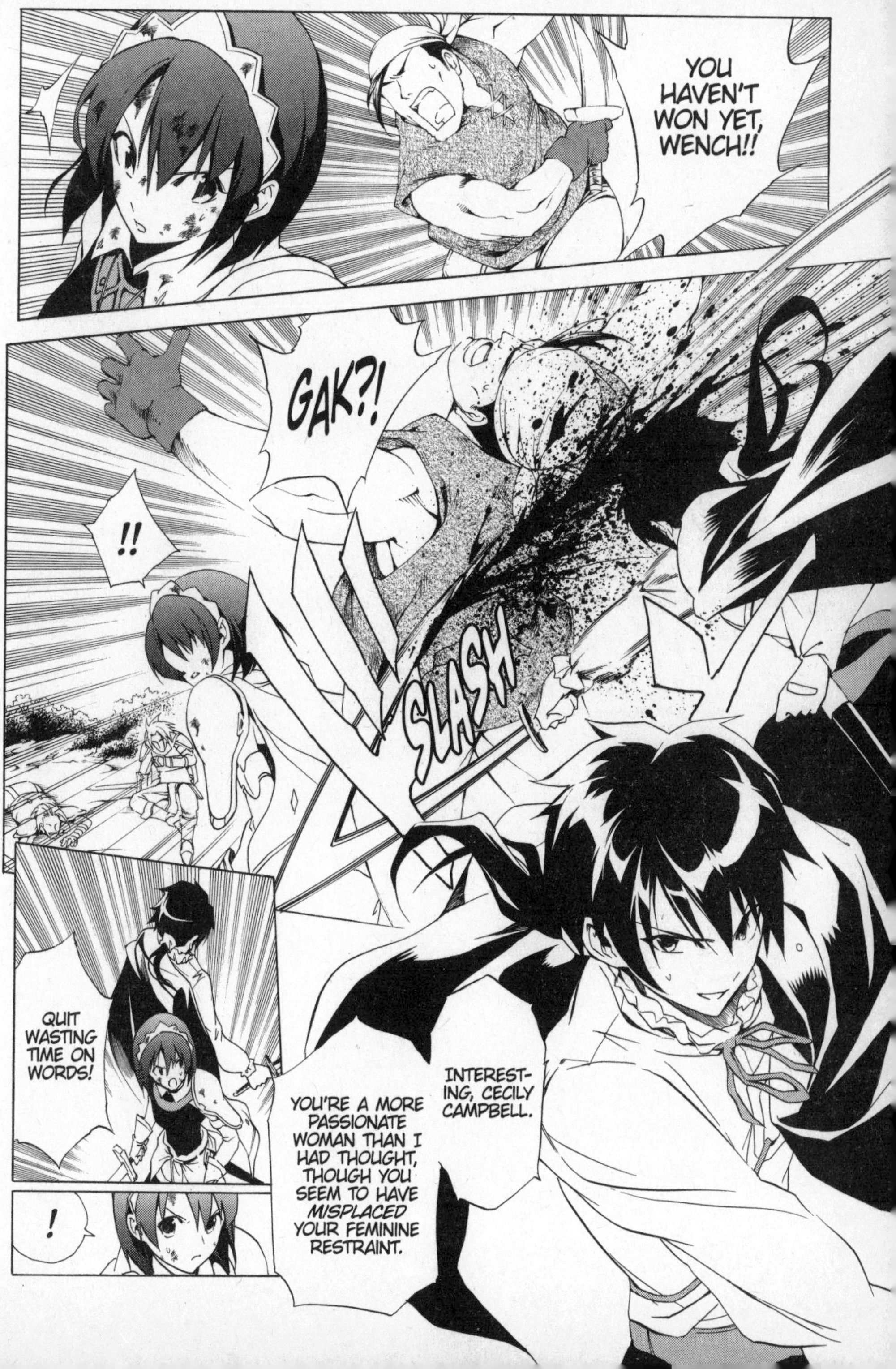
YOU HAVEN'T WON YET, WENCH!!
GAK?!
!!
SLASH
INTEREST-ING, CECILY CAMPBELL.
YOU'RE A MORE PASSIONATE WOMAN THAN I HAD THOUGHT, THOUGH YOU SEEM TO HAVE *MISPLACED* YOUR FEMININE RESTRAINT.
QUIT WASTING TIME ON WORDS!
!

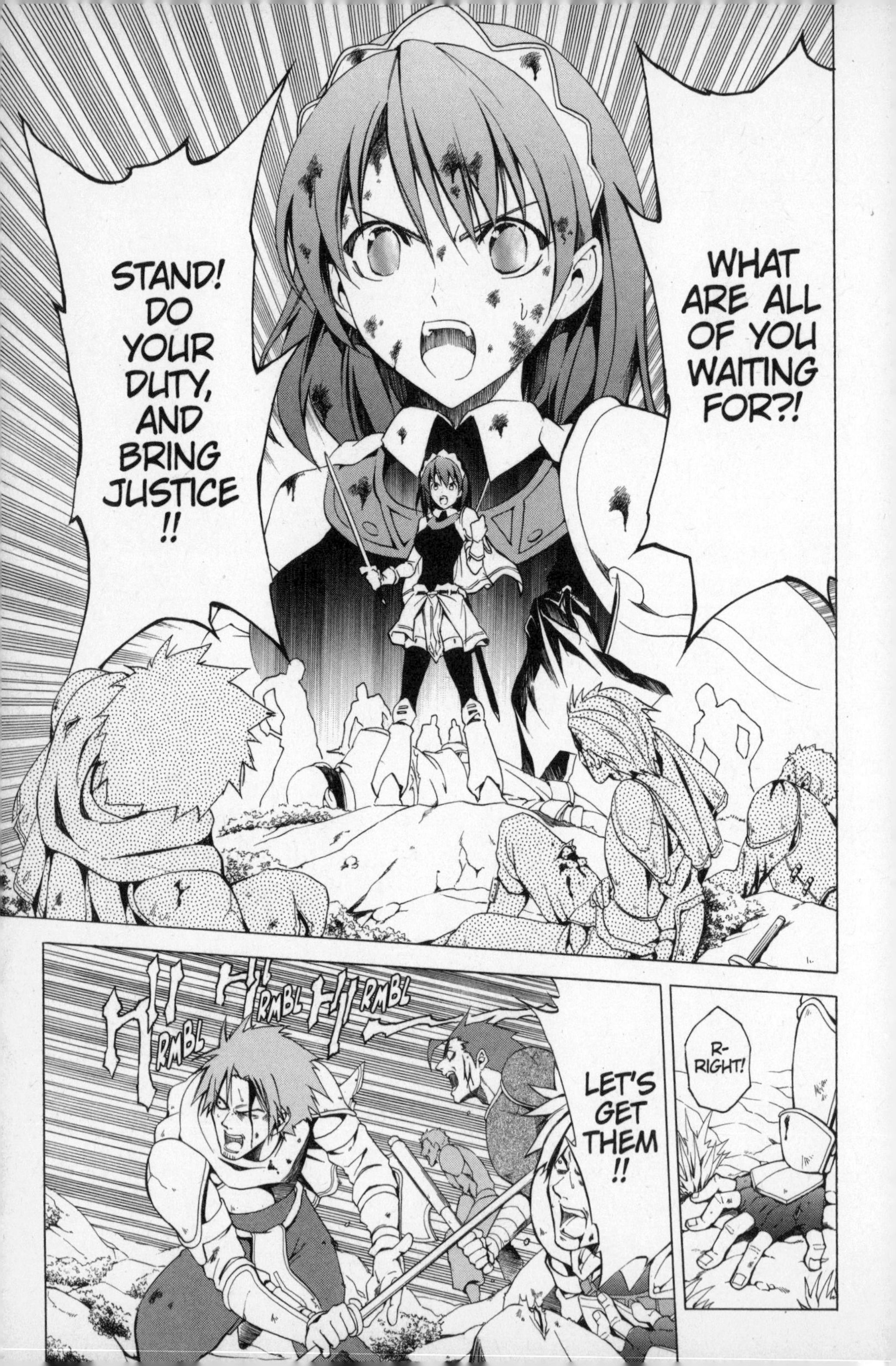
WHAT ARE ALL OF YOU WAITING FOR?!
STAND! DO YOUR DUTY, AND BRING JUSTICE!!
R-RIGHT!
LET'S GET THEM!!
RMBL
RMBL
RMBL
RMBL

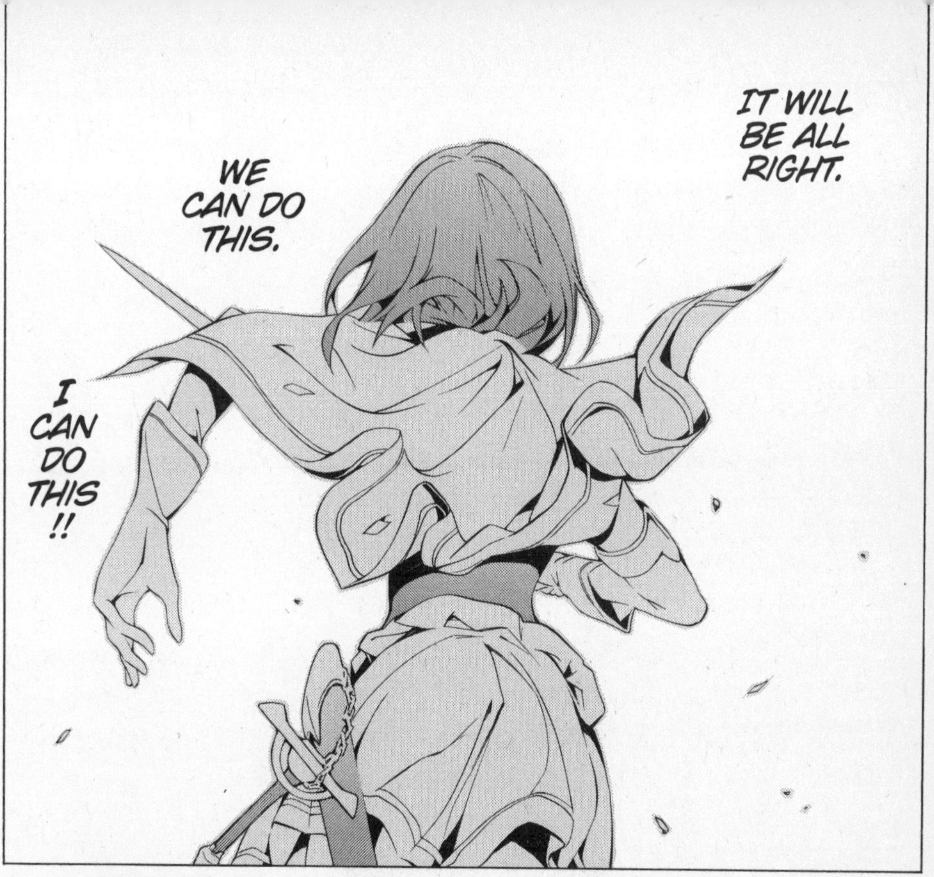
IT WILL BE ALL RIGHT.
WE CAN DO THIS.
I CAN DO THIS!!

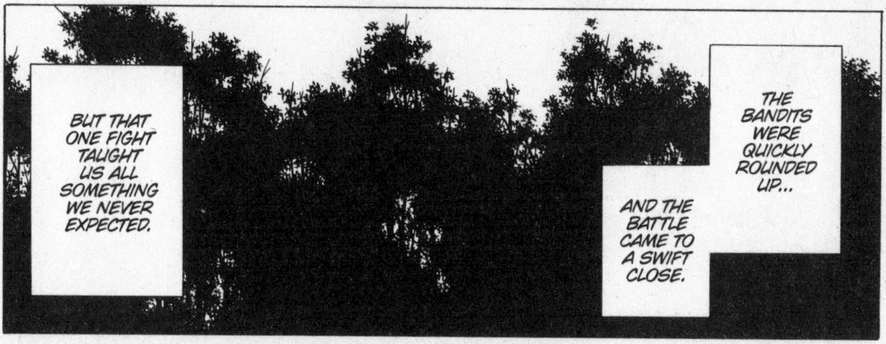
THE BANDITS WERE QUICKLY ROUNDED UP...
AND THE BATTLE CAME TO A SWIFT CLOSE.
BUT THAT ONE FIGHT TAUGHT US ALL SOMETHING WE NEVER EXPECTED.

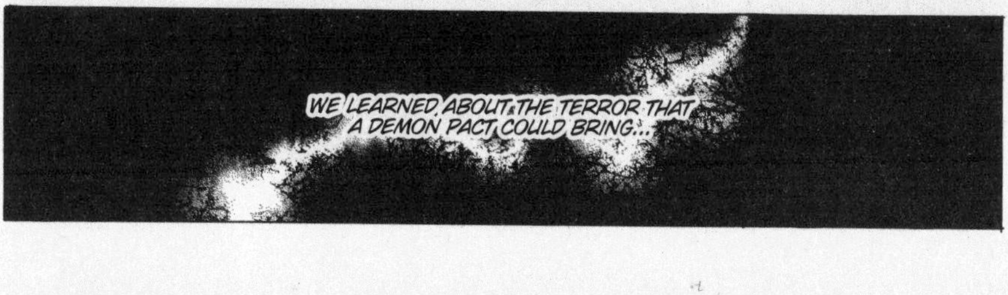
WE LEARNED ABOUT THE TERROR THAT A DEMON PACT COULD BRING...

✳ Cecily Campbell ✳

The Sacred Blacksmith

聖剣の刀鍛冶（ブラックスミス）

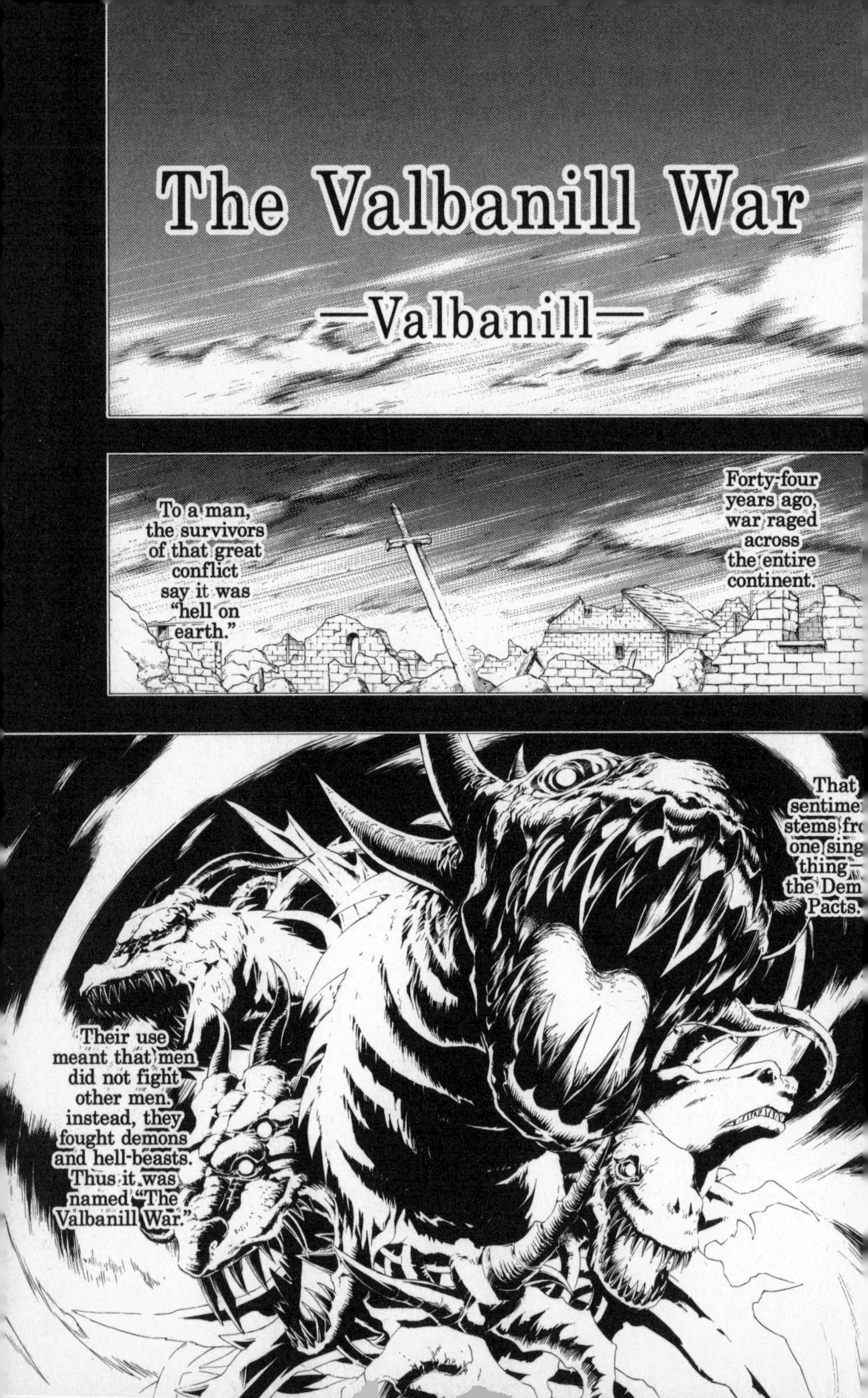
The Valbanill War
—Valbanill—
Forty-four years ago, war raged across the entire continent.
To a man, the survivors of that great conflict say it was "hell on earth."
That sentimen stems fro one sing thing— the Dem Pacts.
Their use meant that men did not fight other men. instead, they fought demons and hell-beasts. Thus it was named "The Valbanill War."

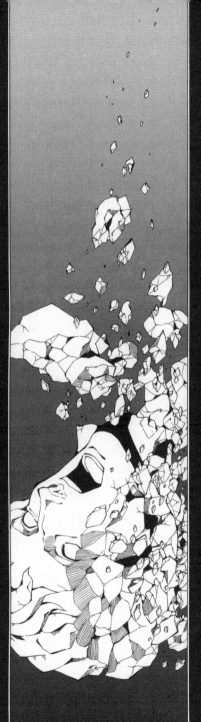

But these
demons
were not
summoned
from the
depths
of hell.
They were
made
through the
sacrifice of
human
flesh.

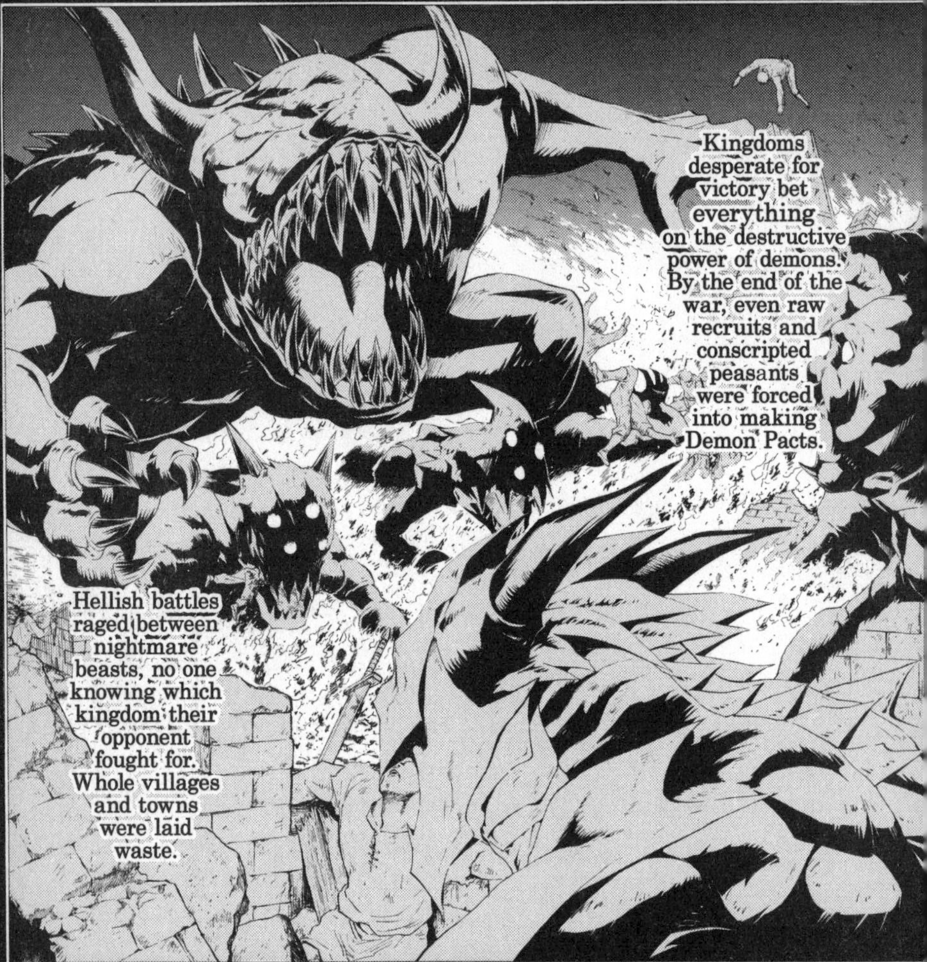
Kingdoms desperate for victory bet everything on the destructive power of demons. By the end of the war, even raw recruits and conscripted peasants were forced into making Demon Pacts.
Hellish battles raged between nightmare beasts, no one knowing which kingdom their opponent fought for. Whole villages and towns were laid waste.

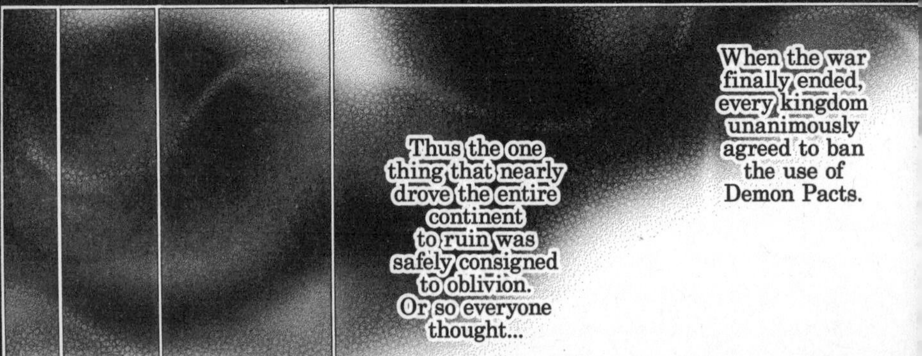
When the war finally ended, every kingdom unanimously agreed to ban the use of Demon Pacts.
Thus the one thing that nearly drove the entire continent to ruin was safely consigned to oblivion. Or so everyone thought...

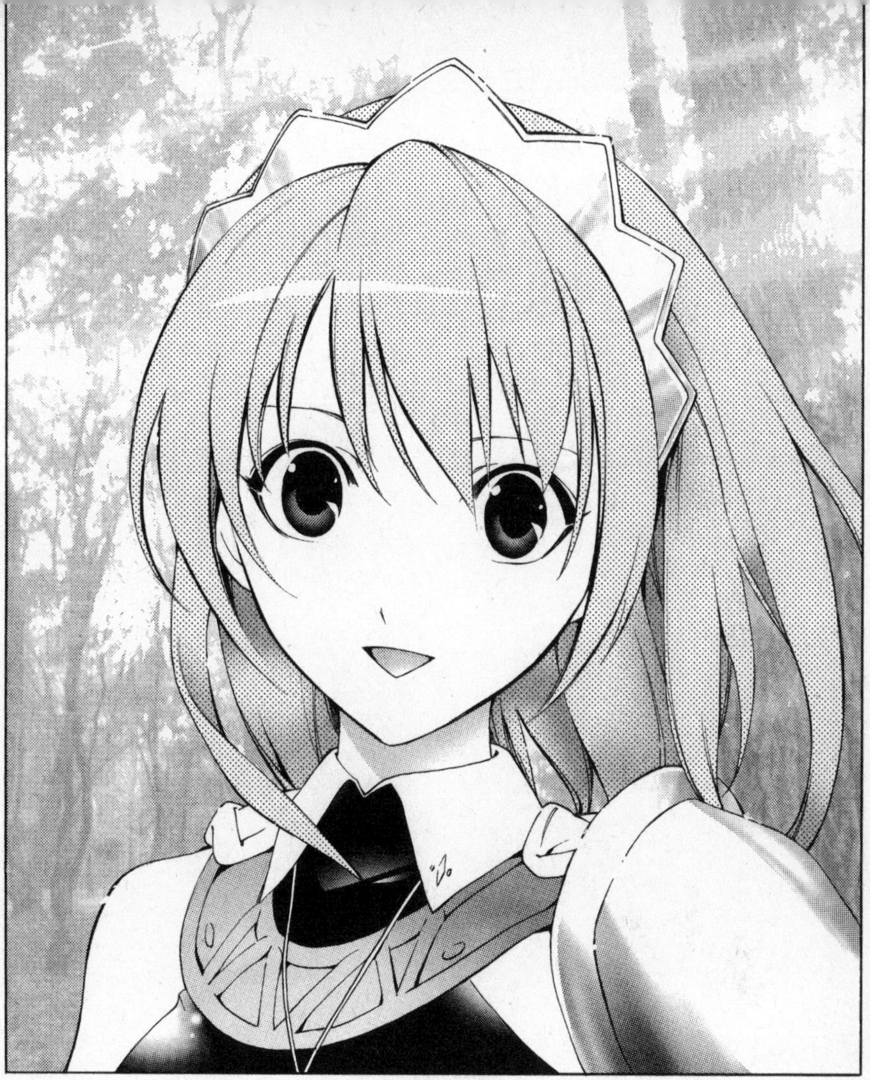

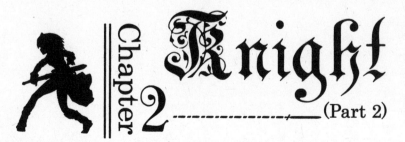

Chapter 2 Knight (Part 2)

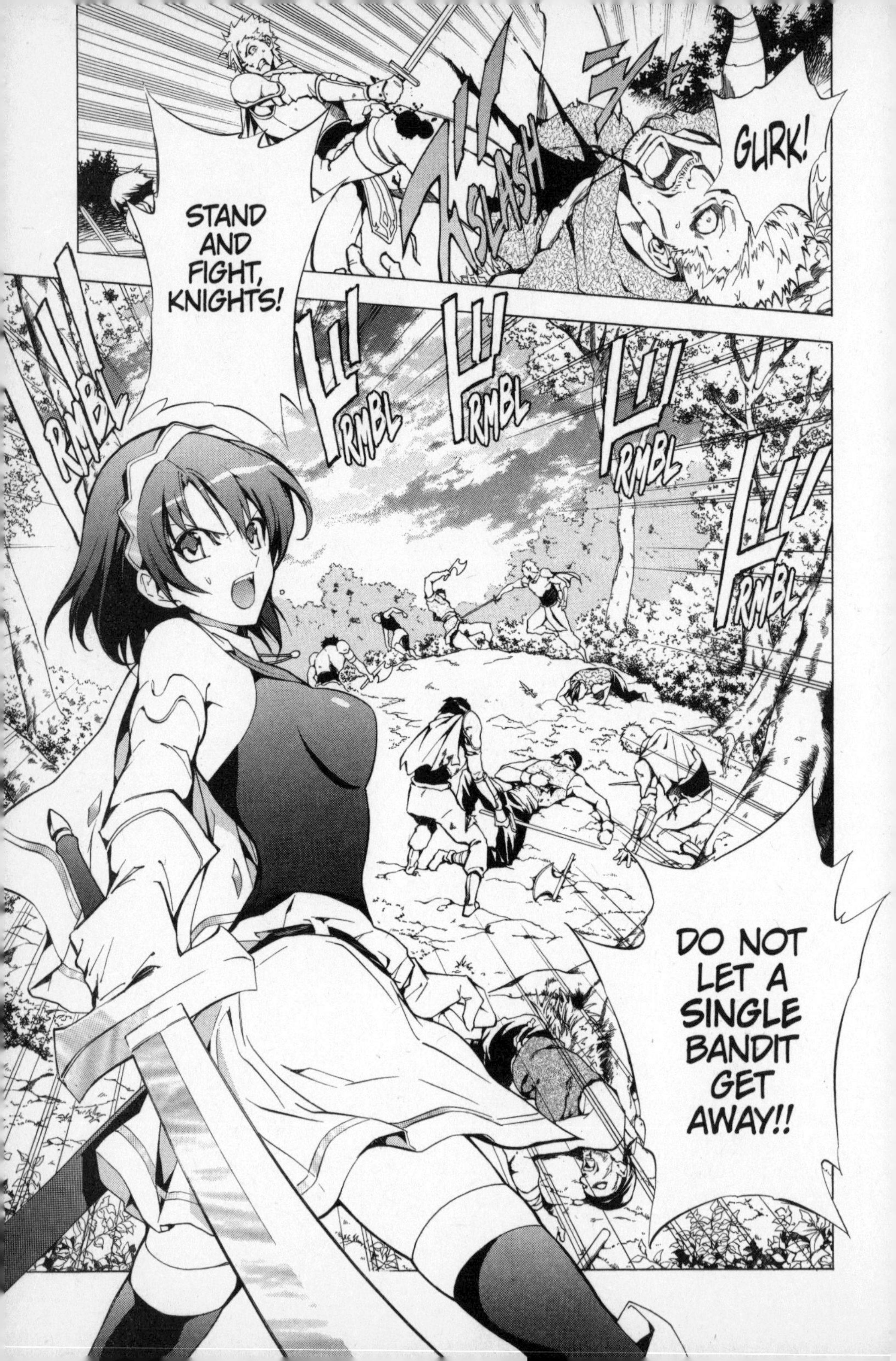
GURK!
SLASH
STAND AND FIGHT, KNIGHTS!
RMBL
RMBL
RMBL
RMBL
RMBL
DO NOT LET A SINGLE BANDIT GET AWAY!!

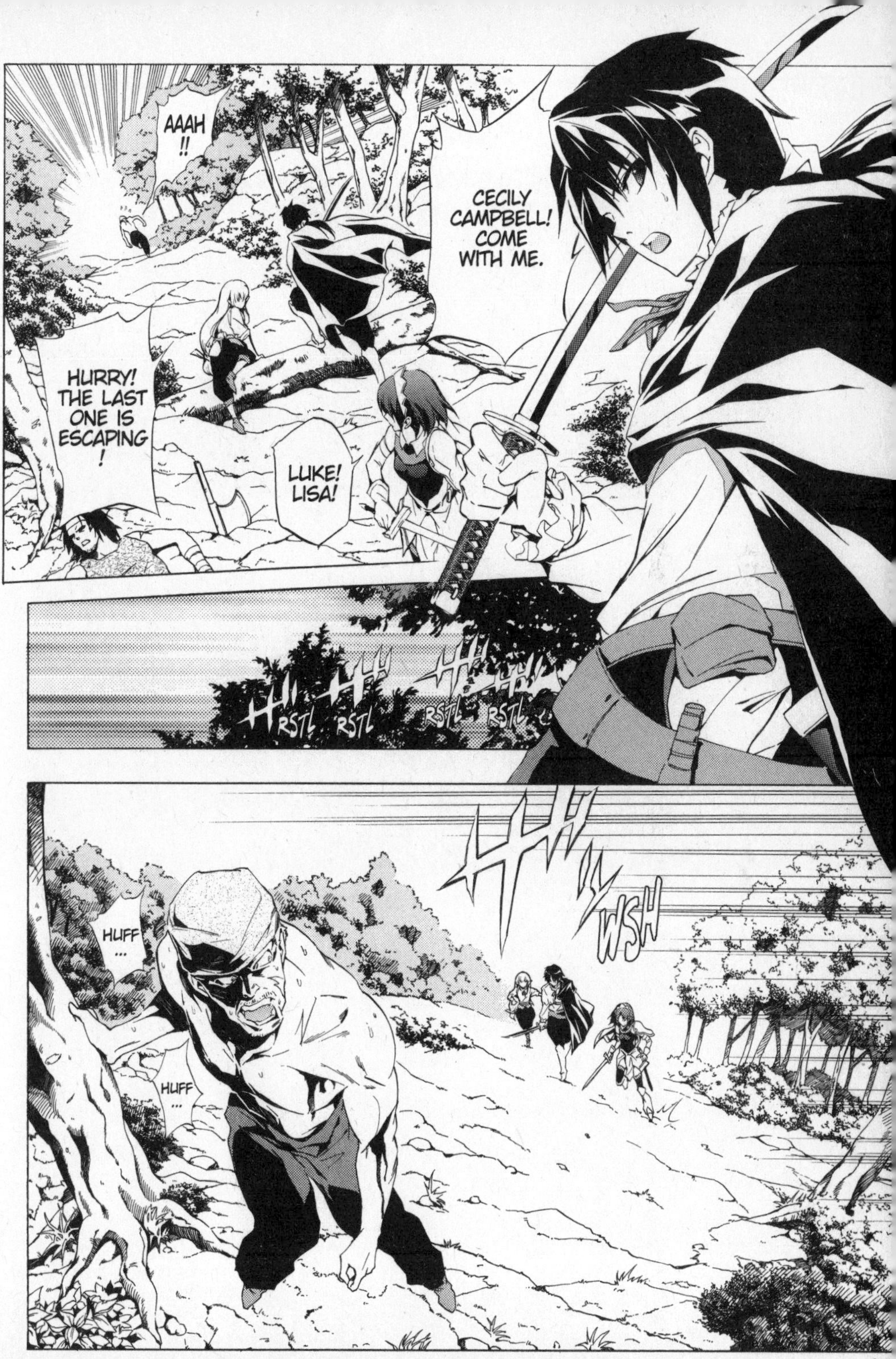
CECILY CAMPBELL! COME WITH ME.
AAAH!!
LUKE! LISA!
HURRY! THE LAST ONE IS ESCAPING!
RSTL RSTL RSTL RSTL
WSH
HUFF...
HUFF...

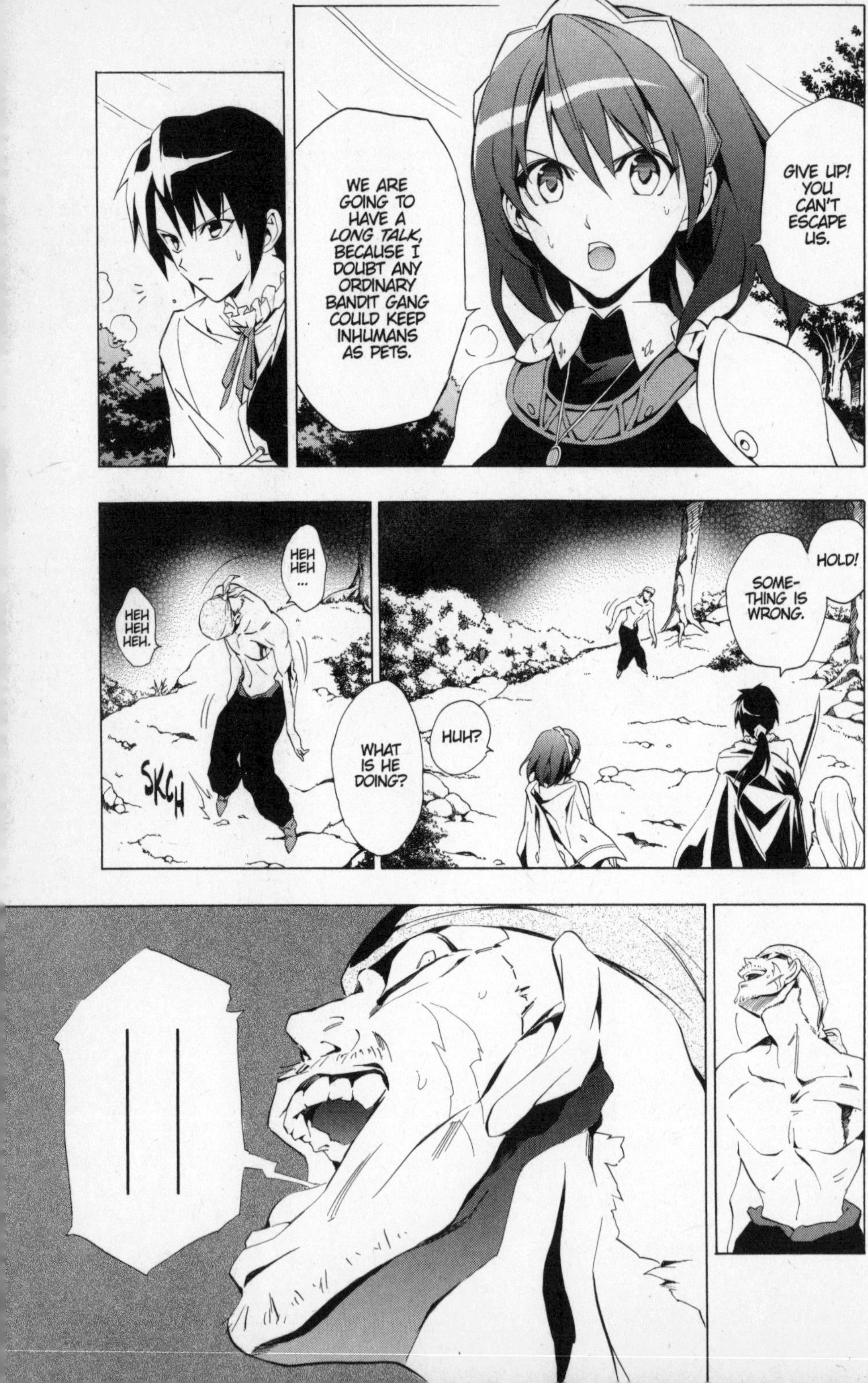
GIVE UP! YOU CAN'T ESCAPE US.
WE ARE GOING TO HAVE A *LONG TALK*, BECAUSE I DOUBT ANY ORDINARY BANDIT GANG COULD KEEP INHUMANS AS PETS.
HOLD!
SOME-THING IS WRONG.
HUH?
WHAT IS HE DOING?
HEH HEH ...
HEH HEH HEH.
SKCH

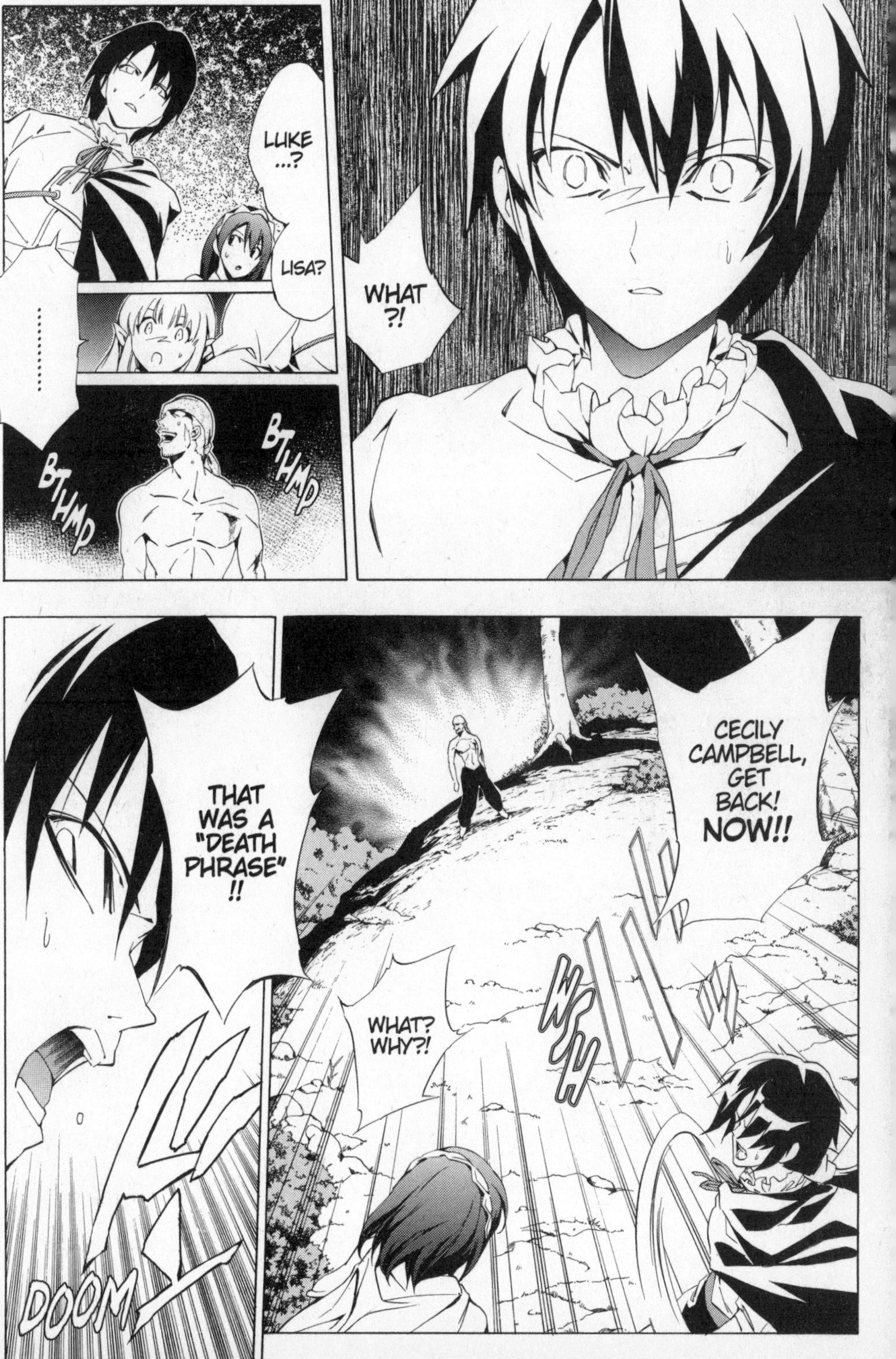
WHAT ?!
LUKE ...?
LISA?
......
BTHMP
BTHMP
CECILY CAMPBELL, GET BACK! NOW!!
WHAT? WHY?!
THAT WAS A "DEATH PHRASE" !!
DOOM

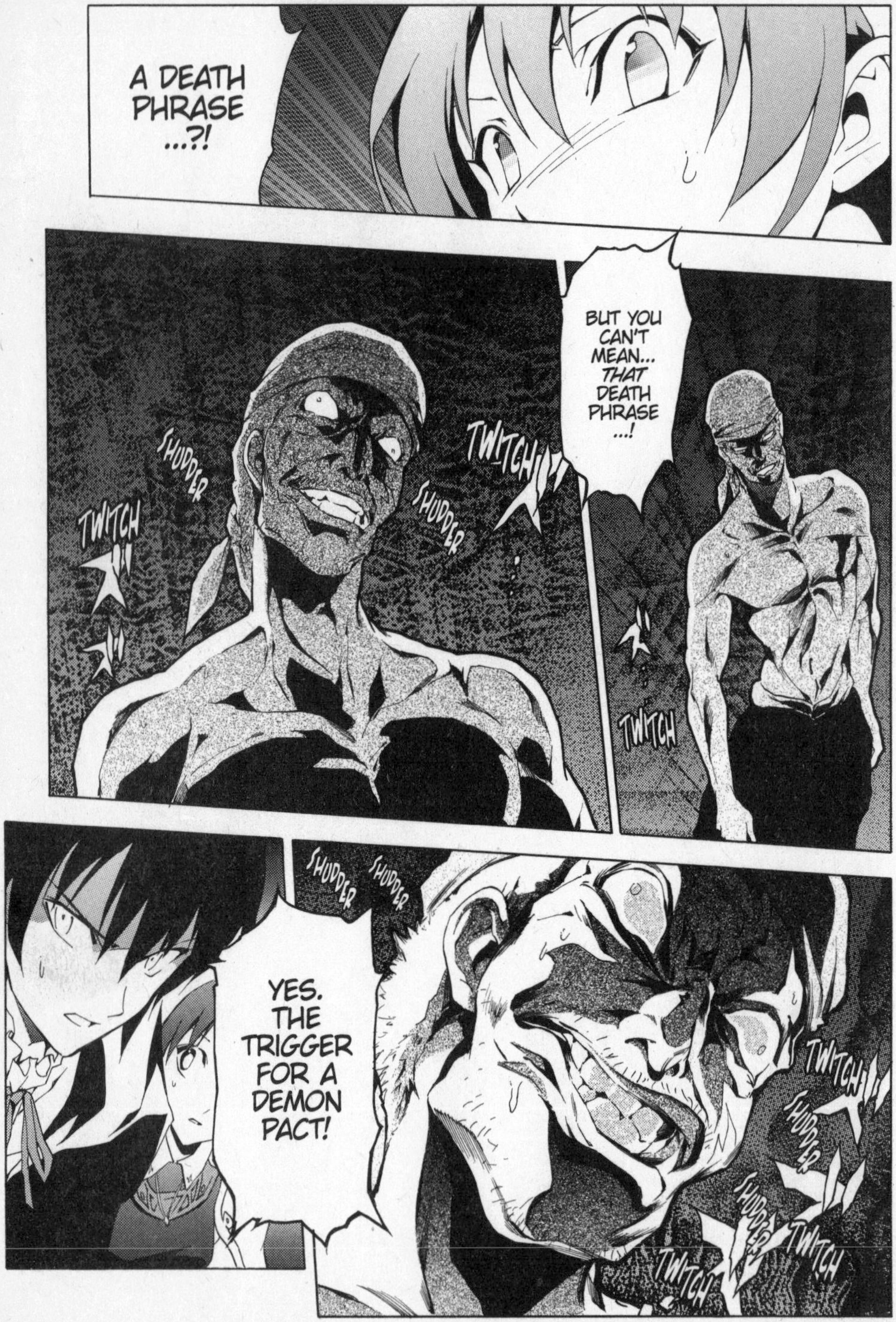
A DEATH PHRASE ...?!
BUT YOU CAN'T MEAN... *THAT* DEATH PHRASE ...!
TWITCH
TWITCH
SHUDDER
SHUDDER
TWITCH
SHUDDER
SHUDDER
TWITCH
SHUDDER
SHUDDER
TWITCH
TWITCH
YES. THE TRIGGER FOR A DEMON PACT!

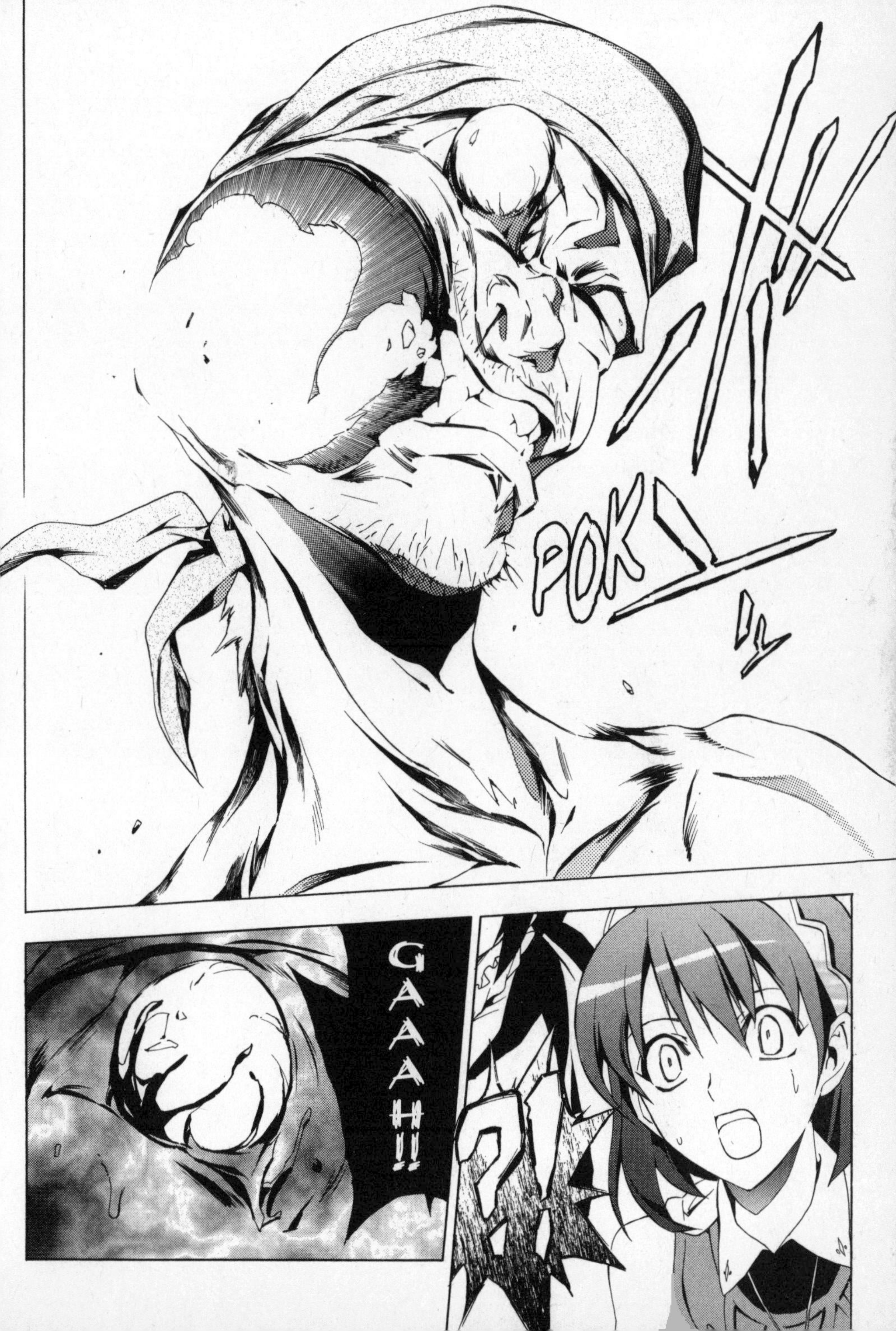
POK
GAAAH!!

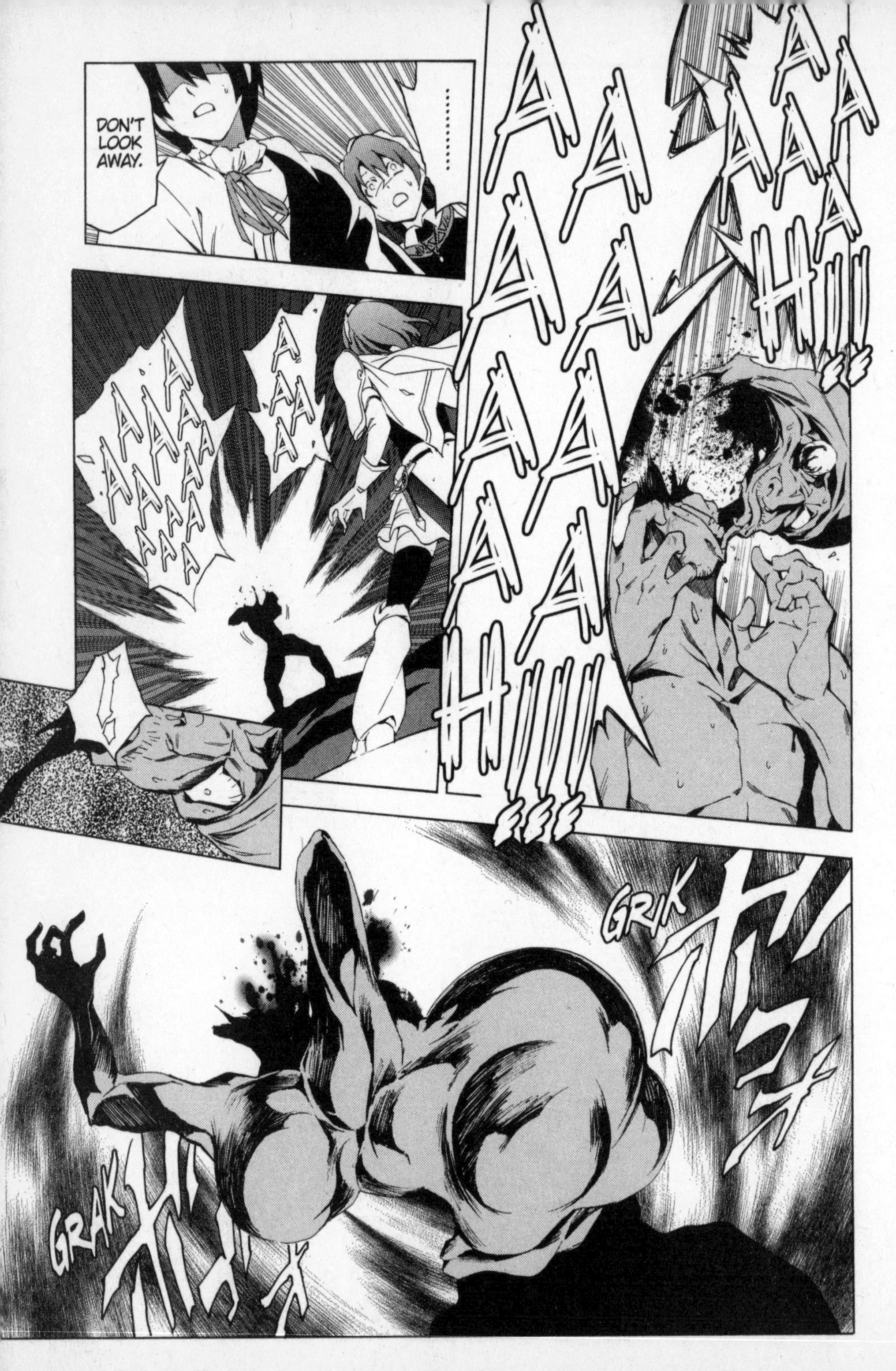
AAAAAAAAAHH!!
AAAAAAH!!
......
DON'T LOOK AWAY.
AAAA
AAAAAAAAAAAAAAA
!!
GRIK
GRAK

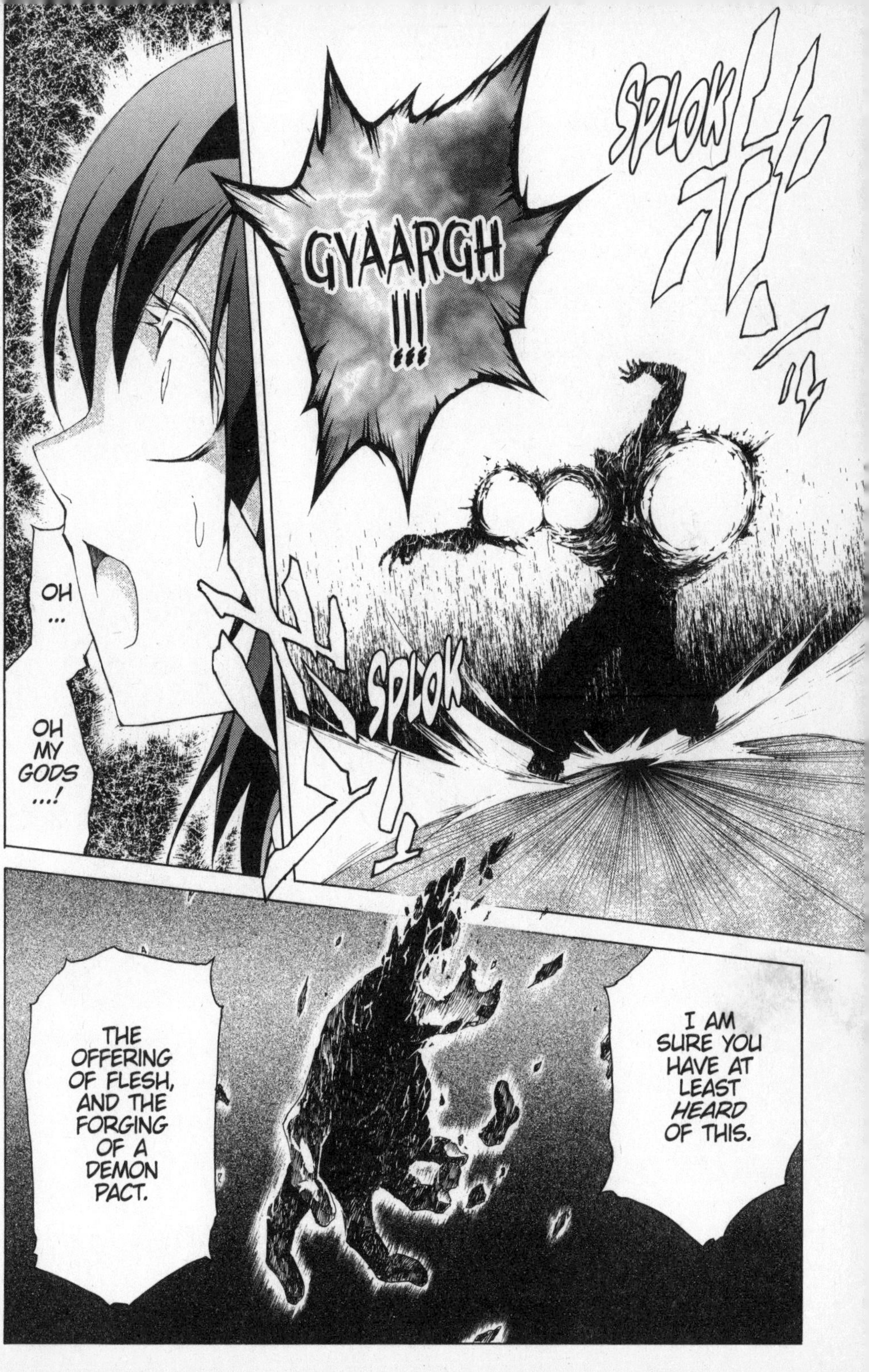
SPLOK
GYAARGH!!!
SPLOK
OH ...
OH MY GODS ...!
I AM SURE YOU HAVE AT LEAST *HEARD* OF THIS.
THE OFFERING OF FLESH, AND THE FORGING OF A DEMON PACT.

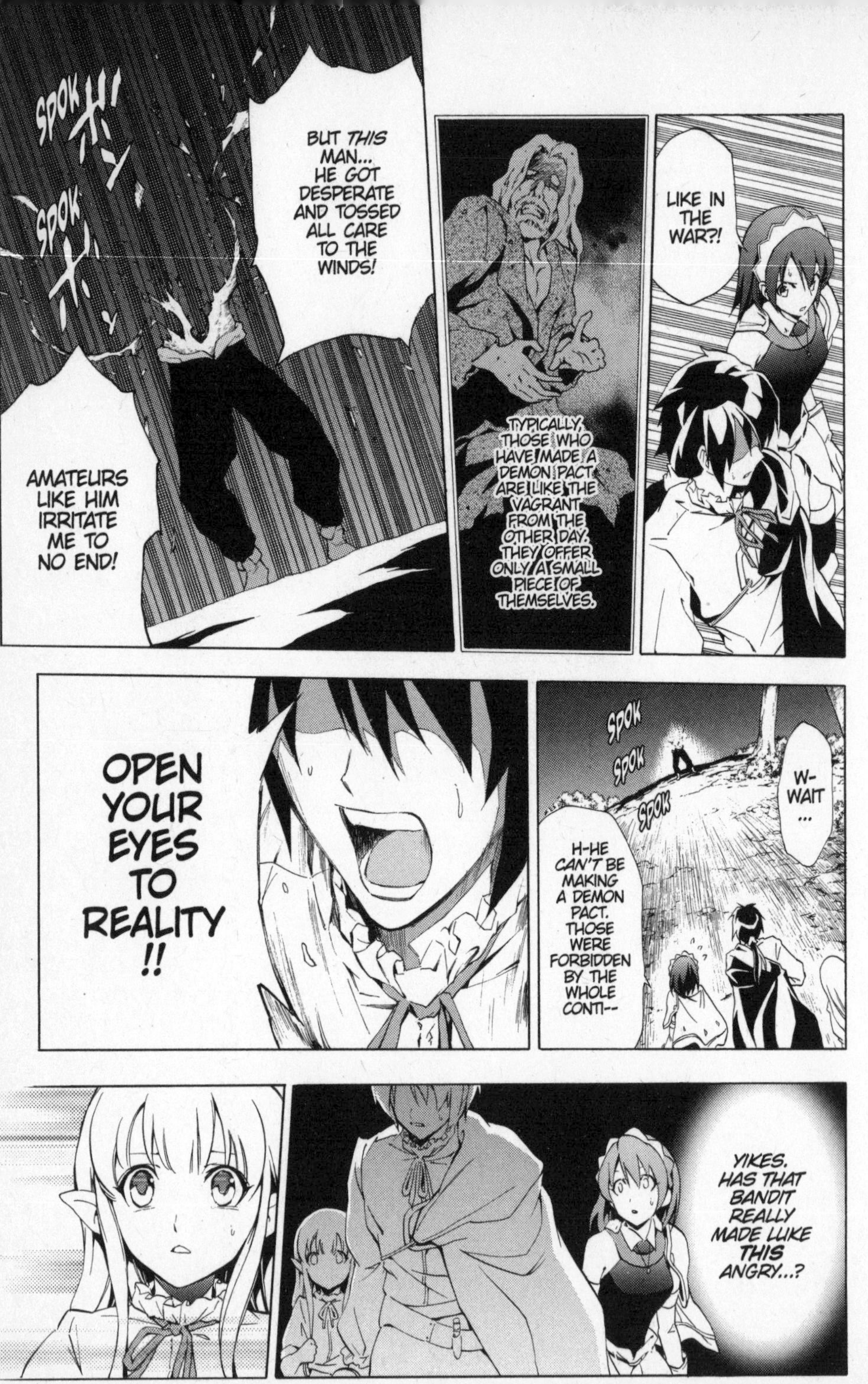
LIKE IN THE WAR?!
TYPICALLY, THOSE WHO HAVE MADE A DEMON PACT ARE LIKE THE VAGRANT FROM THE OTHER DAY. THEY OFFER ONLY A SMALL PIECE OF THEMSELVES.
BUT THIS MAN... HE GOT DESPERATE AND TOSSED ALL CARE TO THE WINDS!
SPOK
SPOK
AMATEURS LIKE HIM IRRITATE ME TO NO END!
W-WAIT...
SPOK
SPOK
SPOK
H-HE CAN'T BE MAKING A DEMON PACT. THOSE WERE FORBIDDEN BY THE WHOLE CONTI--
OPEN YOUR EYES TO REALITY!!
YIKES. HAS THAT BANDIT REALLY MADE LUKE THIS ANGRY...?

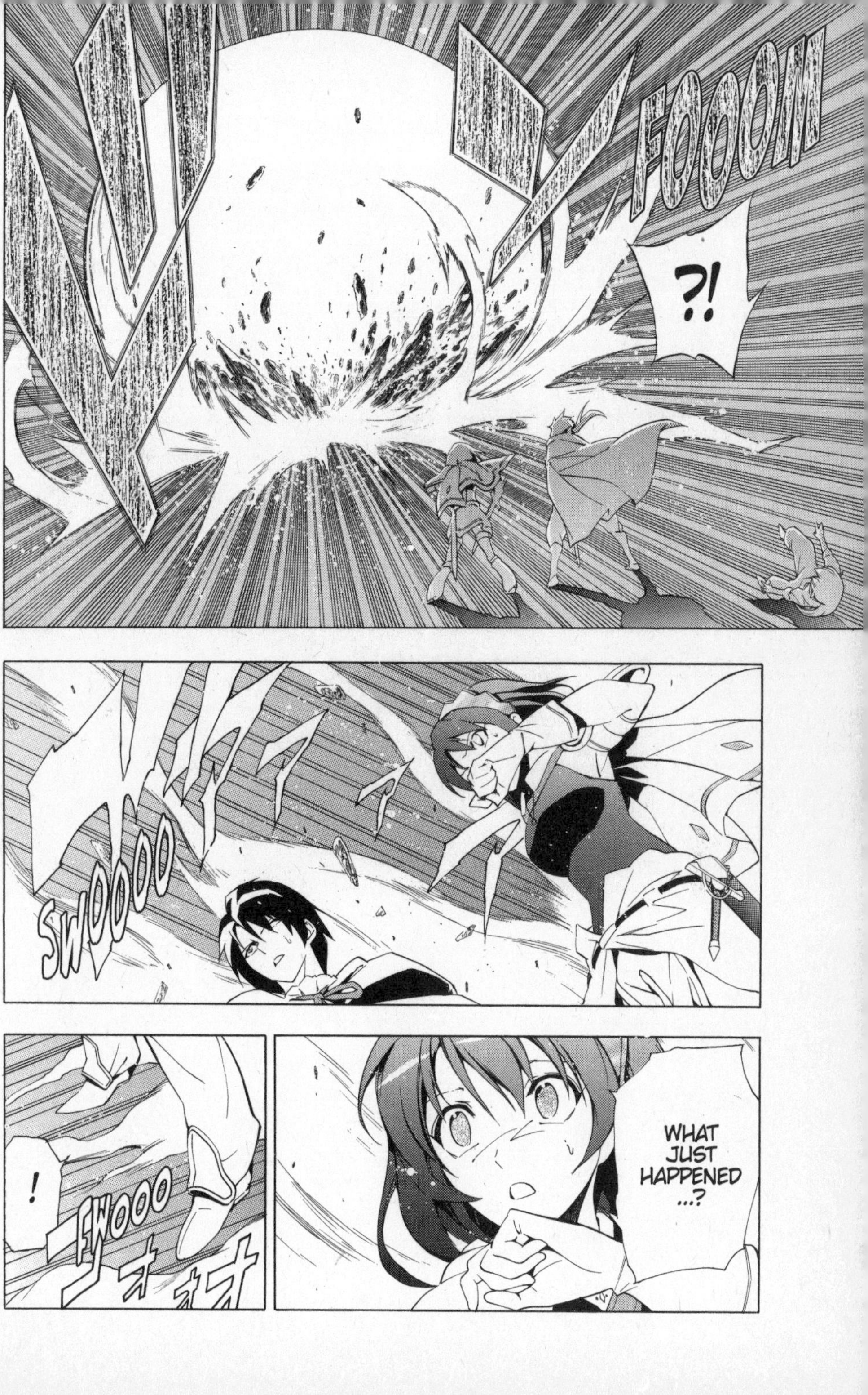
FOOOM
?!
SWOOOO
WHAT JUST HAPPENED ...?
!
FWOOO

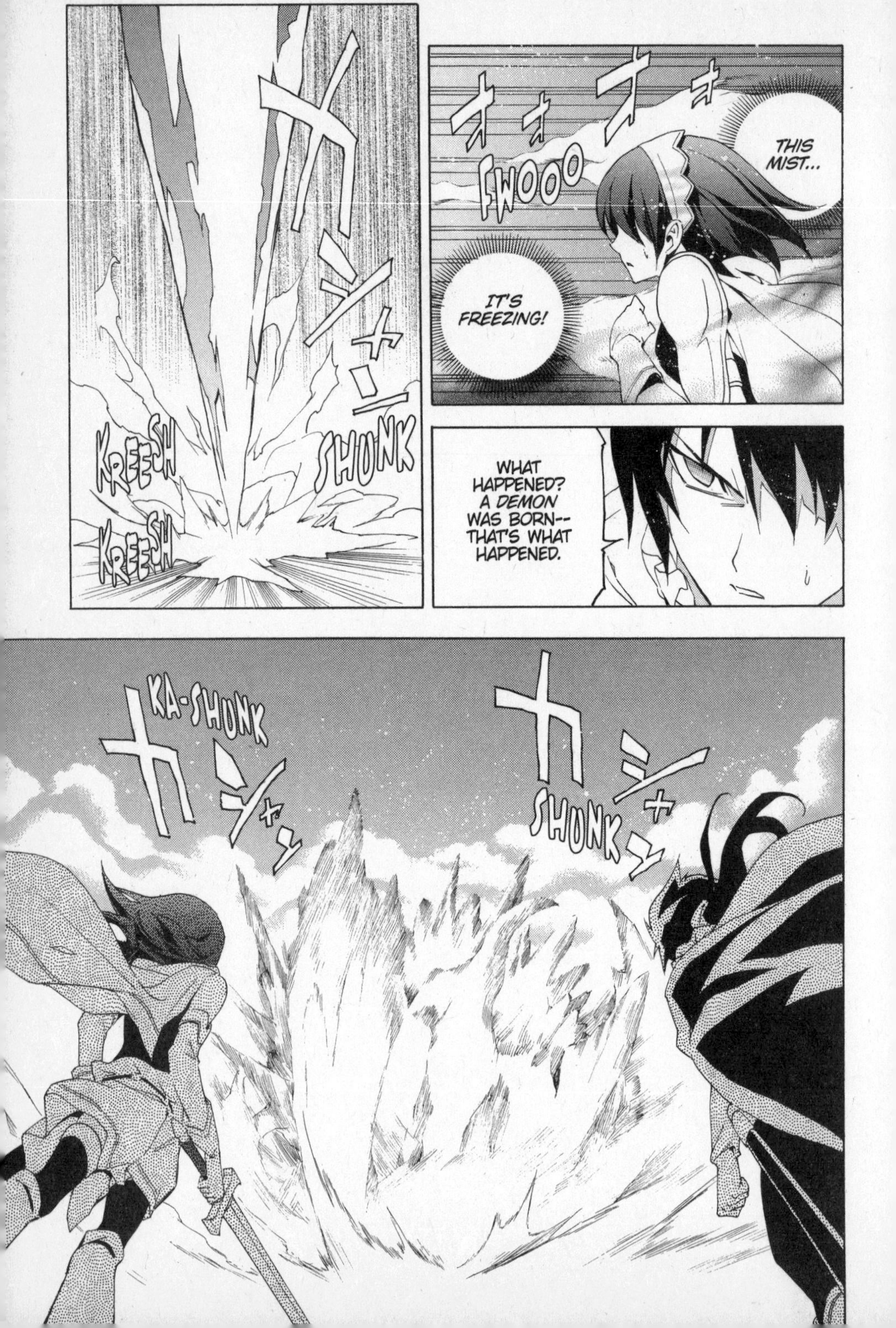
SWOOO
THIS MIST...
IT'S FREEZING!
WHAT HAPPENED? A DEMON WAS BORN--THAT'S WHAT HAPPENED.
SHUNK
KREESH
KREESH
SHUNK
KA-SHUNK

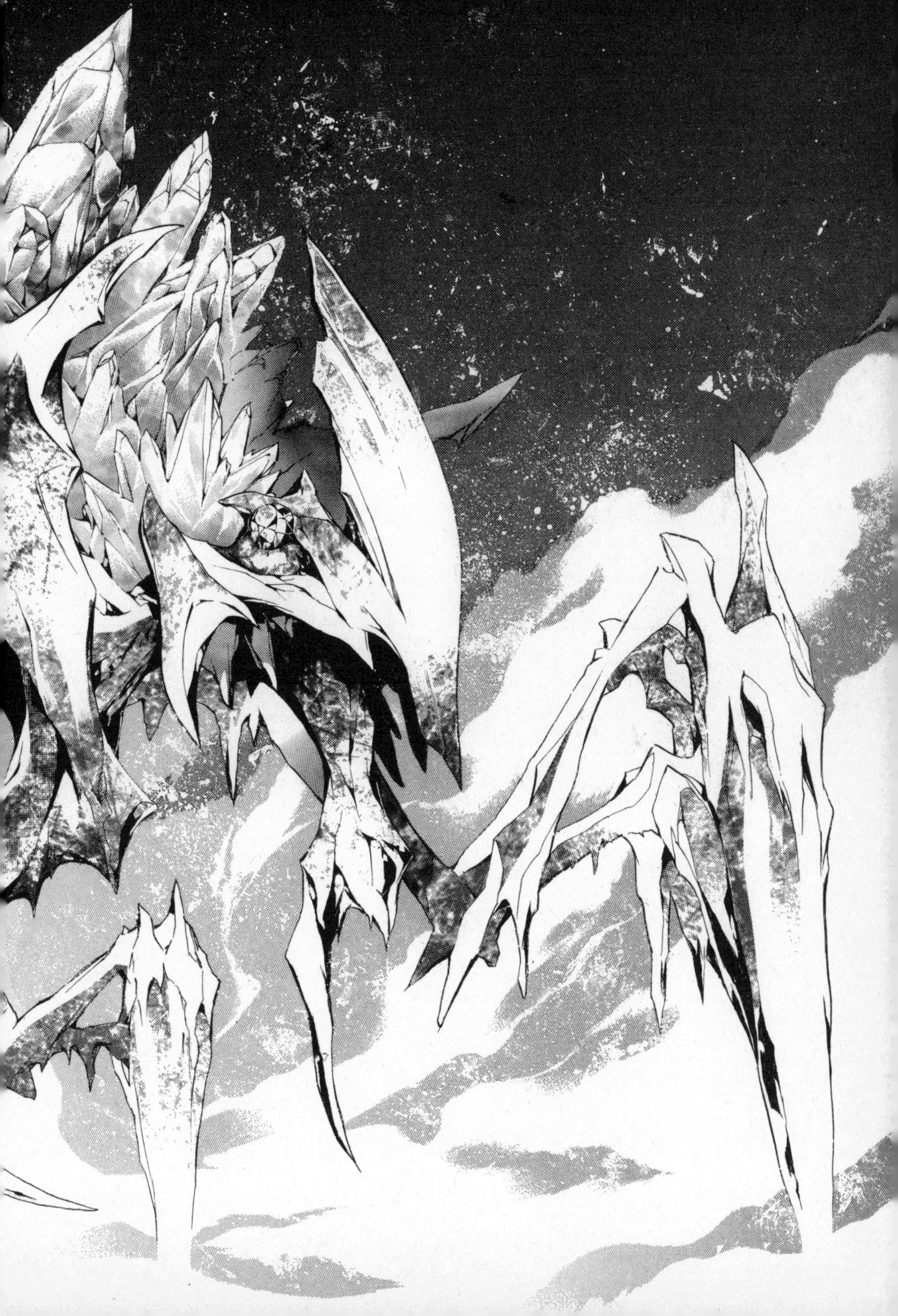

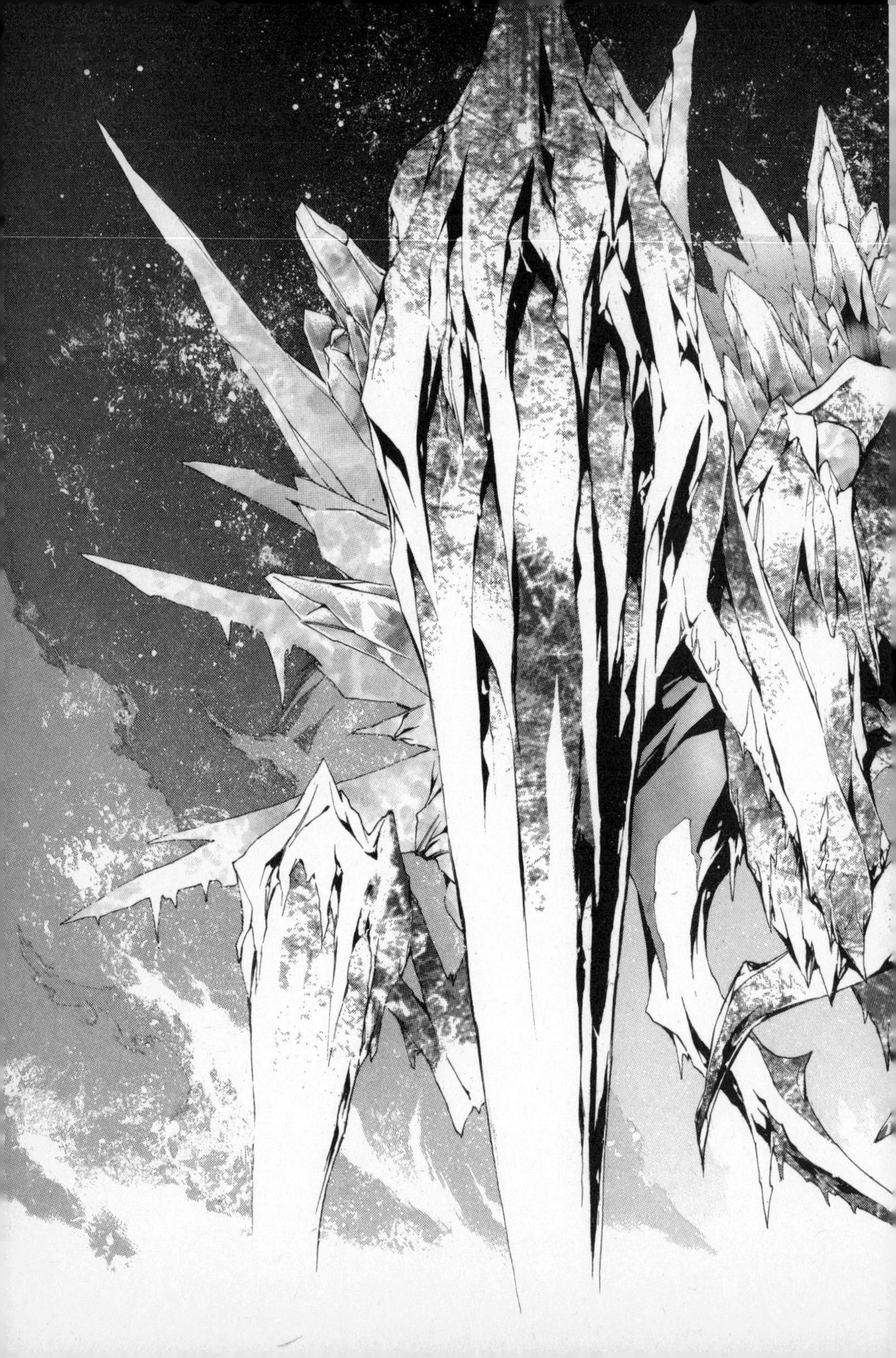

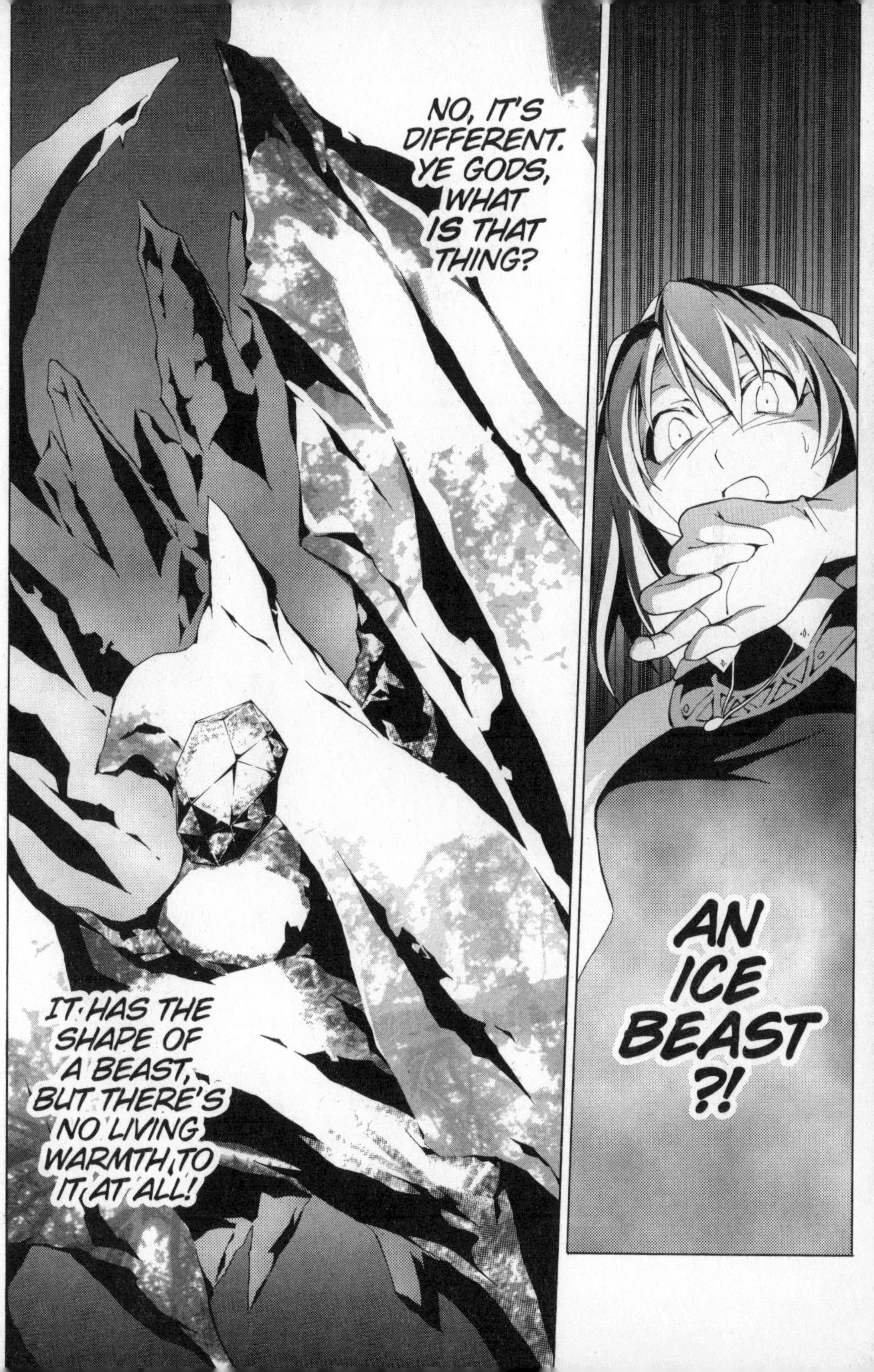
AN ICE BEAST ?!
NO, IT'S DIFFERENT. YE GODS, WHAT IS THAT THING?
IT HAS THE SHAPE OF A BEAST, BUT THERE'S NO LIVING WARMTH TO IT AT ALL!

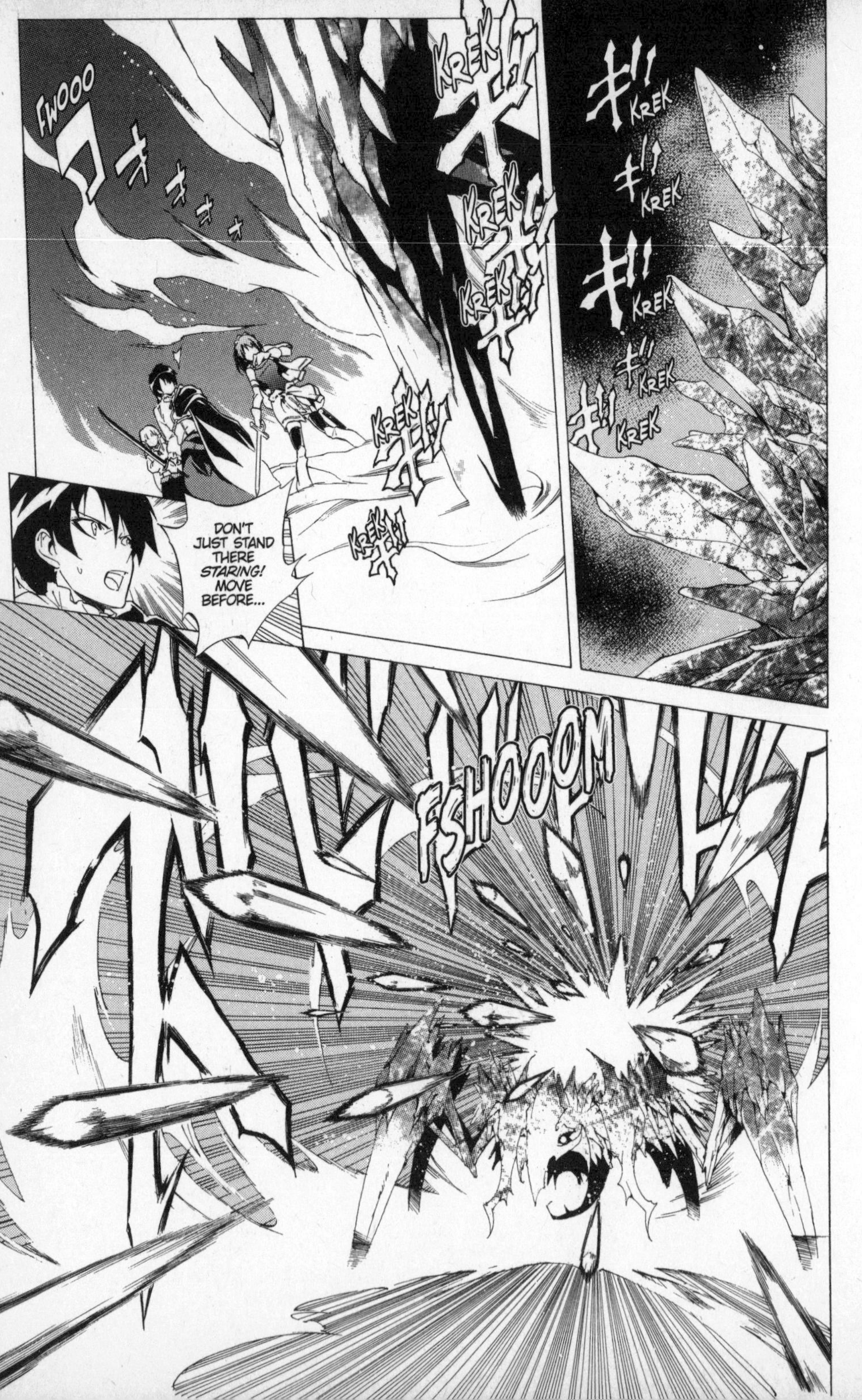
ギ!! KREK
ギ!! KREK
ギ!! KREK
ギ!! KREK
ギ!! KREK
KREK ギ!!
KREK ギ!!
KREK ギ!!
FWOOO コオォォォ
KREK ギ!!
KREK ギ!!
DON'T JUST STAND THERE STARING! MOVE BEFORE...
FSHOOOM

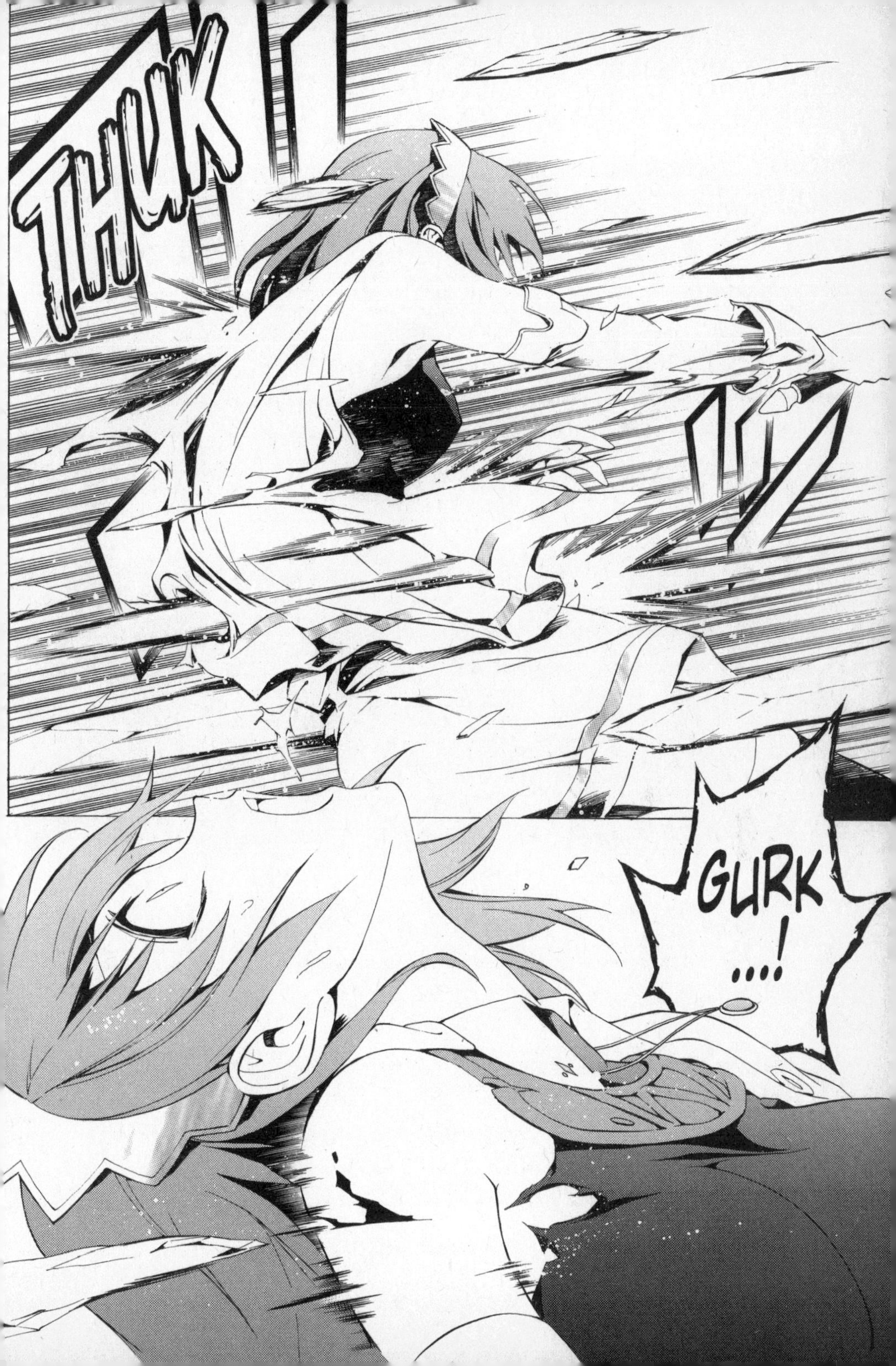
THUK
GURK
....!

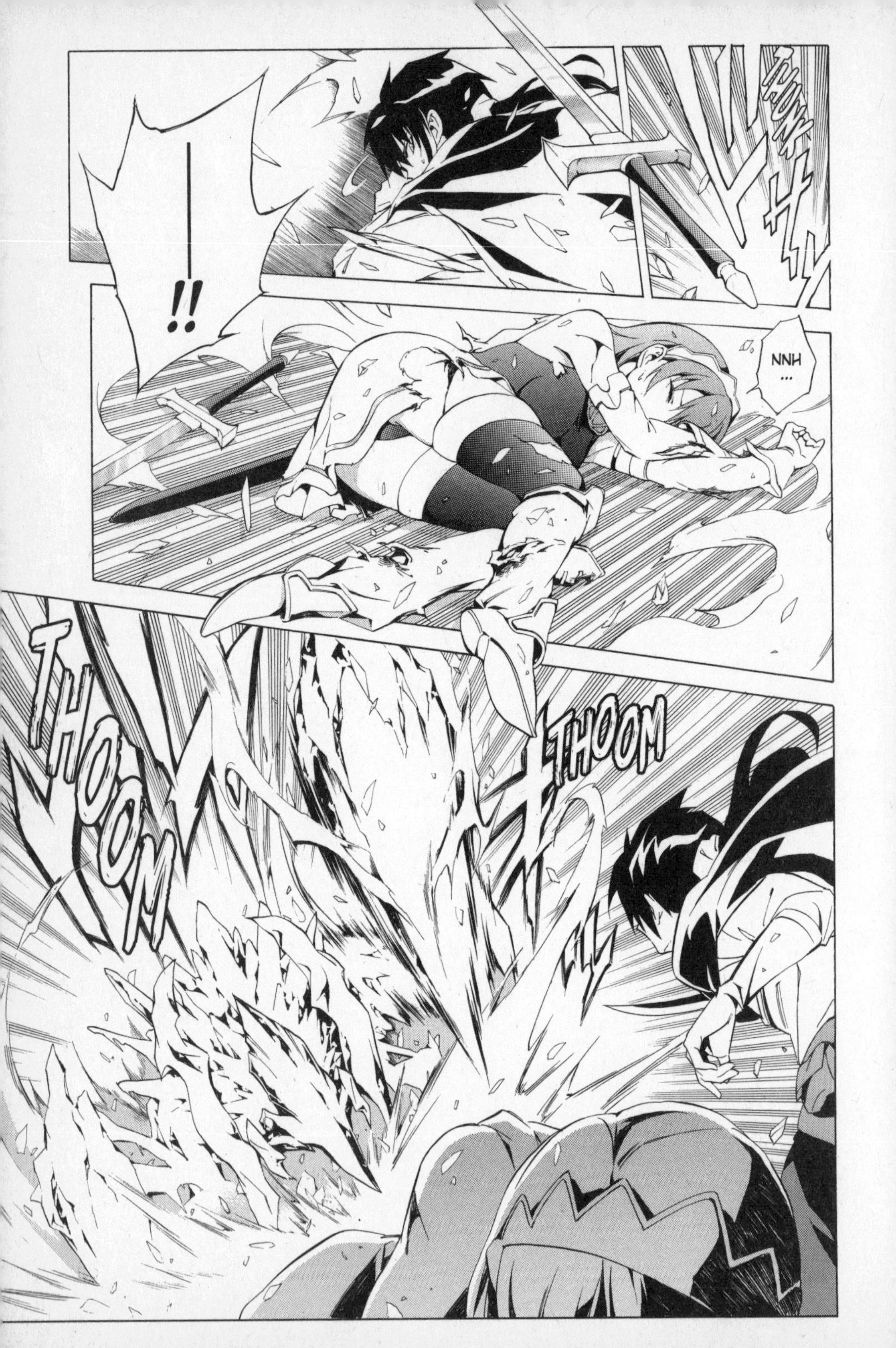
THUNK
——!!
NNH ...
THOOM
THOOM

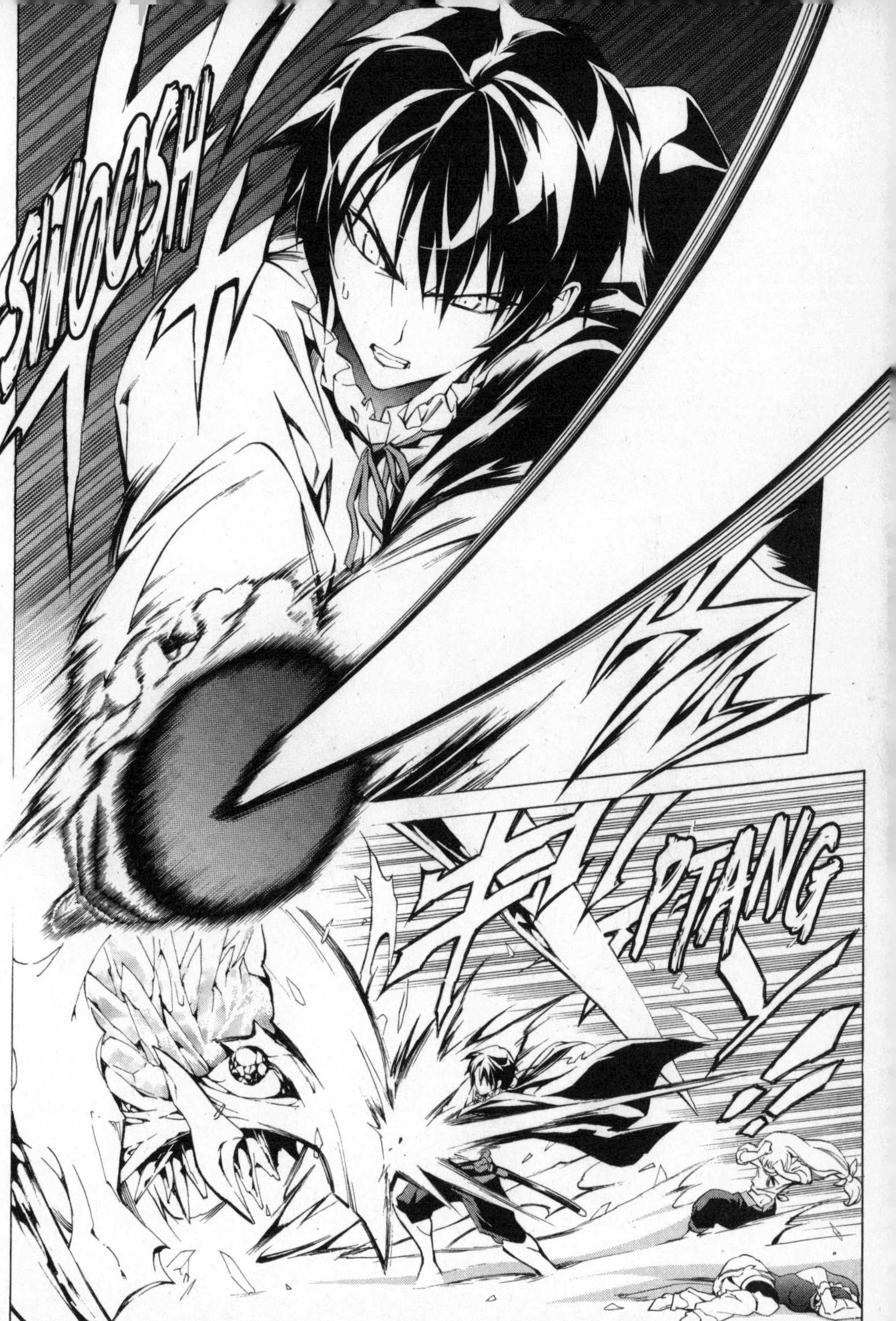
SWOOSH
PTANG

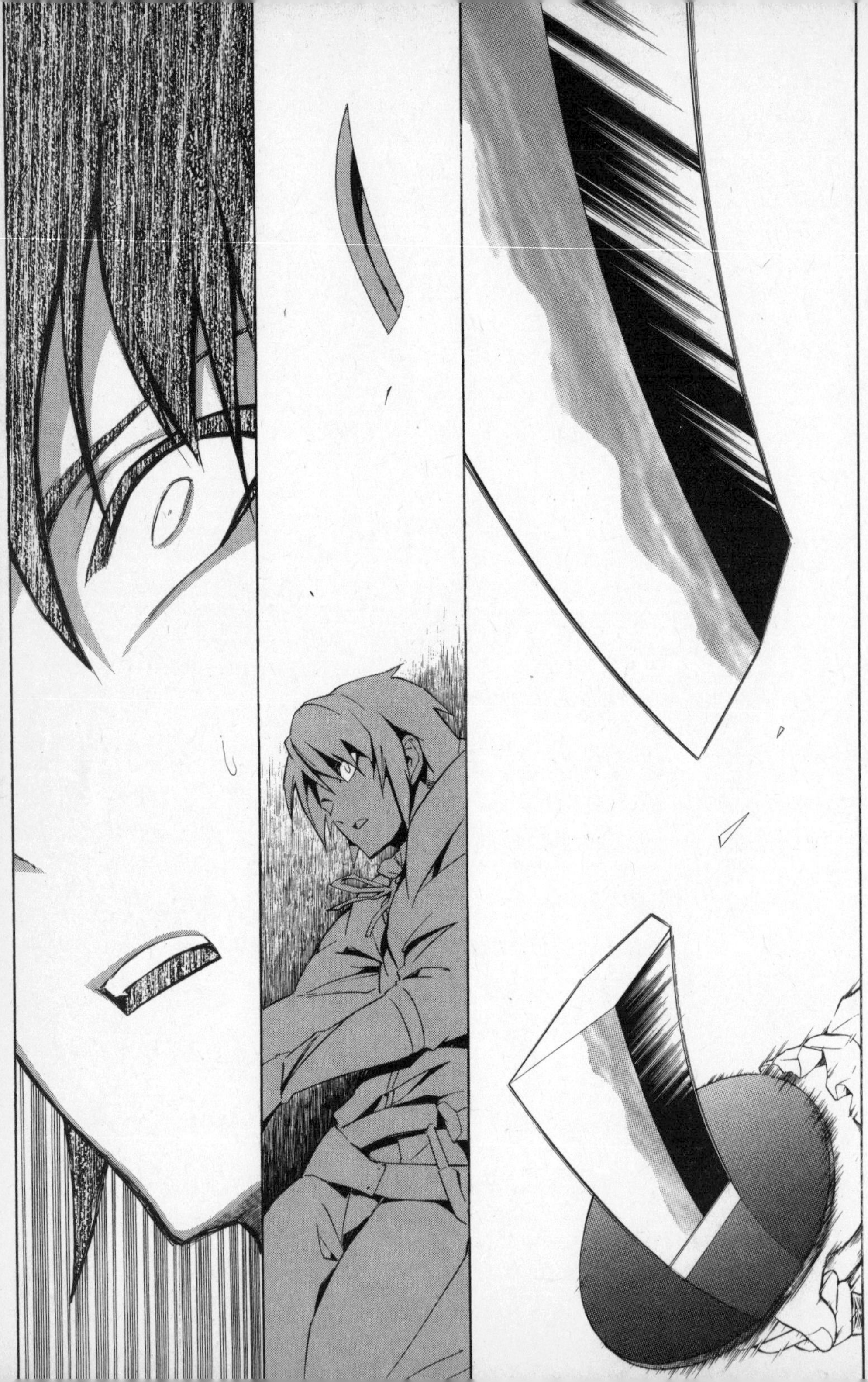

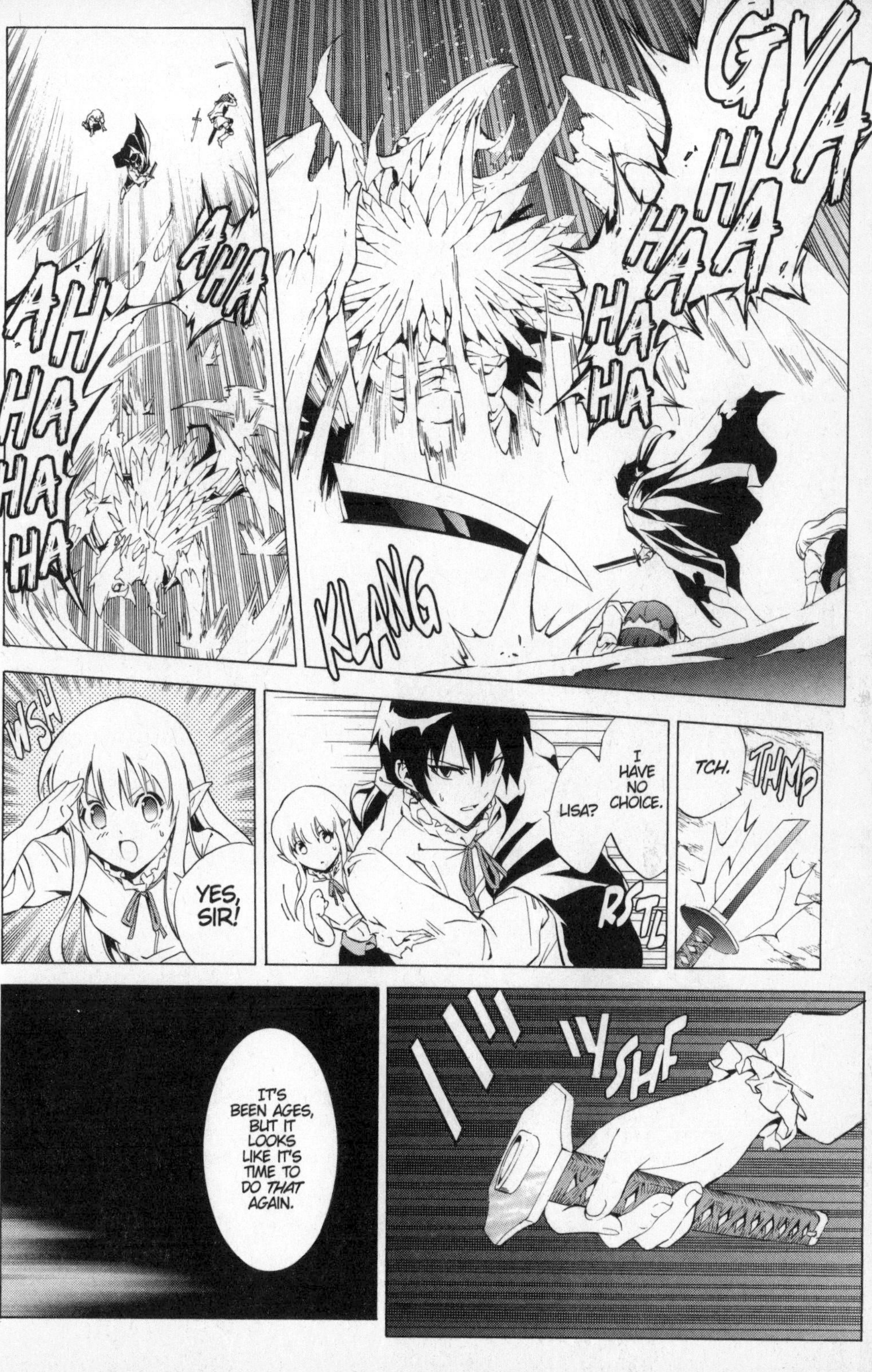
GYA HA HA. HA HA HA
KLANG
AHA
AH HA HA HA HA
THMP
TCH.
I HAVE NO CHOICE.
LISA?
RSTL
WSH
YES, SIR!
SHF
IT'S BEEN AGES, BUT IT LOOKS LIKE IT'S TIME TO DO *THAT* AGAIN.

I WANT...

"I WANT YOU TO SEE ME!"

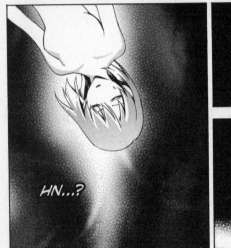

HN...?

SMELT.

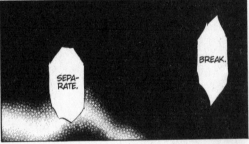

SEPA-RATE.

BREAK.

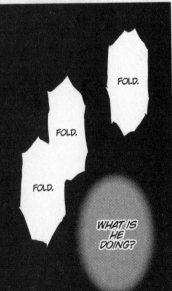

FOLD.

FOLD.

FOLD.

WHAT IS HE DOING?

FOLD.

WELD.

FORGE.

LUKE'S VOICE...

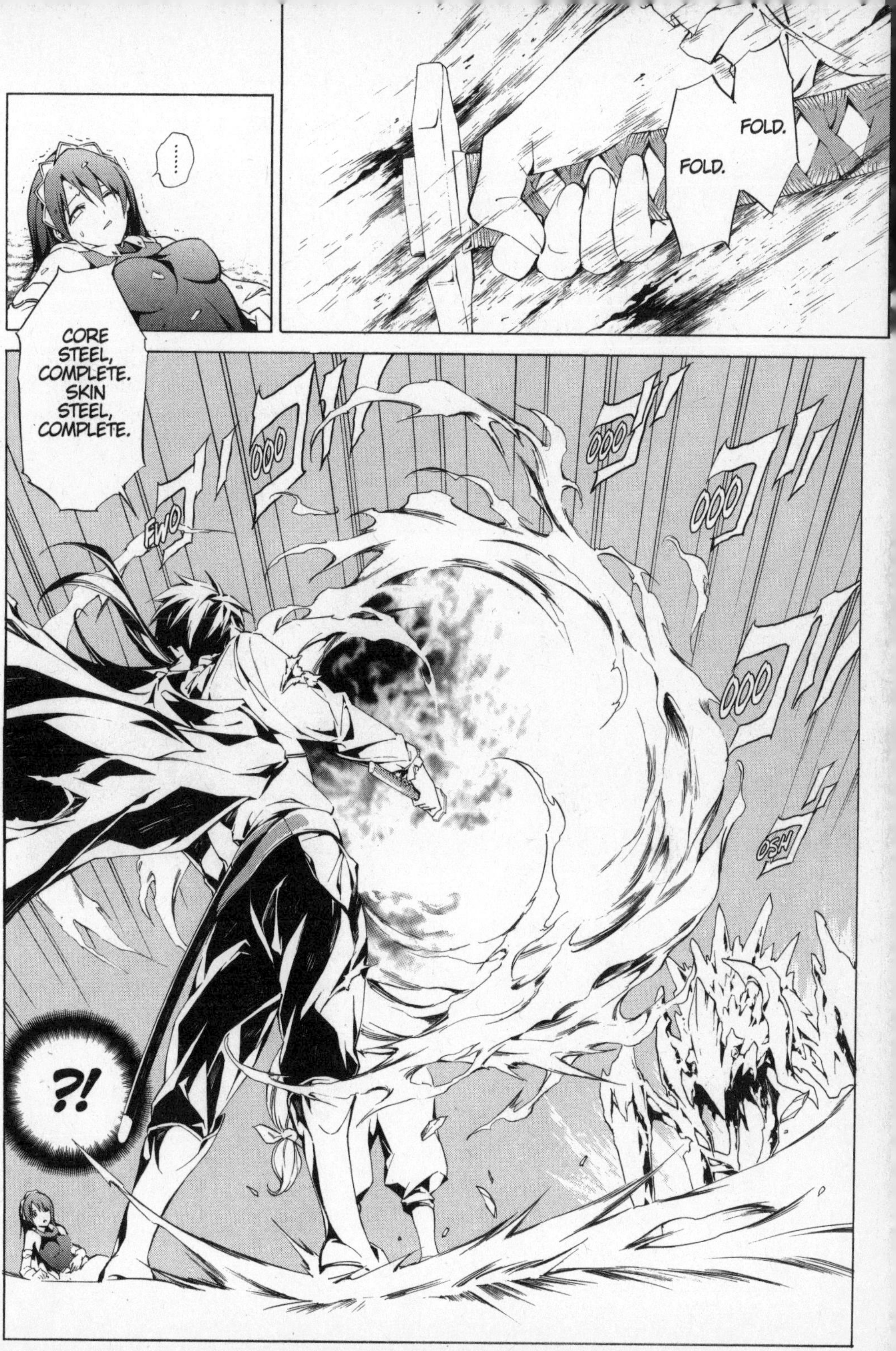
FOLD.
FOLD.
……
CORE STEEL, COMPLETE. SKIN STEEL, COMPLETE.
FWO
OOO
OOO
OOO
OOO
OSH
?!

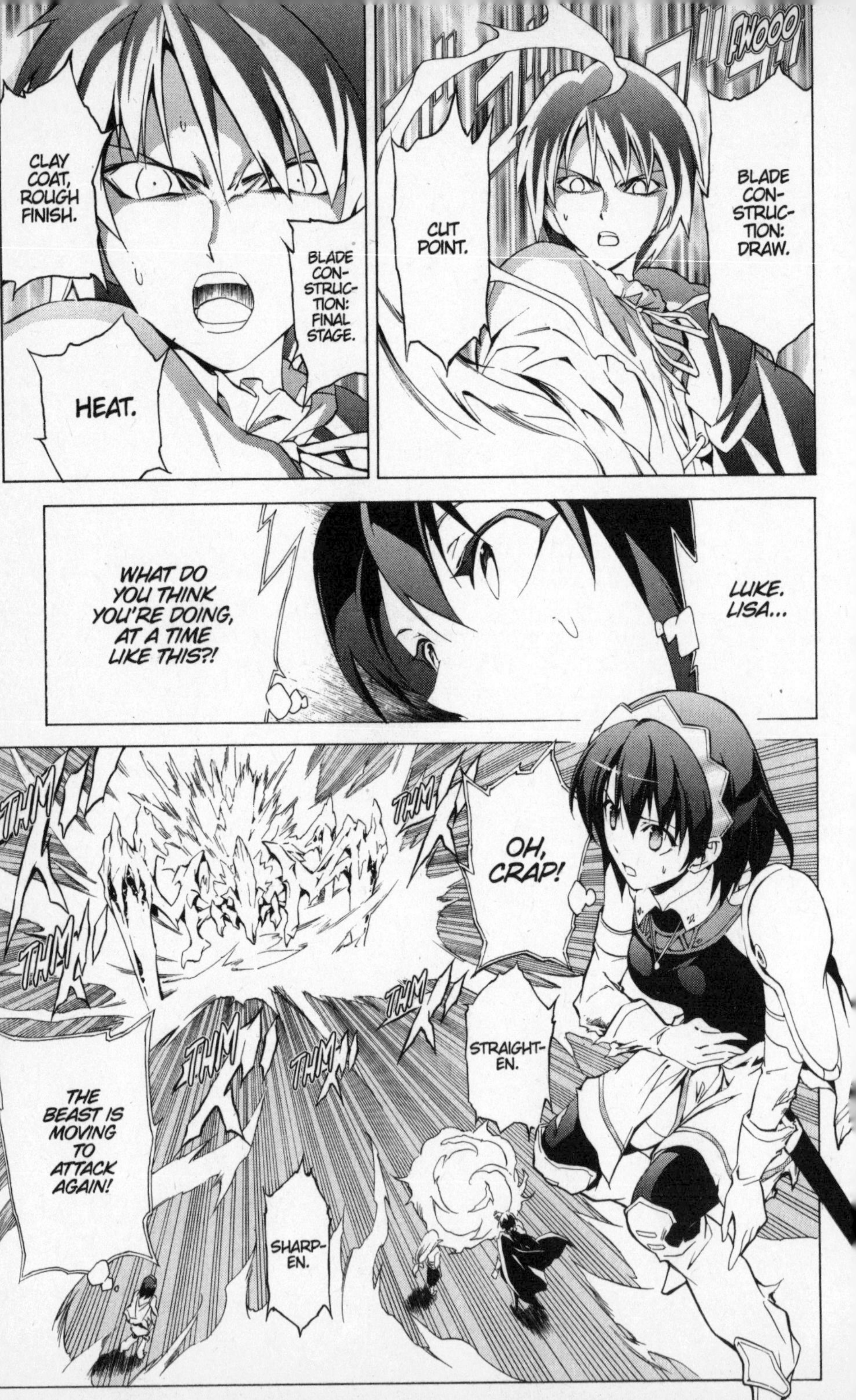
FWOOO
BLADE CON-STRUC-TION: DRAW.
CUT POINT.
CLAY COAT, ROUGH FINISH.
BLADE CON-STRUC-TION: FINAL STAGE.
HEAT.
LUKE. LISA...
WHAT DO YOU THINK YOU'RE DOING, AT A TIME LIKE THIS?!
OH, CRAP!
THM
THM
THM
THM
STRAIGHT-EN.
THM
THM
THE BEAST IS MOVING TO ATTACK AGAIN!
SHARP-EN.

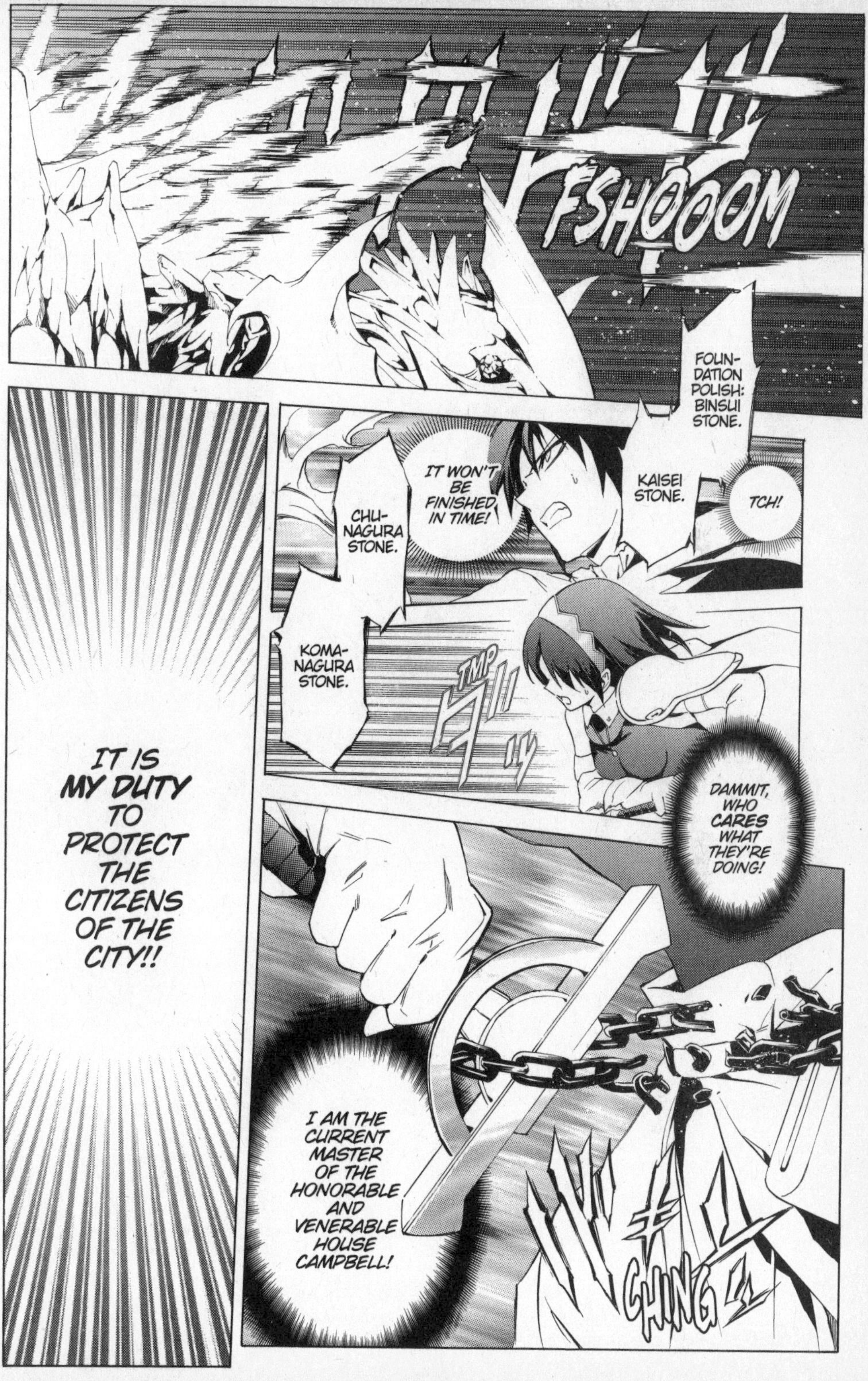
FSHOOOM
FOUN-DATION POLISH: BINSUI STONE.
TCH!
KAISEI STONE.
IT WON'T BE FINISHED IN TIME!
CHU-NAGURA STONE.
KOMA-NAGURA STONE.
TMP
DAMMIT, WHO CARES WHAT THEY'RE DOING!
I AM THE CURRENT MASTER OF THE HONORABLE AND VENERABLE HOUSE CAMPBELL!
CHING
IT IS MY DUTY TO PROTECT THE CITIZENS OF THE CITY!!

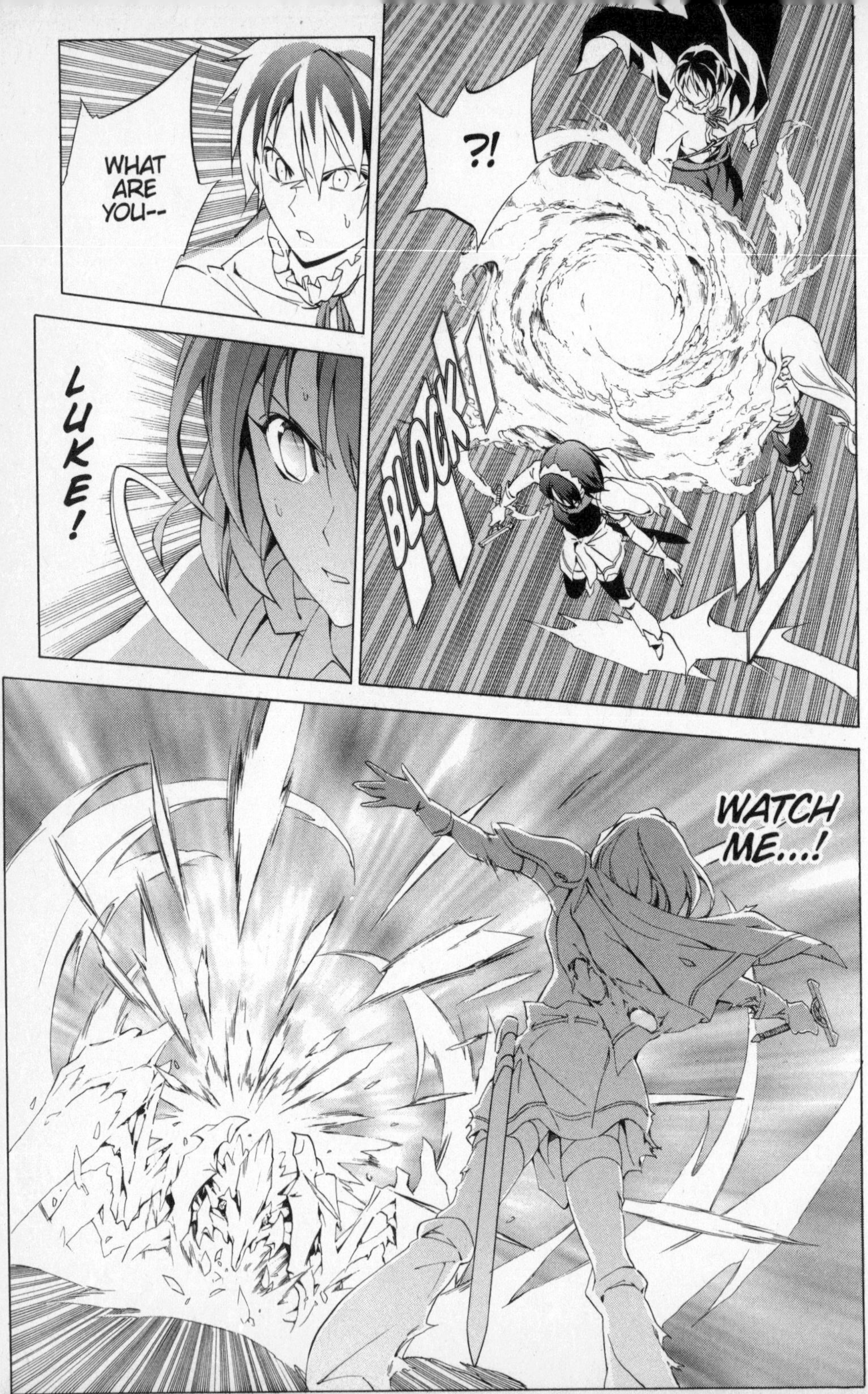
?!
BLOCK!!
WHAT ARE YOU--
LUKE!
WATCH ME...!

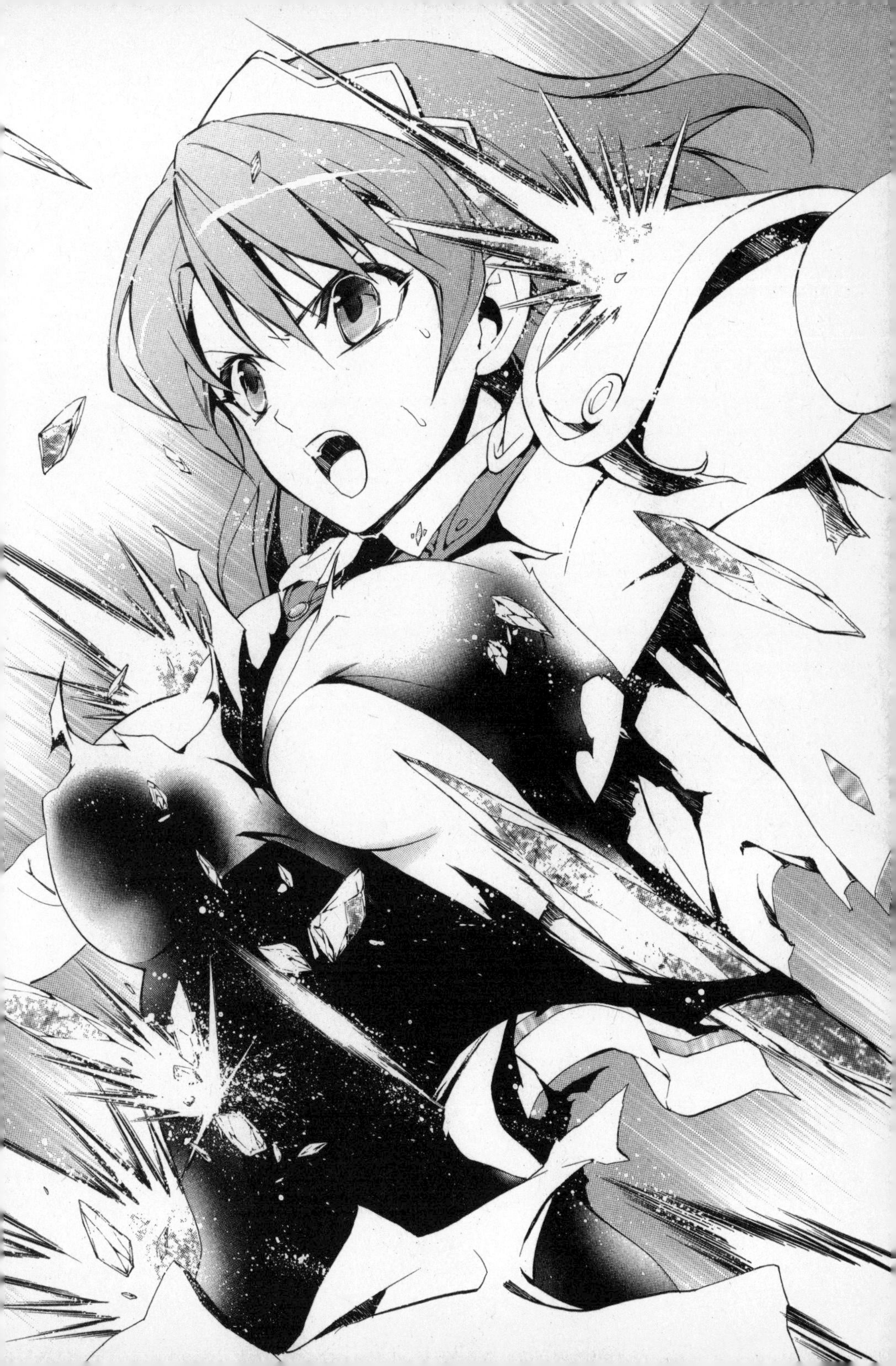

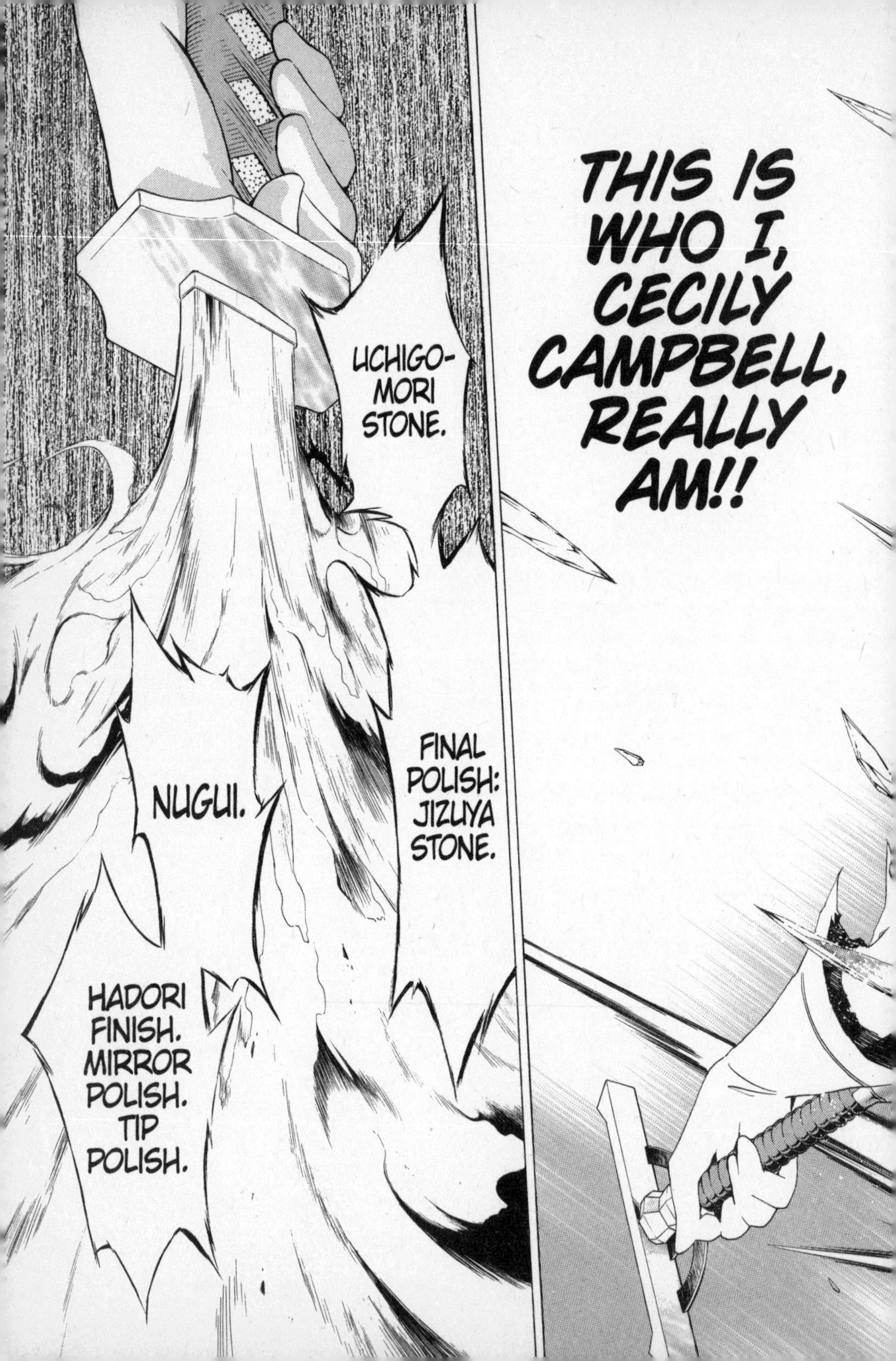
THIS IS WHO I, CECILY CAMPBELL, REALLY AM!!
UCHIGO-MORI STONE.
FINAL POLISH: JIZUYA STONE.
NUGUI.
HADORI FINISH. MIRROR POLISH. TIP POLISH.

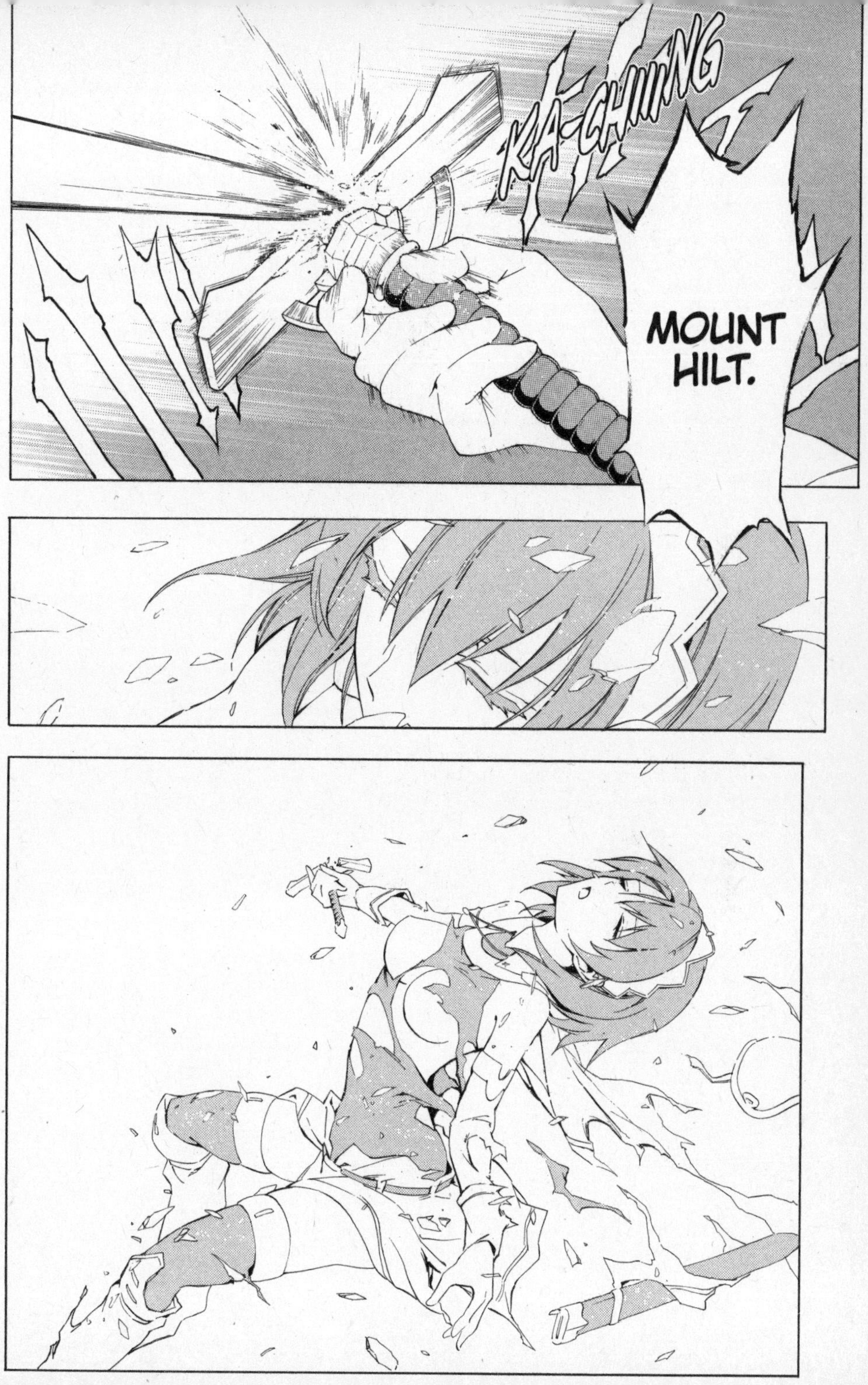
KA-CHIIING
MOUNT HILT.

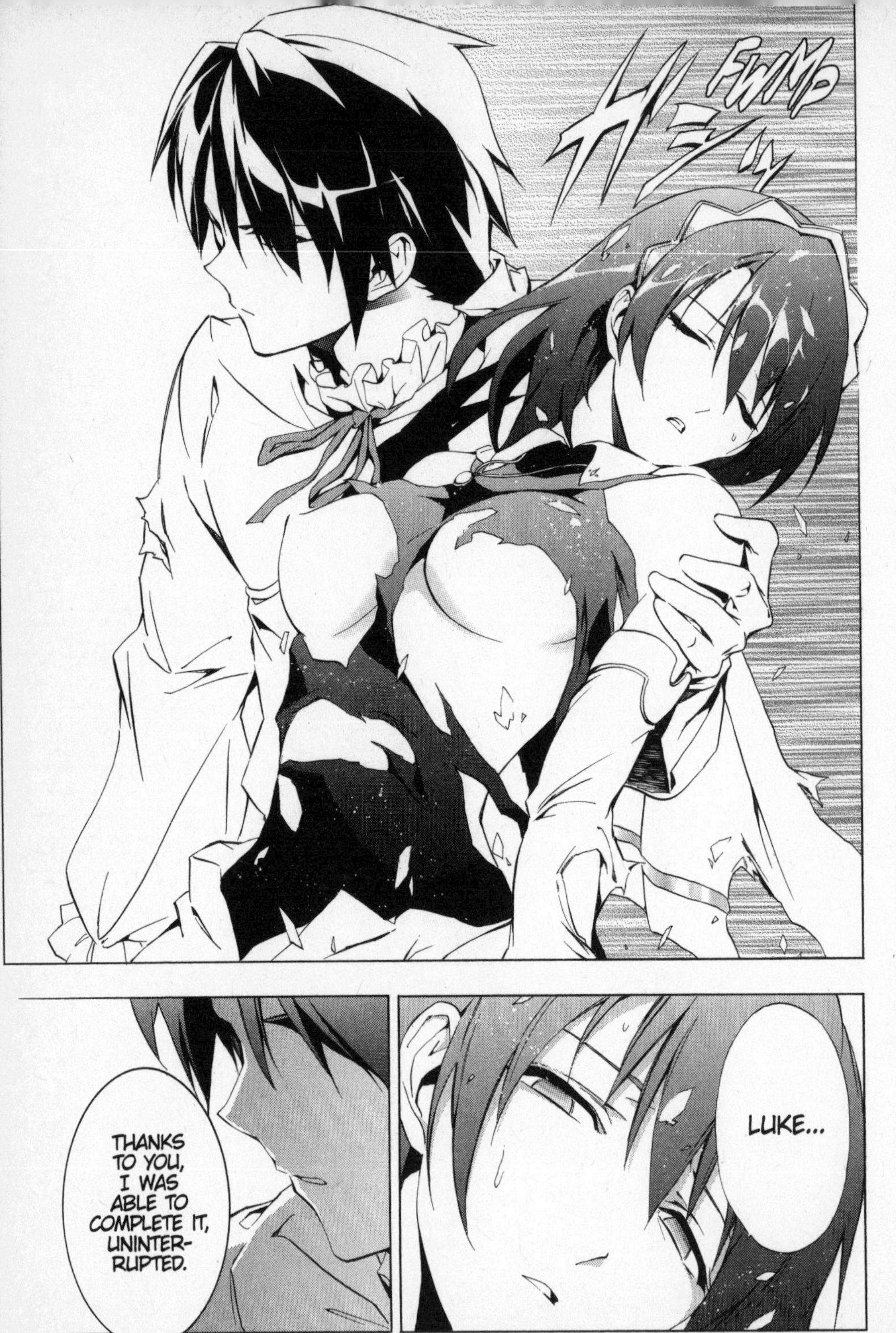
FWMP
LUKE...
THANKS TO YOU, I WAS ABLE TO COMPLETE IT, UNINTER-RUPTED.

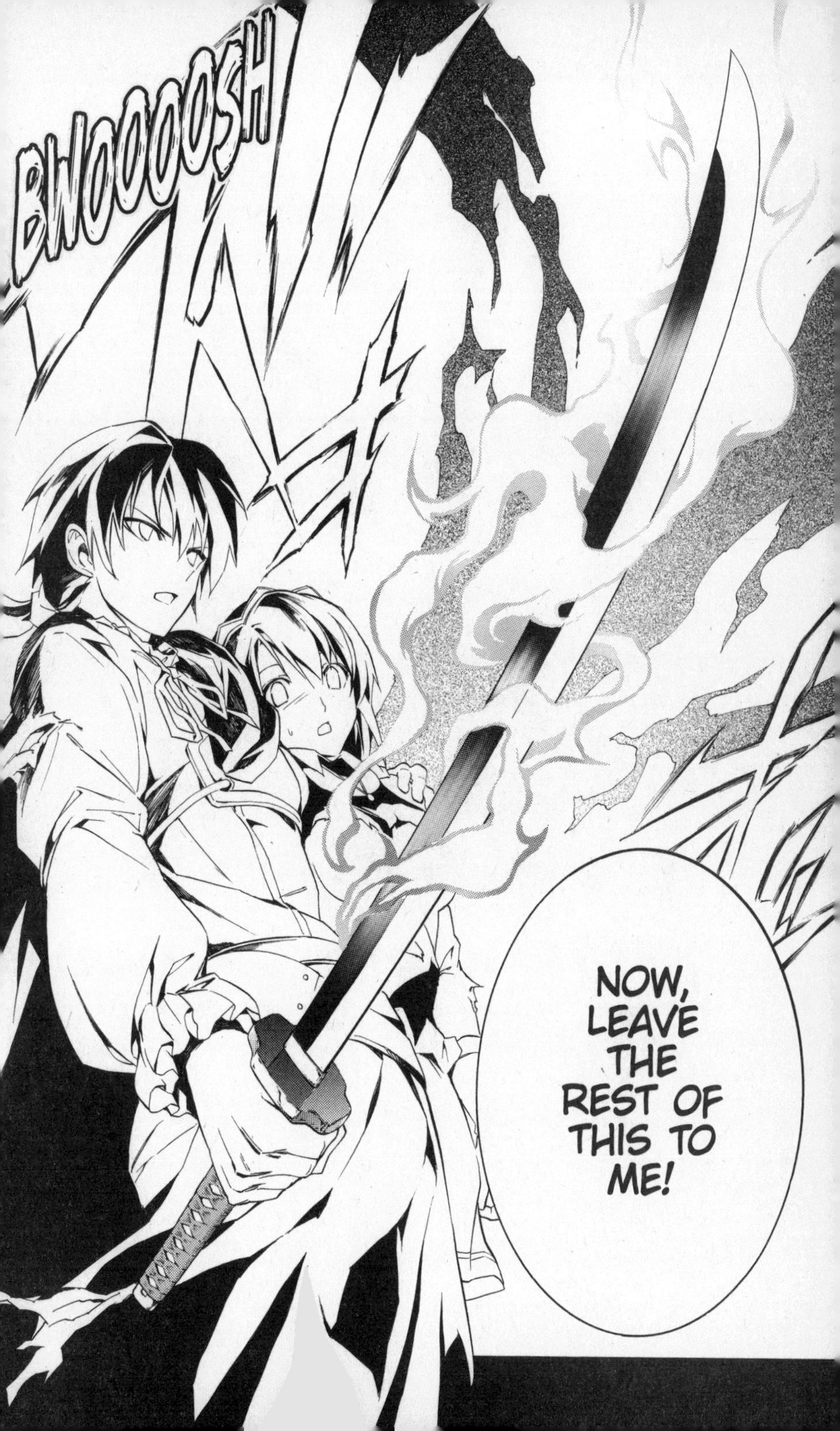
BWOOOOSH
NOW, LEAVE THE REST OF THIS TO ME!

✳ Luke Ainsworth ✳

The Sacred Blacksmith

聖剣の刀鍛冶

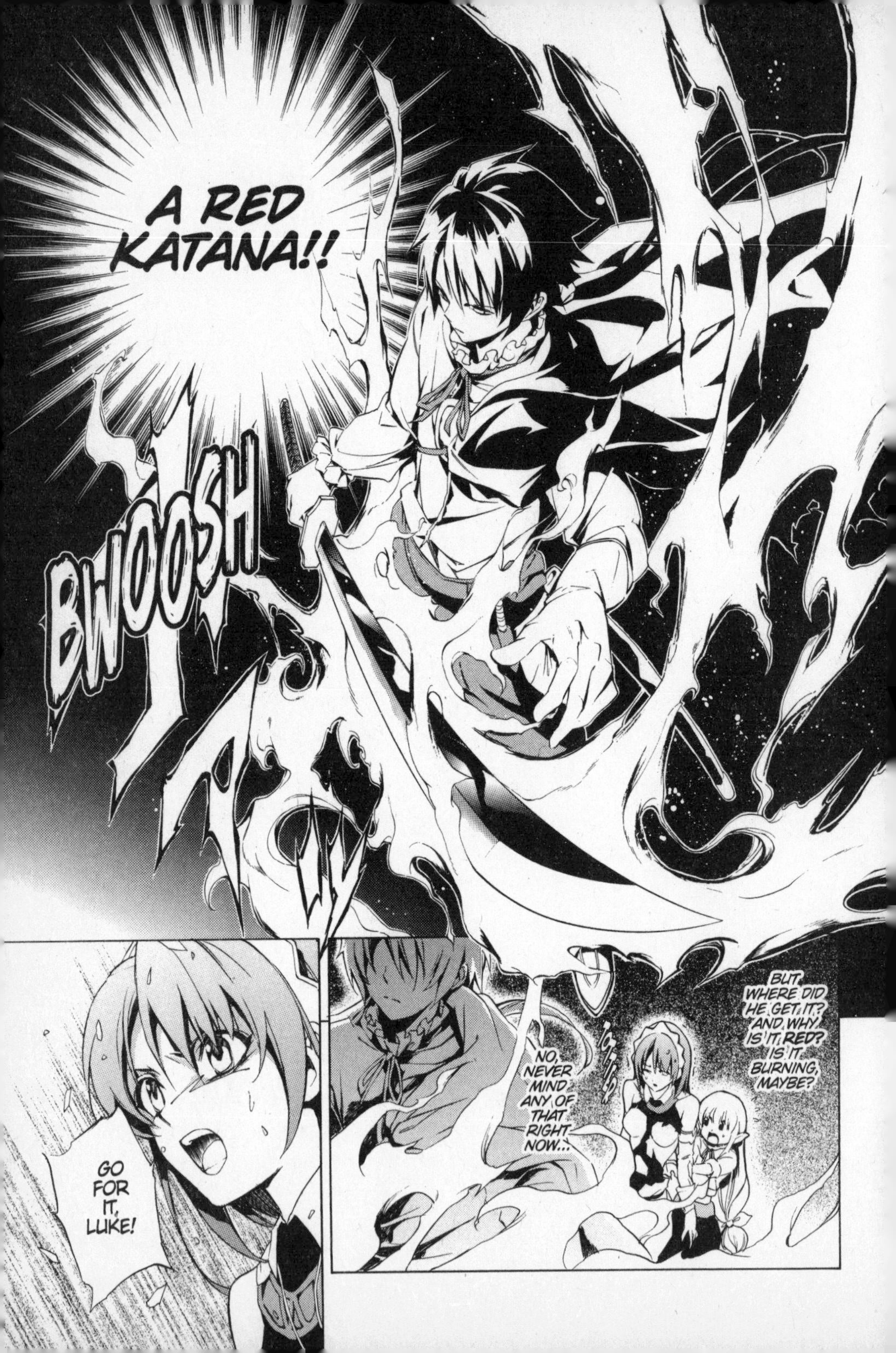
A RED KATANA!!
BWOOSH
BUT, WHERE DID HE GET IT? AND WHY IS IT RED? IS IT BURNING, MAYBE?
NO, NEVER MIND ANY OF THAT RIGHT NOW...
GO FOR IT, LUKE!

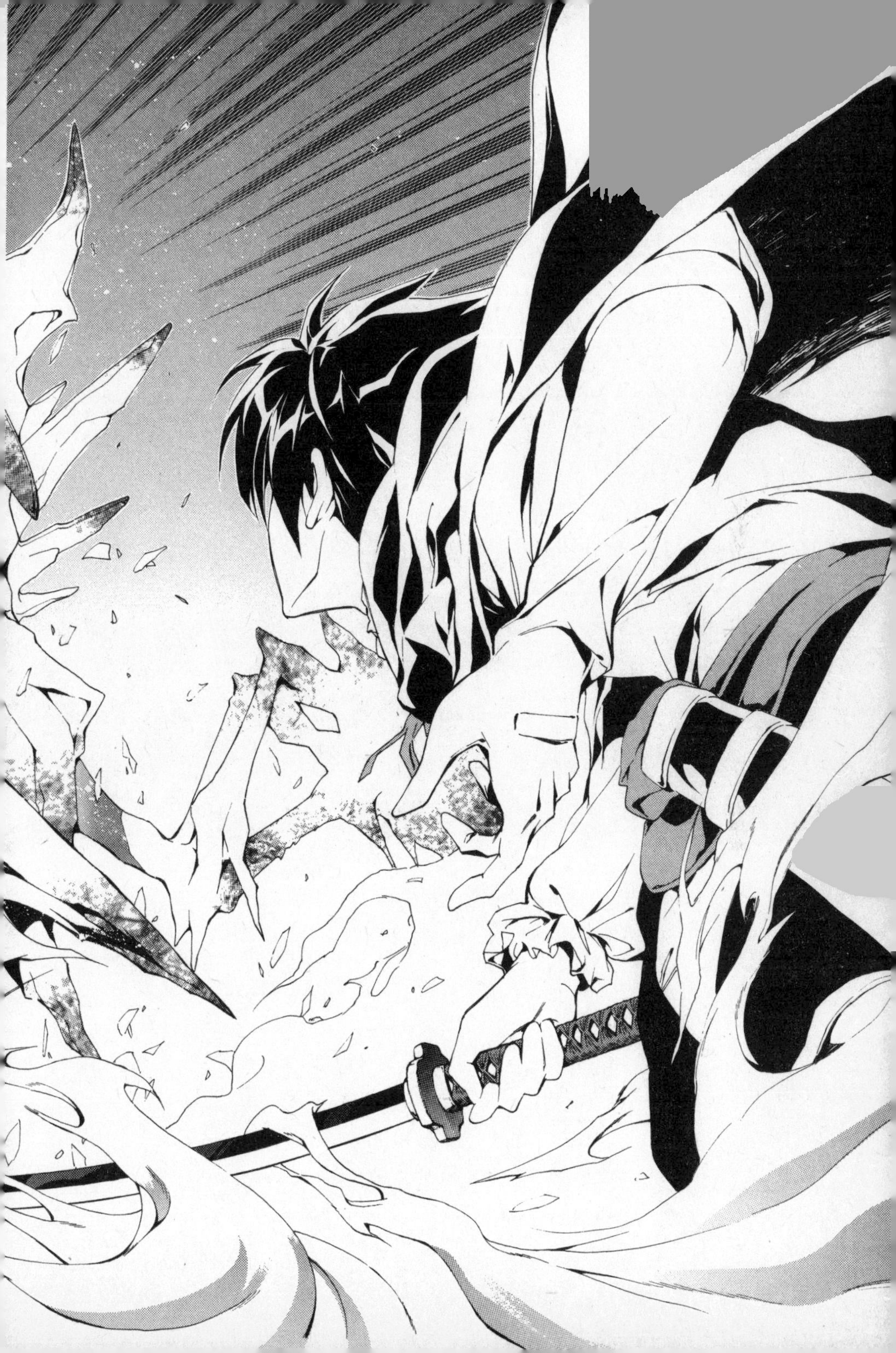

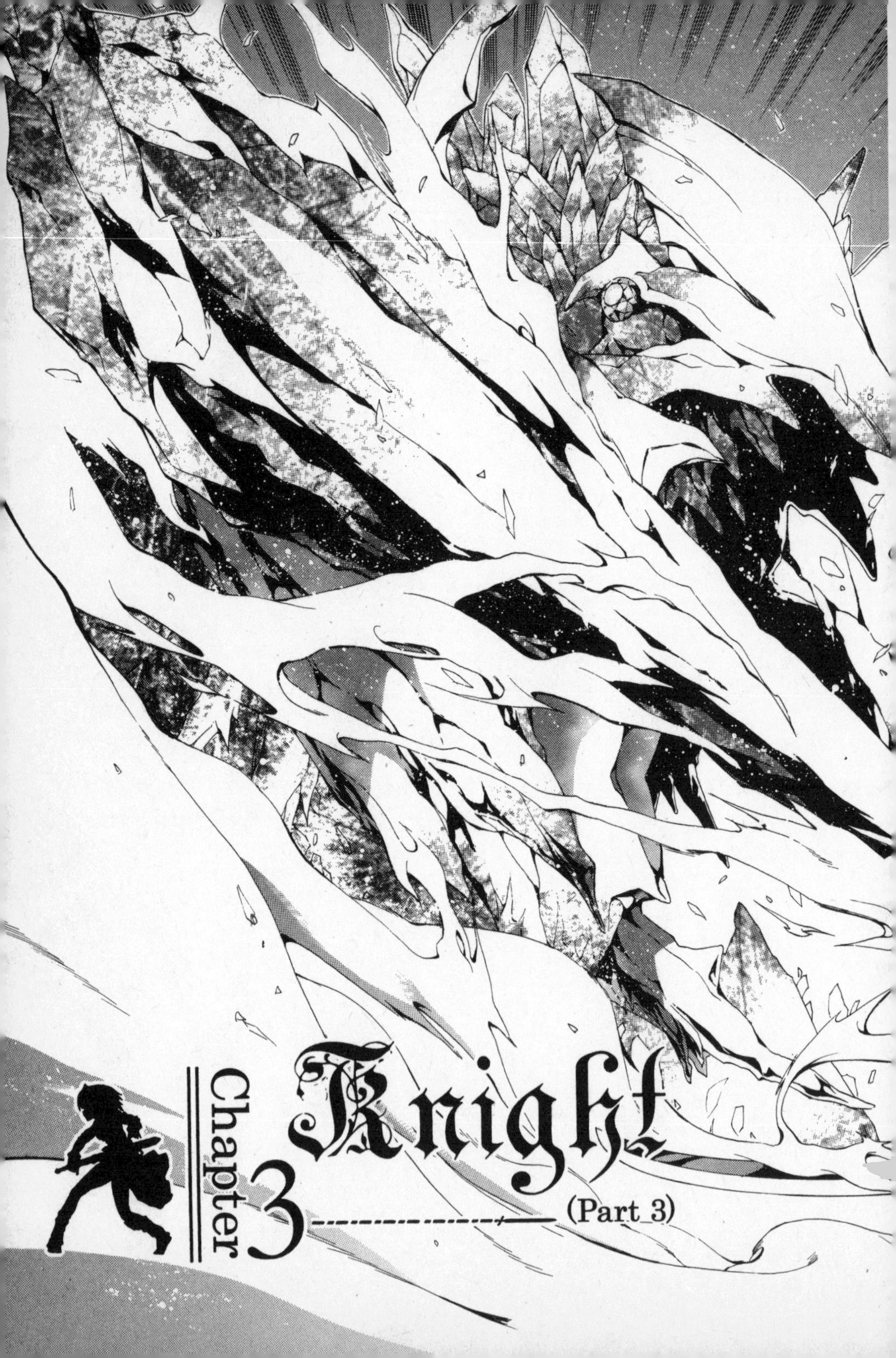
Knight
Chapter 3
(Part 3)

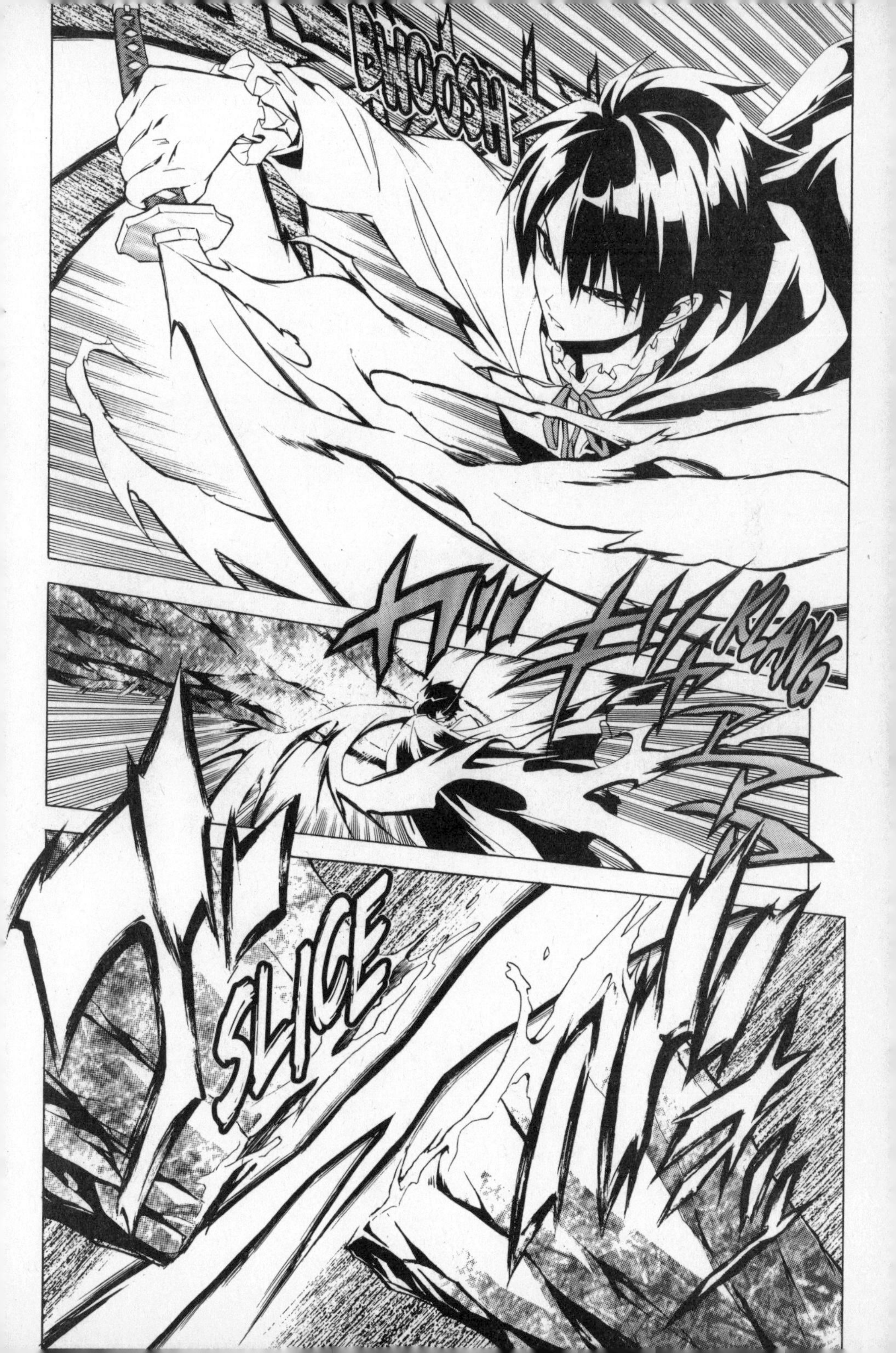
BWOOSH
KLANG
SLICE

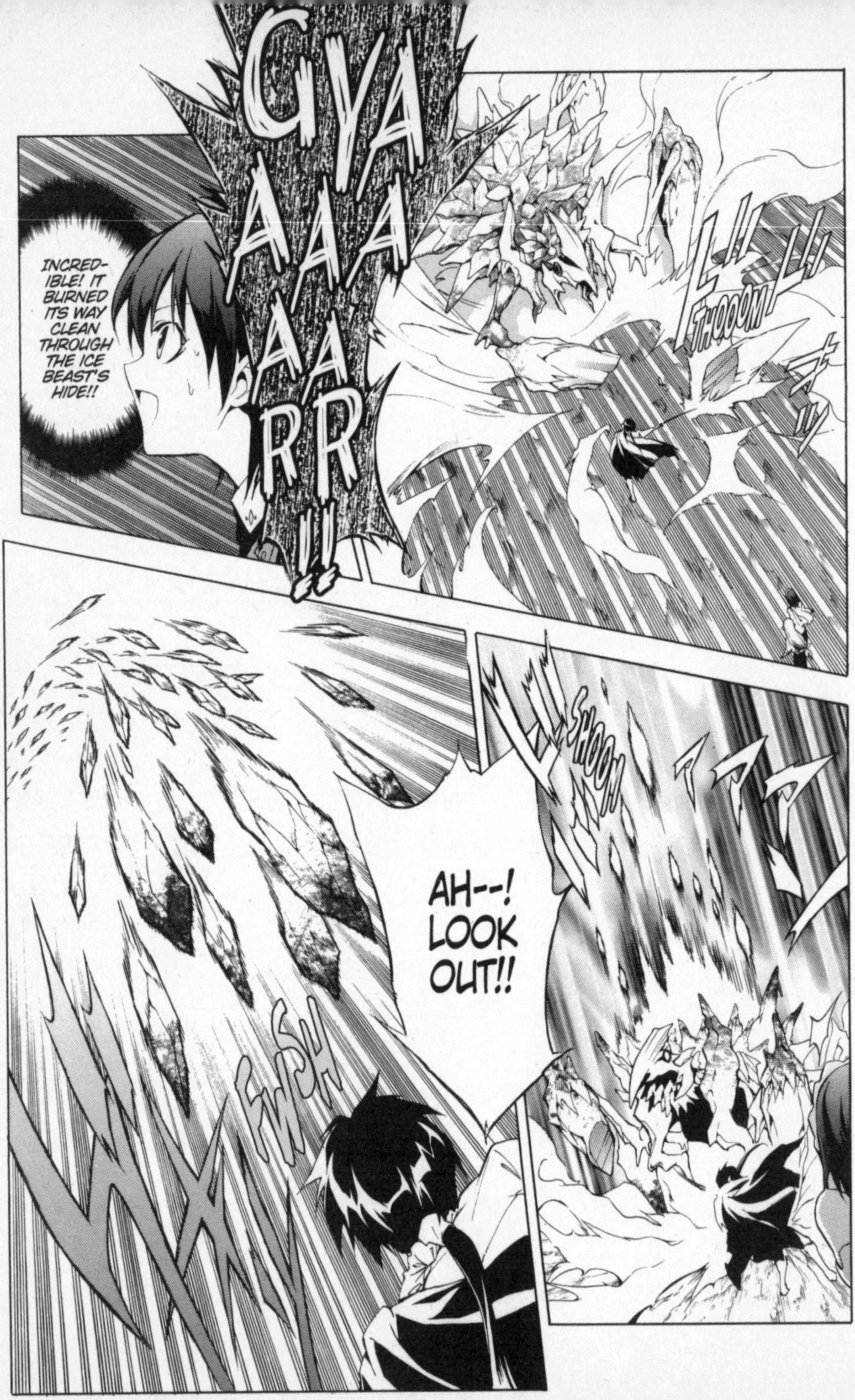
GYAAAAAARR!!
INCREDIBLE! IT BURNED ITS WAY CLEAN THROUGH THE ICE BEAST'S HIDE!!
THOOOM
SHOOOM
AH--! LOOK OUT!!
SWISH

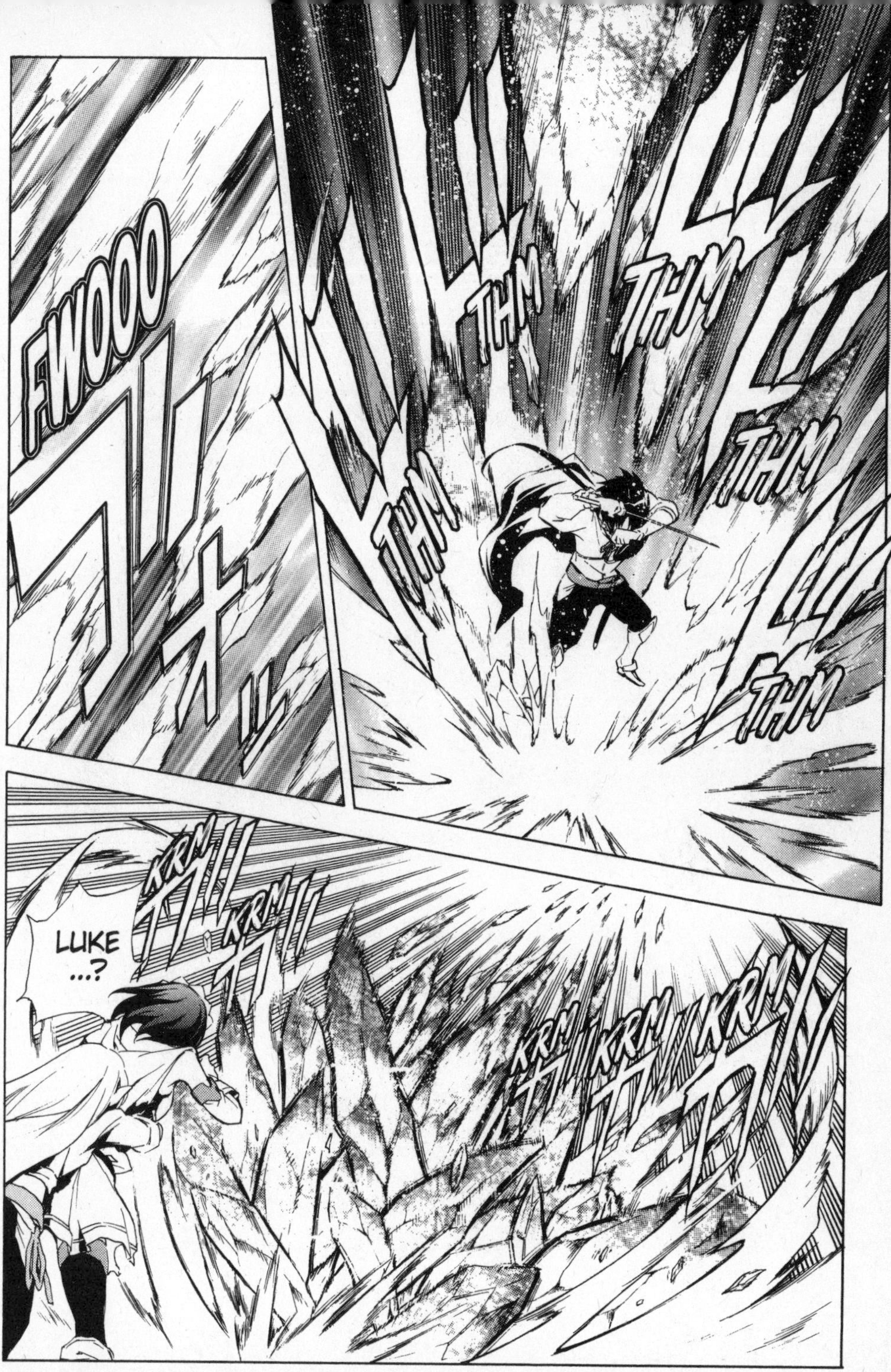
THM
THM
THM
THM
THM
FWOOO
LUKE ...?
KRM
KRM
KRM
KRM
KRM

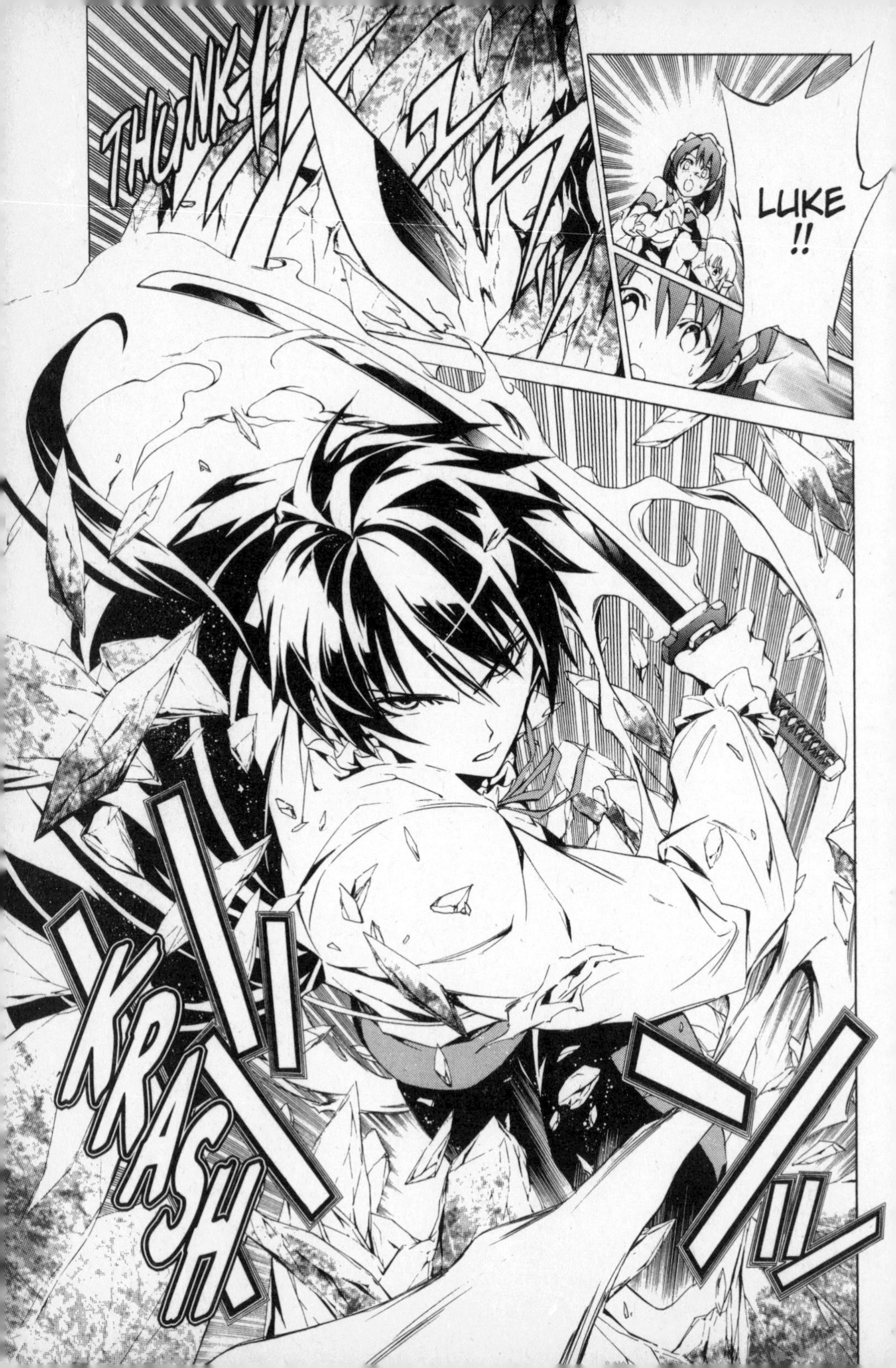
LUKE !!
THUNK!!
KRASH

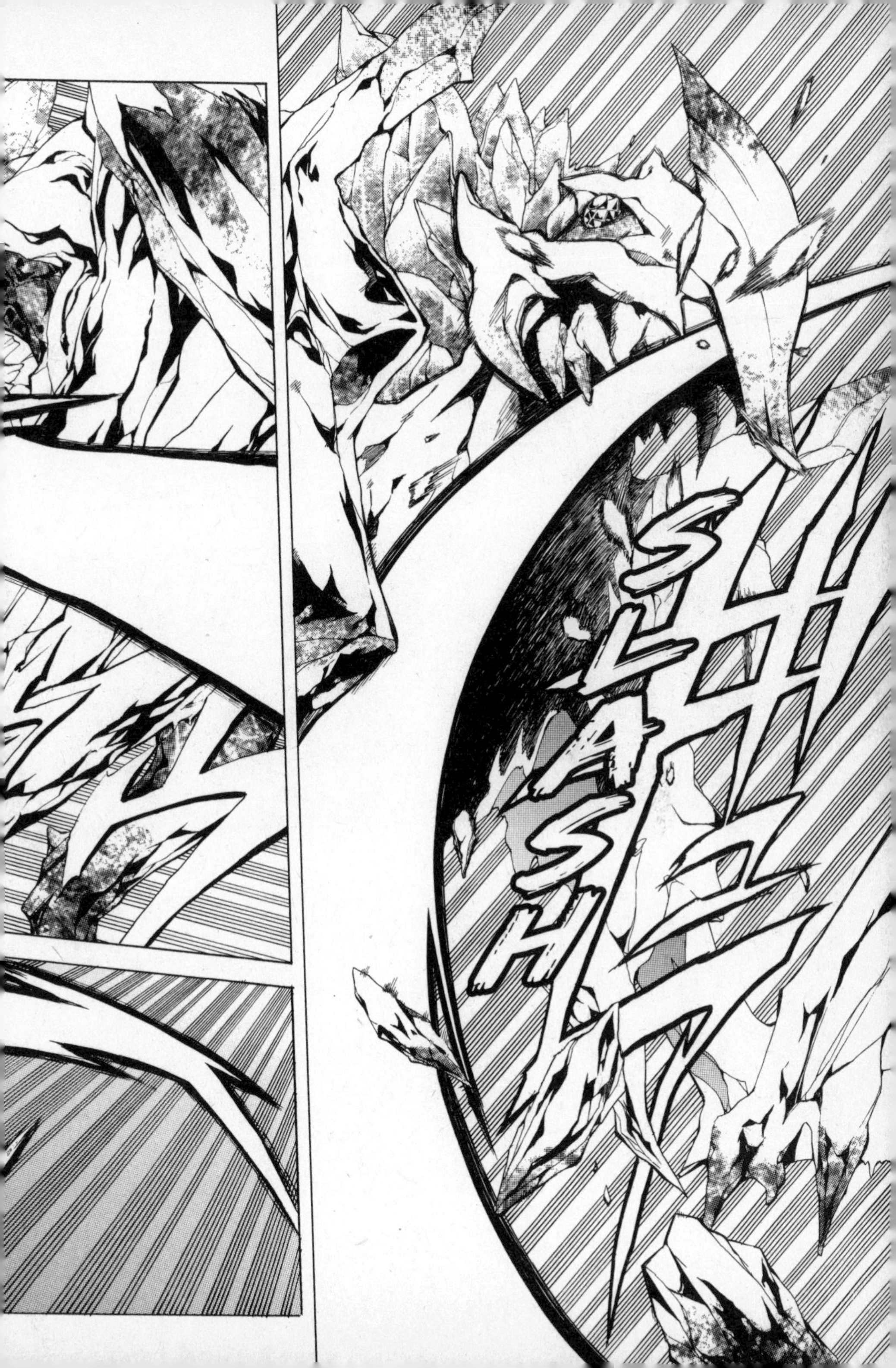
SLASH

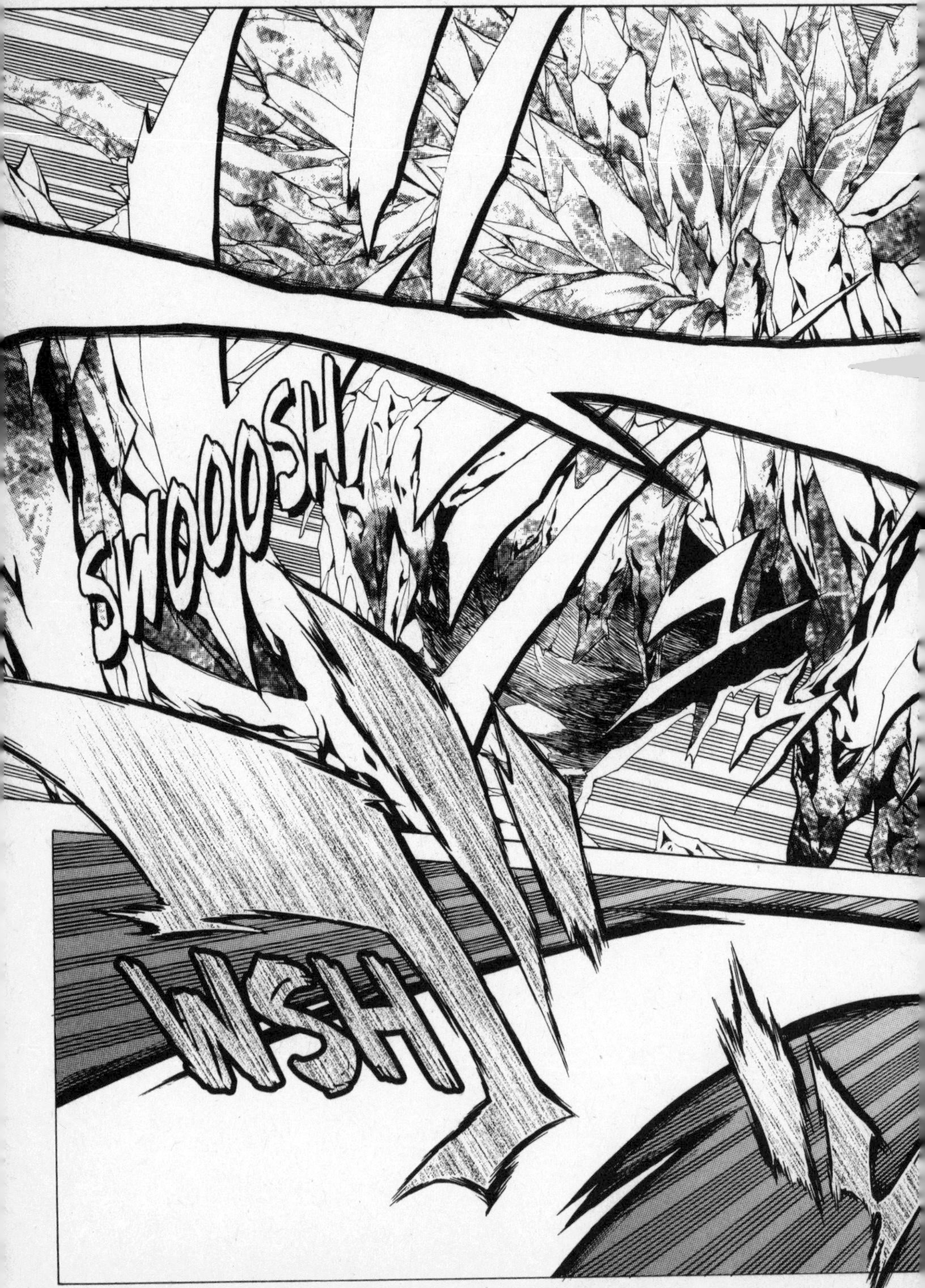
SWOOOSH
WSH

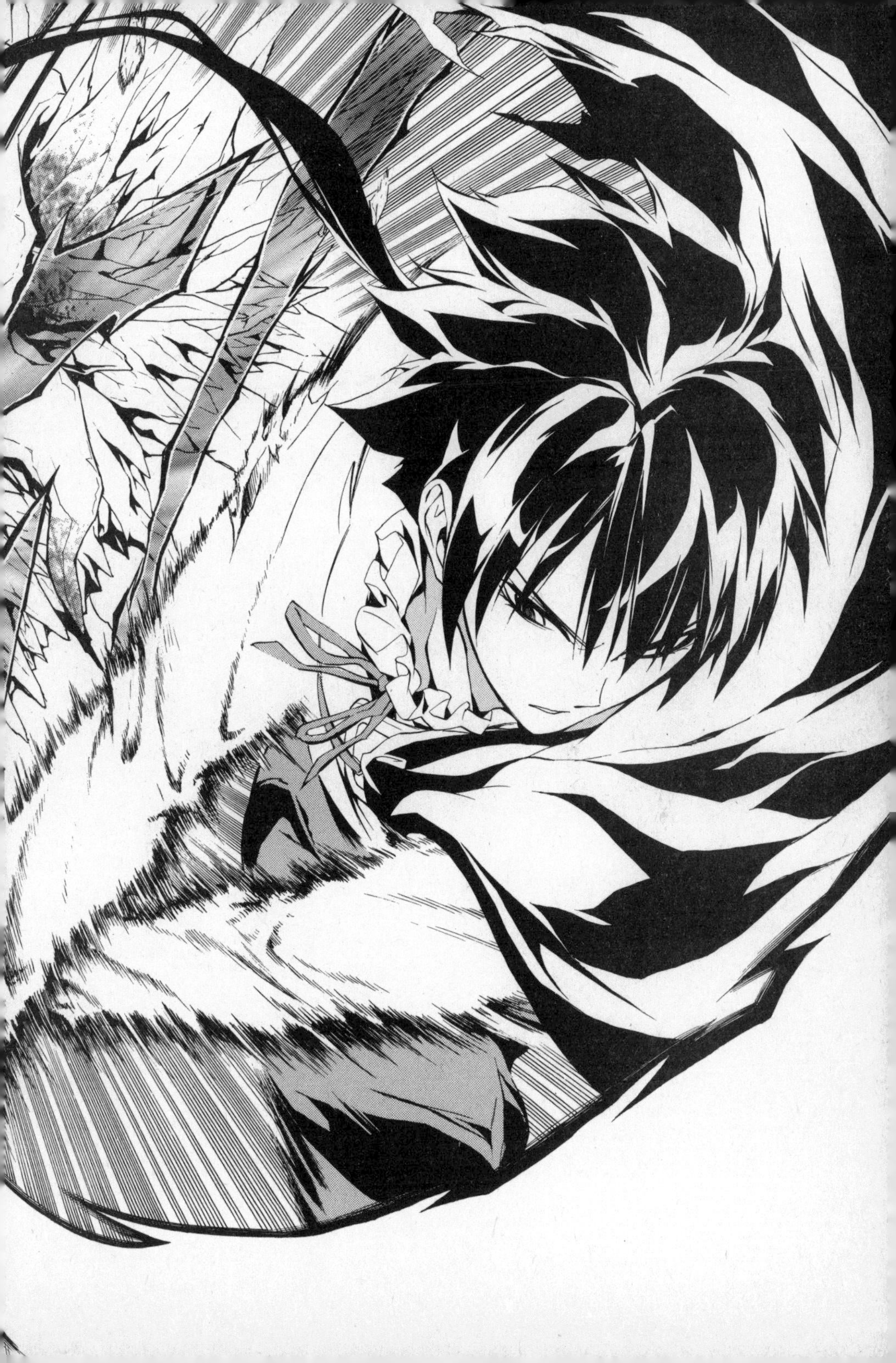

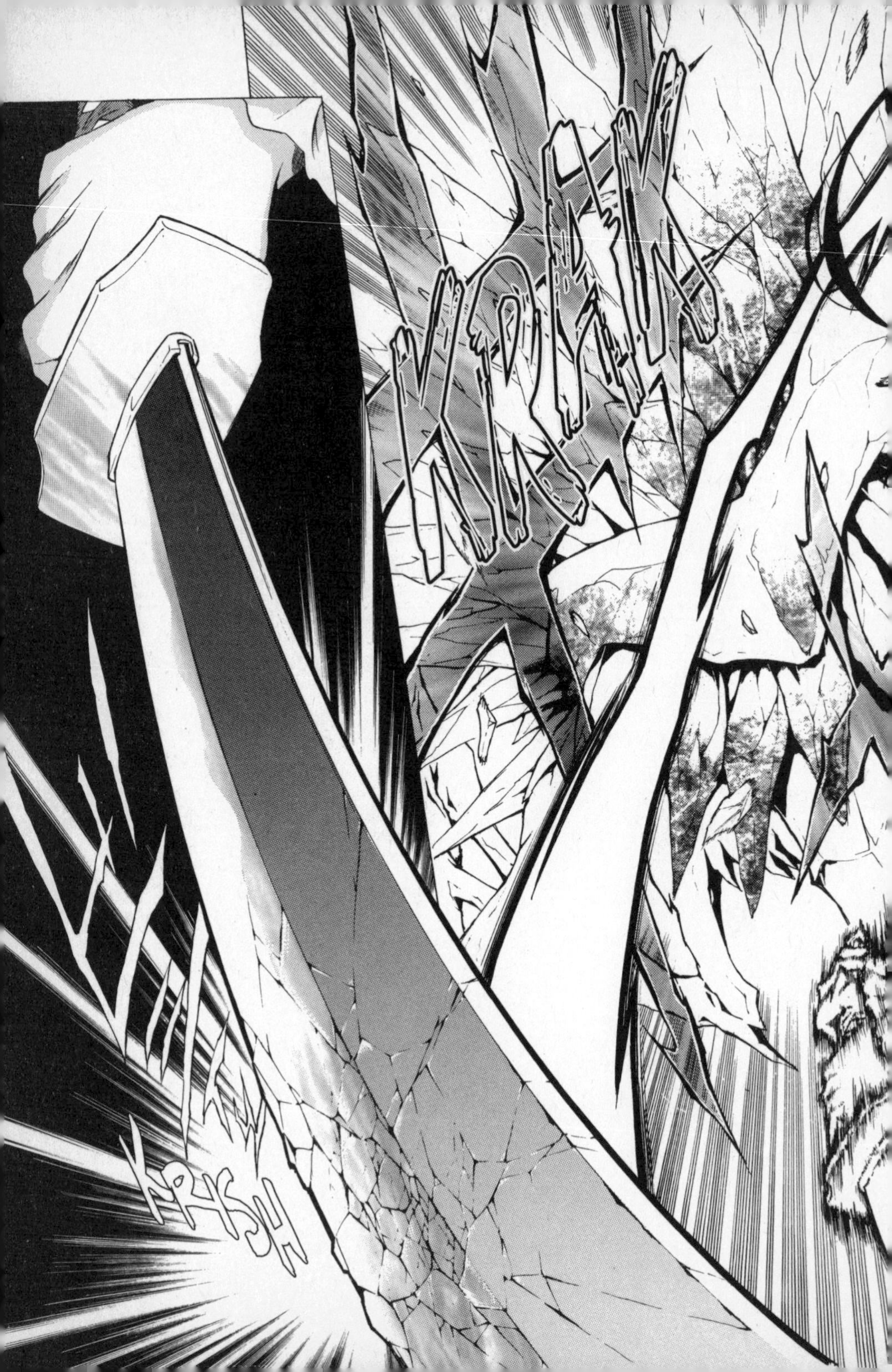
KRAK
KRSH

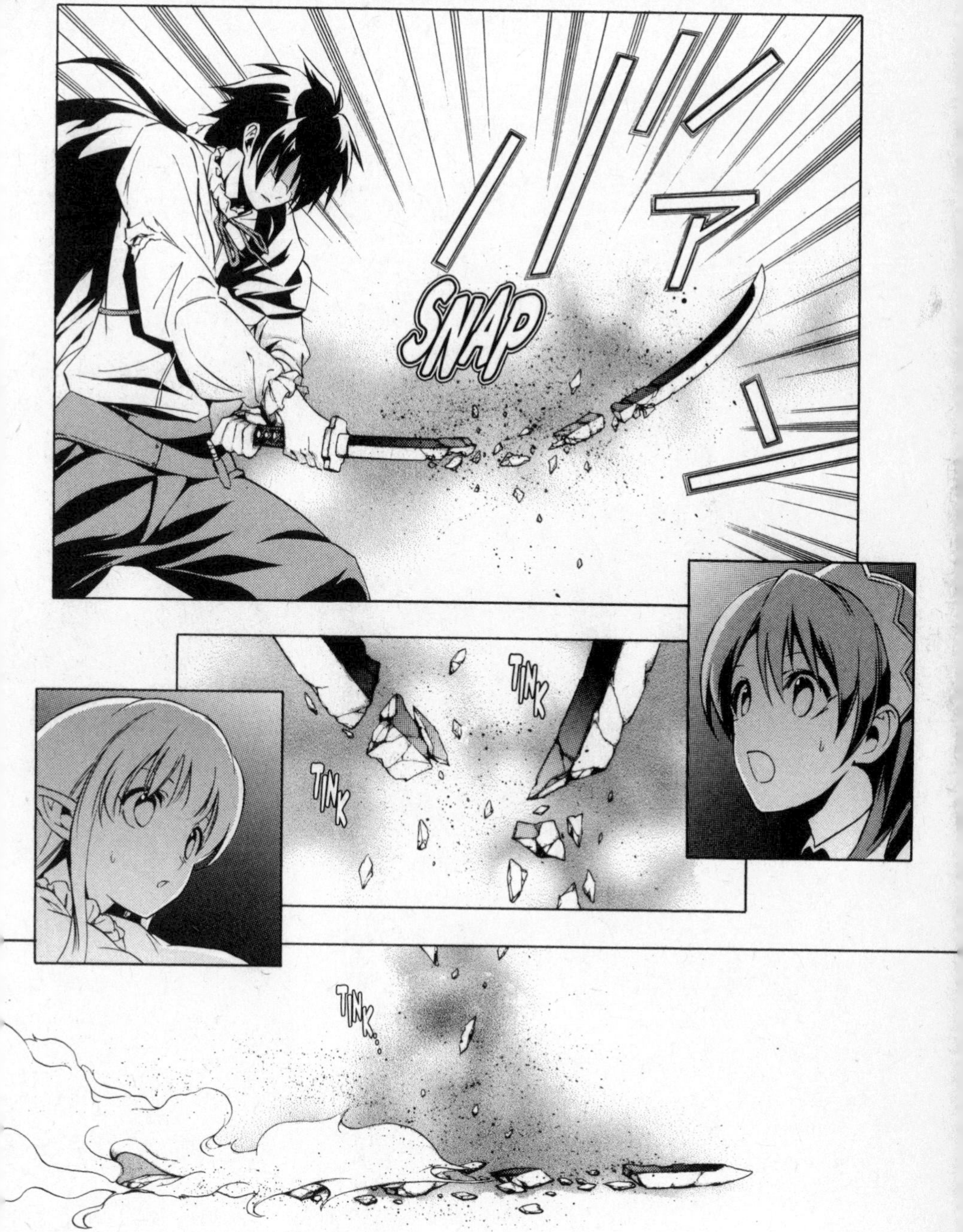
SNAP
TINK
TINK
TINK...

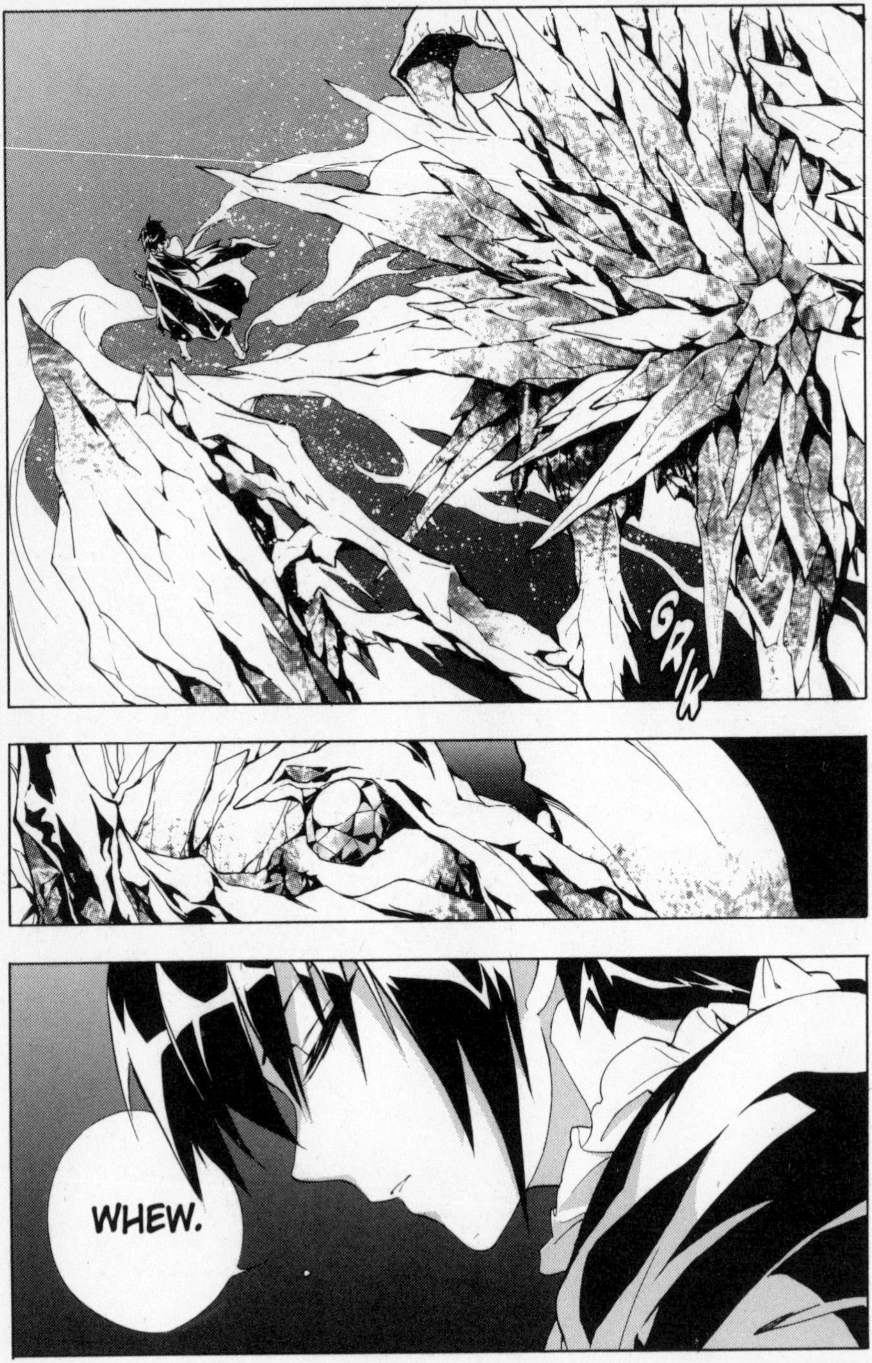
GRIK
WHEW.

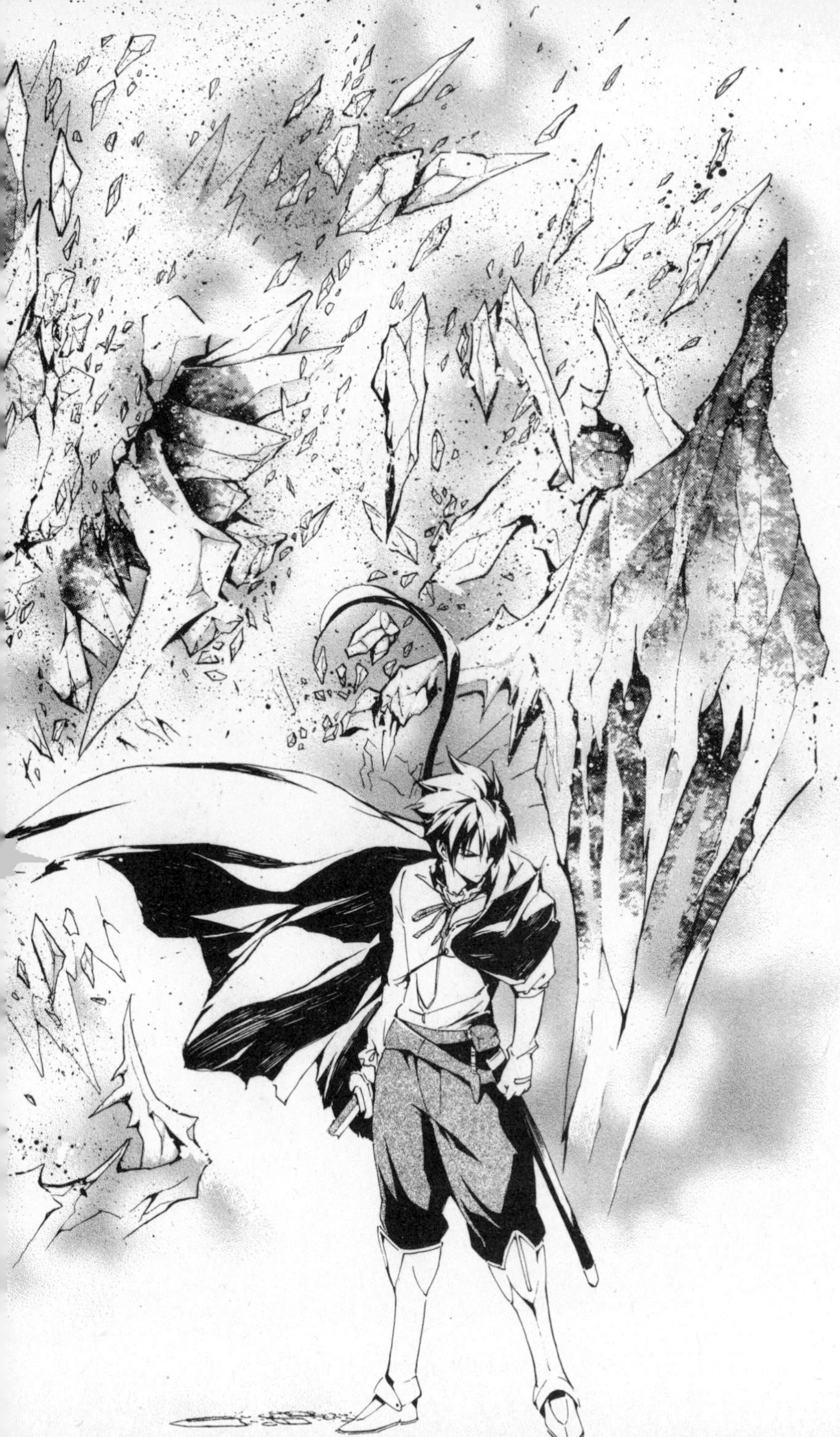

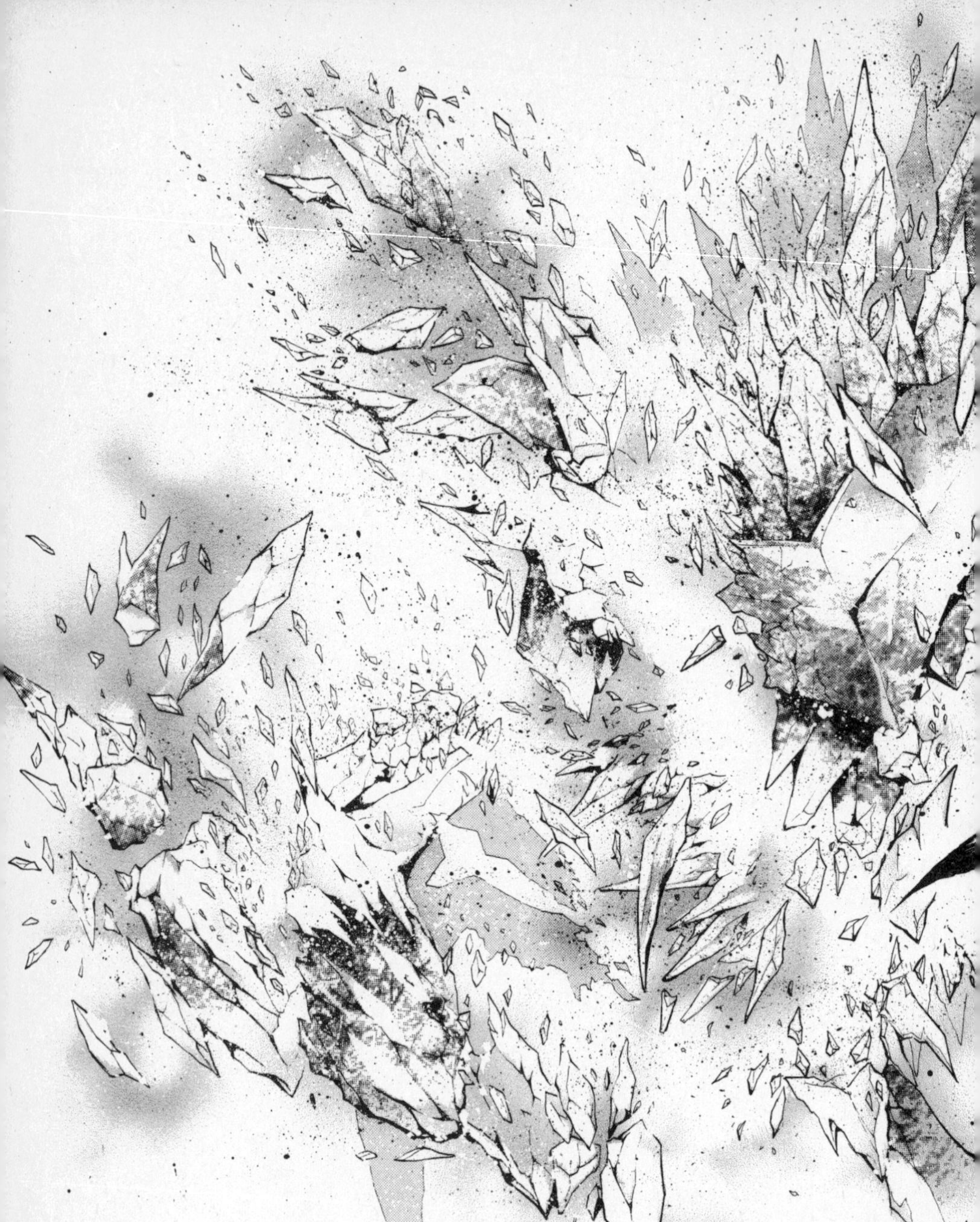

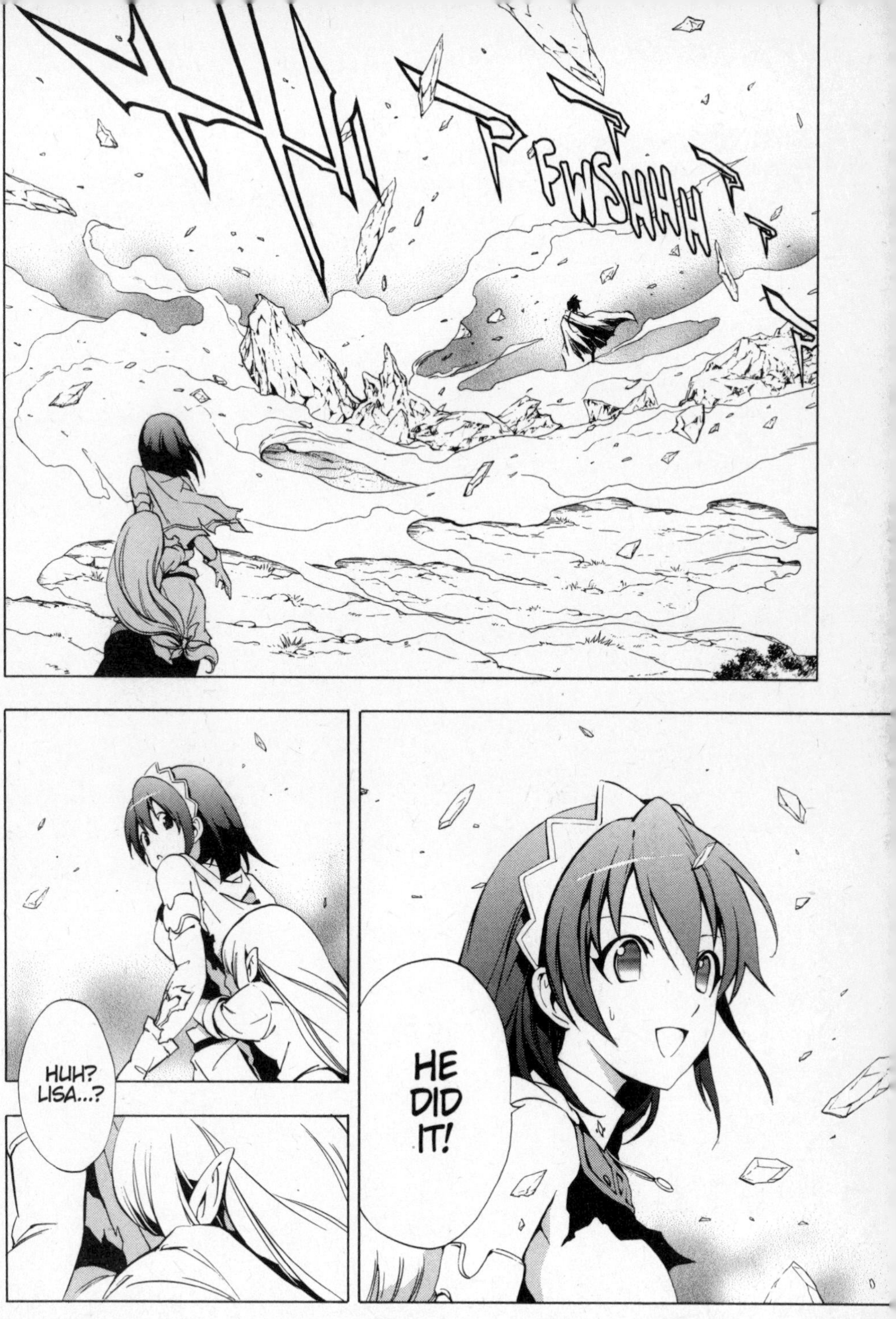
FWSHHHH
HE DID IT!
HUH? LISA...?

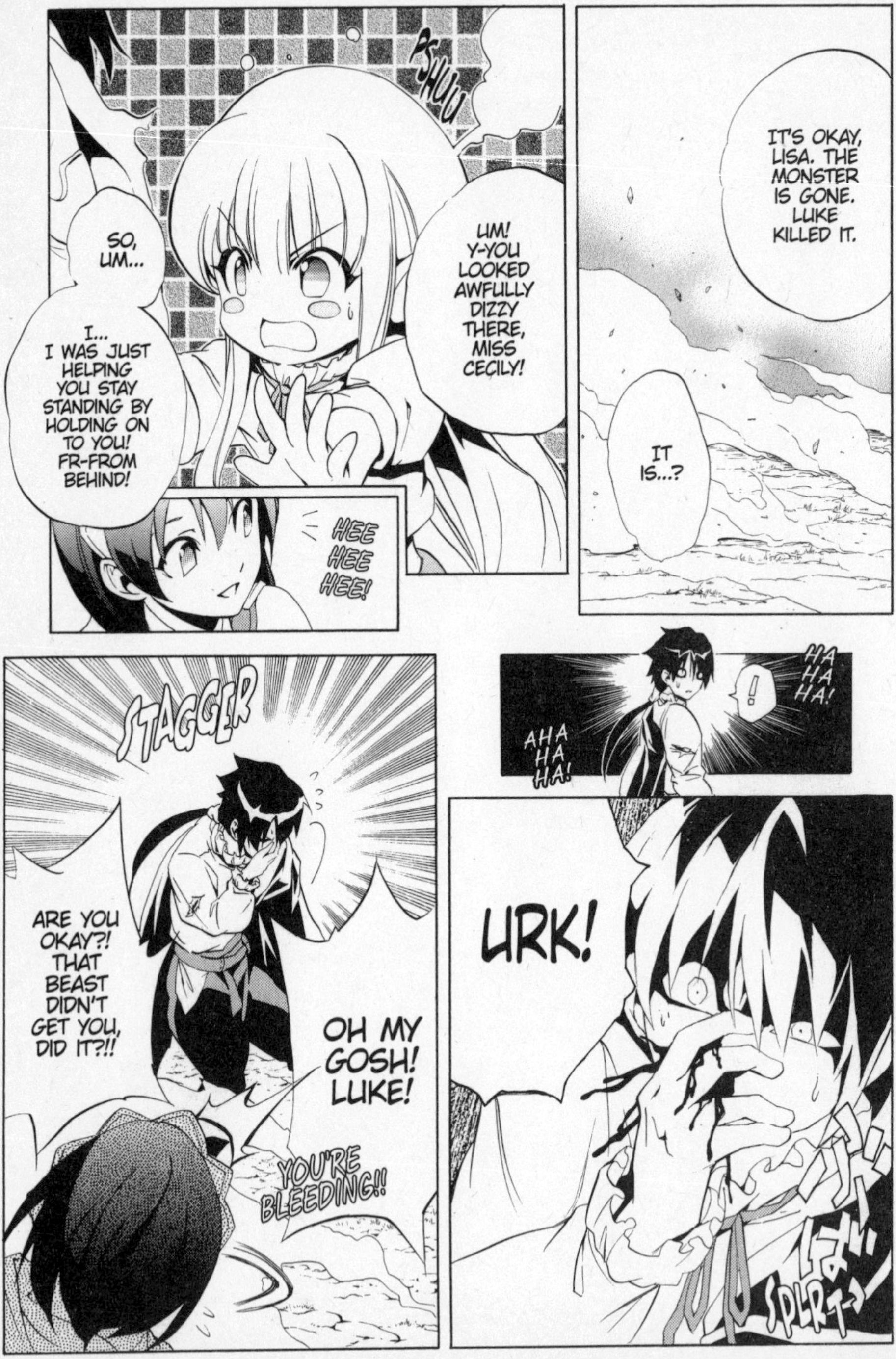
IT'S OKAY, LISA. THE MONSTER IS GONE. LUKE KILLED IT.
IT IS...?
PSHUU
UM! Y-YOU LOOKED AWFULLY DIZZY THERE, MISS CECILY!
SO, UM...
I... I WAS JUST HELPING YOU STAY STANDING BY HOLDING ON TO YOU! FR-FROM BEHIND!
HEE HEE HEE!
HA HA HA!
!
AHA HA HA!
URK!
SPLRT
STAGGER
OH MY GOSH! LUKE!
YOU'RE BLEEDING!!
ARE YOU OKAY?! THAT BEAST DIDN'T GET YOU, DID IT?!!

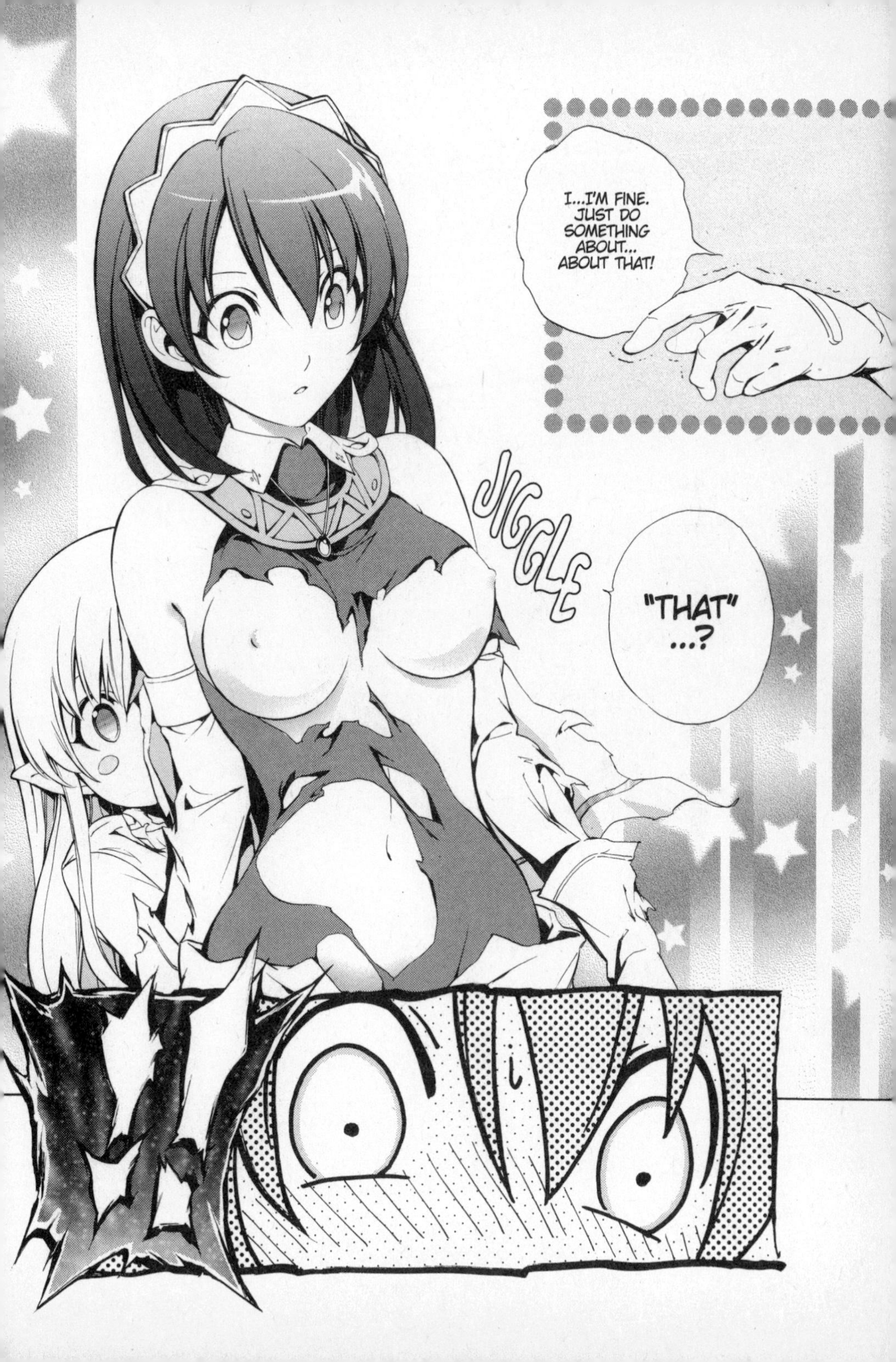
I...I'M FINE. JUST DO SOMETHING ABOUT... ABOUT THAT!
JIGGLE
"THAT" ...?

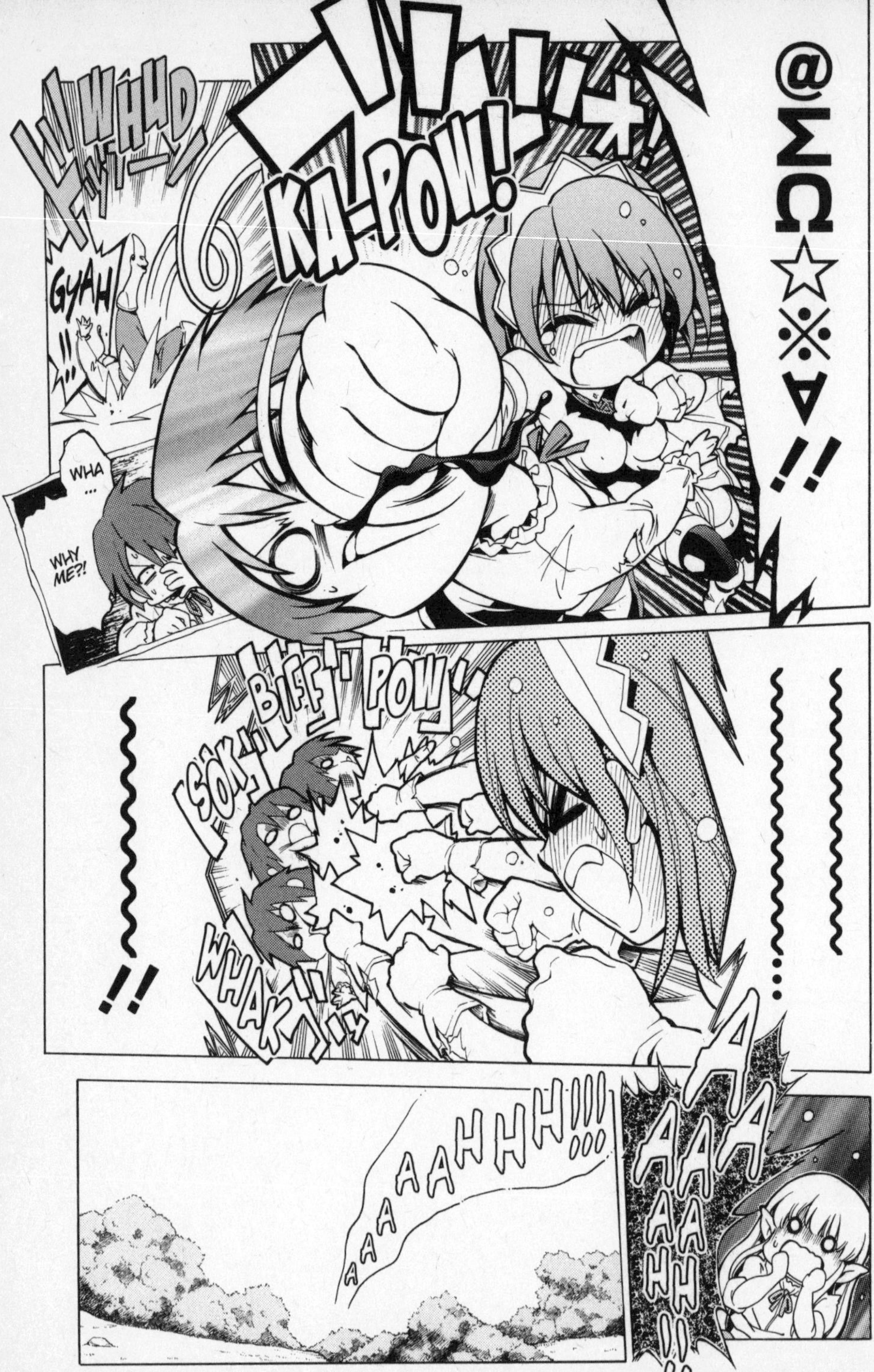

@ΣΩ☆※∀!!
KA-POW!
WHUD!
GYAH!!!
WHA...
WHY ME?!
~~~~~...
SOK!
BIFF!
POW!
WHAK!!
~~~~~!!
AAAAAAAHH!!
AAAAAAHHHH!!!

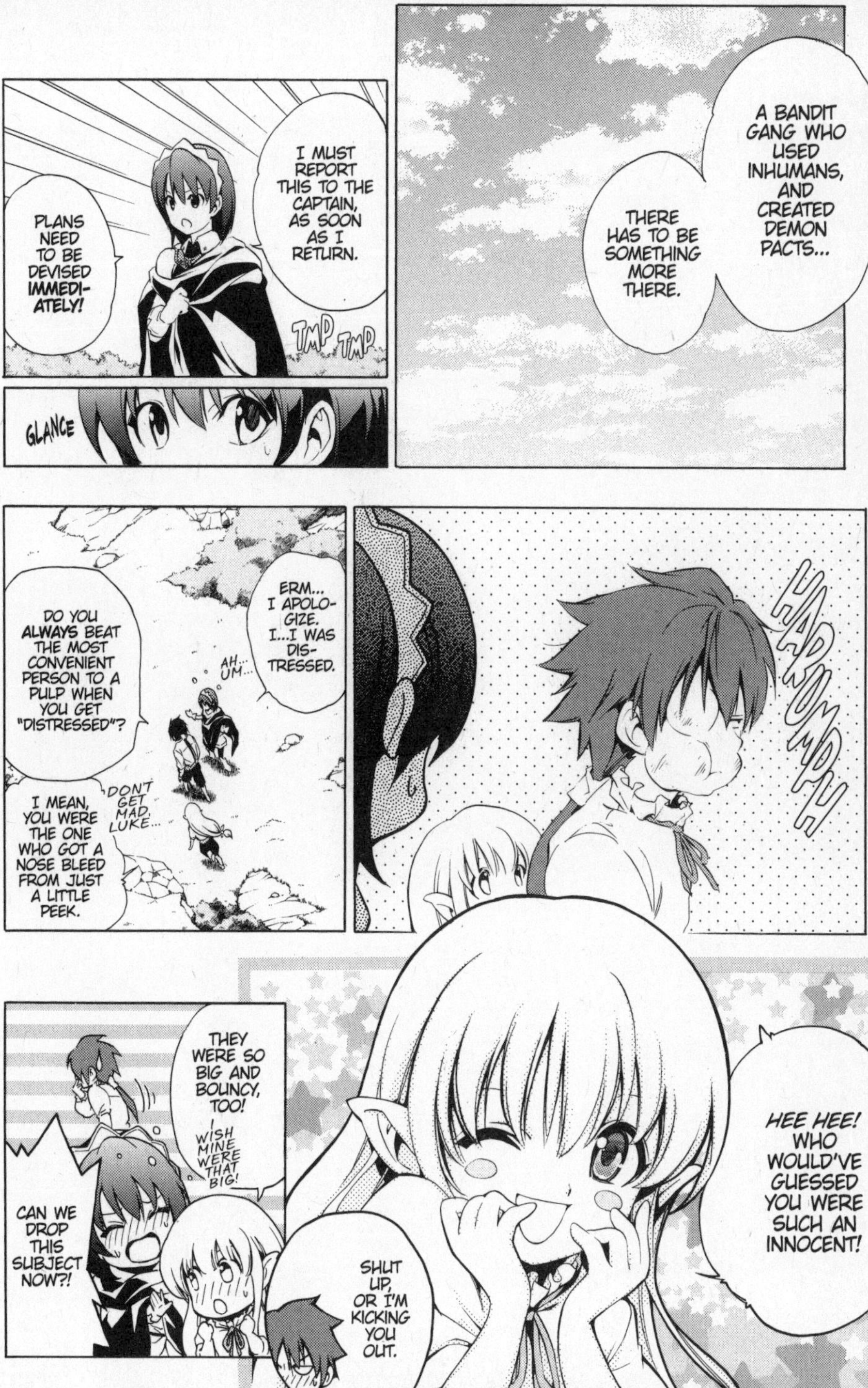
A BANDIT GANG WHO USED INHUMANS, AND CREATED DEMON PACTS...
THERE HAS TO BE SOMETHING MORE THERE.
I MUST REPORT THIS TO THE CAPTAIN, AS SOON AS I RETURN.
PLANS NEED TO BE DEVISED IMMEDIATELY!
TMP TMP
GLANCE
HARUMPH
ERM... I APOLOGIZE. I...I WAS DISTRESSED.
AH... UM...
DO YOU ALWAYS BEAT THE MOST CONVENIENT PERSON TO A PULP WHEN YOU GET "DISTRESSED"?
DON'T GET MAD, LUKE...
I MEAN, YOU WERE THE ONE WHO GOT A NOSE BLEED FROM JUST A LITTLE PEEK.
HEE HEE! WHO WOULD'VE GUESSED YOU WERE SUCH AN INNOCENT!
SHUT UP, OR I'M KICKING YOU OUT.
THEY WERE SO BIG AND BOUNCY, TOO!
I WISH MINE WERE THAT BIG!
CAN WE DROP THIS SUBJECT NOW?!

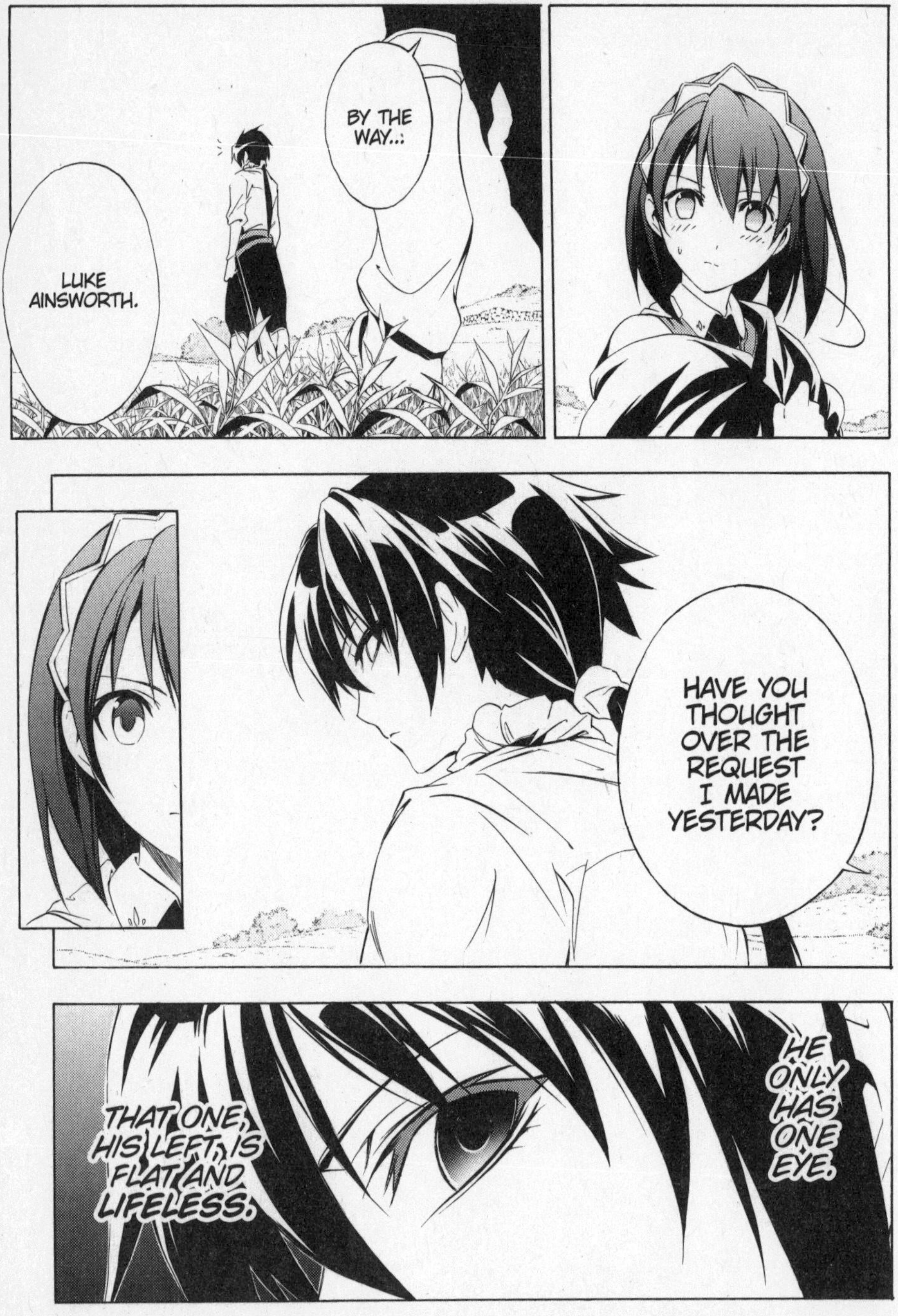
BY THE WAY...:
LUKE AINSWORTH.
HAVE YOU THOUGHT OVER THE REQUEST I MADE YESTERDAY?
HE ONLY HAS ONE EYE.
THAT ONE, HIS LEFT, IS FLAT AND LIFELESS.

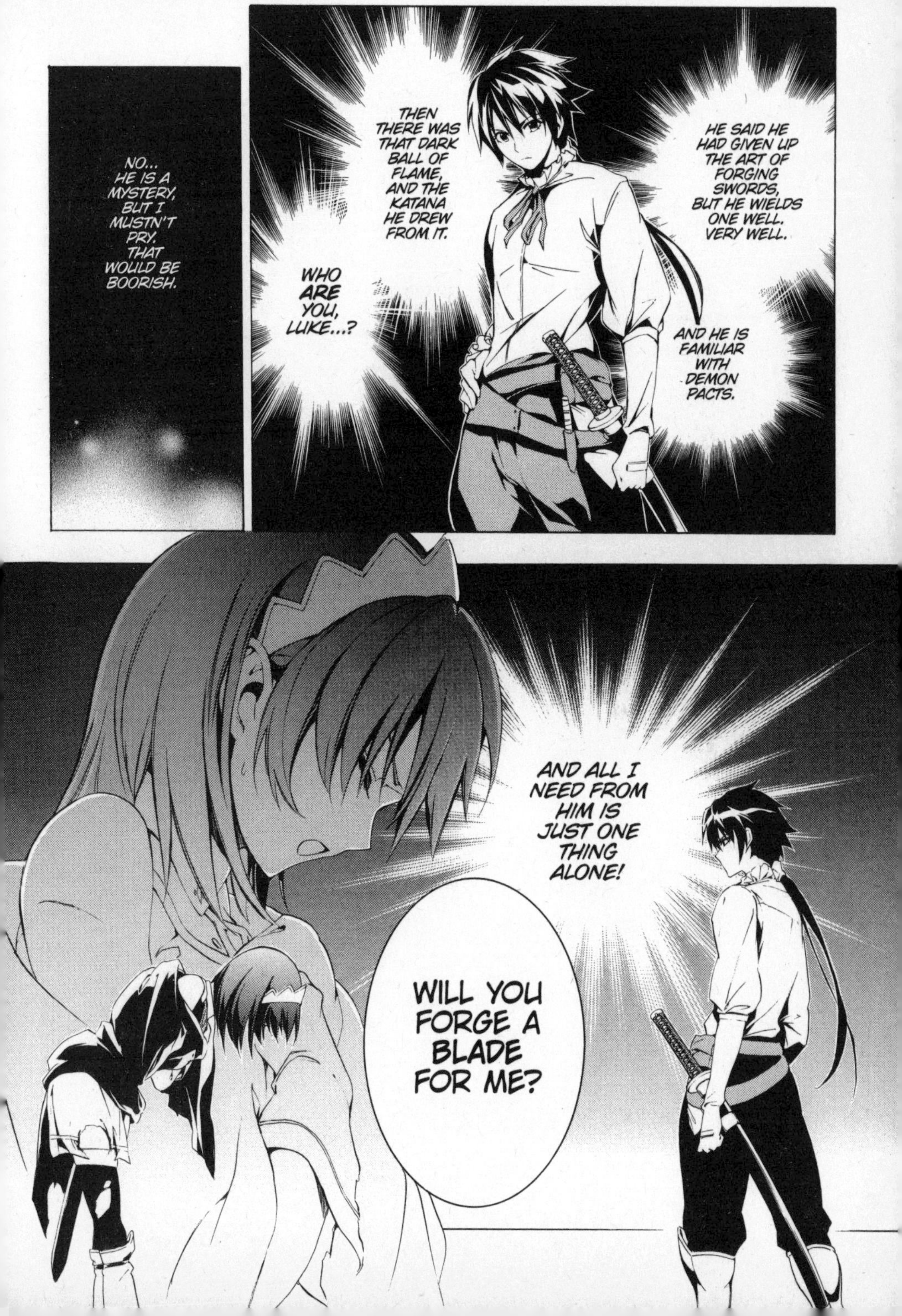
HE SAID HE HAD GIVEN UP THE ART OF FORGING SWORDS, BUT HE WIELDS ONE WELL. VERY WELL.
THEN THERE WAS THAT DARK BALL OF FLAME, AND THE KATANA HE DREW FROM IT.
AND HE IS FAMILIAR WITH DEMON PACTS.
WHO ARE YOU, LUKE...?
NO... HE IS A MYSTERY, BUT I MUSTN'T PRY. THAT WOULD BE BOORISH.
AND ALL I NEED FROM HIM IS JUST ONE THING ALONE!
WILL YOU FORGE A BLADE FOR ME?

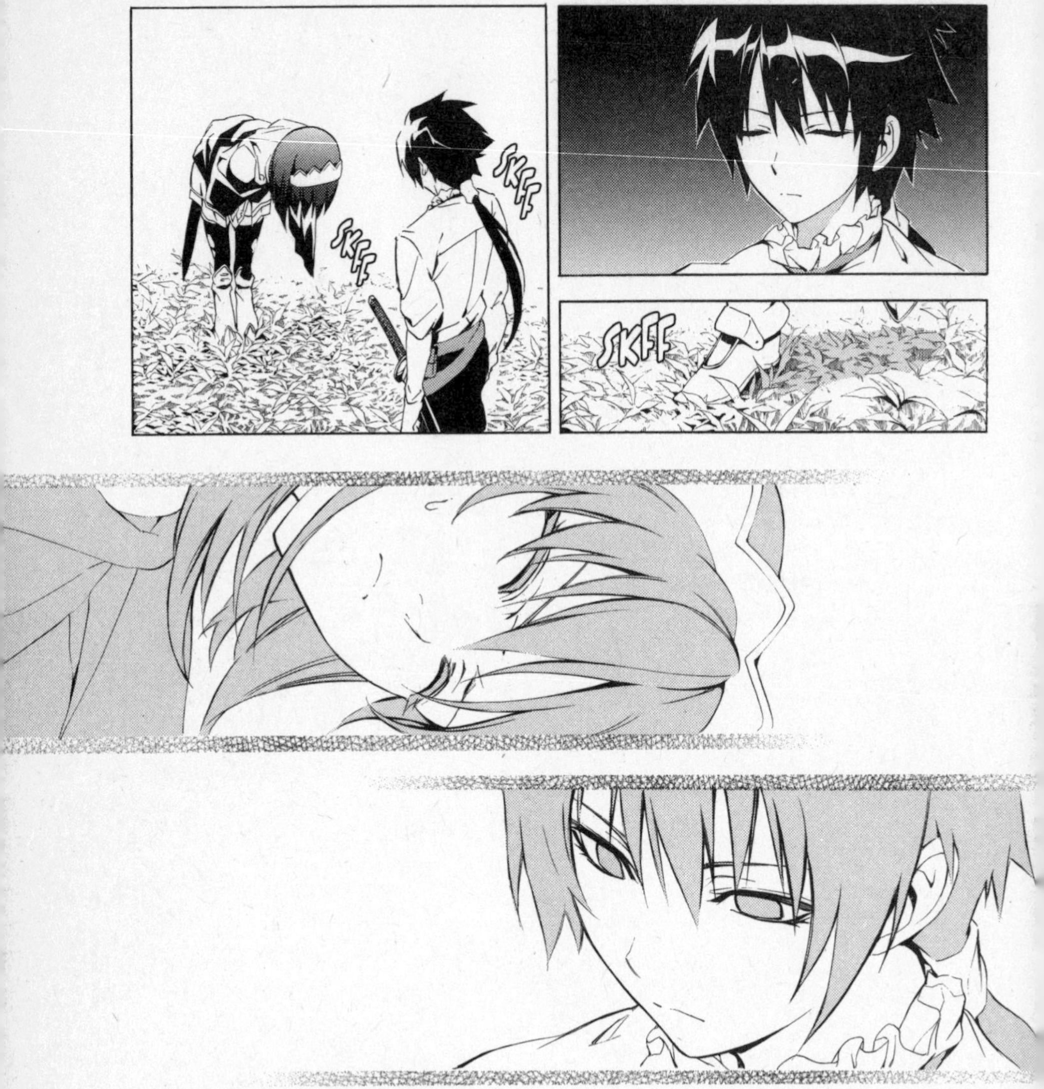
SKFF
SKFF
SKFF
PAT

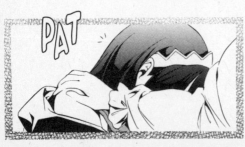

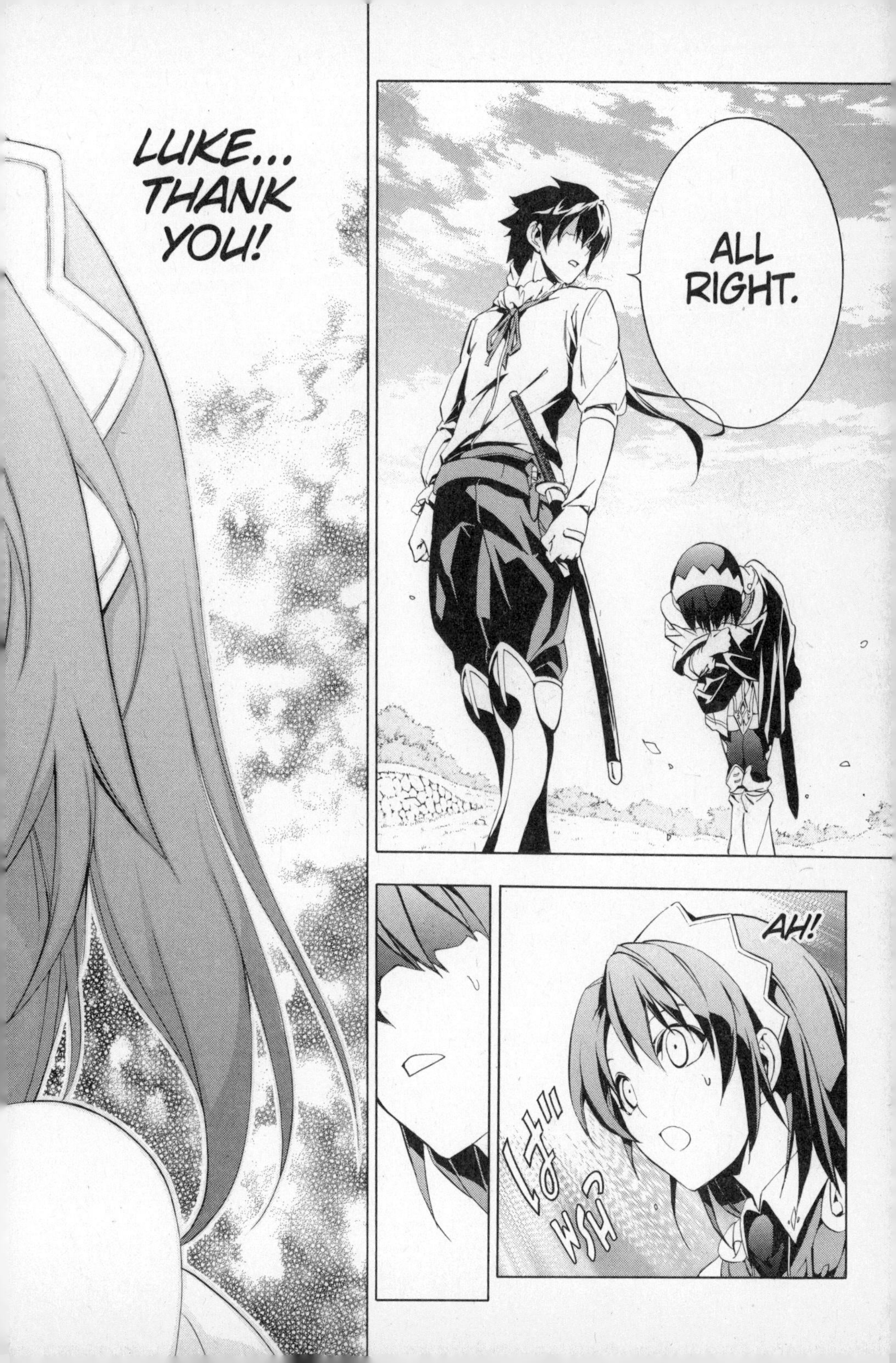
ALL RIGHT.
AH!
WHSH
LUKE... THANK YOU!

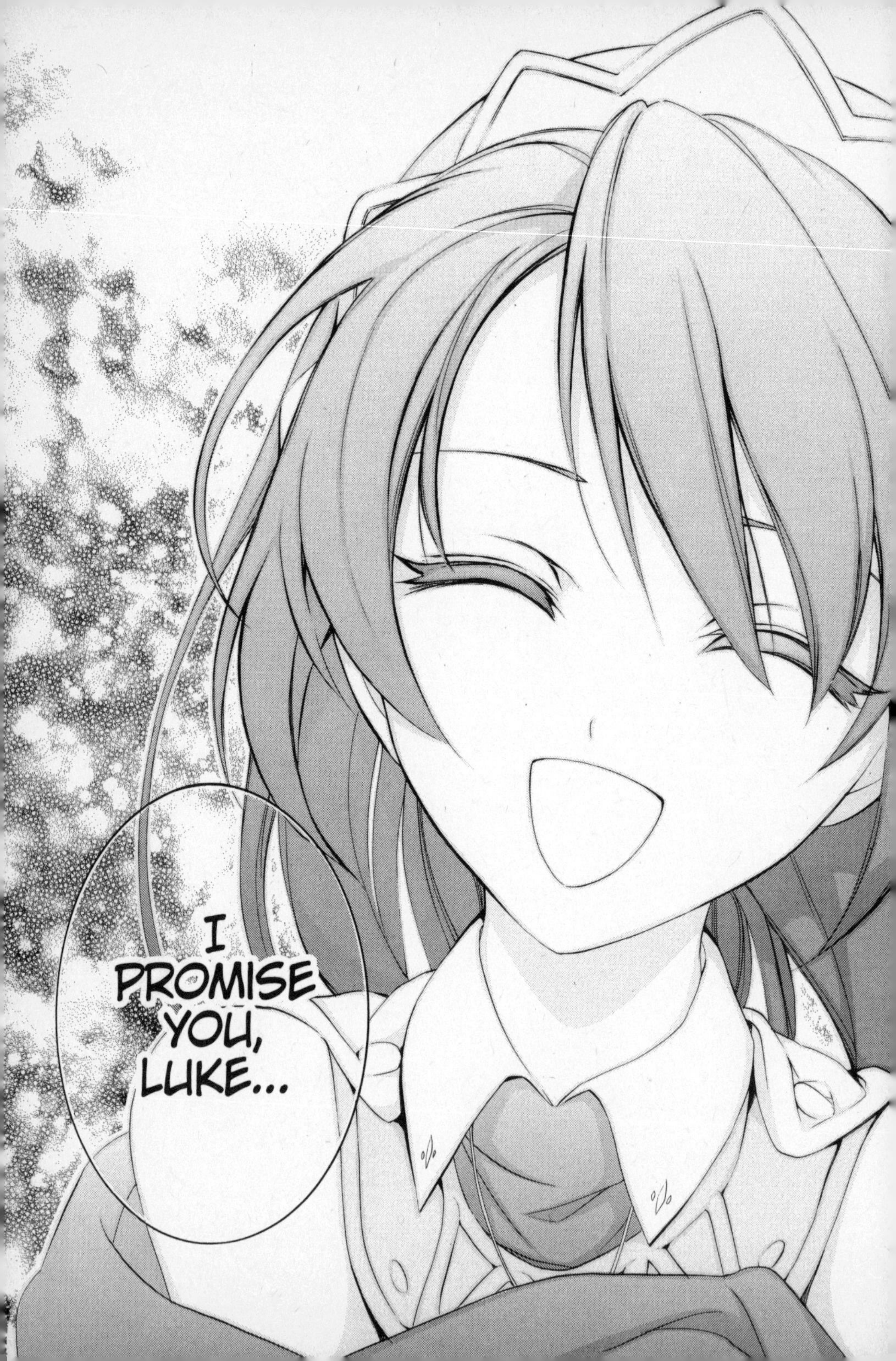
I PROMISE YOU, LUKE...

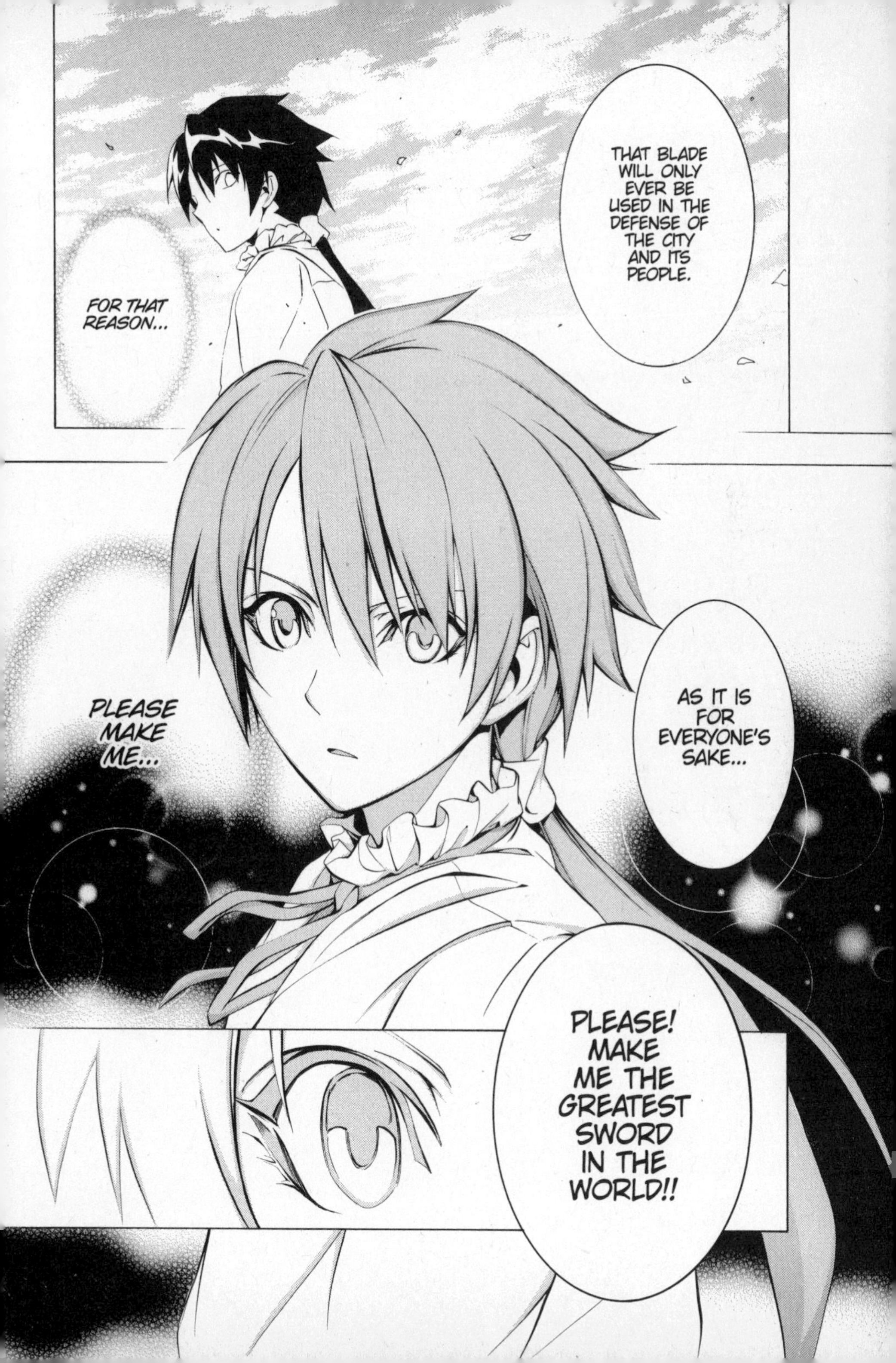
THAT BLADE WILL ONLY EVER BE USED IN THE DEFENSE OF THE CITY AND ITS PEOPLE.
FOR THAT REASON...
AS IT IS FOR EVERYONE'S SAKE...
PLEASE MAKE ME...
PLEASE! MAKE ME THE GREATEST SWORD IN THE WORLD!!

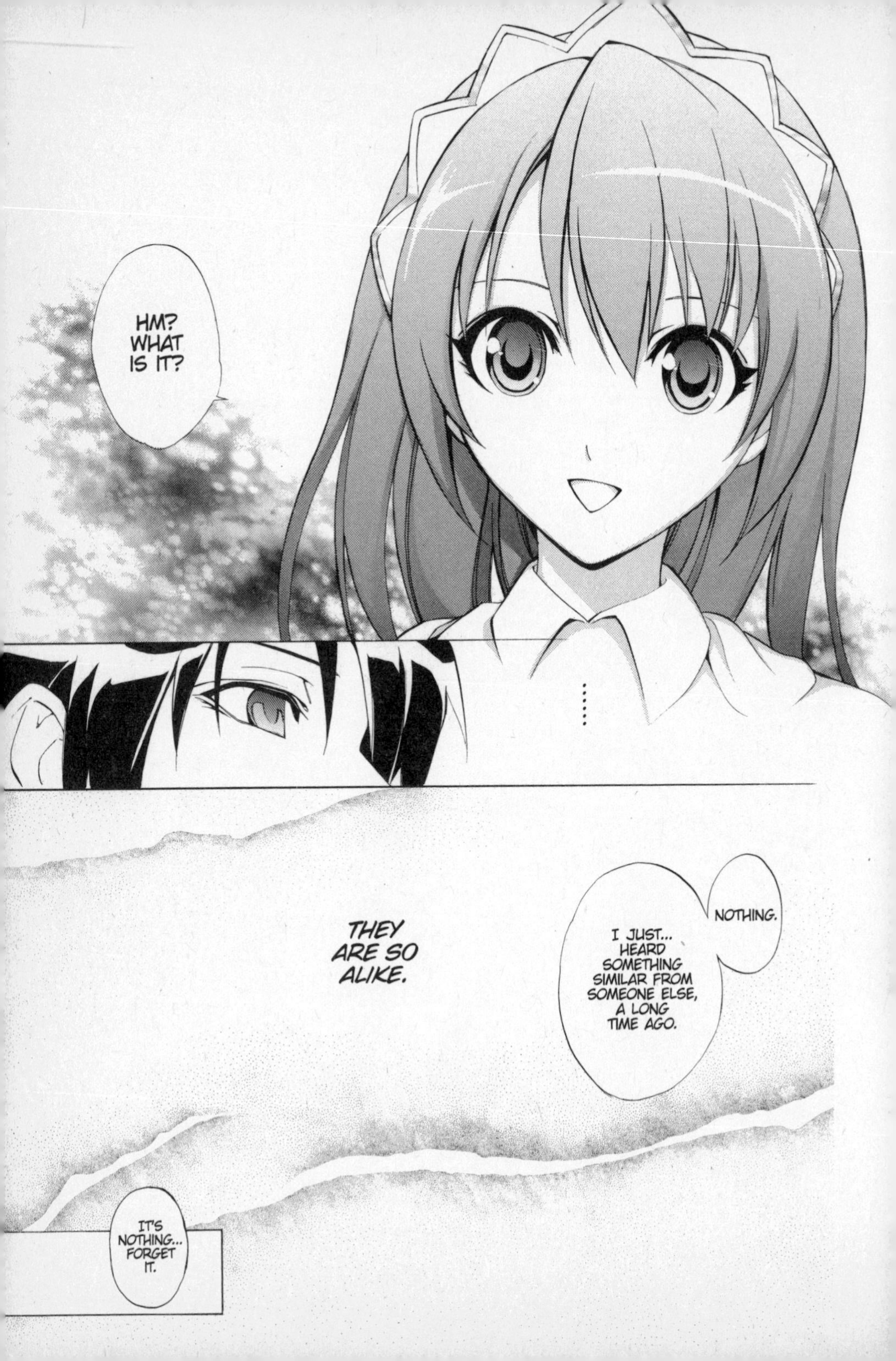
HM? WHAT IS IT?
......
NOTHING.
I JUST... HEARD SOMETHING SIMILAR FROM SOMEONE ELSE, A LONG TIME AGO.
THEY ARE SO ALIKE.
IT'S NOTHING... FORGET IT.

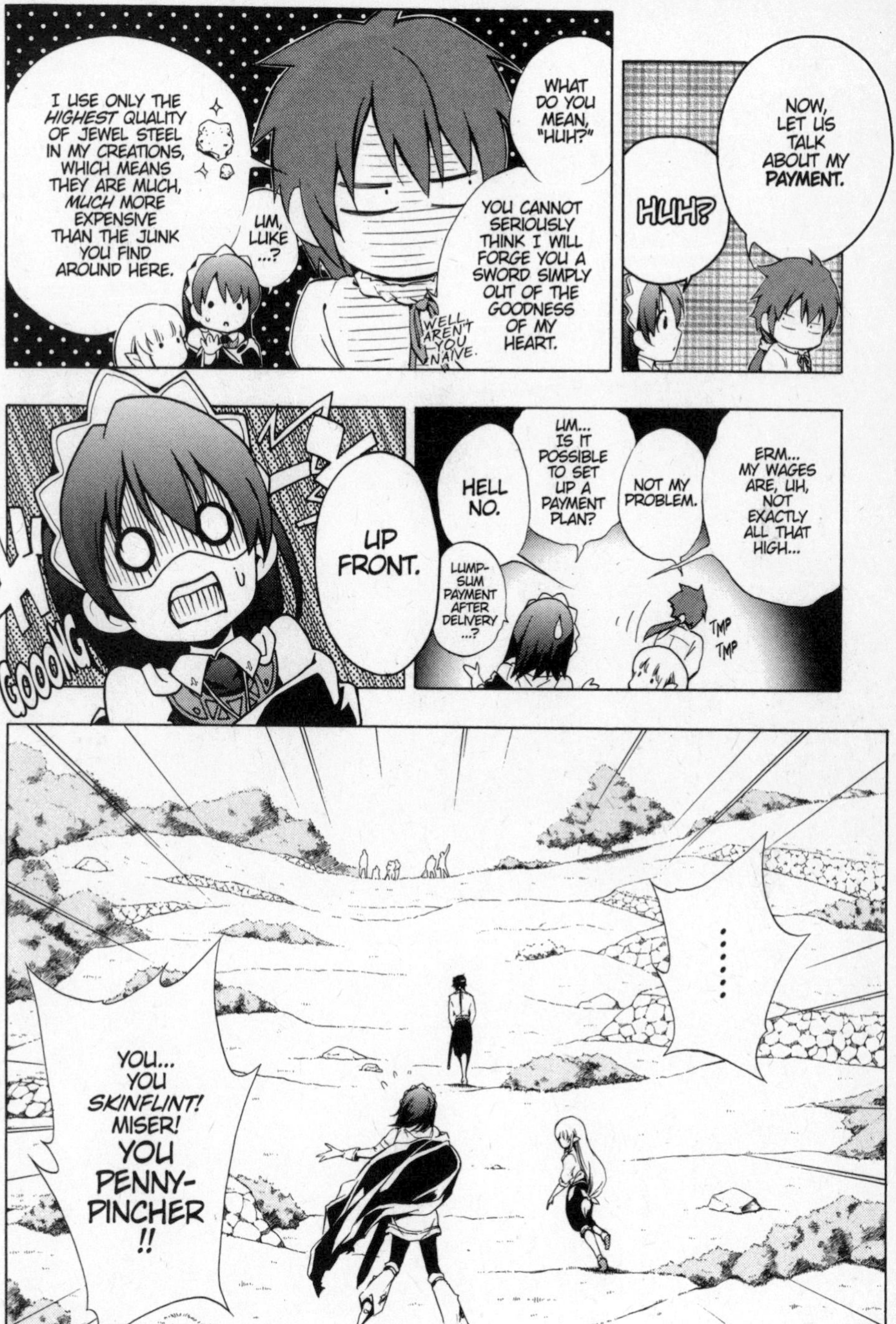
NOW, LET US TALK ABOUT MY PAYMENT.
HUH?
WHAT DO YOU MEAN, "HUH?"
YOU CANNOT SERIOUSLY THINK I WILL FORGE YOU A SWORD SIMPLY OUT OF THE GOODNESS OF MY HEART.
WELL AREN'T YOU NAIVE.
I USE ONLY THE HIGHEST QUALITY OF JEWEL STEEL IN MY CREATIONS, WHICH MEANS THEY ARE MUCH, MUCH MORE EXPENSIVE THAN THE JUNK YOU FIND AROUND HERE.
UM, LUKE ...?
ERM... MY WAGES ARE, UH, NOT EXACTLY ALL THAT HIGH...
NOT MY PROBLEM.
UM... IS IT POSSIBLE TO SET UP A PAYMENT PLAN?
HELL NO.
LUMP-SUM PAYMENT AFTER DELIVERY ...?
TMP TMP
UP FRONT.
GOOONG
......
YOU... YOU SKINFLINT! MISER! YOU PENNY-PINCHER !!

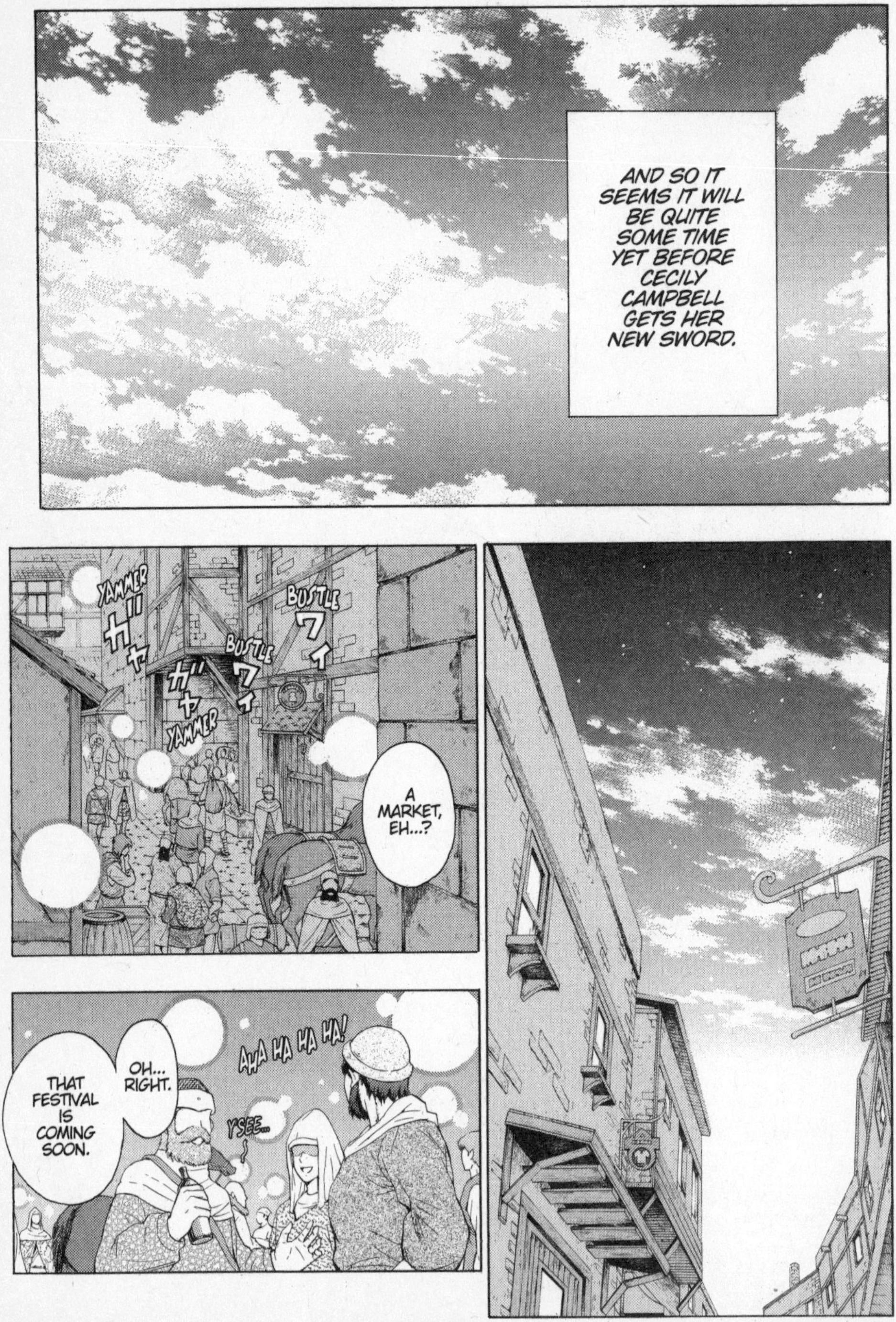
AND SO IT SEEMS IT WILL BE QUITE SOME TIME YET BEFORE CECILY CAMPBELL GETS HER NEW SWORD.
BUSTLE ワイ
BUSTLE ワイ
YAMMER ガヤ
ガヤ YAMMER
A MARKET, EH...?
AHA HA HA HA!
OH... RIGHT.
THAT FESTIVAL IS COMING SOON.
Y'SEE...

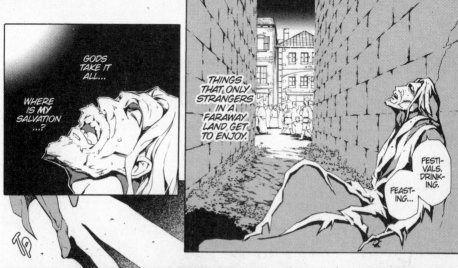

THINGS THAT ONLY STRANGERS IN A FARAWAY LAND GET TO ENJOY.
FESTIVALS. DRINKING.
FEASTING...
GODS TAKE IT ALL...
WHERE IS MY SALVATION ...?
PARDON ME.
?
HEE HEE! YES, THIS SORT OF THING IS BEST LEFT TO THOSE WITH EXPERIENCE.
BEGINNERS ARE NO GOOD.
NO, THEY WERE NO GOOD AT ALL.
NOT ONLY DID THEY RUN WILD-- SO STUPID!-- BUT THEY DID IT WHERE THEY WERE QUICKLY FOUND. SO FOOLISH! AND WORSE YET, THEY WERE CAUGHT TOO SOON.
NO, THEY DID NOT DO WELL AT ALL. THAT IS WHY, THIS TIME, I WILL DO YOU THE FAVOR.

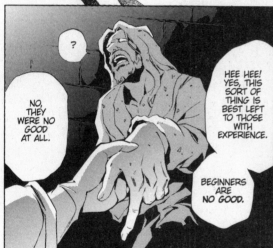

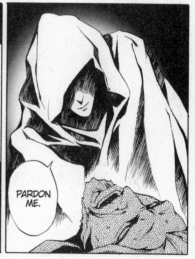

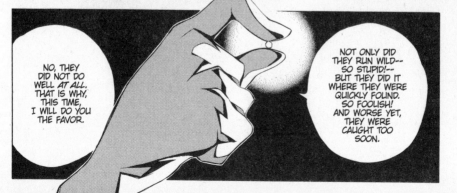

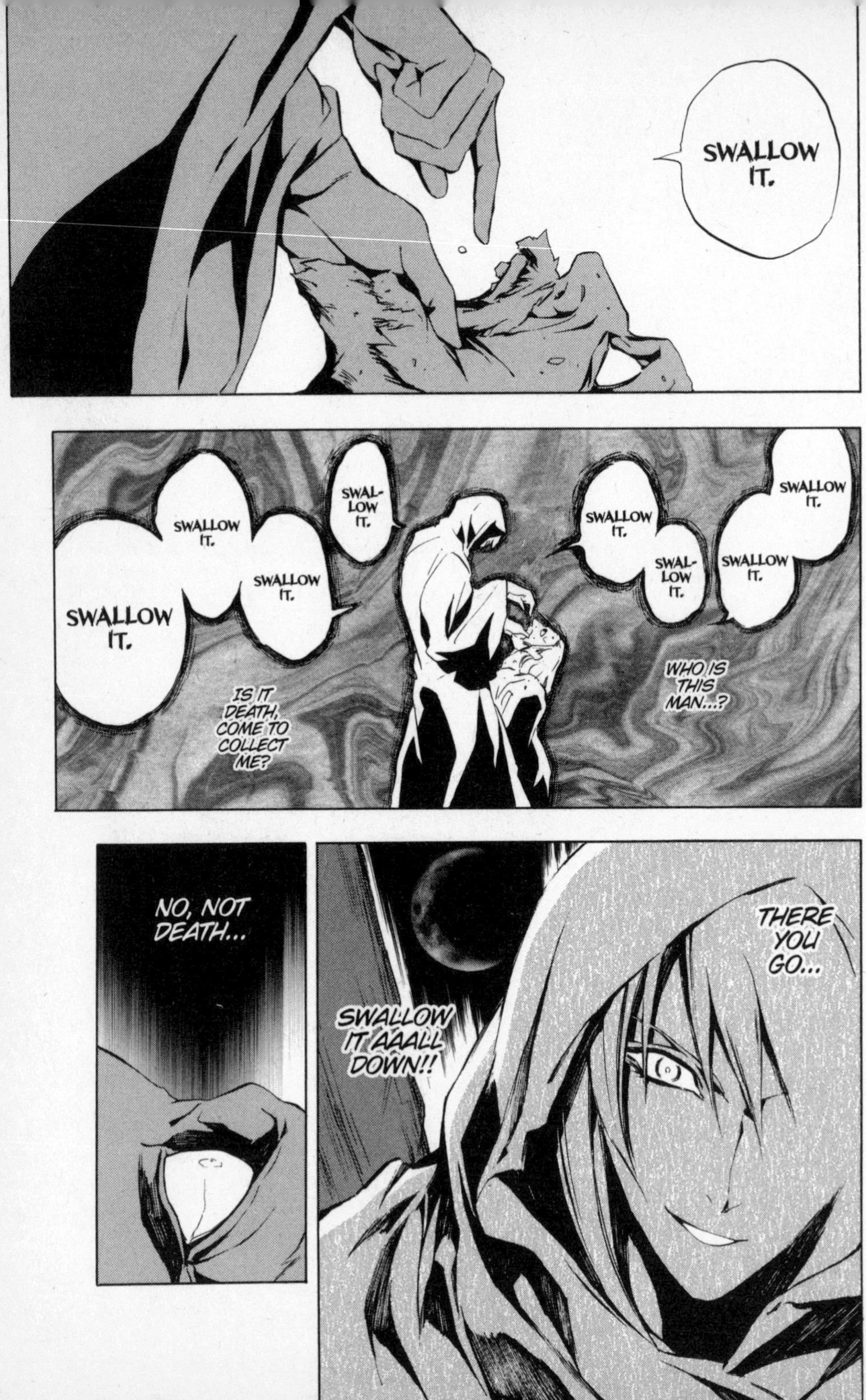
SWALLOW IT.
SWALLOW IT.
SWALLOW IT.
SWALLOW IT.
SWAL-LOW IT.
WHO IS THIS MAN...?
SWAL-LOW IT.
SWALLOW IT.
SWALLOW IT.
SWALLOW IT.
IS IT DEATH, COME TO COLLECT ME?
THERE YOU GO...
SWALLOW IT AAALL DOWN!!
NO, NOT DEATH...

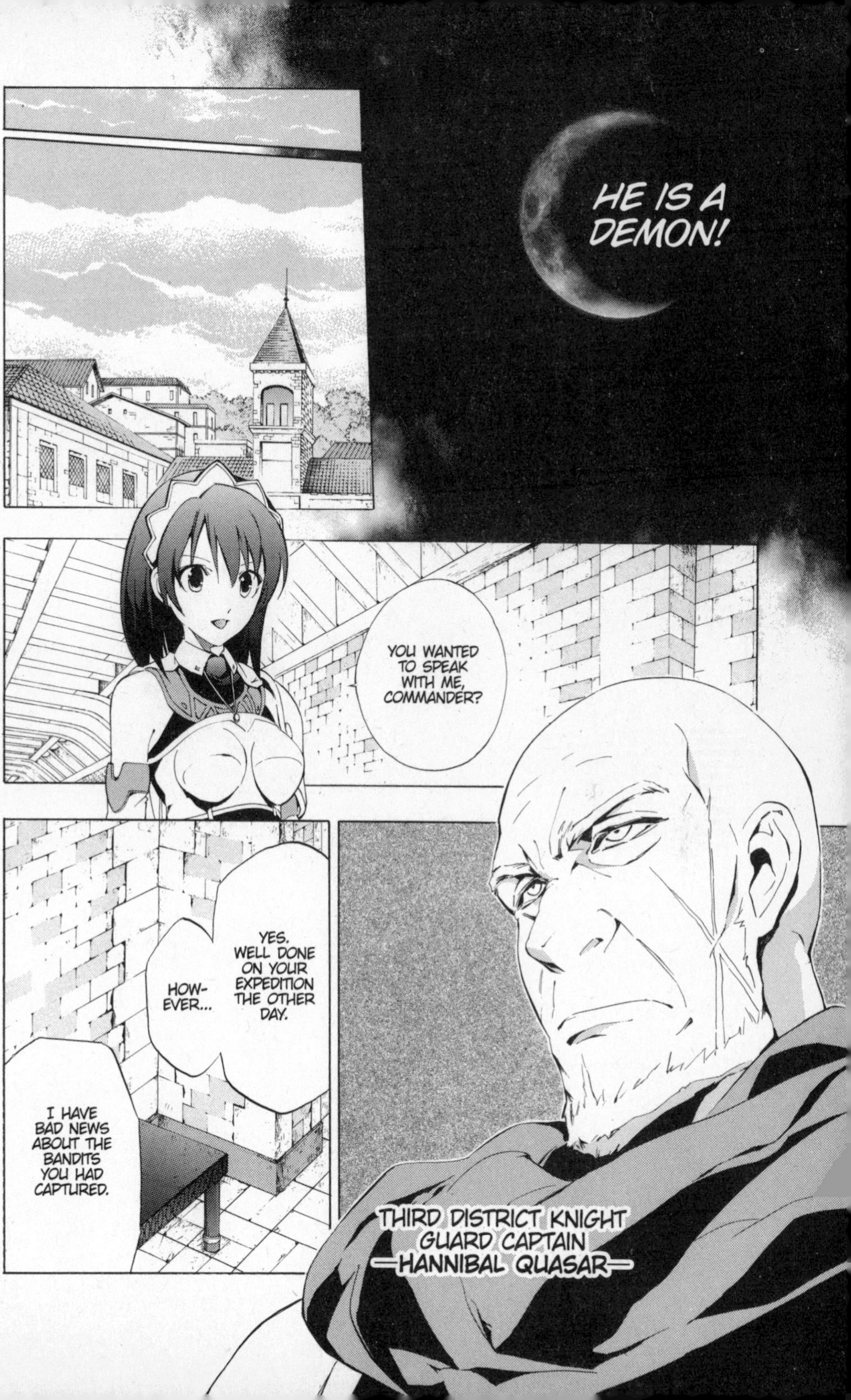
HE IS A DEMON!
YOU WANTED TO SPEAK WITH ME, COMMANDER?
THIRD DISTRICT KNIGHT GUARD CAPTAIN —HANNIBAL QUASAR—
YES. WELL DONE ON YOUR EXPEDITION THE OTHER DAY.
HOW-EVER...
I HAVE BAD NEWS ABOUT THE BANDITS YOU HAD CAPTURED.

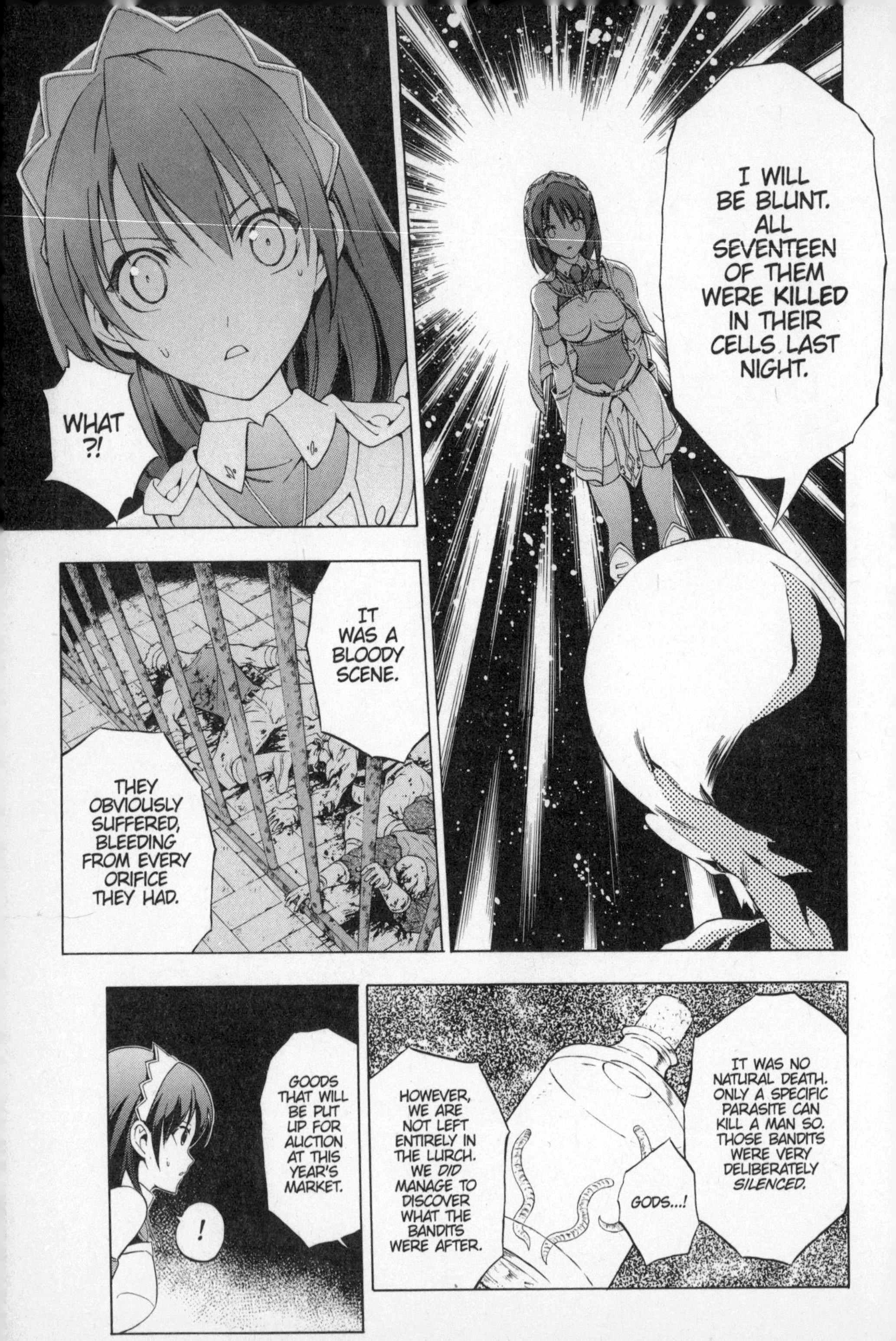
I WILL BE BLUNT. ALL SEVENTEEN OF THEM WERE KILLED IN THEIR CELLS LAST NIGHT.
WHAT ?!
IT WAS A BLOODY SCENE.
THEY OBVIOUSLY SUFFERED, BLEEDING FROM EVERY ORIFICE THEY HAD.
IT WAS NO NATURAL DEATH. ONLY A SPECIFIC PARASITE CAN KILL A MAN SO. THOSE BANDITS WERE VERY DELIBERATELY *SILENCED*.
GODS...!
HOWEVER, WE ARE NOT LEFT ENTIRELY IN THE LURCH. WE *DID* MANAGE TO DISCOVER WHAT THE BANDITS WERE AFTER.
GOODS THAT WILL BE PUT UP FOR AUCTION AT THIS YEAR'S MARKET.
!

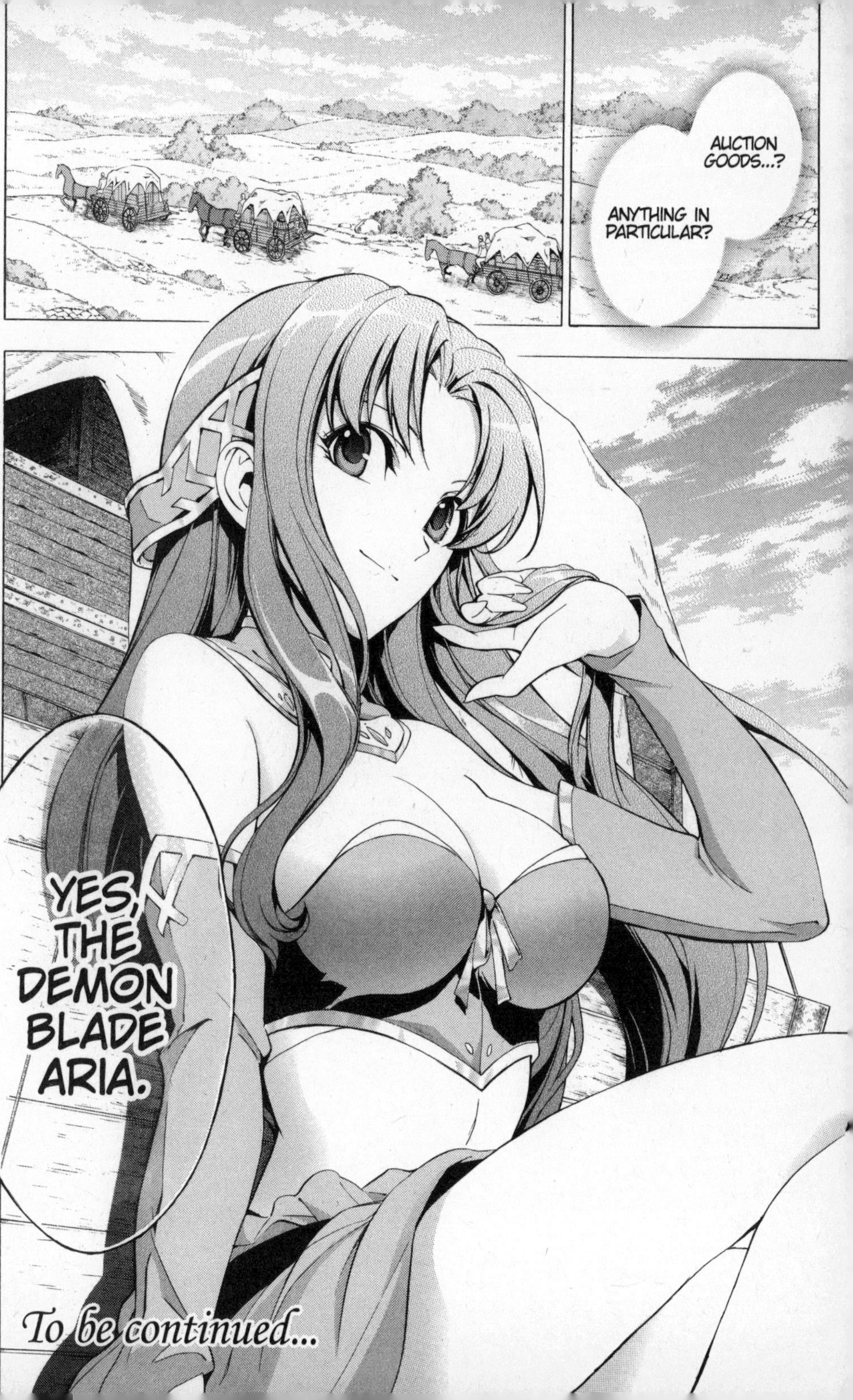
AUCTION GOODS...?
ANYTHING IN PARTICULAR?
YES, THE DEMON BLADE ARIA.
To be continued...

✳ Lisa ✳

The Sacred Blacksmith

聖剣の刀鍛冶

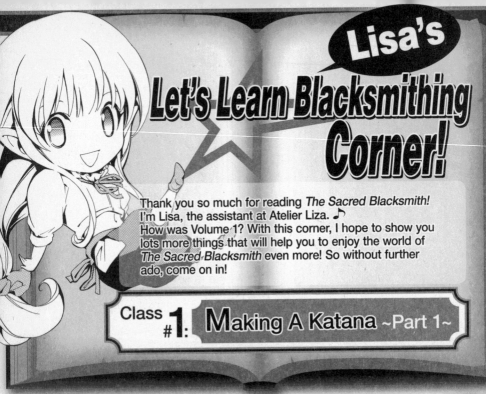

Lisa's Let's Learn Blacksmithing Corner!

Thank you so much for reading *The Sacred Blacksmith!* I'm Lisa, the assistant at Atelier Liza. ♪
How was Volume 1? With this corner, I hope to show you lots more things that will help you to enjoy the world of *The Sacred Blacksmith* even more! So without further ado, come on in!

Class #1: Making A Katana ~Part 1~

Why is Luke's sword so amazing?!

It never bends, it never breaks, and it's extremely sharp!

Unlike the straight swords that knights like Cecily use, Luke's katana has a distinctive curve. It may have broken during his fight with the demon in Chapter 2, but a knight with a normal sword wouldn't have been able to fight at all! A katana is a very powerful blade, strong enough to even cut into axes, like in Chapter 1. But what makes it that strong?

Sharp-eyed readers will have noticed that Luke's katana is modeled on the real-world Japanese katana. Unlike most swords, Japanese katana are made of two different types of steel, giving it the toughness to stay sharp, and the resilience to avoid breaking. But that's not much of an explanation. What exactly goes into making a Japanese katana?

GO!

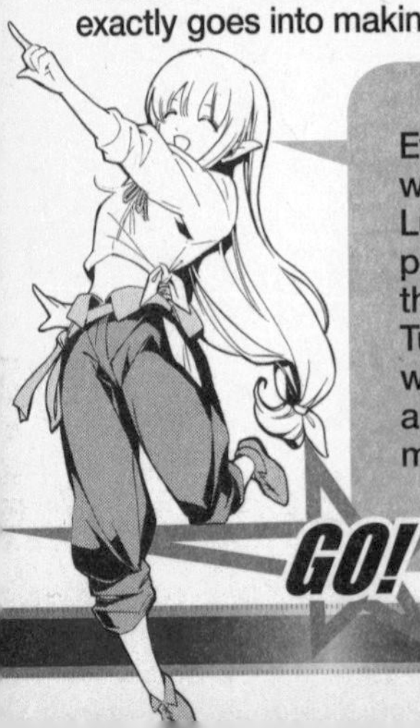

Even Miss Cecily wanted a sword like Luke's. But how do people make blades that are so incredible? Turn to the next page, where I explain all about how they're made! ♪

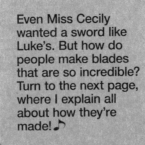

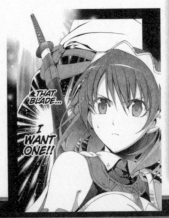

THAT BLADE...
I WANT ONE!!

How To Forge A Japanese Katana

It doesn't break! It doesn't bend! It's super sharp!

Are just a few words not enough? Here's a detailed explanation of the forging process! ☆

The 3-Step Forging Process

1. Assemble the correct steels.
2. Forge the steels.
3. Shape the blade.

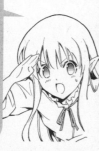

It sounds really easy, but it's actually a super-long process!

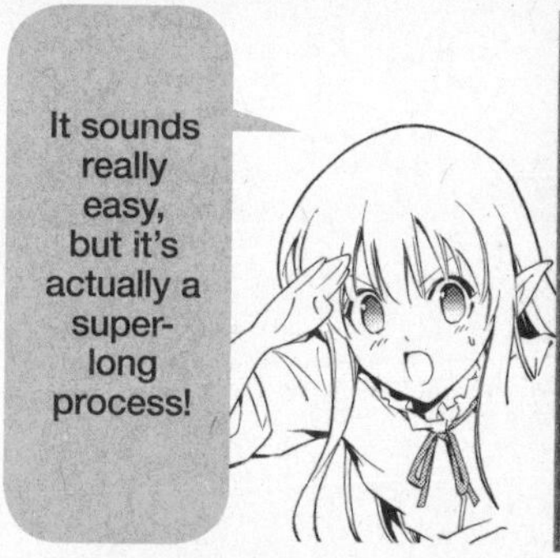

1 Smelting & Separation

Katanas are made from a special metal called "jewel steel." But jewel steel comes in awkward, lumpy "blooms," so they need to be melded together (smelting), and then cut into easy-to-use pieces (separation).

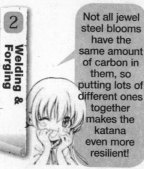

Not all jewel steel blooms have the same amount of carbon in them, so putting lots of different ones together makes the katana even more resilient!

2 Welding & Forging

Next, the pieces of jewel steel are covered in clay, stacked in a pile, and heated in the furnace. When the clay melts off, they're pulled out as one single lump. The blacksmith will then hammer the lump into a block about 6 x 9cm in size.

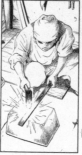

3 Folding

Now that we have the materials, it's time to forge the blade! The jewel steel block is heated in the furnace and then drawn into a long bar. The bar is folded back on itself, reheated, and drawn out into a long bar again. This is repeated about 15 times. Man, does it take a lot of strength! This process evens out the carbon content and pounds any impurities out of the steel.

Building the Skin Steel

The result of the folding process is a hard steel known as "skin steel." Katanas are made from this steel, and the softer steel that the skin steel wraps around is called "core steel." Both types of steel are made at the same time.

RIDGE
CORE STEEL
SKIN STEEL
EDGE

Building the Core Steel

Core steel is a softer metal made from iron mixed with a little jewel steel. They are heated and folded together in a process just like that for skin steel.

Blade Construction

Once both steels are ready, it's time to wrap the hard, carbon-rich skin steel around the soft, carbon-poor core steel. This is the first major difference between the katana and other swords. It's this process that gives the katana the hardness that keeps it from bending, and the flexibility that prevents it from breaking.

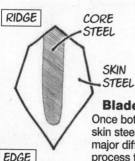

4 Elongation

Now that the two types of steel are put together, the result is heated and carefully drawn out into a "blank," the basic shape of the sword. Blacksmiths keep the final shape they want the blade to be firmly in mind during this step.

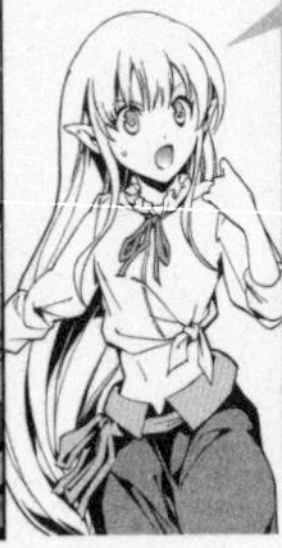
The weight of the steel determines how long the blade will be, so blacksmiths hammer away to draw the blade out to just the right length!

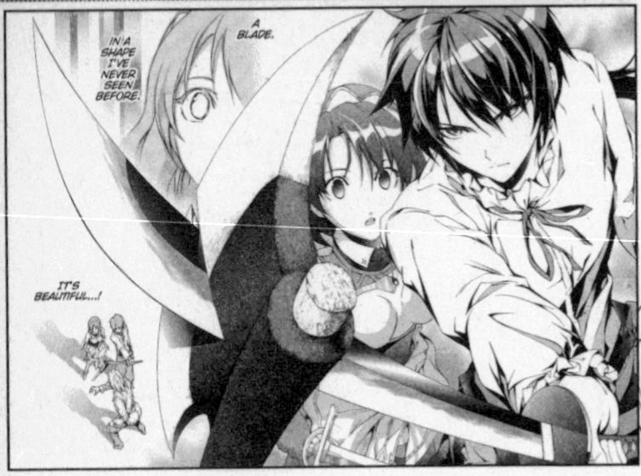
A BLADE.
IN A SHAPE I'VE NEVER SEEN BEFORE.
IT'S BEAUTIFUL...!

5 Cutting the Point

Once the blank is finished, the blacksmith goes chop-chop, and cuts the end off on the diagonal. The tip is then heated in the forge and shaped from the edge back to the ridge into its distinct curve.

6 Shaping the Blade

Once the blank is made and the tip is cut, the general shape of the blade is finished. Next, on to some refinements! The blade is once again heated in the forge, and the edge is made. A rasp is used to even out the thickness. Next up, refining the blade's distinctive curve and the hamon temper line.

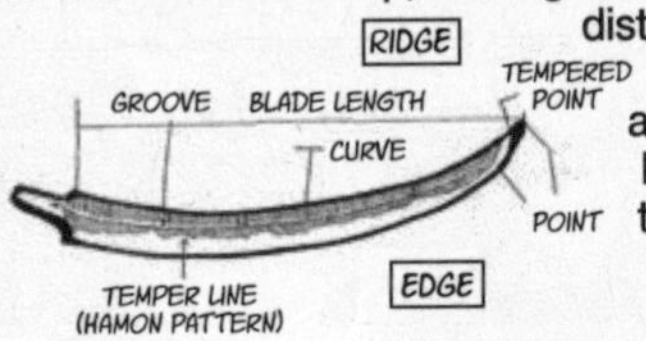
RIDGE
GROOVE
BLADE LENGTH
TEMPERED POINT
CURVE
POINT
EDGE
TEMPER LINE (HAMON PATTERN)

7 Rough Finish

The surface of the blade is cleaned with a very rough type of whetstone, called an "arato." A big plane that can hone even pig steel, the arato will grind down all the little dips and bumps until the blade is perfectly smooth!

8 Clay Coat

Heat-resistant clay is mixed with charcoal powder and polishing stone powder to make "blade clay." This determines the pattern of the blade's "hamon" or temper line, so the blade clay is applied very carefully in waves. The part of the blade that needs the most heat only gets a thin coat. The rest of the blade is coated thickly.

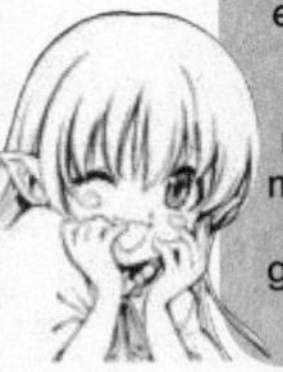
Depending on how the blacksmith puts on the blade clay, the curve of the blade will change. The thinly-covered edge will get really hard, and the thickly-covered ridge will become much more supple! When cooled, it gives the katana its distinctive curve.

9 Finishing the Blade

Once the blade clay has dried on the blade, it is heated in the furnace to about 8,000 degrees! The blacksmith will then pull it out at the right moment, and quench it in a barrel of water. That's what makes the blade curve! Blacksmiths know the exact moment to pull the blade out by its color, but figuring out what that "right color" is takes practice.

There are many more steps after this, including straightening the blade, setting the edge, polishing, and many other important things. Once all of those are done, the Japanese katana is finally complete!

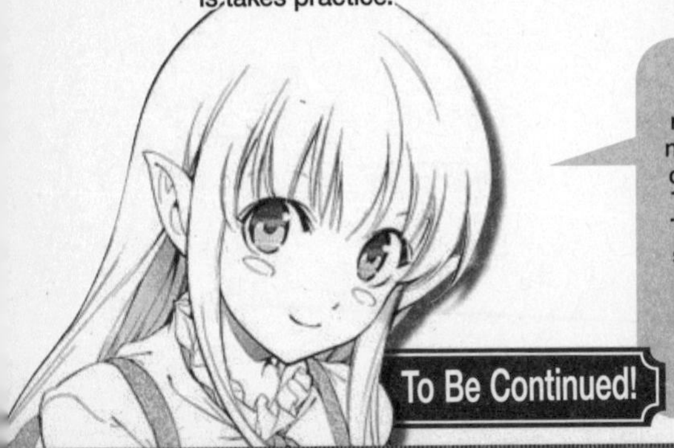
The main storyline mentions the names of many of these stages, but now you have a better idea of what they really involve! This isn't the end, though. There's lots and lots more steps to go! So next time, we'll talk about the "polishing" stages that finish the blade. Hope you're looking forward to it as much as I am!
To Be Continued!

"Whoa, this is more fun than the original novels!"

That was the first thing that popped into my head when I read the first chapter of the manga. "Oh crap," I remember thinking. "I could be in trouble here."

I never dreamed the manga would be able to expand the world so much, or bring it to such vibrant life. I await each new chapter with both trepidation and breathless anticipation.

Yamada-sensei, thank you. Thank you, thank you, thank you. I look forward to more of your awesome and awe-inspiring work. Luna-san and I won't let ourselves fall short of your standard!

—Novel Author
Isao Miura

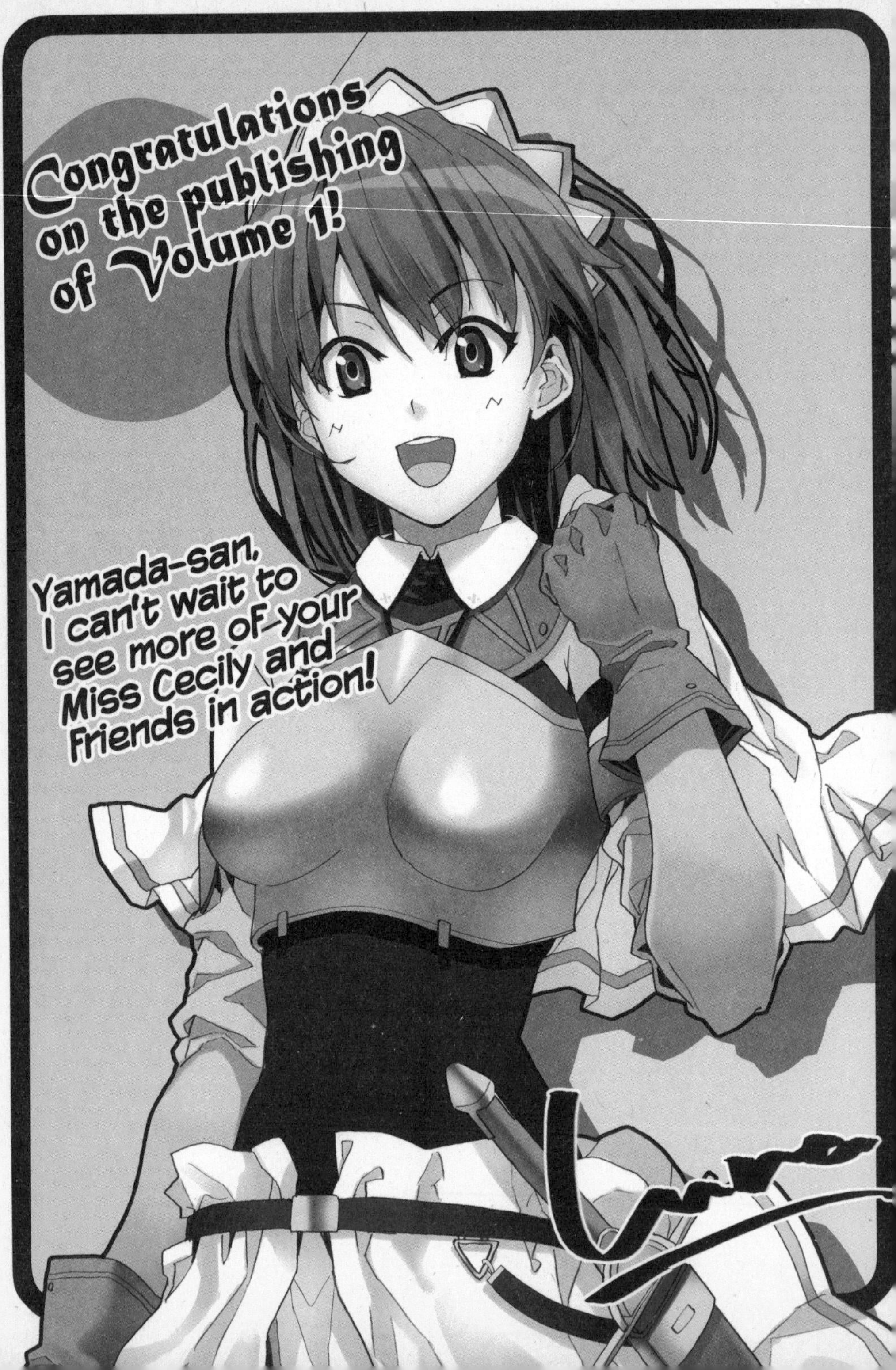
Congratulations on the publishing of Volume 1!
Yamada-san, I can't wait to see more of your Miss Cecily and Friends in action!

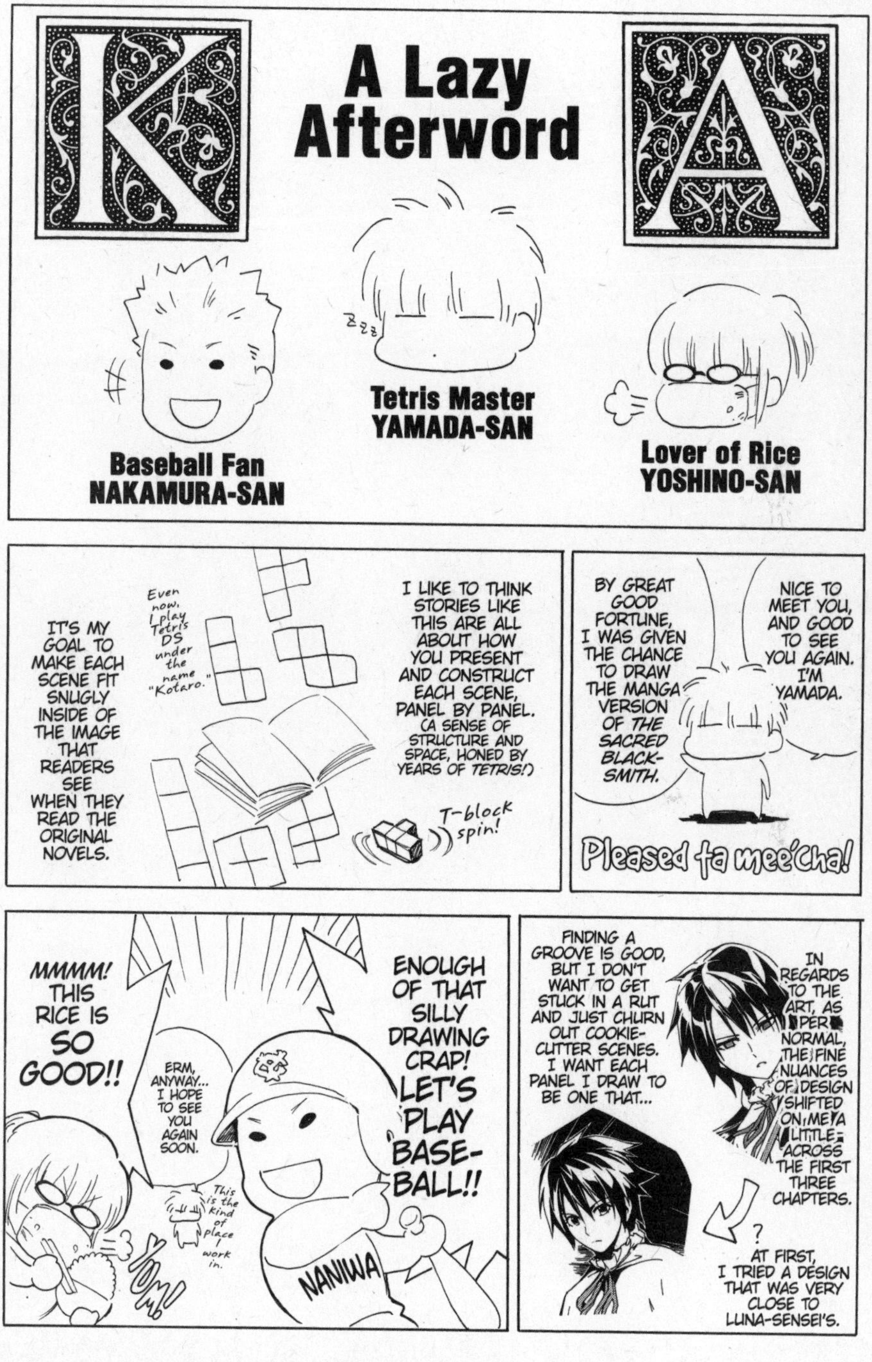
A Lazy Afterword
Lover of Rice
YOSHINO-SAN
Tetris Master
YAMADA-SAN
Zzz
Baseball Fan
NAKAMURA-SAN
NICE TO MEET YOU, AND GOOD TO SEE YOU AGAIN. I'M YAMADA.
BY GREAT GOOD FORTUNE, I WAS GIVEN THE CHANCE TO DRAW THE MANGA VERSION OF *THE SACRED BLACKSMITH*.
Pleased ta mee'Cha!
I LIKE TO THINK STORIES LIKE THIS ARE ALL ABOUT HOW YOU PRESENT AND CONSTRUCT EACH SCENE, PANEL BY PANEL. (A SENSE OF STRUCTURE AND SPACE, HONED BY YEARS OF *TETRIS!*)
Even now, I play Tetris DS under the name "Kotaro."
IT'S MY GOAL TO MAKE EACH SCENE FIT SNUGLY INSIDE OF THE IMAGE THAT READERS SEE WHEN THEY READ THE ORIGINAL NOVELS.
T-block spin!
IN REGARDS TO THE ART, AS PER NORMAL, THE FINE NUANCES OF DESIGN SHIFTED ON ME A LITTLE ACROSS THE FIRST THREE CHAPTERS.
FINDING A GROOVE IS GOOD, BUT I DON'T WANT TO GET STUCK IN A RUT AND JUST CHURN OUT COOKIE-CUTTER SCENES. I WANT EACH PANEL I DRAW TO BE ONE THAT...
?
AT FIRST, I TRIED A DESIGN THAT WAS VERY CLOSE TO LUNA-SENSEI'S.
ENOUGH OF THAT SILLY DRAWING CRAP! LET'S PLAY BASE-BALL!!
ERM, ANYWAY... I HOPE TO SEE YOU AGAIN SOON.
MMMM! THIS RICE IS SO GOOD!!
This is the kind of place I work in.
NANIWA

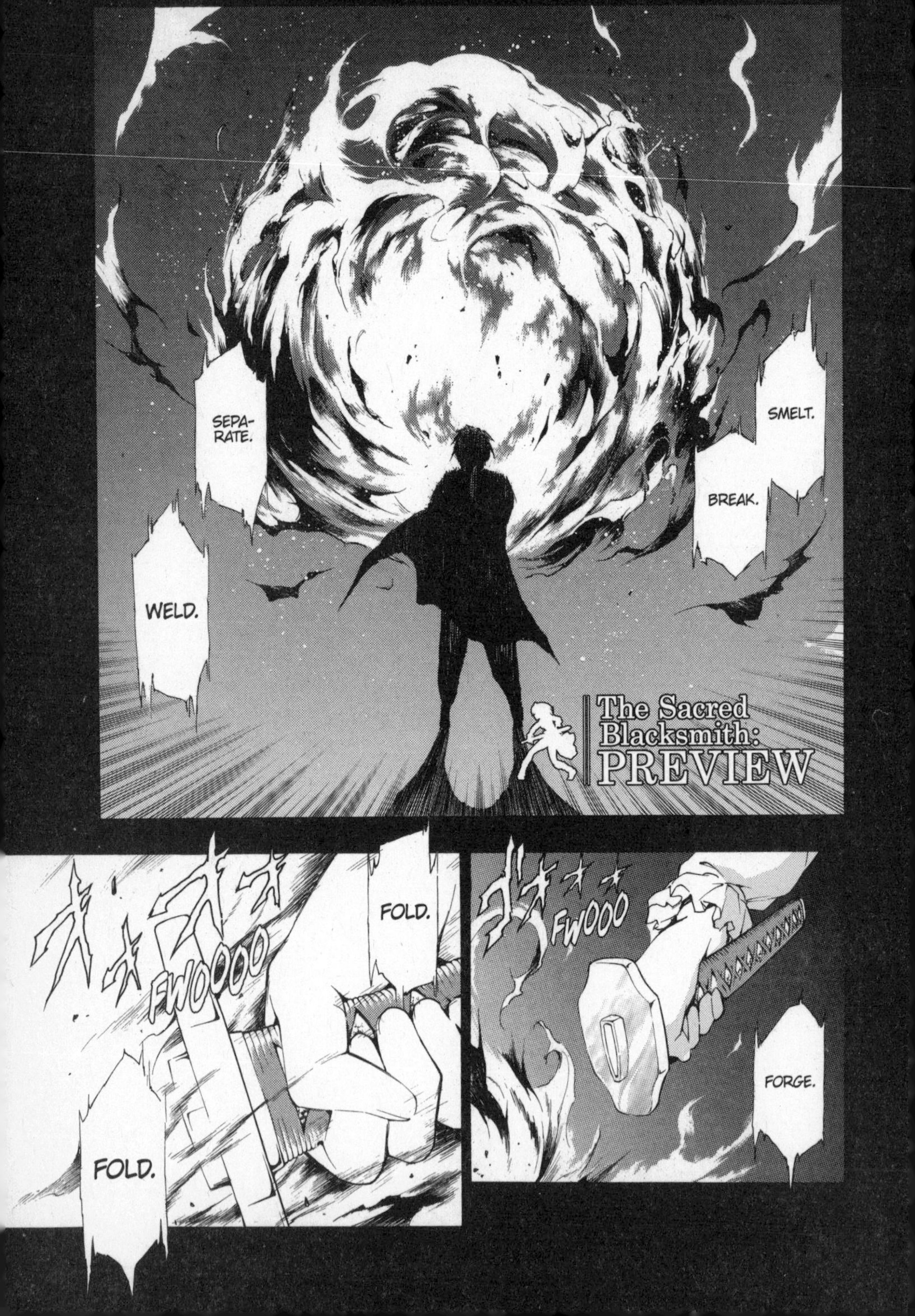

SMELT.
BREAK.
SEPA-
RATE.
WELD.
The Sacred Blacksmith:
PREVIEW
FWOOO
FORGE.
FWOOOO
FOLD.
FOLD.

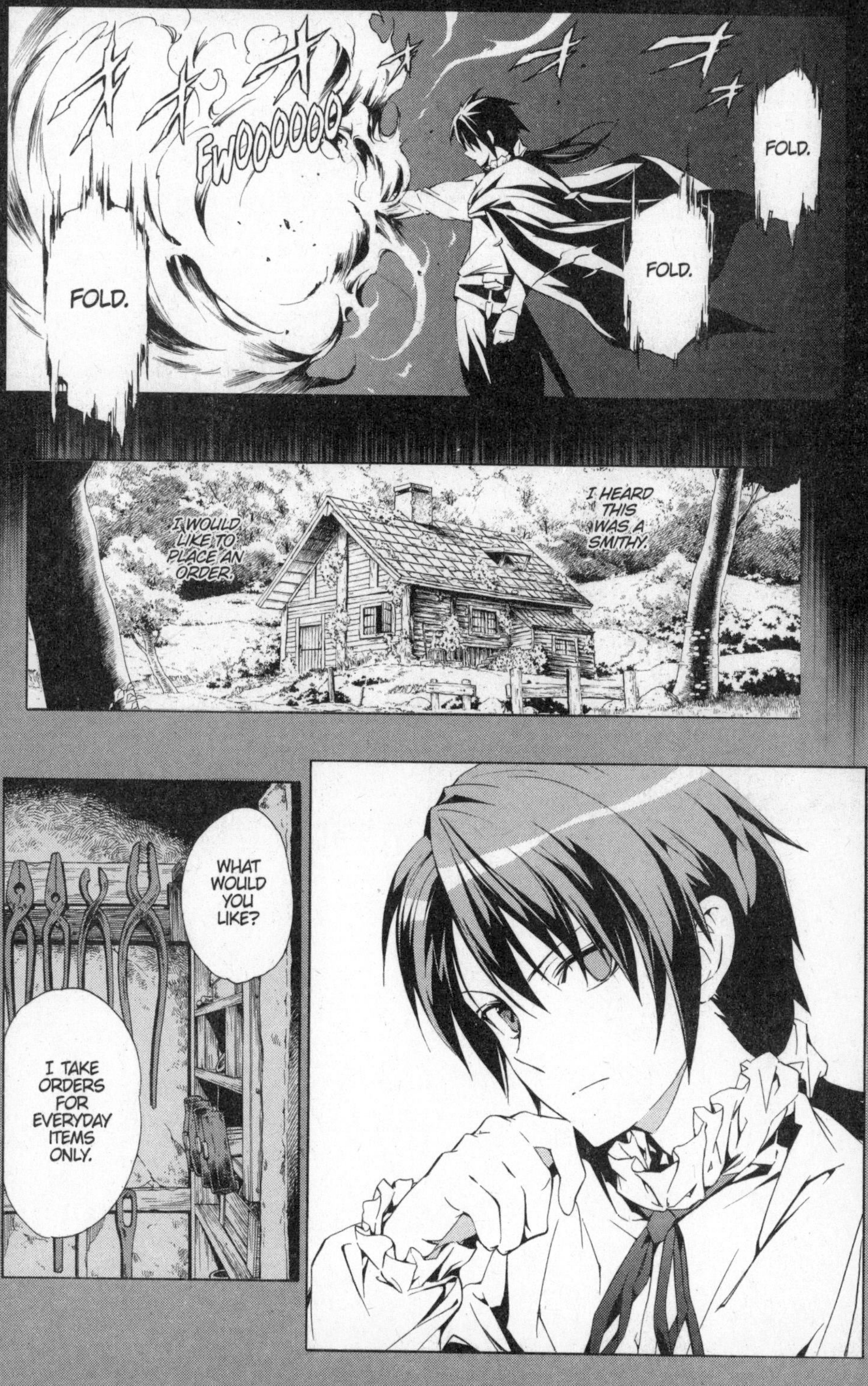
FOLD.
FOLD.
FWOOOOOO
FOLD.
I HEARD THIS WAS A SMITHY.
I WOULD LIKE TO PLACE AN ORDER.
WHAT WOULD YOU LIKE?
I TAKE ORDERS FOR EVERYDAY ITEMS ONLY.

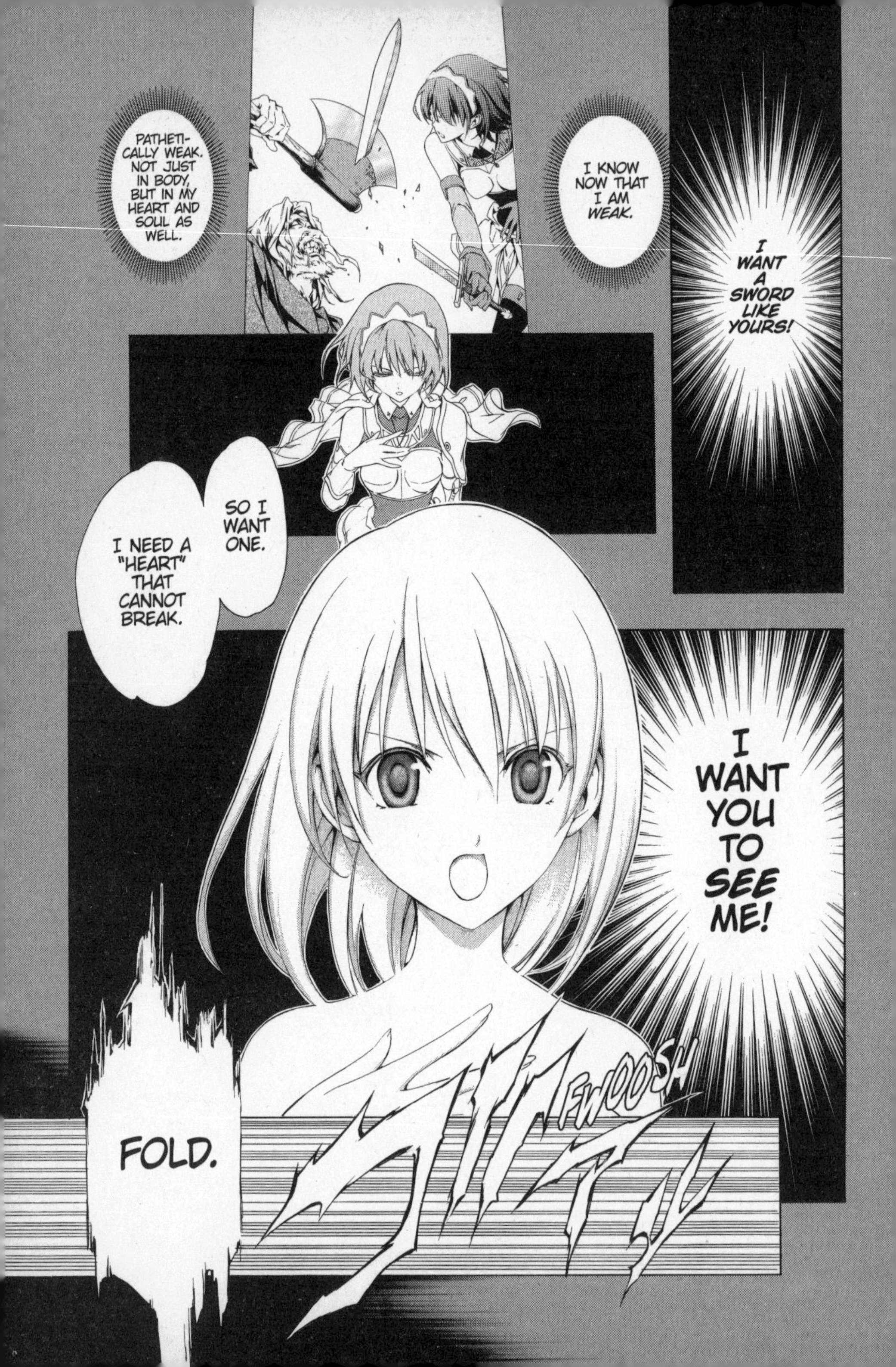
I KNOW NOW THAT I AM WEAK.
PATHETICALLY WEAK. NOT JUST IN BODY, BUT IN MY HEART AND SOUL AS WELL.
I WANT A SWORD LIKE YOURS!
SO I WANT ONE.
I NEED A "HEART" THAT CANNOT BREAK.
I WANT YOU TO SEE ME!
FWOOSH
FOLD.

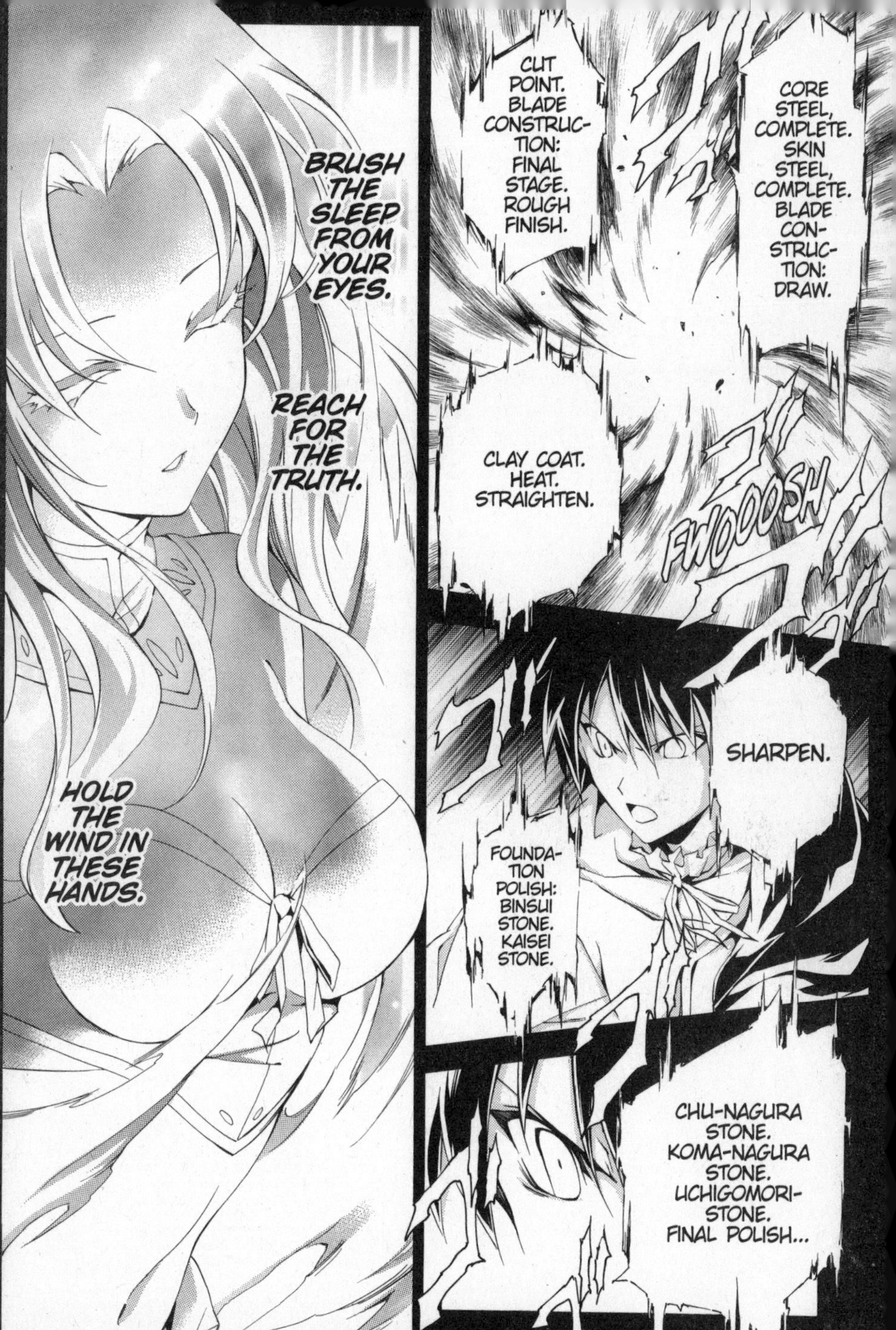
CORE STEEL, COMPLETE. SKIN STEEL, COMPLETE. BLADE CON-STRUC-TION: DRAW.
CUT POINT. BLADE CONSTRUC-TION: FINAL STAGE. ROUGH FINISH.
CLAY COAT. HEAT. STRAIGHTEN.
FWOOOSH
SHARPEN.
FOUNDA-TION POLISH: BINSUI STONE. KAISEI STONE.
CHU-NAGURA STONE. KOMA-NAGURA STONE. UCHIGOMORI-STONE. FINAL POLISH...
BRUSH THE SLEEP FROM YOUR EYES.
REACH FOR THE TRUTH.
HOLD THE WIND IN THESE HANDS.

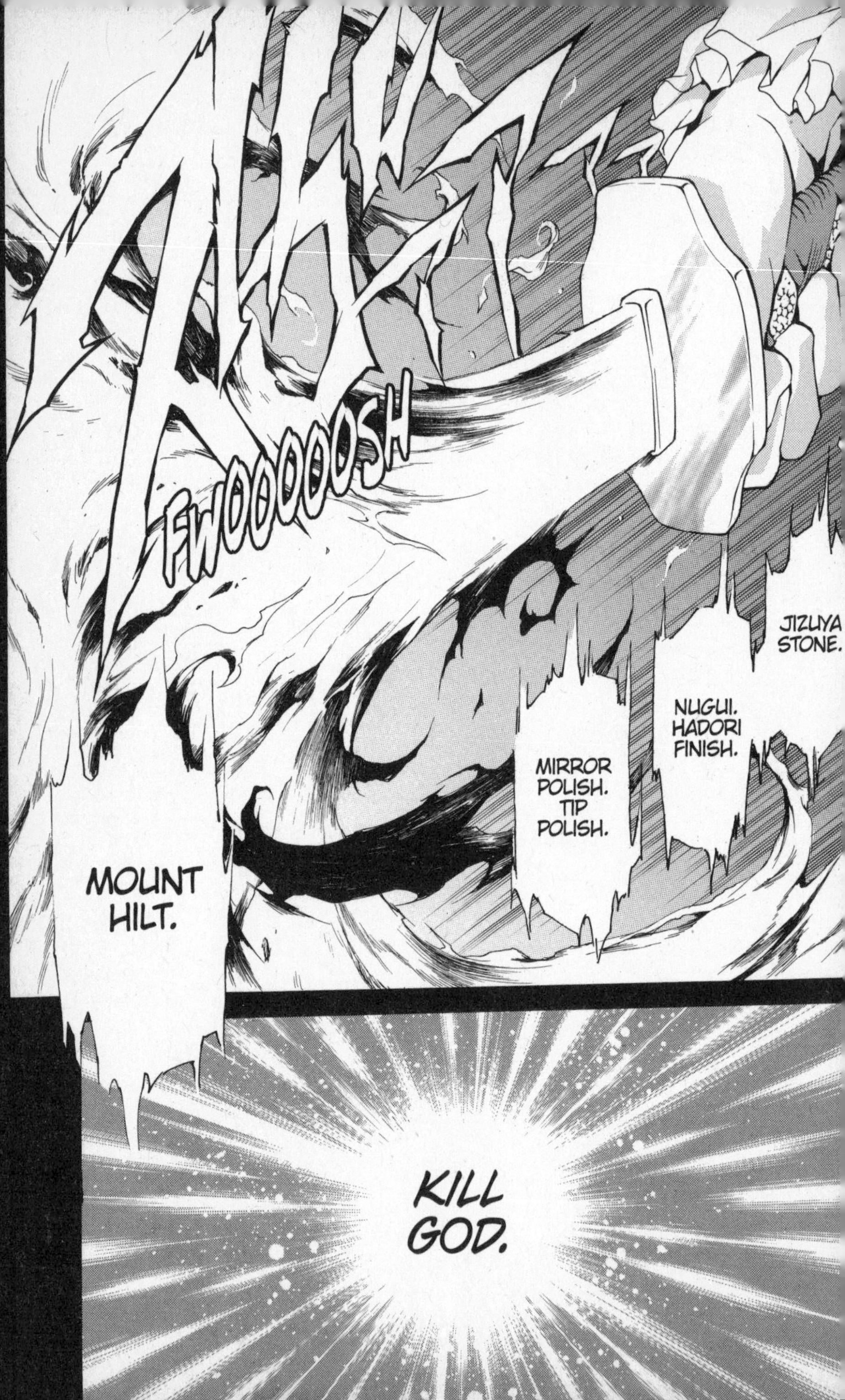

JIZUYA STONE.
NUGUI. HADORI FINISH.
MIRROR POLISH. TIP POLISH.
FWOOOOSH
MOUNT HILT.
KILL GOD.

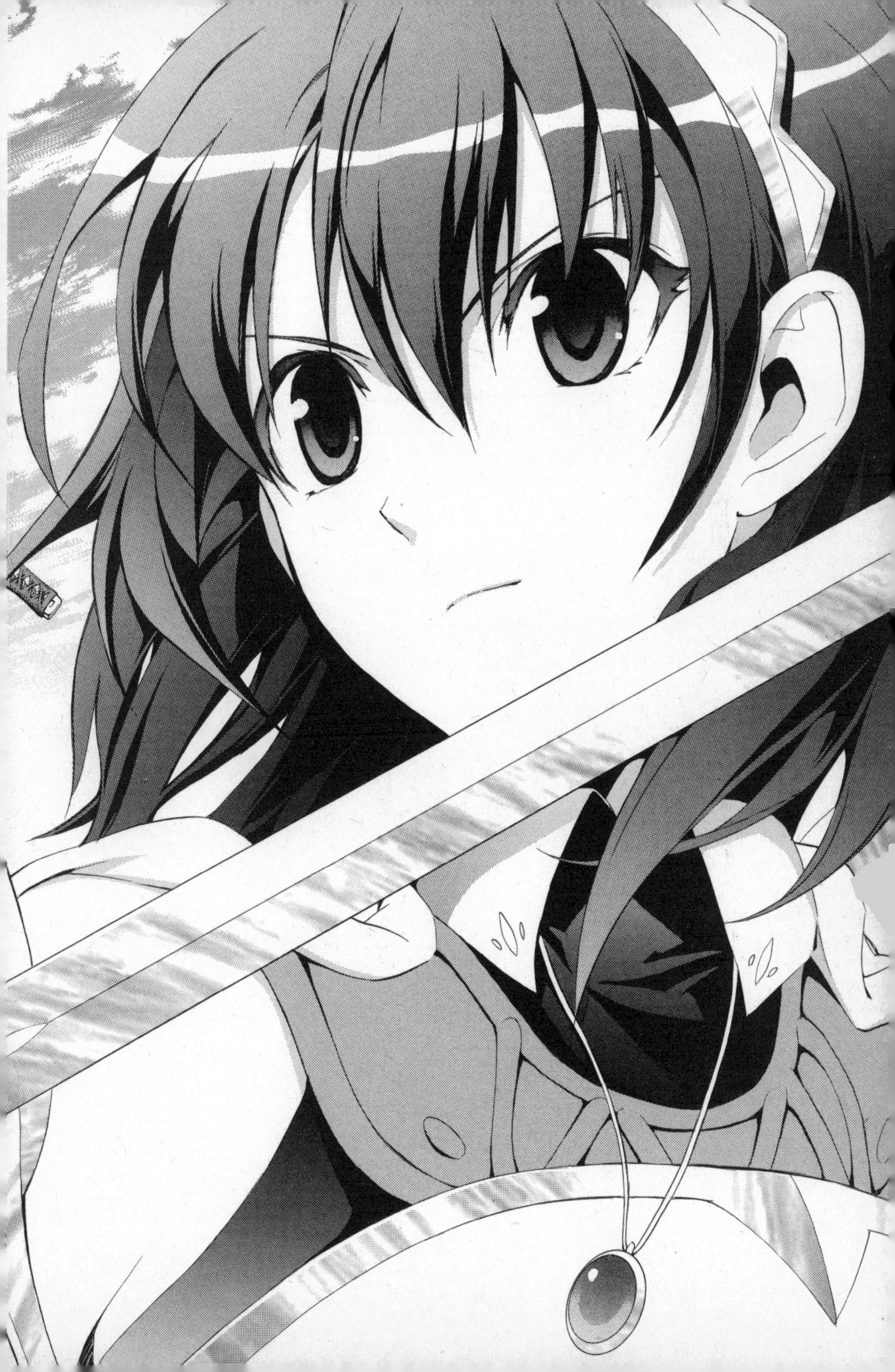

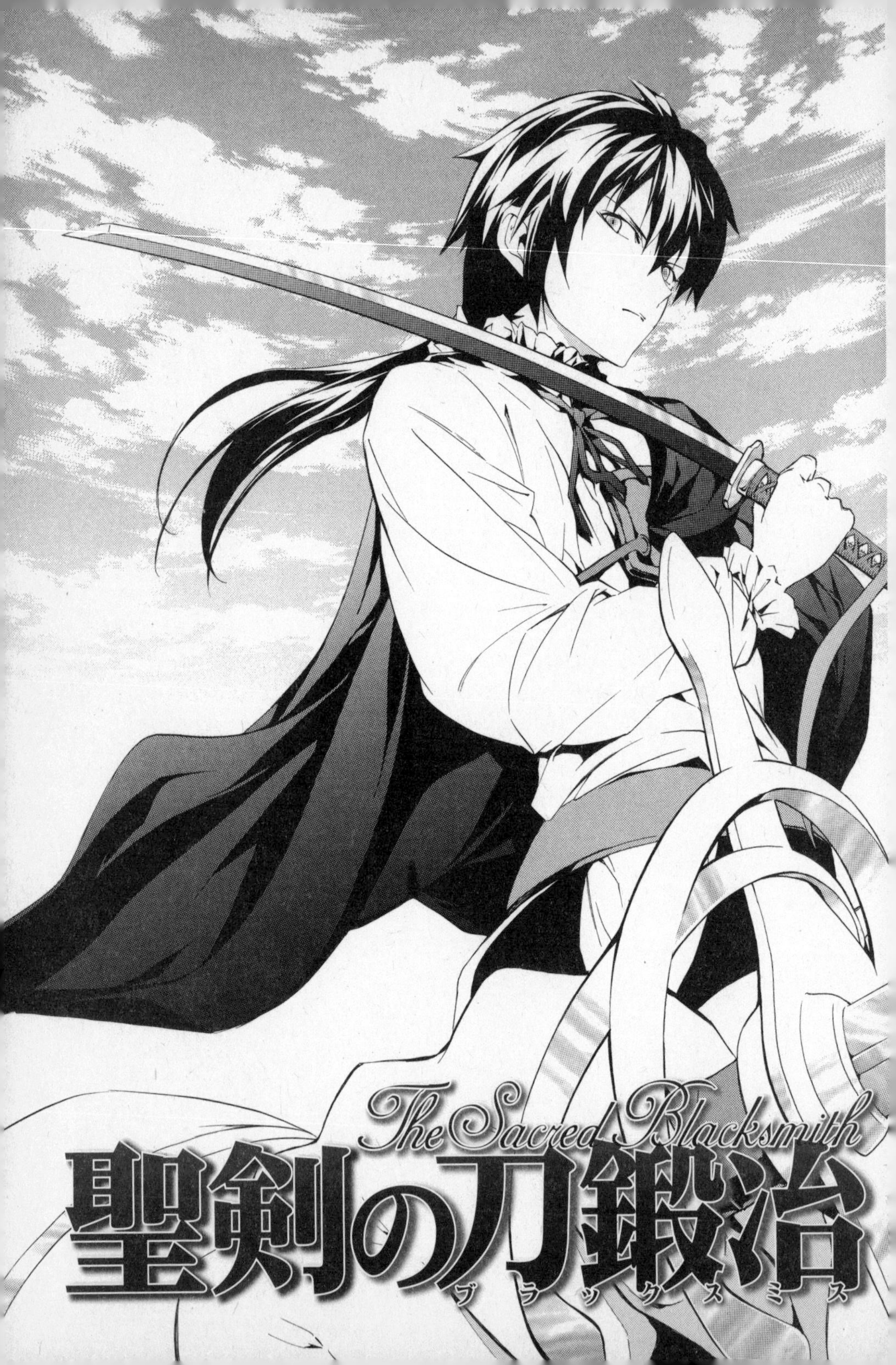
The Sacred Blacksmith
聖剣の刀鍛冶
ブラックスミス

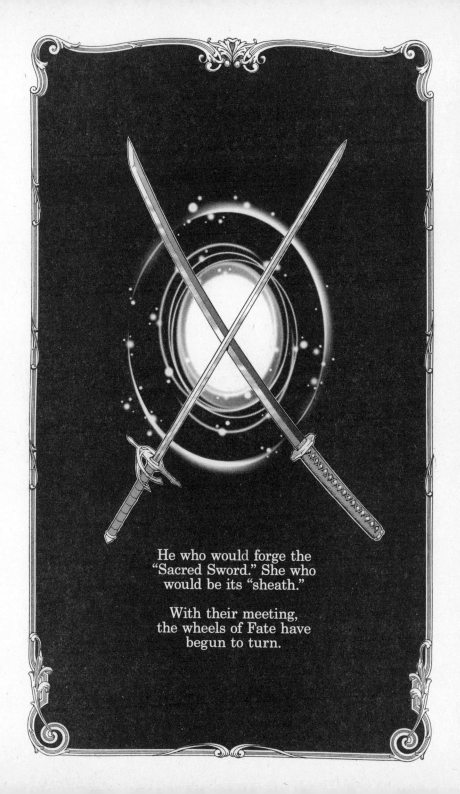

He who would forge the
"Sacred Sword." She who
would be its "sheath."

With their meeting,
the wheels of Fate have
begun to turn.

The Sacred Blacksmith

聖剣の刀鍛冶

NEXT TIME...

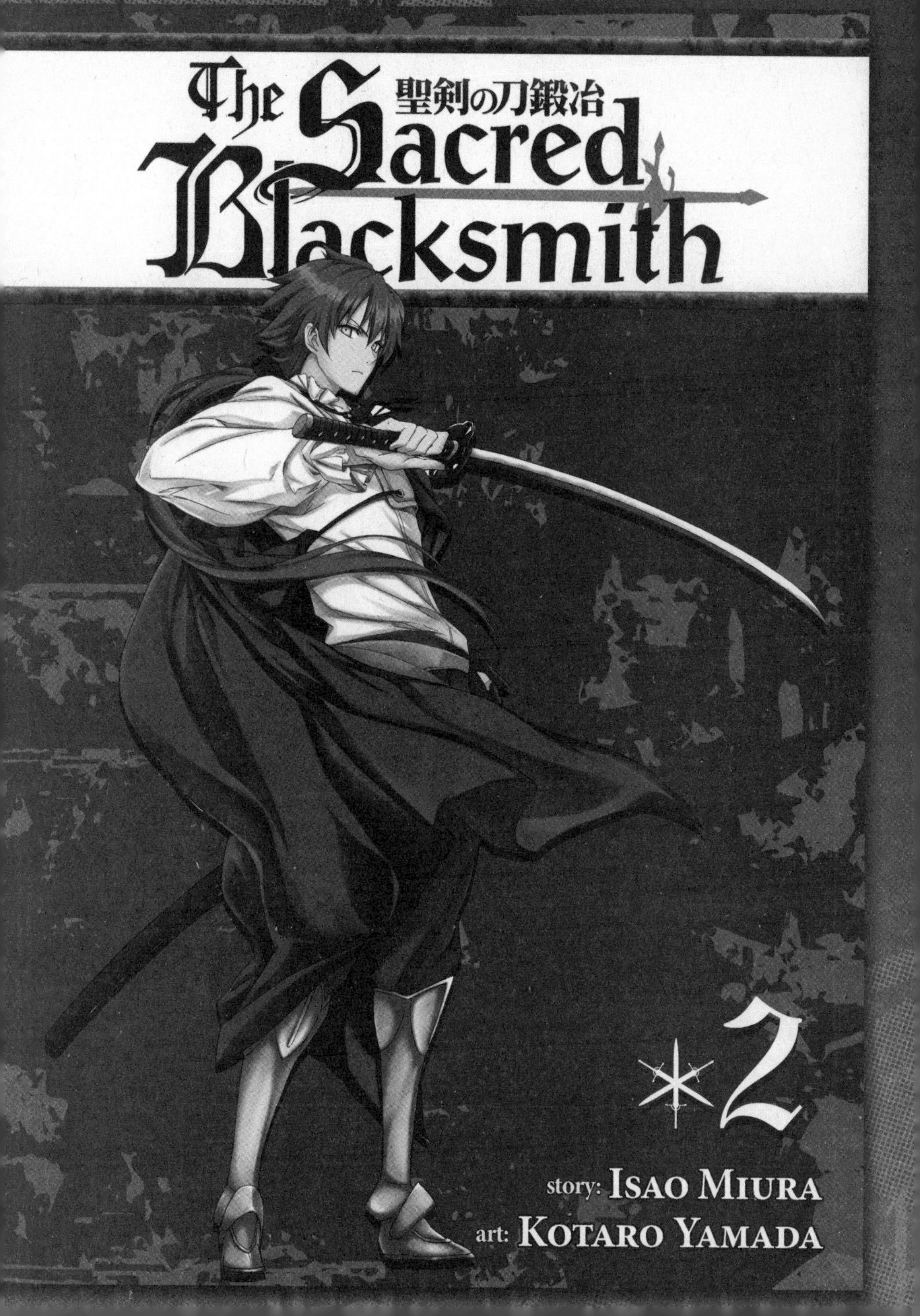

The Sacred Blacksmith
聖剣の刀鍛冶
2
story: Isao Miura
art: Kotaro Yamada